BL-BQ

RELIGION (GENERAL)
HINDUISM
JUDAISM
ISLAM
BUDDHISM

Library of Congress Classification

2001 EDITION

Prepared by the
Cataloging Policy
and Support Office,
Library Services

Library of Congress, Cataloging Distribution Service, Washington, D.C.

The additions and c
press will be cumul
Additions and Chan

Library of Co

Library of Congress
Library of Cong
Judaism, Islam, B
Office, Library Ser
p. cm.
Rev. ed. of: Classi
Religions, Hinduis
Division, Processi
Includes index.
ISBN 0-8444-104
1. Classification, Library of Congress. 2. Classification--Books--Religion.
3. Classification--Books--Religions. I. Title: Religion (general), Hinduism,
Judaism, Islam, Buddhism. II. Library of Congress. Cataloging Policy and
Support Office. III. Library of Congress. Subject Catloging Division.
Classification. Class B. Subclasses BL, BM, BP, BQ. Religion--Religions,
Hinduism, Judaism, Islam, Buddhism. IV. Title.

Z696.U5B25 2001
025.4'62--dc21

2001050695

For sale by the

Library of Congress
Cataloging Distribution Service
Washington, DC 20541

Use the Internet and eliminate mail time and postage costs
http://cip.loc.gov/cip

PREFACE

The first edition of Class B: Subclasses BL-BQ (Religion. Hinduism. Judaism. Islam. Buddhism) was published in 1927 in a volume that also included subclasses BR-BX. The second edition was published in 1962 in the same configuration. The third edition was published in 1984. This 2001 edition has been produced using a new automated system developed at the Library of Congress for this purpose. The system will allow for the production of new editions on a more regular and frequent basis.

In 1992, Rebecca Guenther, Network Development and MARC Standards Office, began overseeing the conversion of Library of Congress Classification data to machine-readable form using the provisionally approved USMARC format for classification data. In 1993-1994, the Cataloging Distribution Service developed programs for producing printed classification schedules from the MARC records in cooperation with Lawrence Buzard, Paul Weiss, senior cataloging policy specialist, and Rebecca Guenther. The Cataloging Distribution Service also coordinated the layout and design of the new schedules.

The classification data were converted to the MARC format largely without editing or revision. As a result, this new edition is for the most part a cumulation of existing data rather than a fully revised edition. Users will notice, however, that many tables that had formerly appeared within the text of the schedule itself have been converted to external tables and now appear at the end of the volume. Since most of these external tables have been renumbered, their designations do not correspond to those in earlier editions of these subclasses.

New or revised numbers and captions are added to the L.C. Classification schedules as a result of development proposals made by the cataloging staff of the Library of Congress and cooperating institutions. Upon approval of these proposals by the weekly editorial meeting of the Cataloging Policy and Support Office, new classification records are created or existing records are revised in the master classification database. The Classification Editorial Team, consisting of Lawrence Buzard, editor, and Barry Bellinger, Kent Griffiths, Nancy Jones, and Dorothy Thomas, assistant editors, is responsible for creating new classification records, maintaining the master database, and creating index terms for the captions.

Barbara Tillett, Chief
Cataloging Policy and Support Office
August 2001

OUTLINE

BL	1-2790	Religions. Mythology. Rationalism
	1-50	Religion (General)
	51-65	Philosophy of religion. Psychology of religion. Religion in relation to other subjects
	70-71	Sacred books (General)
	71.5-73	Biography
	74-99	Religions of the world
	175-265	Natural theology
	175-190	General
	200	Theism
	205-216	Nature and attributes of Deity
	217	Polytheism
	218	Dualism
	220	Pantheism
	221	Monotheism
	224-227	Creation. Theory of the earth
	239-265	Religion and science
	270	Unity and plurality
	290	The soul
	300-325	The myth. Comparative mythology
	350-385	Classification of religions
	410	Religions in relation to one another
	425-490	Religious doctrines (General)
	430	Origins of religion
	435-457	Nature worship
	458	Women in comparative religion
	460	Sex worship. Phallicism
	465-470	Worship of human beings
	473-490	Other
	500-547	Eschatology
	550-619	Worship. Cultus
	624-629.5	Religious life
	630-(632.5)	Religious organization
	660-2680	History and principles of religions
	660	Indo-European. Aryan
	685	Ural-Altaic
	687	Mediterranean region
	689-980	European. Occidental
	700-820	Classical (Etruscan, Greek, Roman)
	830-875	Germanic and Norse
	900-980	Other European
	1000-2370	Asian. Oriental
	1000-1035	General
	1050-1060	By region

OUTLINE

BL	Religions. Mythology. Rationalism
	History and principles of religions
	Asian. Oriental - Continued
1100-1295	Hinduism
1100-1107.5	General
1108.2-1108.7	Religious education
1109.2-1109.7	Antiquities. Archaeology. Inscriptions
1111-1143.2	Sacred books. Sources
1112.2-1137.5	Vedic texts
1140.2-1140.4	Purāṇas
1141.2-1142.6	Tantric texts
1145-1146	Hindu literature
1153.7-1168	By region or country
1212.32-1215	Doctrines. Theology
1216-1225	Hindu pantheon. Deities
1225.2-1243.58	Religious life
1243.72-1243.78	Monasteries. Temples, etc.
1271.2-1295	Modifications. Sects
1284.5-1289.592	Vaishnavism
1300-1380	Jainism
1310-1314.2	Sacred books. Sources
1315-1317	Jain literature
1375.3-1375.7	Jaina pantheon. Deities
1376-1378.85	Forms of worship
1379-1380	Modifications, etc.
1500-1590	Zoroastrianism (Mazdeism). Parseeism
1595	Yezidis
1600-1695	Semitic religions
1600-1605	General
1610	Aramean
1615-1616	Sumerian
1620-1625	Assyro-Babylonian
1630	Chaldean
1635	Harranian. Pseudo-Sabian
1640-1645	Syrian. Palestinian. Samaritan
1650	Hebrew
	For Judaism, see subclass BM
1660-1665	Phoenician. Carthaginian, etc.
1670-1672	Canaanite
1675	Moabite. Philistine
1680-1685	Arabian (except Islam)
1695	Druses
1710	Ethiopian

OUTLINE

BL		Religions. Mythology. Rationalism
		History and principles of religions
		Asian. Oriental - Continued
	1750-2350	By region or country
	1790-1975	China
	1830-1883	Confucianism
	1899-1942.85	Taoism
	2000-2032	India
	2017-2018.7	Sikhism
	2195-2228	Japan
	2216-2227.8	Shinto
	2230-2240	Korea
	2390-2490	African
	2420-2460	Egyptian
	2500-2592	American
		For American Indians, see classes E-F
	2600-2630	Pacific Ocean islands. Oceania
	2670	Arctic regions
	2700-2790	Rationalism
BM	1-990	Judaism
	1-449	General
	70-135	Study and teaching
	150-449	History
	201-449	By region or country
	480-488.8	Pre-Talmudic Jewish literature (non-Biblical)
	495-532	Sources of Jewish religion. Rabbinical literature
	497-509	Talmudic literature
	497-497.8	Mishnah
	498-498.8	Palestinian Talmud
	499-504.7	Babylonian Talmud
	507-507.5	Baraita
	508-508.5	Tosefta
	510-518	Midrash
	520-523.7	Halacha
	525-526	Cabala
	529	Jewish tradition
	534-538	Relation of Judaism to special subject fields
	534-536	Religions
	545-582	Principles of Judaism (General)
	585-585.4	Controversial works against the Jews
	590-591	Jewish works against Christianity and Islam
	600-645	Dogmatic Judaism
	646	Heresy, heresies
	648	Apologetics

OUTLINE

BM		Judaism - Continued
	650-747	Practical Judaism
	651-652.7	Priests, rabbis, etc.
	653-653.7	Congregations. Synagogues
	654-655.6	The tabernacle. The temple
	656-657	Forms of worship
	660-679	Liturgy and ritual
	690-695	Festivals and fasts
	700-720	Rites and customs
	723-729	Jewish way of life. Spiritual life. Mysticism. Personal religion. Moral theology
	730-747	Preaching. Homiletics
	750-755	Biography
	900-990	Samaritans
BP	1-610	Islam. Bahai Faith. Theosophy, etc.
	1-253	Islam
	1-68	General
	42-48	Study and teaching
	50-68	History
	70-80	Biography
	75-77.75	Muḥammad, Prophet, d. 632
	87-89	Islamic literature
	100-(157)	Sacred books
	100-134	Koran
	128.15-129.83	Special parts and chapters
	130-134	Works about the Koran
	135-136.9	Hadith literature. Traditions. Sunna
	137-137.5	Koranic and other Islamic legends
	160-165	General works on Islam
	165.5	Dogma ('Aqā'id)
	166-166.94	Theology (Kalām)
	167.5	Heresy, heresies, heretics
	168	Apostasy from Islam
	169	Works against Islam and the Koran
	170	Works in defense of Islam. Islamic apologetics
	170.2	Benevolent work. Social work. Welfare work, etc.
	170.3-170.5	Missionary work of Islam
	171-173	Relation of Islam to other religions
	173.25-173.45	Islamic sociology
	174-190	The practice of Islam
	176-181	The five duties of a Moslem. Pillars of Islam
	182	Jihad (Holy War)
	184-184.9	Religious ceremonies, rites, etc.
	186-186.97	Special days and seasons, fasts, feasts, festivals, etc. Relics

OUTLINE

BP		Islam. Bahai Faith. Theosophy, etc.
		Islam
		The practice of Islam - Continued
	187-187.9	Shrines, sacred places, etc.
	188-190	Islamic religious life
	188.2-188.3	Devotional literature
	188.45-189.65	Sufism. Mysticism. Dervishes
	189.68-189.7	Monasticism
	191-253	Branches, sects, etc.
	192-194.9	Shiites
	221-223	Black Muslims
	232	Moorish Science Temple of America
	251-253	Nurculuk
	300-395	Bahai Faith
	500-585	Theosophy
	595-597	Anthroposophy
	600-610	Other beliefs and movements
BQ	1-9800	Buddhism
	1-10	Periodicals. Yearbooks (General)
	12-93	Societies, councils, associations, clubs, etc.
	96-99	Financial institutions. Trusts
	100-102	Congresses. Conferences (General)
	104-105	Directories (General)
	107-109	Museums. Exhibitions
	115-126	General collections. Collected works
	128	Encyclopedias (General)
	130	Dictionaries (General)
	133	Terminology
	135	Questions and answers. Maxims (General)
	141-209	Religious education (General)
	210-219	Research
	221-249	Antiquities. Archaeology
	240-244	Literary discoveries
	246-249	Inscriptions, etc.
	251-799	History
	800-829	Persecutions
	840-999	Biography
	840-858	Collective
	860-999	Individual
	860-939	Gautama Buddha
	940-999	Other
	1001-1045	Buddhist literature
	1100-3340	Tripiṭaka (Canonical literature)
	4000-4060	General works

OUTLINE

BQ

- Buddhism - Continued
  - 4061-4570 Doctrinal and systematic Buddhism
    - 4180-4565 Special doctrines
    - 4570 Special topics and relations to special subjects
  - 4600-4610 Relation to other religious and philosophical systems
  - 4620-4905 Buddhist pantheon
  - 4911-5720 Practice of Buddhism. Forms of worship
    - 4965-5030 Ceremonies and rites. Ceremonial rules
    - 5035-5065 Hymns. Chants. Recitations
    - 5070-5075 Altar, liturgical objects, ornaments, memorials, etc.
    - 5080-5085 Vestments, altar cloths, etc.
    - 5090-5095 Liturgical functions
    - 5100-5125 Symbols and symbolism
    - 5130-5137 Temple. Temple organization
    - 5140-5355 Buddhist ministry. Priesthood. Organization
      - 5251-5305 Education and training
      - 5310-5350 Preaching
    - 5360-5680 Religious life
      - 5485-5530 Precepts for laymen
      - 5535-5594 Devotional literature. Meditations. Prayers
      - 5595-5633 Devotion. Meditation. Prayer
      - 5635-5675 Spiritual life. Mysticism. Englightenment. Perfection
    - 5700-5720 Festivals. Days and seasons
    - 5725-5845 Folklore
      - 5821-5845 Miracle literature
    - 5851-5899 Benevolent work. Social work. Welfare work, etc.
    - 5901-5975 Missionary work
    - 6001-6160 Monasticism and monastic life Saṃgha (Order)
    - 6200-6240 Asceticism. Hermits. Wayfaring life
    - 6300-6388 Monasteries. Temples. Shrines. Sites
    - 6400-6495 Pilgrims and pilgrimages
    - 7001-9800 Modifications, schools, etc.
      - 7100-7285 Theravāda (Hinayana) Buddhism
      - 7300-7529 Mahayana Buddhism
      - 7530-7950 Tibetan Buddhism (Lamaism)
      - 7960-7989 Bonpo (Sect)
      - 8000-9800 Special modifications, sects, etc.
        - 8500-8769 Pure Land Buddhism
        - 8900-9099 Tantric Buddhism
        - 9250-9519 Zen Buddhism

	Religions. Mythology. Rationalism
	Religion
	Periodicals. Serials
1.A1	International or polyglot
1.A2-Z	English and American
2	Dutch
3	French
4	German
5	Italian
6	Scandinavian
7	Spanish and Portuguese
9.A-Z	Other languages, A-Z
10	Yearbooks
	Societies
11.A1	General works
11.A2-Z	English and American
12	Dutch
13	French
14	German
15	Italian
16	Scandinavian
17	Spanish and Portuguese
19.A-Z	Other, A-Z
21	Congresses
	Collected works
	Including monographs, papers, essays, etc.
25	Several authors
27	Individual authors
29	Selections
31	Dictionaries. Encyclopedias
35	Directories
37	Computer network resources
	Including the Internet
41	Study of comparative religion. Historiography. Methodology
	Religious education
42	General works
42.5.A-Z	By region or country, A-Z
43.A-Z	Biography of students and historians, A-Z
	Museums. Exhibitions
45	General works
46.A-Z	Individual, A-Z
	Subarrange by place or name
48	General works
50	Addresses, essays, lectures
51	Philosophy of religion. Philosophy and religion
	Cf. BD573, Philosophy and religion
	Psychology of religion. Religious experience
	Cf. BP175, Islam
	Cf. BR110+, Christianity
	Cf. HQ61, Religious emotion and eroticism
53.A1	Periodicals. Societies. Serials
53.A2-Z	General works

Religion
Psychology of religion.
Religious experience -- Continued
53.5 Fanaticism. Religious addiction. Religious neurosis
54 Glossolalia. Gift of tongues
Cf. BT122.5, Glossolalia or tongues as one of the gifts of the Holy Spirit
55 Religion and civilization
Religion and ethics, see BJ47
Religion and literature
see PN49, PN1077, PR145, PR830.R5, etc.
Religion and science, see BL239+
60 Religion and sociology
65.A-Z Religion in relation to other subjects, A-Z
Cf. BR115.A+, Christianity in relation to other subjects
Adoption, see HV875.2+
65.A4 Aesthetics
65.A46 Aging
65.A72 Archaeology
Art, see N72.R4
Atomic energy, see BL65.N83
65.A85 Atomic warfare
65.B34 Balisier plant
65.B47 Bereavement
65.B54 Blasphemy
65.B66 Books and reading
Business, see HF5388
65.C45 Censorship
65.C53 Change
65.C58 Civil rights
Cf. BL65.H78, Human rights
Comic, The, see BL65.L3
65.C7 Crime. Criminals
Cf. HV8865+, Provision for religious and moral instruction of prisoners (Administrative aspects)
65.C8 Culture
65.D67 Dreams
65.D7 Drugs. Hallucinogenic drugs
Economics, see HB72
65.E46 Emotions
65.E68 Equality
65.E75 Ethnicity. Ethnic relations
Fantasy, see BL65.I43
65.F4 Fear
65.F65 Food
65.F67 Forgiveness
Freedom, see BL65.L52
65.G4 Geography
65.G73 Gratitude
Hallucinogenic drugs, see BL65.D7

Religion
Religion in relation to other subjects, A-Z -- Continued

65.H36 Happiness
Health, see BL65.M4
65.H5 History
65.H64 Homosexuality
65.H78 Human rights
Cf. BL65.C58, Civil rights
65.H8 Humanities (General)
Cf. N72.R4, Religion and visual art
Cf. PN49, Religion and literature
Humor, see BL65.L3
Hygiene, see BL65.M4
65.H9 Hypnotism
65.I43 Imagination. Fantasy
Cf. BF408+, Psychology
Information technology, see BL265.I54
65.I55 International affairs
Investments, see HG4515.13
65.J83 Judgment
65.J87 Justice
65.L2 Language
Cf. P53.76, Religious aspects of language study and teaching
65.L3 Laughter. The comic. Wit and humor
65.L33 Law
65.L42 Leadership
Cf. BL626.38, Religious life
65.L52 Liberty
65.L67 Lotus
65.M2 Magic
65.M4 Medicine. Health. Hygiene
Including spiritual healing
65.M45 Mental health
65.N3 Nationalism
Cf. BV629+, Church and state
65.N35 Nature
Cf. BL435+, Nature worship
Cf. GF80, Religious aspects of human ecology
Nonviolence, see BL65.V55
65.N83 Nuclear energy
65.N85 Numbers
Nursing, see RT85.2
65.P3 Parapsychology
65.P4 Peace
Peace of mind, see BL627.55
65.P47 Persecution
65.P6 Play
65.P7 Politics
65.P73 Postmodernism
65.P75 Poverty
Psychoanalysis, see BF175.4.R44

Religion
Religion in relation
to other subjects, A-Z -- Continued
65.R3 Race
65.R48 Revolutions
Science, see BL239+
65.S37 Secrecy. Secrets
65.S38 Self
65.S4 Sex
65.S42 Sex crimes
65.S62 Social conflict
65.S64 Social movements
Spiritual healing, see BL65.M4
Sports, see GV706.42
65.S8 State, The
65.S84 Success
65.S85 Suffering
Technology, see BL265.T4
65.T47 Terrorism
65.T55 Time
UFO cults, see BL65.U54
(65.U5) Underdeveloped areas
see BL2680
65.U54 Unidentified flying objects. UFO cults
Cf. BP605.A33, Aetherius Society
Cf. BP605.U52, Unarius Educational Foundation
Utopias, see HX807
65.V44 Vegetarianism
65.V55 Violence. Nonviolence
65.W2 War
Cf. BL65.A85, Atomic warfare
65.W42 Wealth
65.W57 Wisdom
Wit and humor, see BL65.L3
65.W67 Work
Sacred books (General)
Cf. BL1010, Ancient oriental religions
70 Collected works
71 History and criticism
Biography
71.5 History and criticism
72 Collective
73.A-Z Individual, A-Z
Class here only works on persons whose religious affiliation cannot be determined
Cf. BP610, Other beliefs and movements
Religions of the world
Including historical and comparative works
74 Collected works
Cf. BL70, Sacred books
General works
75 Early through 1800
80 1801-1950

Religion
Religions of the world
General works -- Continued
80.2 1951-2000
80.3 2001-
82 Handbooks, manuals, etc.
85 General special
87 Addresses, essays, lectures
90 Pictorial works
92 Juvenile works
95 Outlines, syllabi, etc.
History. By period
Cf. GN470+, Religion of primitive peoples
For Christianity, see BR1+
For early works, see BL75
Origins of religion, see BL430
96 Ancient
97 Medieval
98 Modern
98.5 Civil religion
99 Liberalism (Religion)
100 Religion and the supernatural
Cf. BT960+, Invisible world
105 Authority
Natural theology
175 Collected works
e.g.
Bridgewater treatises
175.B7 Collected. By date
175.B81-B88 Miscellaneous volumes. By number and date
General works
180 Early through 1800
181 1801-1950
182 1951-2000
183 2001-
185 Juvenile works
190 Insufficiency of natural theology
200 Theism
Including belief in God apart from revelation
Cf. BL51, Philosophy of religion
Cf. BL2700+, Rationalism, deism, etc.
Cf. BT98+, Christian doctrine of God
Nature and attributes of Deity
Cf. BT98+, Doctrinal theology
205 General works
210 Analogies and correspondences
Anthropomorphism
215 General works
215.3 Fatherhood. Masculinity
Cf. BL325.F35, Comparative mythology

Religion
Natural theology
Nature and attributes of Deity
Anthropomorphism -- Continued
215.5 Motherhood. Femininity
Cf. BL325.F4, Female deities
Cf. BL325.M6, Mother goddesses
Cf. BL473.5, Goddesses
Cf. BT153.M6, Christianity
216 Theodicy
217 Polytheism
218 Dualism
220 Pantheism
221 Monotheism
Cf. BT98+, Doctrinal theology
Creation. Theory of the earth
Cf. BD493+, Cosmology
Cf. BL263, Evolution
Cf. BS651+, Genesis and science
Cf. BT695+, Doctrinal theology
General works
224 Early through 1800
225 1801-1950
226 1951-2000
227 2001-
Providence
Cf. BT135, Doctrinal theology
230 General works
235 Fatalism. Destiny
237 Religion and the intellectual
237.5 Puritan movements
Cf. BX9301+, Puritans
238 Fundamentalism
Cf. BT82.2, Christian fundamentalism
Religion and science
Cf. BT1095+, Apologetics
General works
239 Early through 1800
240 1801-1950
240.2 1951-2000
240.3 2001-
241 Addresses, essays, lectures
243 Juvenile works
245 History
Special sciences
250 Archaeology
Astronomy
253 General works
254 Astronautics
255 Biology
255.5 Computer science
256 Ethnology. Anthropology
259 Geology

Religion
Natural theology
Religion and science
Special sciences -- Continued
261 Life sciences
Natural history
262 General works
263 Evolution
Cf. BS659, Bible and evolution
Cf. GN281+, Human evolution
Cf. QH359+, General biology
265.A-Z Other, A-Z
265.C4 Chemistry
265.E6 Electricity
265.I54 Information technology
265.L5 Light
265.M3 Mathematics
Medicine, see BL65.M4
265.P4 Physics
265.T4 Technology
270 Unity and plurality
Good and evil, see BJ1400+
Evil, see BJ1406
Prayer, adoration, see BL560
Sacrifice, see BL570+
290 The Soul
Cf. BD419+, Philosophy
Cf. BT740+, Doctrinal theology
Future life, see BL535+
The myth. Comparative mythology
Cf. GR1+, Folklore
300 Periodicals. Societies. Serials
301 Congresses
303 Dictionaries
Biography
303.5 Collective
303.6.A-Z Individual, A-Z
Myth. The nature of myth
304 General works
304.2 Myth and ritual school
General works
305 Early through 1800
310 1801-1950
311 1951-2000
312 2001-
313 General special
315 Addresses, essays, lectures
320 Study and teaching
325.A-Z Topics in comparative mythology, A-Z
325.A35 Agriculture
325.A45 Amphibians
Androgyny, see BL325.B45
325.A6 Animals

Religion
The myth. Comparative mythology
Topics in comparative mythology, A-Z -- Continued

325.B43	Birds
325.B45	Bisexuality. Androgyny. Hermaphroditism
325.B5	Blood
325.C56	Clouds
325.C7	Creation
	Darkness, see BL325.L47
325.D33	Days of the week
325.D35	Dead, The. Death
325.D4	Deluge
325.E3	Eagle
325.E35	Eclipses
325.E4	Edens
325.E45	Eggs
325.E47	Electricity
	Evil, see BL325.G58
325.E93	Eye
325.F3	Fall of man
325.F35	Fathers
325.F4	Female deities. Nymphs. Fairies, etc. Cf. BL325.L5, Lilith
325.F5	Fire
325.F6	Fleeing
325.G5	Giants
325.G55	Golden age
325.G58	Good and evil
325.G6	Gorgons
	Great mother of the gods, see BL820.C8
325.G7	Griffins
325.H23	Hand
325.H25	Head
325.H3	Headless gods
325.H4	Healing deities
	Hermaphroditism, see BL325.B45
325.H46	Heroes Cf. GR515, Heroes in folklore
325.I48	Incest
325.I5	Incubation
325.I57	Insects
325.K5	Kings and rulers Cf. GR520, Kings in folklore
325.L3	Labyrinths
325.L4	Leadership
325.L47	Light and darkness
325.L5	Lilith
325.L56	Lions
325.M3	Matriarchy
325.M35	Mensuration
325.M4	Metamorphosis
325.M5	Mice
325.M53	Millstones. Mills

Religion
The myth. Comparative mythology
Topics in comparative mythology, A-Z -- Continued
325.M56 Moon, The
Cf. BL438, Moon worship
325.M6 Mother goddesses
325.M63 Mountains
325.N35 Navel
325.N37 Navigation
325.N5 Night
325.O4 Oedipus
325.O74 Order
325.P45 Phoenix
Cf. GR830.P4, Folklore
325.P6 Plants. Trees
Cf. BL444, Nature worship
325.P7 Polarity. Opposites
325.R2 Rainbow
325.R6 Rome
325.S3 Samson
325.S37 Saturn (Planet)
325.S42 Sex
325.S47 Sisters
325.S5 Sky gods
325.S7 Spirals
325.S8 Sun, The
Cf. BL438, Sun worship
325.T45 Thirteen (The number)
325.T55 Time
Trees, see BL325.P6
325.T8 Twins
Cf. BL820.C2, Castor and Pollux
325.V5 Virgin birth
325.V55 Virginity
325.V68 Voyages and travels
325.W45 Wheels
325.W56 Wisdom
325.W65 Women heroes
Classification of religions
350 General works
355 Polytheistic
360 Monotheistic
365 Revealed
Preliterate peoples (General), see GN470+
380 Ethnic
385 National
390 Proposed, universal, or world religions
410 Religions in relation to one another
For Christianity in relation to other religions, see BR127+
Religious doctrines (General)
425 General works
427 Creeds

Religion
Religious doctrines (General) -- Continued
430 Origins of religion
Cf. GN470.5, Preliterate peoples
432 Paganism
Cf. BP605.N46, Neo-paganism
Nature worship
Including religious interpretations of nature
435 General works
438 Celestial bodies. Sun, moon, stars
Cf. BL325.M56, The moon in comparative mythology
Cf. BL325.S8, The sun in comparative mythology
438.2 Earth
Animals
Cf. GR820+, Mythical animals
439 General works
439.5 Killing of animals. Animal experimentation. Vivisection
440 Crocodile
441 Serpent
442 Birds
443.A-Z Other, A-Z
443.B4 Bears
443.B8 Bulls
443.C3 Cats
443.H6 Horses
443.L6 Llamas
444 Plants. Trees
Cf. BL325.P6, Comparative mythology
Cf. BL583, Sacred wood and field cults
446 Deserts
447 Mountains
450 Water
453 Fire
457.A-Z Other, A-Z
457.C3 Caduceus
457.C6 Corn
457.E3 Earthquakes
457.H3 Hawthorn
457.M4 Metals
457.S7 Stones (Sacred)
457.S75 Storms
457.W5 Wine
458 Woman in comparative religion
Cf. BL325.F4, Female deities, etc. in comparative religion
460 Sex worship. Phallicism. Horned god
Cf. BL65.S4, Sex in religion
Cf. BL441, Serpent worship
Cf. BL444, Tree worship
462 Marriage

Religion
Religious doctrines (General) -- Continued
Worship of human beings. Apotheosis. Superman
465 General works
Cult of the Roman emperors, see DG124
467 Ancestor worship
470 Worship of the dead. Fear of the dead
473 God. Gods
Cf. GR500+, Supernatural beings (Folklore)
473.5 Goddesses
474 Trinities
474.5 Quaternities
475 Saviors. Messiahs
475.5 Revelation
475.6 Judgment of God
475.7 Sin
476 Redemption. Salvation
476.5 Reconciliation
476.7 Repentance
477 Angels. Good spirits
Cf. BT965+, Doctrinal theology
478 Cherubim
480 Demons. Evil spirits. Devil worship
Cf. BF1501+, Demonology
Cf. BL1595, Yezidis
Cf. GR525+, Demonology (Folklore)
For individual religions, see BP166.89, BQ4900, BT975, etc.
482 Spirit possession
485 Idolatry. Image worship
487 Miracles
488 Saints
490 Superstitions in relation to religion
Cf. BR135+, Christian superstition
Eschatology
Cf. BT819+, Christian eschatology
500 General works
501 Apocalypticism. Apocalyptic literature
Cf. BS646, Revelation
Cf. BS1705, Apocalypses
503 End of the world
503.2 Millennialism
503.5 Ascension
504 Death
505 Resurrection
510 Incarnation
Reincarnation. Metamorphoses. Transmigration
515 General works
518 Addresses, essays, lectures
Biography
519 Collective
520.A-Z Individual, A-Z
530 Immortality

Religion
Eschatology -- Continued
Future life
535 General works
540 Other worlds. Paradise, etc.
Cf. BD655, Plurality of worlds, life on other planets
545 Infernal regions
547 Judgment of the dead
Worship. Cultus
For classical cults, see DE - DG
550 General works
560 Prayer. Prayers. Hymns, etc.
For prayer books and devotions for special classes of persons, see BL625.2+
Sacrifice. Offerings. Vows
570 General works
571 Foundation sacrifices
Sacred places
Cf. GR505+, Sacred places in folklore
580 General works
(581) By region or country
see BL660-BL2670
582 Cities and towns
583 Groves. Rivers
Including wood and field cults
Cf. BL444, Plant and tree worship
584 Underground areas. Grottoes
586 Temples. Pagodas, etc.
588 Home. Dwellings
Sacred times, seasons, days
590 General works
595.A-Z Special, A-Z
595.S9 Sunday
595.W55 Winter solstice
Rites and ceremonies. Ritual, cult, symbolism
600 General works
602 Altar
Symbols. Emblems
603 General works
604.A-Z Special, A-Z
604.B64 Body, Human
604.C5 Circle
604.C7 Cross
Cf. BV160, Christian art and symbolism
604.D6 Dove
604.D7 Drinking vessels
604.H6 Horns
Human body, see BL604.B64
604.M36 Mandala
Cf. BL2015.M3, Indian religion
604.S4 Serpent
604.S8 Swastika

Religion
Worship. Cultus
Rites and ceremonies. Ritual, cult, symbolism
Symbols. Emblems
Special, A-Z -- Continued
604.S85 Sword
604.T7 Triangle
604.V2 V symbol
604.W3 Walls
604.W4 Wheel
604.W7 Wreaths
604.Y2 Y symbol
604.Y5 Yin Yang symbol
605 Music. Dances
610 Mysteries
613 Divination. Oracles, etc.
Cf. BF1745+, Occult sciences
615 Initiations
617 Covenants
619.A-Z Other, A-Z
619.B43 Beads
619.B57 Birth customs
619.C3 Castration
619.C57 Circumcision
619.C6 Confession
619.E9 Eye
619.F57 Fire walking
619.F85 Funeral services
619.H4 Headgear
619.H68 House blessings
619.L8 Lustration
619.M37 Marriage service
619.M45 Memorials
619.N7 Nocturnal ceremonies
619.O6 Ordure (Use)
619.O7 Orientation
619.P3 Paper (Use)
619.P5 Pilgrims and pilgrimages
619.R42 Regeneration
619.R44 Relics and reliquaries
619.S3 Sacraments
619.S45 Ships
619.S5 Silence (Use)
619.W3 Water
Religious life
624 General works
Meditations
624.2 General works
624.5 Twelve-step program meditations (for all classes of recovering persons)
625 Asceticism. Mysticism
Special classes of persons
625.2 African Americans

Religion
Religious life
Special classes of persons -- Continued
625.3 Middle aged persons
625.4 Aged
625.47 Youth
625.5 Children
625.6 Family
625.65 Men
625.68 Mothers
625.7 Women
625.8 Parents
625.9.A-Z Other, A-Z
625.9.A37 Adult child abuse victims
625.9.A38 Adult children of dysfunctional families
625.9.A43 Alcoholics
625.9.A84 Athletes
625.9.B47 Bereaved children
625.9.B48 Bereaved parents
625.9.B87 Businesspeople
625.9.C35 Caregivers
625.9.C47 Chronic pain patients
625.9.C62 Codependents
625.9.C64 College students
625.9.C65 Compulsive gamblers
625.9.D45 Depressed persons
625.9.D58 Divorced people
625.9.F35 Families of alcoholics
625.9.G39 Gays
625.9.R43 Recovering addicts
625.9.S53 Sick. Patients
Including the terminally ill
625.9.T44 Teenage girls
Terminally ill, see BL625.9.S53
625.9.V52 Victims of family violence
Other special topics
625.92 Boredom
625.93 Coincidence
625.94 Dance
625.95 Desire
626 Ecstasy
626.3 Faith
626.33 Interpersonal relations
626.35 Joy
626.38 Leadership
626.4 Love
626.5 Martyrdom
627 Meditation
Cf. BF637.M4, Applied psychology
Cf. BF637.T68, Transcendental Meditation
627.5 Pain
627.55 Peace of mind
627.57 Personality. Typology (Psychology)

Religion
Religious life
Other special topics -- Continued
Prayer, see BL560
628 Retreats
628.2 Silence
628.4 Small groups
628.5 Spiritual journals
628.7 Storytelling
628.8 Travel
Typology (Psychology), see BL627.57
629 Vocation. Calling
629.5.A-Z Other, A-Z
629.5.C53 Change
629.5.F33 Failure
629.5.G37 Gardening. Gardens
629.5.S44 Self-esteem
Religious organization
630 General works
631 Monasticism and religious orders
Cf. BL1238.72+, Hinduism
Cf. BP189.68+, Islam
Cf. BQ6001+, Buddhism
Cf. BV4518, Christianity (General)
Cf. BX385+, Orthodox Eastern Church
Cf. BX580+, Russian Church
Cf. BX2400+, Catholic Church
Cf. BX5183+, Church of England
Cf. BX5970+, Protestant Episcopal Church
Communities and institutions
632 General works
(632.5) By region or country
see BL660-BL2670
633 Prophets and prophecy
635 Priests and priestcraft
637 Missionary activities
Cf. BM729.P7, Judaism
Cf. BV2000, Christianity
Mass media
638 General works
(638.5) By region or country
see BL660-BL2670
639 Conversion. Converts
639.5 Apostasy
640 Religious liberty
History and principles of religion
660 Indo-European. Aryan
Celtic, see BL900+
Hamitic, see BL2410
Semitic, see BL1600+
Slavic, see BL930+
685 Ural-Altaic
For Asian groups, see BL2370.A+

Religion
History and principles of religion -- Continued
687 Mediterranean region
European. Occidental
689 General works
By period
690 To 1500
695 Modern, 1500-
By region or country, see BL980.A+
Classical religion and mythology
Cf. N7760+, Art
Cf. DE-DG, Classical history and antiquities
For cultural studies, see DE-DG
700 Periodicals. Societies. Serials
710 Collections
715 Dictionaries
Cf. DE5, Classical dictionaries
717 Historiography. Methodology
General works
720 Early through 1800
721 1801-1950
722 1951-2000
723 2001-
725 Elementary works
727 General special
730 Addresses, essays, lectures
735 Future life. Elysium. Hades
Etruscan
740 General works
745 General special
750 Addresses, essays, lectures
760.A-Z Special topics, A-Z
760.V6 Votive offerings
Cf. DG223.7.V67, Etruscan antiquities
Greek
Cf. PA4037, Homeric mythology
General works
780 Early through 1800
781 1801-1950
782 1951-2000
783 2001-
785 General special
788 Ritual
790 Addresses, essays, lectures
793.A-Z Local, A-Z
e. g.
793.A7 Arcadia
793.C6 Corinth
793.C7 Crete
Cf. BL793.M8, Mycenae
793.C75 Crimea
793.C8 Cumae
793.C85 Cyrenaica

Religion
History and principles of religion
European. Occidental
Classical religion and mythology
Greek
Local, A-Z -- Continued
793.D4 Delphi
793.L2 Laconia
793.L4 Lemnos
793.M8 Mycenae
Cf. BL793.C7, Crete
793.P3 Petrae
793.P4 Pergamon
793.S3 Samothrace
793.S5 Sicily
793.T4 Thera
793.T43 Thessaly
793.T7 Troy
Including the Trojan War
795.A-Z Special topics, A-Z
795.A54 Animals
795.A56 Anthesteria
795.A7 Aromatic plants
795.B57 Bisexuality
Child and parent, see BL795.P37
795.C55 Children
795.C57 Colonies. Colonization
Colonization, see BL795.C57
795.C58 Constellations. Stars
For folklore of the stars, see GR625
795.C6 Contests
795.C7 Crime and criminals
Cult tables, see BL795.T32
795.D35 Dancing
Darkness, see BL795.L54
795.D4 Death
Delphian oracle, see DF261.D35
795.D5 Demons
795.D6 Dolphin
795.D7 Dragons
795.E25 Economics
795.E5 Eleusinian mysteries
795.E6 Elysium
795.E7 Eschatology
795.E8 Europa
Fatalism, see BL795.F37
795.F37 Fate and fatalism
795.F55 Fire
795.F6 Foot
795.F8 Future life
795.G57 Girls
795.G6 God
795.G63 Goddesses

Religion
History and principles of religion
European. Occidental
Classical religion and mythology
Greece
Special topics, A-Z -- Continued

795.H47 Heroines
795.H6 Homosexuality
795.H83 Human sacrifice
795.H85 Hunting
795.I49 Immortalism
795.I5 Immortality
795.L3 Landscapes
Including gardens, meadows, etc.
795.L54 Light and darkness
Marriage, Sacred, see BL795.S22
795.M4 Mental illness
795.M47 Metamorphosis
795.M6 Moderation
795.M65 Monsters
795.M9 Mysteries
795.N3 Navel
795.O7 Orpheus
795.P37 Parent and child
795.P48 Pilgrims and pilgrimages
795.P57 Politics
795.P6 Prayer
795.P7 Priests and priestesses
795.R58 Rivers
795.S22 Sacred marriage
795.S23 Sacred meals
795.S25 Sacrifice
Sanctuaries, see BL795.S47
795.S47 Shrines, sanctuaries, temples
795.S62 Soul
795.S63 Sphere
795.S65 Springs
Stars, see BL795.C58
795.S85 Sun worship
795.T32 Tables. Cult tables
Temples, see BL795.S47
795.T54 Thesmophoria
795.T8 Tree worship
795.T85 Trials
Trojan War, see BL793.T7
795.V57 Virginity
795.V6 Votive offerings
795.W28 War
795.W3 Water
795.W56 Winds
795.W65 Women
795.W74 Wreaths
795.Z63 Zodiac

Religion
History and principles of religion
European. Occidental
Classical religion and mythology -- Continued
Roman
798 Dictionaries
General works
800 Early through 1800
801 1801-1950
802 1951-2000
803 2001-
805 General special
808 Ritual
810 Addresses, essays, lectures
813.A-Z Local, A-Z
e. g.
813.A3 Africa (North)
813.A7 Aricia
813.C3 Campania
813.E8 Etruria
813.O7 Ostia
813.P6 Pompeii
813.S3 Sabine territory
815.A-Z Special topics, A-Z
815.C74 Crime. Criminals
815.E8 Evocation
815.F8 Future life
Government of God, see BL815.P74
815.H47 Heroes
Human sacrifice, see BL815.S3
815.I4 Immortality
815.L3 Laurel
815.L8 Lupercalia
815.M6 Monotheism
815.M64 Moon
815.M8 Mysticism
815.P68 Prayer
815.P7 Priests
815.P74 Providence and government of God
815.R4 Regifugium
815.S15 Sacred meals
815.S3 Sacrifice, Human
815.S8 Sun worship
815.T3 Tanaquil legend
815.T35 Taurobolium
815.T45 Terminus
815.V3 Ver sacrum
815.V4 Vestals
815.W6 Women
820.A-Z Special deities and characters of classical mythology, A-Z
Including cults
820.A25 Adonis

Religion
History and principles of religion
European. Occidental
Classical religion and mythology
Special deities and characters of classical mythology, A-Z -- Continued

820.A3	Aeacus
820.A34	Aeneas
820.A4	Aesculapius
820.A46	Agamemnon
820.A54	Aion
820.A56	Alcmene
820.A6	Amazons
820.A63	Amycus
820.A64	Andromeda
820.A65	Antenor
820.A67	Anteus
	Aphrodite, see BL820.V5
820.A7	Apollo
	Ares, see BL820.M2
820.A8	Argonauts
820.A83	Ariadne
	Artemis, see BL820.D5
820.A835	Atalanta
	Athene, see BL820.M6
820.A84	Attis
820.B2	Bacchus. Dionysus
820.B28	Baucis and Philemon
	Biton, see BL820.C62
820.B64	Bona Dea
820.C127	Cacus
820.C13	Cadmus
820.C15	Calydonian boar
820.C16	Camilla
820.C18	Cassandra
820.C2	Castor and Pollux. The Dioscuri Cf. BL325.T8, Twin myths
820.C4	Cerebus
820.C5	Ceres. Demeter
820.C55	Charon
	Charybdis, see BL820.S39
820.C57	Chimera
820.C6	Circe
820.C62	Cleobis and Biton
820.C63	Concordia. Concordia Augusta
820.C65	Cupid. Eros
820.C7	Curetes
820.C8	Cybele. Rhea Cybele Including Great mother of the gods
820.C83	Cyclopes
820.C85	Cyrene (nymph)
820.D25	Daedalus

Religion
History and principles of religion
European. Occidental
Classical religion and mythology
Special deities and characters of classical mythology, A-Z -- Continued

820.D3 Danaids
Demeter, see BL820.C5
820.D5 Diana. Artemis
820.D54 Diktynna
Dionysus, see BL820.B2
Dioscuri, see BL820.C2
820.E5 Eileithyia
820.E7 Epaphus
820.E8 Erichthonius
Erinyes, see BL820.F8
Eros, see BL820.C65
Eumenides, see BL820.F8
820.F7 Fortuna. Tyche
820.F8 Furies. Erinyes
820.G47 Geryon
820.G5 Giants
820.G7 Gorgons
820.G8 The graces
820.H43 Hecate
820.H45 Helen of Troy
Helios, see BL820.S62
Hephaestus, see BL820.V8
Hera, see BL820.J6
820.H5 Hercules. Heracles
Hermes, see BL820.M5
820.H55 Hippolyta
820.H7 Horatii
820.H9 Hyacinthus
820.H93 Hydra
(820.H95) Hygieia
see BL820.S25
820.I33 Icarus
Ino, see BL820.M3
820.I65 Iphigenia
820.I8 Itys
820.J2 Janus
Jason, see BL820.A8
820.J6 Juno. Hera
Cf. BL820.E5, Eileithyia
820.J8 Jupiter. Zeus
820.J83 Jupiter Dolichenus
820.L25 Ladon
820.L28 Lamia
820.L3 Lares
Leucothea, see BL820.M3
820.M2 Mars. Ares

Religion
History and principles of religion
European. Occidental
Classical religion and mythology
Special deities and characters of classical mythology, A-Z -- Continued

820.M26 Marsyas
820.M3 Matuta. Leucothea. Ino
820.M37 Medea
820.M38 Medusa
820.M39 Melampus
820.M4 Memmon
820.M45 Mens
820.M5 Mercury. Hermes
820.M55 Midas
820.M6 Minerva. Athene (Athena)
820.M63 Minotaur
820.M65 Mother goddesses
820.M8 Muses
820.N47 Nemean lion
820.N48 Nemesis
820.N5 Neptune. Poseidon
820.N95 Nymphs
820.O3 Odysseus. Ulysses
820.O43 Oedipus
820.O6 Ops
820.O7 Orpheus
820.P2 Pan
820.P23 Pandora
820.P4 Pegasus
820.P43 Penates
820.P45 Penelope
Persephone, see BL820.P7
820.P5 Perseus
820.P53 Phaethon
Philemon and Baucis, see BL820.B28
Poseidon, see BL820.N5
820.P65 Procrustes
820.P68 Prometheus
820.P7 Proserpina. Proserpine. Persephone
820.P8 Psyche
820.P9 Pyrrus. Pyrros
Rhea, see BL820.C8
820.R65 Roma
820.R67 Romulus & Remus
820.S25 Salus. Hygieia
820.S29 Saturn
820.S3 Satyrs
820.S39 Scylla. Charybdis
820.S47 Silvanus
820.S5 Sirens
820.S53 Sisyphus

Religion
History and principles of religion
European. Occidental
Classical religion and mythology
Special deities and characters of classical mythology, A-Z -- Continued

820.S62 Sol. Helios
820.S66 Sphinxes
820.T37 Tantalus
820.T47 Themis
820.T5 Theseus
820.T6 Tiber River. Tiberinus
820.T63 Titans
Tyche, see BL820.F7
Ulysses, see BL820.O3
820.V34 Valetudo
820.V5 Venus. Aphrodite
820.V55 Vesta
820.V6 Victory
820.V8 Vulcan. Hephaestus
Zeus, see BL820.J8

Germanic and Norse mythology
830 Periodicals. Societies. Serials
Collected works
840 Several authors
845 Individual authors
850 Dictionaries
855 Sources
Cf. PT, Literature
860 General works
863 General special
865 Addresses, essays, lectures
870.A-Z Special topics, A-Z
Including individual gods
870.B3 Balder
870.C74 Creation
870.D7 Drinks and drinking
870.F28 Fafnir
870.F3 Fate and fatalism
870.F5 Freyr
870.F6 Frigg
870.F7 Funeral rites and ceremonies
870.F8 Future life
870.G53 Giants
870.H4 Heimdallr
870.H65 Holde
870.I6 Immortality
870.L6 Loki
870.L64 Love
870.M3 Mannus
870.M5 Miogarosormr
870.M8 Muspilli

Religion
History and principles of religion
European. Occidental
Germanic and Norse mythology
Special topics, A-Z -- Continued

870.N4 Nerthus
870.O3 Odin
870.R4 Reincarnation
870.S2 Sacrifice
870.S5 Skadi
870.S8 Sun worship
870.S87 Symbolism
870.T4 Temples
870.T5 Thor
870.U4 Ull
870.V3 Valkyrites
875.A-Z Individual countries (except Germany and Scandinavia), A-Z
e. g.
875.F5 Finland
875.F8 France or Gaul (Germanic only)
Cf. BL980.F8, Non-Christian religions (except Germanic and Norse) in France

Other early European religions
By ethnic group
Celtic
900 General works
910 Druids
Individual countries (except for Druids), see BL980.A+
915.A-Z Special topics, A-Z
Including individual deities
915.B67 Borvo
915.T4 Teutates
915.V54 Vilemurk
Slavic
930 General works
935.A-Z Special topics, A-Z
Including individual gods
Slovak mythology, see BL940.C95
Sorbian cults, see BL940.G35
935.S92 Svantovit
935.S94 Svarog
Wendic cults, see BL940.G35
940.A-Z By region or country, A-Z
e. g.
940.C95 Czechoslovakia
940.G35 Germany (East)
945 Baltic
Including the Latvians, Lithuanians, Yatvyags, and Prussians (Baltic tribe)

Religion
History and principles of religion
European. Occidental
Other early European religions
By ethnic group -- Continued
Ural-Altaic
Cf. BL2370.A+, Other Asian religions
(960) General works
see BL685
Special, see BL980.A+
975.A-Z Other, A-Z
975.A75 Armenians
975.A8 Asturians
975.B26 Balkar (Turkic people)
975.B84 Bulgars (Turkic people)
975.C4 Celtiberi
975.C46 Chuvash
975.D3 Dacians
975.F8 Finno-Ugrian
975.G5 Getae (Zalmoxis cult)
975.I2 Iberians
975.I57 Illyrians
975.K34 Kalmyks
975.M6 Mordvinians
975.S38 Scythians
975.T5 Thracians
975.U34 Udmurts
975.V46 Veneti (Italic people)
980.A-Z By region or country, A-Z
Including modern period and material on religions in general or two or more religions in a region or country
e. g.
980.F8 France or Gaul
980.G7 Great Britain. England
980.H8 Hungary. The Magyars
980.I7 Ireland
980.L3 Lapland
980.N5 Netherlands. Holland
980.S3 Scotland
Serbia, see BL980.Y83
980.Y83 Yugoslavia
Asian. Oriental
1000 Periodicals. Societies. Serials
1005 Dictionaries. Encyclopedias
Collections
Several authors
1010 Ancient. Sacred books
e. g. Müller's Sacred books of the East
1015 Modern
1020 Individual authors
General works
1030 Early through 1800

Religion
History and principles of religions
Asian. Oriental
General works -- Continued
1031 1801-1950
1032 1951-2000
1033 2001-
1035 Addresses, essays, lectures
By region
1050 Northern and Central Asia
1055 Southern and Eastern Asia
1060 Southwestern Asia. Asia Minor. Levant
Cf. BL1600+, Semitic religions
By religion
Hinduism
1100 Periodicals. Yearbooks
Societies. Councils. Associations. Clubs
Class here international and Indian national organizations
For works limited to a sect or independent religious organization, see BL1272.152+
For other national or local organizations, see BL1153.7+
1101 General works. History
1101.3.A-Z Individual, A-Z
1101.5 Congresses. Conferences (General)
For works limited to a sect, see BL1272.152+
1101.7 Directories (General)
Museums. Exhibitions
1102.3 General works. India
1102.5.A-Z Local, India, A-Z, or individual, A-Z, if location is unnamed
Under each locality:
.x *General works*
.x2A-Z *Individual, A-Z*
1102.7.A-Z Other regions or countries, A-Z
Under each country:
.x *General works*
.x2A-Z *Local or individual, A-Z*
1105 Encyclopedias. Dictionaries. Terminology
General collections. Collected works
For sacred books, see BL1111+
For sectarian collections, see BL1272.152+
For collections limited to a particular country except India, see BL1154.2+
Several authors
1107 Comprehensive volumes
1107.3 Collected essays. Festschriften
1107.5 Individual authors
For works by founders and most important leaders of sects, see BL1272.152+

Religion
History and principles of religions
Asian. Oriental
By religion
Hinduism -- Continued
Religious education. Study and teaching
For works dealing with general education managed by Hindu institutions, see LC951.A+
For works dealing with ministerial education, see BL1241.64
For works limited to a sect, see BL1272.152+
1108.2 General works
By region or country
India
General works, see BL1108.2
1108.5.A-Z Local, A-Z
1108.7.A-Z Other regions or countries, A-Z
Under each country:
.x General works
.x2A-Z Local, A-Z
Antiquities. Archaeology. Inscriptions, etc.
Class here works limited to religious points of view only; for descriptive or philological works, see subclasses DS, PK, or PL
1109.2 General works
1109.3 General special
By region or country
India
General works, see BL1109.2
1109.5.A-Z Local, A-Z
Under each:
.x General works
.x2A-Z Individual, A-Z
1109.7.A-Z Other regions or countries, A-Z
Apply table at BL1108.7.A-Z
Sacred books. Sources
Collections
Original
1111 Comprehensive
Class here comprehensive collections of two or more major groups of sacred books
1111.2 Selections. Anthologies
Class here selections from two or more major groups of sacred books
Translations
1111.3.A-Z Comprehensive. By language, A-Z
1111.32.A-Z Selections. Anthologies. By language, A-Z
1111.4 General works. History and criticism
1111.5 General special

Religion
History and principles of religions
Asian. Oriental
By religion
Hinduism
Sacred books. Sources -- Continued
1111.6 Dictionaries
Including terminology, indexes, concordances, etc.
Biography. Characters of two or more sacred books
Cf. BL1112.3+, Characters of Vedic texts
Cf. BL1138.3+, Characters of the Mahābhārata
Cf. BL1139.4+, Characters of the Rāmāyaṇa
1111.7 General works
1111.72.A-Z Special groups of characters, A-Z
1111.72.R57 Rishis
1111.75.A-Z Individual, A-Z
1111.8.A-Z Special topics, A-Z
Vedic texts
1112.2-29 General (Table BL1)
Class here comprehensive collections of or works about two or more Vedas not limited to samhitas
Biography. Characters in Vedic texts
1112.3 Collective
1112.35.A-Z Individual, A-Z
Saṃhitās
1112.4-49 General (Table BL1)
Class here collections of or works about saṃhitās of two or more Vedas
1112.5-59 R̥gveda saṃhitā (Table BL2)
Class here also collections of or works about R̥gveda texts including Brāhmaṇas, Upaniṣads, etc.
Yajurveda saṃhitās
1112.6-69 General (Table BL1)
Class here also collections of or works about Yajurveda texts including Brāhmaṇas, Upaniṣads, etc.
Individual recensions
1112.7-79 Kāṭhakasaṃhitā (Table BL2)
1112.8-89 Kapisthalakathasaṃhitā (Table BL2)
1113.3-39 Maitrāyaṇīsaṃhitā (Table BL2)
1113.4-49 Taittirīyasaṃhitā (Table BL2)
1113.6-69 Vājasaneyisaṃhitā (White Yajurveda saṃhitā) (Table BL2)

Religion
History and principles of religions
Asian. Oriental
By religion
Hinduism
Sacred books. Sources
Vedic texts
Saṃhitās
Yajurveda saṃhitās
Individual
recensions -- Continued
1113.7-79 Kāṇvasaṃhitā (Table BL2)
1114.2-1121.29 General (Table BL1)
Sāmaveda saṃhitās
1114.2-29 General (Table BL1)
Class here also collections of or works about Sāmaveda texts including Brāhmaṇas, Upaniṣads, etc.
Individual recensions
1114.3-39 Jaiminīyasaṃhitā (Table BL2)
1114.4-49 Kauthumasaṃhitā (Table BL2)
Atharvaveda saṃhitās
1114.6-69 General (Table BL1)
Class here also collections of or works about Atharvaveda texts including Brāhmaṇas, Upaniṣads, etc.
Individual recensions
1114.7-79 Paippalāda (Table BL2)
1114.8-89 Śaunaka (Table BL2)
Brāhmaṇas
1116.2-29 General (Table BL1)
Ṛgveda Brāhmaṇas
1116.3-39 General (Table BL1)
Individual texts
1116.4-49 Aitareyabrāhmaṇa (Table BL2)
1116.6-69 Kauṣītakibrāhmaṇa (Table BL2)
1116.7-79 Śāṅkhāyanabrāhmaṇa (Table BL2)
Yajurveda Brāhmaṇas
1118.2-29 General (Table BL1)
Individual texts
1118.3-39 Kathabrāhmaṇa (Kāṭhakabrāhmaṇa) (Table BL2)
1118.4-49 Taittirīyabrāhmaṇa (Table BL2)
1118.5-59 Śatapathabrāhmaṇa (Table BL2)
Sāmaveda Brāhmaṇas
1121.2-29 General (Table BL1)
1121.3.A-Z Individual texts. By title, A-Z
1121.3.A78-A789 Ārṣeyabrāhmaṇa (Table BL3)

1120 is old #, see 1124.5-59 Upanisads

	Religion
	History and principles of religions
	Asian. Oriental
	By religion
	Hinduism
	Sacred books. Sources
	Vedic texts
	Brāhmaṇas
	Sāmaveda Brāhmaṇas
	Individual texts.
	By title, A-Z -- Continued
1121.3.D35-D359	Daivatabrāhmaṇa (Devatādhyāyabrāhmaṇa) (Table BL3)
1121.3.J35-J359	Jaiminīyabrāhmaṇa (Table BL3)
1121.3.J36-J369	Jaiminīyārṣeyabrāhmaṇa (Table BL3)
1121.3.J37-J379	Jaiminīyopaniṣadbrāhmaṇa (Table BL3)
1121.3.S34-S349	Ṣaḍviṃśabrāhmaṇa (Table BL3)
1121.3.S35-S359	Sāmavidhānabrāhmaṇa (Table BL3)
1121.3.S36-S369	Saṃhitopanisadbrāhmaṇa (Table BL3)
1121.3.T35-T359	Tāṇḍyabrāhmaṇa (Table BL3)
1121.3.U63-U639	Upaniṣadbrāhmaṇa (Chāndogyabrāhmaṇa. Mantrabrāhmaṇa) (Table BL3)
1121.3.V36-V369	Vaṃśabrāhmaṇa (Table BL3)
1121.7-79	Atharvaveda Brāhmaṇa (Table BL2)
	Including Gopathabrāhmaṇa
	Āraṇyakas
1122.2-29	General (Table BL1)
	Ṛgveda Āraṇyaka
1122.3-39	General (Table BL1)
	Individual texts
1122.4-49	Aitareyāraṇyaka (Table BL2)
1122.5-59	Śāṅkhāyanāraṇyaka (Table BL2)
	Yajurveda Āraṇyaka
1123.2-29	General (Table BL1)
	Individual texts
1123.3-39	Kaṭhāraṇyaka (Table BL2)
1123.4-49	Taittirīyāraṇyaka (Table BL2)
1123.5-59	Śatapathāraṇyaka (Bṛhadāraṇyaka) (Table BL2)
	Sāmaveda Āraṇyakas
1123.7-79	General (Table BL1)
	Individual texts
1123.8-89	Talavakārāraṇyaka (Jaiminīyopaniṣadbrāhmaṇa) (Table BL2)
	Upaniṣads

	Religion
	History and principles of religions
	Asian. Oriental
	By religion
	Hinduism
	Sacred books. Sources
	Vedic texts
	Upaniṣads -- Continued
1124.5-59	General (Table BL1)
1124.7.A-Z	Individual Upaniṣads. By title, A-Z
1124.7.A45-A459	Adhyātmopaniṣad (Table BL3)
1124.7.A58-A589	Aitareyopaniṣad (Table BL3)
1124.7.A65-A659	Akṣyupaniṣad (Akṣikopaniṣad) (Table BL3)
1124.7.A67-A679	Āruṇopaniṣat (Table BL3)
1124.7.A75-A759	Ātmapūjopaniṣad (Table BL3)
1124.7.A88-A889	Avyaktapaniṣad (Table BL3)
1124.7.B53-B539	Bhāvanopaniṣad (Table BL3)
1124.7.B75-B759	Bṛhadāraṇyakopaniṣad (Table BL3)
1124.7.C53-C539	Chāndogyopaniṣad (Table BL3)
1124.7.D35-D359	Dakṣiṇāmūrtyupaniṣad (Table BL3)
1124.7.D37-D379	Darśanopaniṣad (Table BL3)
1124.7.D48-D489	Devyupaniṣad (Table BL3)
1124.7.G36-G369	Gaṇapatyātharvásirṣopaniṣad (Table BL3)
1124.7.G37-G379	Garbhopaniṣad (Table BL3)
1124.7.G66-G669	Gopālatāpanīyopaniṣad (Table BL3)
1124.7.I76-I769	Īśopaniṣad (Table BL3)
1124.7.K35-K359	Kaivalyopaniṣad (Table BL3)
1124.7.K38-K389	Kaṭhopaniṣad (Table BL3)
1124.7.K39-K399	Kauṣītakibrāhmaṇopaniṣad (Table BL3)
1124.7.K46-K469	Kenopaniṣad (Table BL3)
1124.7.K82-K829	Kubjikopaniṣad (Table BL3)
1124.7.M34-M349	Mahānārāyaṇopaniṣad (Table BL3)
1124.7.M35-M359	Maitrayāṇiyopaniṣad (Table BL3)
1124.7.M36-M369	Maṇḍalabrāhmaṇopaniṣad (Table BL3)
1124.7.M37-M379	Māṇḍūkyopaniṣad (Table BL3)
1124.7.M86-M869	Muṇḍakopaniṣad (Table BL3)
1124.7.N37-N379	Nārāyaṇopaniṣad (Table BL3)
1124.7.P73-P739	Praśnopaniṣad (Table BL3)
1124.7.R36-R369	Rāmatāpinīyopaniṣad (Table BL3)
1124.7.S27-S279	Ṣaṭpraśnopaniṣad (Table BL3)
1124.7.S84-S849	Śvetāśvataropaniṣad (Table BL3)
1124.7.T35-T359	Taittirīyopaniṣad (Table BL3)
1124.7.T74-T749	Tripurātāpinyupaniṣad (Table BL3)
1124.7.V35-V359	Vallabheśopaniṣad (Table BL3)
1124.7.Y63-Y639	Yogacuḍāmaṇyupaniṣad (Table BL3)
	Kalpasūtras (Vedic ritual sūtras)

Religion
History and principles of religions
Asian. Oriental
By religion
Hinduism
Sacred books. Sources
Vedic texts
Kalpasūtras (Vedic ritual sūtras) -- Continued

1126.2-29 General (Table BL1)
For other Vedaṅga texts, e. g. Prātiśākhyasūtras, Anukuramaṇīs, etc., see the corresponding saṃhitās

1126.3.A-Z Individual Kalpasūtras. By title, A-Z
1126.3.A63-A639 Āpastambakalpasūtra (Table BL3)
1126.3.A77-A779 Ārṣeyakalpasūtra (Table BL3)
Śrautasūtras
1126.4-49 General (Table BL1)
Ṛgvedic Śrautasūtras
1126.6-69 General (Table BL1)
Individual Śrautasūtras
1126.7-79 Āśvalāyanaśrautasūtra (Table BL2)
1126.8-89 Āśvalāyanaśrautapariśiṣṭa (Table BL2)
1127.2-29 Śāṅkhāyanaśrautasūtra (Table BL2)
Yajurvedic Śrautasūtras
1127.4-49 General (Table BL1)
Individual Śrautasūtras
1127.5-59 Kāṭhakaśrautasūtra (Table BL2)
1127.6-69 Kātyāyanaśrautasūtra (Table BL2)
1127.7-79 Mānavaśrautasūtra (Table BL2)
1127.8-89 Vārāhaśrautasūtra (Table BL2)
1128.2-29 Baudhāyanaśrautasūtra (Table BL2)
1128.3-39 Vādhūlaśrautasūtra (Table BL2)
1128.4-49 Bhāradvājaśrautasūtra (Table BL2)
1128.6-69 Āpastambaśrautasūtra (Table BL2)
1128.7-79 Hiraṇyakeśinśrautasūtra (Table BL2)
1128.8-89 Vaikhānasaśrautasūtra (Table BL2)
Sāmavedic Śrautasūtras
1129.2-29 General (Table BL1)
Individual Śrautasūtras

Religion
History and principles of religions
Asian. Oriental
By religion
Hinduism
Sacred books. Sources
Vedic texts
Kalpasūtras (Vedic ritual sūtras)
Śrautasūtras
Sāmavedic Śrautasūtras
Individual Śrautasūtras
-- Continued

1129.3-39 Lāṭyāyanaśrautasūtra (Table BL2)

1129.4-49 Drāhyāyaṇaśrautasūtra (Table BL2)

1129.6-69 Jaiminīyaśrautasūtra (Table BL2)

1129.7-79 Atharvavedic Śrautasūtra (Table BL2)
Including Vaitānaśrautasūtra

Gṛhyasūtras

1131.2-29 General (Table BL1)

Ṛgvedic Gṛhyasūtras

1131.3-39 General (Table BL1)

Individual Gṛhyasūtras

1131.5-59 Āśvalāyanagṛhyasūtra (Table BL2)

1131.6-69 Āśvalāyanagṛhyapariśiṣṭa (Table BL2)

1131.7-79 Śāṅkhāyanagṛhyasūtra (Table BL2)

1131.8-89 Kauṣītakagṛhyasūtra (Table BL2)

Yajurvedic Gṛhysūtras

1131.9-99 General (Table BL1)

Individual texts

1133.2-29 Kāṭhakagṛhyasūtra (Laugākṣigṛhyasūtra) (Table BL2)

1133.3-39 Mānavagṛhyasūtra (Maitrāyaṇīyagṛhyasūtra) (Table BL2)

1133.4-49 Vārāhagṛhyasūtra (Table BL2)

1133.6-69 Baudhāyanagṛhyasūtra (Table BL2)

1133.7-79 Bhāradvājagṛhyasūtra (Table BL2)

1133.8-89 Āpastambagṛhyasūtra (Table BL2)

1133.9-99 Hiraṇyakeśingṛhyasūtra (Table BL2)

Religion
History and principles of religions
Asian. Oriental
By religion
Hinduism
Sacred books. Sources
Vedic texts
Kalpasūtras (Vedic ritual sūtras)
Gr̥hyasūtras
Yajurvedic Gr̥hysūtras
Individual texts -- Continued
1134.2-29 Vādhūlagr̥hyasūtra (Table BL2)
1134.3-39 Agniveśyagr̥hyasūtra (Table BL2)
1134.4-49 Vaikhānasagr̥hyasūtra (Table BL2)
1134.5-59 Pāraskaragr̥hyasūtra (Kātīyagr̥hyasūtra) (Table BL2)
Sāmavedic Gr̥hyasūtras
1134.8-89 General (Table BL1)
Individual texts
1134.9-99 Gobhilagr̥hyasūtra (Table BL2)
1136.2-29 Khādiragr̥hyasūtra (Drāhyāyaṇagr̥hyasūtra) (Table BL2)
1136.3-39 Jaiminīyagr̥hyasūtra (Table BL2)
Dharmasūtras (including Code of Manu)
see class K
Śulbasūtras
1136.7-79 General (Table BL1)
1136.8.A-Z Individual Śulbasūtras. By title, A-Z
1136.8.A63-A639 Āpastambaśulbasūtra (Table BL3)
1136.8.B38-B389 Baudhāyanaśulbasūtra (Table BL3)
Pitr̥medhasūtras
1137.2-29 General (Table BL1)
1137.3.A-Z Individual Pitr̥medhasūtras. By title, A-Z
1137.3.B38-B389 Baudhāyanapitr̥medhasūtra (Table BL3)
1137.3.B53-B539 Bhāradvājapitr̥medhasūtra (Table BL3)
1137.3.H57-H579 Hiraniyakeśipitr̥medhasūtra (Table BL3)
1137.5.A-Z Other individual Vedic ritual sutras. By title, A-Z
Subarrange each title by Table BL3
Prātiśākhya, etc.
see the corresponding saṃhitās

Religion
History and principles of religions
Asian. Oriental
By religion
Hinduism
Sacred books. Sources -- Continued
Mahābhārata
Class here the Mahābhārata alone or the Mahābhārata and Rāmāyaṇa combined
For the Rāmāyaṇa alone, see BL1139.2+
1138.2-29 General (Table BL2)
Biography. Characters of the Mahābhārata
1138.3 Collective
1138.4.A-Z Individual, A-Z
1138.6-69 Bhagavadgītā (Table BL2)
Rāmāyaṇa
Class here the Rāmāyaṇa alone
For the Mahābhārata and Rāmāyaṇa combined, see BL1138.2+
1139.2-29 General (Table BL2)
Biography. Characters of the Rāmāyaṇa
1139.4 Collective
1139.5.A-Z Individual, A-Z
Purāṇas
1140.2-29 General (Table BL1)
1140.4.A-Z Individual Purāṇas. By title, A-Z
1140.4.A46-A469 Agnipurāṇa (Āgneyapurāṇa) (Table BL3)
1140.4.B43-B439 Bhāgavatapurāṇa (Table BL3)
1140.4.B44-B449 Bhaviṣyapurāṇa (Table BL3)
1140.4.B45-B459 Bhaviṣyottarapurāṇa (Table BL3)
1140.4.B73-B739 Brahmāṇḍapurāṇa (Table BL3)
1140.4.B74-B749 Brahmapurāṇa (Ādipurāṇa) (Table BL3)
1140.4.B75-B759 Brahmavaivartapurāṇa (Brahmāvaivasvata) (Table BL3)
1140.4.B76-B769 Bṛhaddharmapurāṇa (Table BL3)
1140.4.B77-B779 Bṛhannāradīyapurāṇa (Table BL3)
1140.4.D37-D379 Dattapurāṇa (Table BL3)
1140.4.D47-D479 Devībhāgavatapurāṇa (Table BL3)
1140.4.D48-D489 Devīpurāṇa (Table BL3)
1140.4.D53-D539 Dharmaranyapurāṇa (Table BL3)
1140.4.E42-E429 Ekāmrapurāṇa (Table BL3)
1140.4.G36-G369 Gaṇeśapurāṇa (Table BL3)
1140.4.G38-G389 Garuḍapurāṇa (Table BL3)
1140.4.K34-K349 Kālikāpurāṇa (Table BL3)
1140.4.K35-K359 Kalkipurāṇa (Table BL3)
1140.4.K36-K369 Kapilapurāṇa (Table BL3)
1140.4.K87-K879 Kūrmapurāṇa (Table BL3)
1140.4.L56-L569 Liṅgapurāṇa (Table BL3)
1140.4.M32-M329 Mahābhāgavatapurāṇa (Table BL3)
1140.4.M35-M359 Mallapurāṇa (Table BL3)

	Religion
	History and principles of religions
	Asian. Oriental
	By religion
	Hinduism
	Sacred books. Sources
	Purāṇas
	Individual Purāṇas. By title, A-Z -- Continued
1140.4.M37-M379	Mārkaṇḍeyapurāṇa (Table BL3)
1140.4.M38-M389	Matsyapurāṇa (Table BL3)
1140.4.M84-M849	Mudgalapurāṇa (Table BL3)
1140.4.N37-N379	Nāradapurāṇa (Nāradīyapurāṇa) (Table BL3)
1140.4.N39-N399	Narasiṃhapurāṇa (Table BL3)
1140.4.N55-N559	Nīlamatapurāṇa (Table BL3)
1140.4.P34-P349	Padmapurāṇa (Table BL3)
1140.4.S23-S239	Sāmbapurāṇa (Table BL3)
1140.4.S27-S279	Ṣaurapurāṇa (Table BL3)
1140.4.S48-S489	Śivapurāṇa (Vāyavīyapurāṇa) (Table BL3)
1140.4.S53-S539	Skandapurāṇa (Table BL3)
1140.4.V35-V359	Vāmanapurāṇa (Table BL3)
1140.4.V37-.V379	Varāhapurāṇa (Table BL3)
1140.5.V3793-.V37939	Vāsukipurāṇa (Table BL3)
1140.4.V38-V389	Vāyupurāṇa (Table BL3)
1140.4.V56-V569	Viṣṇudharmottarapurāṇa (Table BL3)
1140.4.V57-V579	Viṣṇupurāṇa (Table BL3)
1140.4.V75-V759	Vr̥hannāradīyapurāṇa (Table BL3)
1140.4.Y87-Y879	Yugapurāṇa (Table BL3)
	Dharmaśāstras see class K
	Tantric texts. Śaiva Āgamas. Vaiṣṇava saṃhitās
1141.2-29	General (Table BL1)
	Āgamas
1141.4-49	General (Table BL1)
1141.5.A-Z	Individual Āgamas. By title, A-Z
1141.5.C35-C359	Candrajñānāgama (Table BL3)
1141.5.K35-K359	Kāmikāgama (Table BL3)
1141.5.K37-K379	Kāraṇāgama (Table BL3)
1141.5.K57-K579	Kiraṇāgama (Table BL3)
1141.5.L35-L359	Lalitāgama (Table BL3)
1141.5.M38-M389	Mataṅgaparameśvarāgama (Table BL3)
1141.5.R37-R379	Rauravāgama (Table BL3)
1141.5.V38-V389	Vātulāgama (Table BL3)
1141.5.V57-V579	Vīrāgama (Table BL3)
	Pāñcarātra
1141.7-79	General (Table BL1)
1141.8.A-Z	Individual saṃhitās. By title, A-Z
1141.8.A55-A559	Ahirbudhnyasaṃhitā (Table BL3)
1141.8.B53-B539	Brahmasaṃhitā (Table BL3)

Religion
History and principles of religions
Asian. Oriental
By religion
Hinduism
Sacred books. Sources
Tantric texts. Śaiva
Āgamas. Vaiṣṇava saṃhitās
Pāñcarātra
Individual saṃhitās.
By title, A-Z -- Continued

1141.8.J38-J389	Jayākhyasaṃhitā (Table BL3)
1141.8.L35-L359	Lakṣmītantra (Table BL3)
1141.8.N37-N379	Nāradapañcarātra (Table BL3)
1141.8.N38-N389	Nāradīyasaṃhitā (Table BL3)
1141.8.P34-P349	Pādmasaṃhitā (Table BL3)
1141.8.P37-P379	Paramasaṃhitā (Table BL3)
1141.8.P38-P389	Pārameśvarasaṃhitā (Table BL3)
1141.8.P42-P429	Pauṣkarasaṃhitā (Table BL3)
1141.8.S36-S369	Sanatkumārasaṃhitā (Table BL3)
1141.8.S38-S389	Sātvatasaṃhitā (Table BL3)
1141.8.S47-S479	Śeṣasaṃhitā (Table BL3)
1141.8.S75-S759	Śrīpraśnasaṃhitā (Table BL3)
1141.8.S76-S769	Śrīśrībrahmasaṃhitā (Table BL3)
1141.8.V54-V549	Viṣnusaṃhitā (Table BL3)
1141.8.V57-V579	Viṣvaksenasaṃhitā (Table BL3)
	Vaikhānasa
1142.2-29	General (Table BL1)
1142.3.A-Z	Individual saṃhitās. By title, A-Z
1142.3.A87-A879	Atrisaṃhitā (Table BL3)
1142.3.M36-M369	Mantrasaṃhitā (Table BL3)
1142.3.M37-M379	Marīcisaṃhitā (Table BL3)
	Tantric texts
1142.5-59	General (Table BL1)
1142.6.A-Z	Individual tantras. By title, A-Z
1142.6.A35-A359	Ākāśabhairavakalpa (Table BL3)
1142.6.A55-A559	Annadākalpatantra (Table BL3)
1142.6.B48-B489	Bhūtaḍāmaratantra (Table BL3)
1142.6.B75-B759	Bṛhannīlatantra (Table BL3)
1142.6.C56-C569	Cīnācārasāratantra (Table BL3)
1142.6.D35-D359	Dāmaratantra (Table BL3)
1142.6.D38-D389	Dattātreyatantra (Table BL3)
1142.6.G35-G359	Gandharvatantra (Table BL3)
1142.6.G36-G369	Gautamīyatantra (Table BL3)
1142.6.G37-G379	Gāyatrītantra (Table BL3)
1142.6.G87-G879	Guptasādhanatantra (Table BL3)
1142.6.G88-G889	Gurutantra (Table BL3)
1142.6.J53-J539	Jñānārṇavatantra (Table BL3)
1142.6.J54-J549	Jñānasaṅkalinītantra (Table BL3)
1142.6.K34-K349	Kālītantra (Table BL3)
1142.6.K35-K359	Kāmadhenutantra (Table BL3)
1142.6.K3592-.K35929	Kāmākhyātantra (Table BL3)

Religion
History and principles of religions
Asian. Oriental
By religion
Hinduism
Sacred books. Sources
Tantric texts. Śaiva
Āgamas. Vaiṣṇava saṃhitās
Tantric texts
Individual tantras.
By title, A-Z -- Continued

1142.6.K36-K369	Kaṅkālamālinītantra (Table BL3)
1142.6.K74-K749	Kriyoḍḍīśantantra (Table BL3)
1142.6.K75-K759	Kriyoḍḍīśatantra (Table BL3)
1142.6.K76-K769	Kṛṣṇyāmalatantra (Table BL3)
1142.6.K78-K789	Kubjikāmatatantra (Table BL3)
1142.6.K82-K829	Kubjikātantra (Table BL3)
1142.6.K83-K839	Kulacūḍāmaṇitantra (Table BL3)
1142.6.K84-K849	Kulaprakāśatantra (Table BL3)
1142.6.K85-K859	Kulārṇavatantra (Table BL3)
1142.6.M34-M349	Mahāmokṣatantra (Table BL3)
1142.6.M35-M359	Mahānirvāṇatantra (Table BL3)
1142.6.M3594-.M35949	Mahāvidyātantra (Table BL3)
1142.6.M36-M369	Mālinīvijayottaratantra (Table BL3)
1142.6.M37-M379	Mātṛkābhedatantra (Table BL3)
1142.6.M38-M389	Māyātantra (Table BL3)
1142.6.M47-M479	Merutantra (Table BL3)
1142.6.M75-M759	Mṛgendratantra (Table BL3)
1142.6.M86-M869	Muṇḍamālātantra (Table BL3)
1142.6.N47-N479	Netratantra (Table BL3)
1142.6.N55-N559	Nīlatantra (Table BL3)
1142.6.N5595-.N55959	Niruttaratantra (Table BL3)
1142.6.N56-N569	Nirvāṇatantra (Table BL3)
1142.6.N57-N579	Nityāṣoḍaśikārṇava (Table BL3)
1142.6.P37-P379	Paramānandatantra (Table BL3)
1142.6.P73-P739	Prapañcasāratantra (Table BL3)
1142.6.R33-R339	Rādhātantra (Table BL3)
1142.6.R38-R389	Rauravatantra (Table BL3)
1142.6.R84-R849	Rudrayāmalatantra (Table BL3)
1142.6.S35-S359	Śaktisaṅgamatantra (Table BL3)
1142.6.S36-S369	Sammohanatantra (Table BL3)
1142.6.S37-S379	Śāṅkhyāyanatantra (Table BL3)
1142.6.S38-S389	Śāradātilakatantra (Table BL3)
1142.6.S39-S399	Sarasvatītantra (Table BL3)
1142.6.S43-S439	Ṣaṭsāhasrasaṃhitā (Table BL3)
1142.6.S45-S459	Saubhāgyalakṣmītantra (Table BL3)
1142.6.S94-S949	Svacchandatantra (Table BL3)
1142.6.T35-T359	Tantrarājatantra (Table BL3)
1142.6.T37-T379	Tārātantra (Table BL3)
1142.6.T64-T649	Toḍalatantra (Table BL3)
1142.6.T75-T759	Tripurārṇavatantra (Table BL3)
1142.6.U44-U449	Uḍḍīśatantra (Table BL3)

Religion
History and principles of religions
Asian. Oriental
By religion
Hinduism
Sacred books. Sources
Tantric texts. Śaiva
Āgamas. Vaiṣṇava saṃhitās
Tantric texts
Individual tantras.
By title, A-Z -- Continued

1142.6.U77-U779 Uttaraṣaṭkatantra (Table BL3)
1142.6.V33-V339 Vāmakeśvaratantra (Table BL3)
1142.6.V55-V559 Vijñānabhairava (Table BL3)
1142.6.V56-V569 Vīṇāśikhatantra (Table BL3)
1142.6.Y65-Y659 Yoginīhṛdaya (Table BL3)
1142.6.Y66-Y669 Yoginītantra (Table BL3)
1142.6.Y68-Y689 Yonitantra (Table BL3)
1143.2.A-Z Other sacred books, and sources. By title, A-Z
Subarrange each title by Table BL3

Hindu literature. Hindu authors
Including devotional or theologico-philosophical works of Hindu authors not limited specifically by subject
Cf. B130+, Philosophy of India (Ancient)
Cf. B5130+, Philosophy of India (Modern)
For works by founders of special sects or movements, see BL1271.2+
For works on specific subjects, regardless of authorship, see the appropriate subject
Sacred books, see BL1111+
Biography, see BL1170+
Collections of several authors
1145 Two or more volumes
1145.5 Single volumes

Religion
History and principles of religions
Asian. Oriental
By religion
Hinduism
Hindu literature.
Hindu authors -- Continued
1146.A-Z Individual authors, A-Z
Including individual anonymous works
For biography, see BL1175.A+
Under each author, using two successive Cutter numbers:
.xA1-.xA3 *Collected works*
.xA1 *Original texts. By date*
.xA2 *Partial editions, selections, etc. By date*
.xA3-.xA39 *Translations. By language, alphabetically*
.xA4-.xZ *Separate works, A-Z*
.x2 *General works. Criticism, interpretation, etc.*
1147 History and criticism
History
1149 Collections. Collected works. Sources
1150 General works. India
For local of India, see BL1153.7.A+
1151.3 General special
1151.5 Addresses, essays, lectures
By period
Early and medieval
1152.3 General works
1152.5 Origins. Early
1152.7 Rise and development of Hindu sects, ca. 200 B.C. to 11th century A.D.
1153.2 11th century to 18th century
1153.5 Modern period
By region or country
South Asia
General, see BL1150
Special countries
India
General, see BL1150
1153.7.A-Z Local, A-Z
Bangladesh
1154.2 Periodicals. Societies. Collections. Sources
1154.3 General works. History
1154.5 General special
1154.7 Biography (Collective)
1154.8.A-Z Local, A-Z
Nepal
1156.2 Periodicals. Societies. Collections. Sources

Religion
History and principles of religions
Asian. Oriental
By religion
Hinduism
History
By region or country
South Asia
Special countries
Nepal -- Continued

1156.3 General works. History
1156.5 General special
1156.7 Biography (Collective)
1156.8.A-Z Local, A-Z

Pakistan

1158.2 Periodicals. Societies. Collections. Sources
1158.3 General works. History
1158.5 General special
1158.7 Biography (Collective)
1158.8.A-Z Local, A-Z

Sikkim

1159.2 Periodicals. Societies. Collections. Sources
1159.3 General works. History
1159.5 General special
1159.7 Biography (Collective)
1159.8.A-Z Local, A-Z

Sri Lanka

1160.2 Periodicals. Societies. Collections. Sources
1160.3 General works
1160.5 General special
1160.7 Biography (Collective)
1160.8.A-Z Local, A-Z

1161.A-Z Other South Asia regions and countries, A-Z

Under each country:

.x	*Periodicals. Societies. Collections. Sources*
.x2	*General works. History*
.x3	*General special*
.x4	*Biography (Collective)*
.x5A-Z	*Local, A-Z*

1161.H56 Himalaya region
1161.K37 Kashmir
1161.L34 Ladakh

Southeast Asia

1162.2 Periodicals. Societies. Collections. Sources
1162.3 General works. History
1162.5 General special
1162.7 Biography (Collective)

Religion
History and principles of religions
Asian. Oriental
By religion
Hinduism
History
By region or country
Southeast Asia -- Continued
Special countries
Indonesia
1163.2 Periodicals. Societies. Collections. Sources
1163.3 General works. History
1163.5 General special
1163.7 Biography (Collective)
1163.8.A-Z Local, A-Z
Malaysia. Malaya
1164.2 Periodicals. Societies. Collections. Sources
1164.3 General works. History
1164.5 General special
1164.7 Biography (Collective)
1164.8.A-Z Local, A-Z
1165.A-Z Other Southeast Asia regions and countries, A-Z
Apply table at BL1161.A-Z
1168.A-Z Other regions or countries, A-Z
Apply table at BL1161.A-Z
1168.A37 Africa, East
1168.F53-F535 Fiji
1168.U53-U535 United States
Biography
Cf. BL1112.3+, Characters of Vedic texts
Cf. BL1138.3+, Characters of Mahābhārata
Cf. BL1139.4+, Characters of Rāmāyaṇa
Collective
For sectarian collective biography, see the sect
1170 General and India
1171 Saints. Gurus. Leaders, etc.
1175.A-Z Individual, A-Z
Subarrange each person by Table BL4
For works limited to founders and most important leaders of individual sects, see BL1272.152+
General works
1200 Early through 1800
1201 1801-1946
1202 1947-
1203 Juvenile works

Religion
History and principles of religions
Asian. Oriental
By religion
Hinduism -- Continued
1205 General special
1210 Addresses, essays, lectures
1211 Controversial works against Hinduism
For works limited to a sect, see BL1272.152+
1211.5 Apologetic works
For works limited to a sect, see BL1272.152+
Doctrines. Theology
For works limited to a sect, see BL1272.152+
1212.32 Periodicals. Societies
1212.34 Collected works. Festschriften
History
For works limited to local places in India or limited to a particular country except India see BL1153.7+
1212.36 General works
1212.38 General special
By period
1212.52 Early Vedic period (Brahmanism) to 2nd century B.C.
Cf. B130+, Ancient Indic philosophy
1212.54 2nd century B.C. to 1800 A.D.
1212.56 Modern period
1212.72 General works. Introductions
1212.74 General special
1212.76 Addresses, essays, lectures
Special doctrines
Cf. B132.A+, Ancient Indic philosophy
God (Concept). Istadeva
For works dealing with attributes, cults, etc., of deities, see BL1216+
1213.32 General works
1213.34 Trimurti
1213.36 Avatars
Cf. BL1219+, Vishnu avatars
1213.38 Pantheism
1213.52 Dharma
1213.54 Man. Puruṣa
1213.56 Ātman-Brahman. Soul. Self. Ātman. Jiva
1213.58 Mokṣa. Mukti. Deliverance
1213.72 Salvation
1213.74 Truth
Religious life, Theoretical
For works dealing with practice, see BL1225.2+
1214.22 General works

Religion
History and principles of religions
Asian. Oriental
By religion
Hinduism
Doctrines. Theology
Special doctrines
Religious life,
Theoretical -- Continued
1214.24 General special
1214.26 Addresses, essays, lectures
1214.32.A-Z Special topics, A-Z
Ahiṃsā, see BJ123.A45
Āśramas. Four stages, see BL1237.75
1214.32.A85 Atonement
1214.32.B53 Bhakti
1214.32.D88 Duty
1214.32.E35 Egoism
1214.32.G87 Guru worship
Cf. BL1241.48, Guruship
1214.32.P68 Poverty, Life of
1214.32.S25 Śaraṇāgati
1214.32.S72 Śraddhā. Faith
1214.32.V45 Vegetarianism
1214.32.V56 Violence and nonviolence
Yoga, see B132.Y6, BL1238.52+
1214.34 Śakti
Cf. BL1282.2+, Saktism
1214.36 Kāma
1214.38 Māya
Eschatology
1214.56 General works
1214.58 Future life
1214.72 Death
Cf. BL1226.82.F86, Funeral rites
Cf. BL1237.82.D43, Special observances
1214.74 Transmigration. Rebirth. Samsara
1214.76 Heaven
1214.78 Hell
1215.A-Z Other special topics and relations to special subjects, A-Z
Alphabets, see BL1215.L36
Altars, see BL1236.76.A48
Amṛta, see BL1215.I66
Amulets, see BL1236.76.A49
Ancestor worship, see BL1239.5.A52
1215.A56 Animism
Asceticism, see BL1239.5.A82
Atonement, see BL1214.32.A85
Avatars, see BL1213.36
Bhakti, see BL1214.32.B53
Brahmans as a caste, see DS432.B73

Religion
History and principles of religions
Asian. Oriental
By religion
Hinduism
Doctrines. Theology
Other special topics and relations to special subjects, A-Z -- Continued
Brahman priesthood, see BL1241.46
1215.C3 Caste
Cattle, see BL1215.C7
Celibacy, see BL1237.82.C46
1215.C45 Chakras (Cakra)
1215.C53 Clairvoyance
1215.C6 Cosmogony. Cosmology
1215.C7 Cows. Cattle
1215.C76 Culture
1215.D3 Dawn
Death, see BL1214.72
1215.D45 Deluge
1215.D46 Demonology
1215.D8 Dualism
Cf. B132.D8, Dvaita
Ecology, see BL1215.N34
1215.E27 Economics
1215.E3 Ecstasy
1215.E5 Endogamy and exogamy
1215.E68 Equality
Fasting, see BL1237.76
1215.F34 Fate and fatalism
1215.F66 Food
Future life, see BL1214.58
Gurus, see BL1241.48
Hair. Haircutting, see BL1239.5.H35
Hell, see BL1214.78
1215.H57 History. Yuga concept
1215.H84 Human rights
1215.H86 Humanism
1215.I66 Immortality. Amṛta
1215.J3 Jatakarma
1215.K56 Kings and rulers
Kuṇḍalinī, see BL1238.56.K86
1215.L36 Language. Alphabets
1215.L54 Life, Meaning of
Man, see BL1213.54
Meditation, see BL1238.32+
1215.M48 Metaphor
1215.M57 Miracles
1215.M87 Music
1215.M9 Mysticism
1215.N3 Names
1215.N34 Nature. Ecology

Religion
History and principles of religions
Asian. Oriental
By religion
Hinduism
Doctrines. Theology
Other special topics and relations to special subjects, A-Z -- Continued

1215.P3 Parables
1215.P4 Peace
1215.P54 Plants
1215.P56 Play
1215.P65 Politics
Prayer, see BL1237.77
1215.P77 Prophecies
1215.P8 Psychology
1215.R34 Race
1215.R4 Revelation
Rishis, see BL1241.52
1215.R5 Rivers
Rulers, see BL1215.K56
Sacrifices, see BL1236.76.S23
Saktism, see BL1282.2+
Salvation, see BL1213.72
Sannyasi, see BL1241.54
1215.S36 Science
Serpent worship, see BL1239.5.S37
1215.S48 Sex
1215.S49 Sex role
1215.S64 Sociology
Soma, see BL1236.76.S66
Soul, see BL1213.56
1215.S67 Sound
Śraddhā, see BL1214.32.S72
1215.S83 State
Class here works dealing with theoretical aspects of Hinduism and state
For works dealing with history, see BL1149+
1215.S85 Storytelling
1215.S87 Superstition
1215.S9 Symbolism
1215.T4 Tēr
Tree planting, see BL1239.5.T74
1215.T75 Trees
Vrata, see BL1237.78
1215.W38 Water
Yakshas, see BL1225.Y27+
1215.Y43 Year
Yuga, see BL1215.H57

Religion
History and principles of religions
Asian. Oriental
By religion
Hinduism -- Continued
Relation of Hinduism to other religious and philosophical systems
Including comparative studies of Hinduism and other religious and philosophical systems
For works limited to a sect, see BL1272.152+
1215.3 General works
1215.5 General special
1215.7.A-Z Special, A-Z
Buddhism, see BQ4610.H6
Christianity, see BR128.H5
Islam, see BP173.H5
Jainism, see BL1358.2
Judaism, see BM536.H5
Hindu pantheon. Deities. Mythical characters
1216 General works. History
1216.2 General special
By region or country
India
General works, see BL1216
1216.4.A-Z Local, A-Z
1216.6.A-Z Other regions or countries, A-Z
Apply table at BL1108.7.A-Z
Individual deities
For deities adopted in Buddhist pantheon, see BQ4718+
Brahmā
1217 General works
1217.2 Cult. Liturgy. Prayers
By region or country
India
General works, see BL1217
1217.3.A-Z Local, A-Z
1217.4.A-Z Other regions or countries, A-Z
Apply table at BL1108.7.A-Z
Siva (Shiva)
Cf. BL1280.5+, Saivism
1218 General works
1218.2 Cult. Liturgy. Prayers
By region or country
India
General works, see BL1218
1218.3.A-Z Local, A-Z
1218.4.A-Z Other regions or countries, A-Z
Apply table at BL1108.7.A-Z
Vishnu
Cf. BL1284.5+, Vaishnavism
1219 General works

Religion
History and principles of religions
Asian. Oriental
By religion
Hinduism
Hindu pantheon. Deities.
Mythical characters
Individual deities
Vishnu -- Continued
1219.2 Cult. Liturgy. Prayers
By region or country
India
General works, see BL1219
1219.3.A-Z Local, A-Z
1219.4.A-Z Other regions or countries, A-Z
Apply table at BL1108.7.A-Z
Krishna (Kṛṣṇa)
1220 General works
1220.2 Cult. Liturgy. Prayers
By region or country
India
General works, see BL1220
1220.3.A-Z Local, A-Z
1220.4.A-Z Other regions or countries, A-Z
Apply table at BL1108.7.A-Z
1225.A-Z Other individual deities, A-Z
1225.A37-A374 Aatim (Table BL7)
1225.A4-A44 Aditi (Table BL7)
1225.A443-A4434 Ādityas (Table BL7)
1225.A45-A454 Agni (Table BL7)
1225.A57-A574 Aiyanār (Table BL7)
1225.A64-A644 Annapūrṇā (Table BL7)
1225.A65-A654 Apsarases (Table BL7)
1225.A7-A74 Aśvins (Table BL7)
1225.A9-A94 Ayyappan (Table BL7)
1225.B3-B34 Bagalāmukhī (Table BL7)
1225.B345-B3454 Balarāma (Table BL7)
1225.B35-B354 Bargabhima (Table BL7)
1225.B37-B374 Bāṭa Ṭhākurāṇī (Table BL7)
1225.B47-B474 Bhādū (Table BL7)
1225.B48-B484 Bhagavati (Table BL7)
1225.B494-B4944 Bhairava (Table BL7)
1225.B5-B54 Bhavānī (Table BL7)
1225.B58-B584 Bhuvaneśvarī (Table BL7)
1225.B65-B654 Bōre Dēvaru (Table BL7)
1225.B7-B74 Bṛhaspati (Bṛihaspati) (Table BL7)
1225.C24-C244 Cāmuṇḍā (Cāmuṇḍī) (Table BL7)
1225.C247-C2474 Caṇḍeśvara (Table BL7)
1225.C25-C254 Caṇḍī (Caṇḍikā, Caṇḍā) (Table BL7)
1225.C38-C384 Cauḍamma (Table BL7)
1225.C54-C544 Chinnamastā (Table BL7)
1225.C57-C574 Citragupta (Table BL7)

Religion
History and principles of religions
Asian. Oriental
By religion
Hinduism
Hindu pantheon. Deities. Mythical characters
Individual deities
Other individual deities, A-Z -- Continued

1225.D3-D34 Dattātreya (Table BL7)
1225.D48-D484 Devanārāyana (Table BL7)
1225.D8-D84 Durgā (Table BL7)
1225.G29-G294 Gandharvas (Table BL7)
1225.G34-G344 Gaṇeśa (Table BL7)
1225.G35-G354 Gaṅgā (Table BL7)
1225.G37-G374 Gaurī (Table BL7)
1225.G38-G384 Gāyatrī (Table BL7)
1225.G67-G674 Gosānī (Table BL7)
1225.G78-G784 Guga Chauhan (Table BL7)
1225.G8-G84 Guruvayurappan (Table BL7)
1225.H3-H34 Hanumān (Table BL7)
1225.H343-H3434 Hariharanātha (Table BL7)
1225.H347-H3474 Hayagrīva (Hayaśiras) (Table BL7)
1225.H35-H354 Hayavadana (Table BL7)
1225.I6-I64 Indra (Table BL7)
1225.J3-J34 Jagannātha (Table BL7)
1225.J96-J964 Jyotibā (Table BL7)
1225.K3-K34 Kālī (Table BL7)
1225.K35-K354 Kalki (Table BL7)
1225.K36-K364 Kāma (Table BL7)
1225.K37-K374 Kaṇṇaki (Table BL7)
1225.K377-K3774 Kanyakāparamēśvari (Table BL7)
1225.K38-K384 Kārttikeya (Table BL7)
1225.K39-K394 Karumāri (Table BL7)
1225.K48-K484 Khamlāṃba (Table BL7)
1225.K5-K54 Khaṇḍobā (Table BL7)
1225.K56-K564 Khōḍiyāra Mātā (Table BL7)
1225.L28-L284 Lajjā Gaurī (Table BL7)
1225.L3-L34 Lakshmi (Table BL7)
1225.L345-L3454 Lakṣmaṇa (Table BL7)
1225.M25-M254 Mahiṣāsura (Table BL7)
1225.M27-M274 Maleya Mādēśvara (Table BL7)
1225.M3-M34 Manasā (Table BL7)
1225.M35-M354 Manus (Table BL7)
1225.M3715-M37154 Māriyammaṉ (Table BL7)
1225.M38-M384 Marut (Table BL7)
1225.M48-M484 Mīnākṣī (Table BL7)
1225.M5-M54 Mitra (Table BL7)
1225.M8-M84 Murugan (Table BL7)
Nabagraha, see BL1225.N38+
1225.N34-N344 Nandadevi (Table BL7)
1225.N35-N354 Narasiṃha (Table BL7)

Religion
History and principles of religions
Asian. Oriental
By religion
Hinduism
Hindu pantheon. Deities.
Mythical characters
Individual deities
Other individual
deities, A-Z -- Continued

1225.N36-N364 Nārāyaṇa (Table BL7)
1225.N37-N374 Narmadā (Table BL7)
1225.N378-N3784 Naṭarāja (Table BL7)
1225.N38-N384 Navagraha (Table BL7)
1225.P23-P234 Paccaināyaki (Table BL7)
1225.P24-P244 Padmanābha (Table BL7)
1225.P25-P254 Panthoibi (Table BL7)
1225.P27-P274 Paraśurāma (Table BL7)
1225.P3-P34 Parvati (Table BL7)
1225.P344-P3444 Pattini (Table BL7)
1225.P72-P724 Pradyumna (Table BL7)
1225.P73-P734 Prajāpati (Table BL7)
1225.P8-P84 Pūṣan (Table BL7)
1225.R24-R244 Rādhā (Table BL7)
1225.R3-R34 Rāma (Rāmacandra) (Table BL7)
1225.R344-R3444 Raṇachoḍarāya (Table BL7)
1225.R345-B3454 Raṅganātha (Table BL7)
1225.R45-R454 Rēṇukāmbe (Table BL7)
1225.R47-R474 Revanta (Table BL7)
1225.R5-R54 Ribhus (Table BL7)
1225.R8-R84 Rudra (Table BL7)
1225.S16-S164 Ṣagara (Table BL7)
1225.S18-S184 Śakti (Table BL7)
Cf. BL1214.34, Śakti concept
Cf. BL1282.2+, Saktism
1225.S19-S194 Ṣampatkumāra (Table BL7)
1225.S22-S224 Śani (Table BL7)
1225.S23-S234 Santoshī Mātā (Table BL7)
1225.S25-S254 Sarasvatī (Table BL7)
1225.S28-S284 Satyā-nārāyan (Table BL7)
1225.S3-S34 Sāvitrī (Table BL7)
1225.S48-S484 Shambulinga (Table BL7)
1225.S5-S54 Ṣhamlaji (Table BL7)
1225.S55-S554 Śirgula (Table BL7)
1225.S57-S574 Ṣītā (Table BL7)
1225.S59-S594 Śītalā (Table BL7)
1225.S63-S634 Soma (Table BL7)
Cf. BL1226.82.V3, Vājapeya
Cf. BL1236.76.S66, Soma (Liturgical object)
1225.S65-S654 Ṣonārāẏa (Table BL7)
1225.S7-S74 Śrī Vēṅkaṭēśvara (Table BL7)
1225.S76-S764 Śrīvidyā (Table BL7)

Religion
History and principles of religions
Asian. Oriental
By religion
Hinduism
Hindu pantheon. Deities. Mythical characters
Individual deities
Other individual deities, A-Z -- Continued
1225.S8-S84 Sūrya (Savitar) (Table BL7)
1225.T3-T34 Tārā (Tārākā) (Table BL7)
1225.T45-T454 Tejāji (Table BL7)
1225.T68-T684 Tripurā Bhairavī (Table BL7)
1225.T73-T734 Tripurasundarī (Table BL7)
1225.T83-T834 Tulasī (Table BL7)
1225.T86-T864 Tushu (Table BL7)
1225.T93-T934 Tyāgarāja (Table BL7)
1225.U82-U824 Uṣas (Table BL7)
1225.V24-V244 Vaḷḷi (Table BL7)
1225.V3-V34 Varuṇa (Table BL7)
1225.V38-V384 Vāyu (Table BL7)
1225.V48-V484 Vīrabhadra (Table BL7)
1225.V49-V494 Viśvakarman (Table BL7)
1225.V495-V4954 Viśvāmitra (Table BL7)
1225.V5-V54 Viṭhobā (Table BL7)
1225.Y27-Y274 Yakshas (Table BL7)
1225.Y28-Y284 Yakṣī (Table BL7)
1225.Y3-Y34 Yama (Table BL7)
Practice. Forms of worship. Religious life
1225.2 Collections. Collected works
1225.3 Encyclopedias. Dictionaries
1225.5 History
1226 General works
1226.12 General special
1226.13 Addresses, essays, lectures
By region or country
India
History, see BL1225.5
1226.15.A-Z Local, A-Z
1226.17.A-Z Other regions or countries, A-Z
Apply table at BL1108.7.A-Z
Liturgy. Rites and ceremonies
For works limited to a sect, see BL1272.152+
For ritual texts of antiquities, e. g. Brāhmaṇas, Śrautasūtras, Gṛhyasūtras, etc., see BL1116+, BL1126+
1226.18 Collections. Collected works
1226.2 General works
1226.72 General special
1226.74 Service books. Liturgical books

Religion
History and principles of religions
Asian. Oriental
By religion
Hinduism
Practice. Forms of worship. Religious life
Liturgy. Rites and ceremonies -- Continued

1226.82.A-Z Special rites and ceremonies, A-Z
For pūjas and rituals of an individual deity, see BL1217+

1226.82.A33 Agnicayana
1226.82.A35 Agnihotra
1226.82.A8 Aśvamedha
1226.82.A85 Atonement
Cf. BL1214.32.A85, Atonement doctrine
1226.82.B38 Bathing (Snāna)
1226.82.B48 Bhasma
1226.82.B7 Brāhmanaśāsana rite
1226.82.C66 Confession
1226.82.D55 Dīkṣā
1226.82.D66 Domestic rites
Cf. BL1131.2+, Gṛhyasūtras
1226.82.F5 Fire rite (General)
Cf. BL1226.82.A33, Agnicayana
Cf. BL1226.82.A35, Agnihotra
1226.82.F6 Foot worship rite
1226.82.F86 Funeral rites
1226.82.I54 Initiation rites (General)
Cf. BL1226.82.S2, Sacred thread ceremony
1226.82.M27 Mahāpradoṣa
1226.82.M3 Marriage rites
1226.82.M93 Mudrās
1226.82.P85 Pūjā
1226.82.P87 Purification rites
1226.82.R75 Ṛshipañcamī
1226.82.S2 Sacred thread ceremony. Upanayana
1226.82.S24 Saṃskāras. Sacraments
1226.82.S25 Sandhyā
1226.82.S3 Self-worship
Soma sacrifices, see BL1226.82.V3
1226.82.S73 Śrāddhā rite
1226.82.S75 Śrāvaṇi
1226.82.T5 Timiti
Upanayana, see BL1226.82.S2
1226.82.V3 Vājapeya (Soma sacrifices)
1226.82.V36 Vāstu-pūjā
1226.82.V52 Vibhūti (Ash rite)
1226.82.Y35 Yajña

Religion
History and principles of religions
Asian. Oriental
By religion
Hinduism
Practice. Forms of worship. Religious life
Liturgy. Rites
and ceremonies -- Continued
Prayers. Hymns. Mantras. Chants.
Recitations
For hymns with music, see M2145.H55
For prayers, hymns, etc. for an individual deity, see BL1217+
For Vedic hymns, see BL1112.2+
For works limited to a sect, see BL1272.152+
1236.22 Collections of prayers, hymns, mantras, etc.
1236.34 Dictionaries
1236.36 General works. History and criticism
1236.38 General special
1236.52.A-Z Special prayers and hymns, A-Z
1236.52.G38 Gāyatrī
1236.52.M67 Morning prayer
1236.52.O46 Om
1236.52.R35 Rain-wishing prayer
1236.54 Individual texts of prayers, hymns, mantras
Liturgical objects and functions. Altars, etc.
1236.72 General works
1236.74 General special
1236.76.A-Z Special topics, A-Z
1236.76.A48 Altars
1236.76.A49 Amulets
1236.76.B45 Bells
1236.76.D45 Dhvaja-stambha
1236.76.F66 Food offering
1236.76.G7 Grasses
1236.76.M84 Mudrās
1236.76.S23 Sacrifices
1236.76.S66 Soma
Cf. BL1225.S63+, Soma (Hindu deity)
Cf. BL1226.82.V3, Vājapeya (Soma sacrifices)
1236.76.T54 Tilakas
1236.76.Y36 Yantra
Religious life. Spiritual life. Discipline
For doctrinal works, see BL1214.22+
For works limited to a sect, see BL1272.152+
1237.32 General works

Religion
History and principles of religions
Asian. Oriental
By religion
Hinduism
Practice. Forms of worship. Religious life
Religious life. Spiritual life. Discipline -- Continued

1237.34 General special
1237.36 Addresses, essays, lectures
Religious life of special groups
Cf. BL1241.44+, Priesthood. Holymen
1237.42 Aged
1237.44 Men
1237.46 Women
1237.48 Parents
1237.52 Youth. Students
1237.54 Children
1237.58.A-Z Other groups, A-Z
1237.58.B57 Bishnois
1237.58.D48 Devadāsīs
1237.58.S65 Soldiers
Special observances. Duties
1237.75 Āśramas. Four stages
Cf. BL1238.72+, Ashram life (General)
Cf. BL1243.72+, Modern institutional ashrams
Cf. BL1272.152+, Individual modern sectarian ashrams
1237.76 Fasting
Cf. BL1239.72+, Fasts and feasts
1237.77 Prayer
Cf. BL1236.22+, Prayers, etc.
1237.78 Vratas (Bratas)
1237.82.A-Z Other topics, A-Z
1237.82.C46 Celibacy
Cf. BL1241.44+, Priesthood. Holymen
1237.82.D43 Death
Cf. BL1214.72, Eschatology
Cf. BL1226.82.F86, Funeral rites
Meditation. Spiritual exercises
For doctrinal works, see BL1214.22+
For works limited to a sect, see BL1272.152+
1238.32 General works
1238.34 General special
1238.36 Addresses, essays, lectures

Religion
History and principles of religions
Asian. Oriental
By religion
Hinduism
Practice. Forms of worship. Religious life
Religious life. Spiritual life. Discipline
Meditation. Spiritual exercises -- Continued
Yoga
Class here works dealing with yoga as religious and spiritual discipline
For works dealing with yoga for health purposes, see RA781.7
For works dealing with yoga for therapeutic purposes, see RM727.Y64
For works dealing with yoga philosophy, see B132.Y6
1238.52 General works
1238.54 General special
1238.56.A-Z Special yoga, A-Z
1238.56.B53 Bhakti yoga
Cf. BL1214.32.B53, Bhakti doctrine
1238.56.H38 Haṭha yoga
Cf. RA781.7, Exercise
Cf. RM727.Y64, Therapeutics
1238.56.K37 Karma yoga
1238.56.K74 Kriya yoga
1238.56.K86 Kuṇḍalinī yoga
1238.56.L38 Laya yoga
1238.56.R35 Rāja yoga
1238.58.A-Z Special topics, A-Z
1238.58.P67 Posture (Asana)
1238.58.P73 Prāṇāyāma
Cf. RA782, Breathing exercises
1238.58.S24 Sādhanā
For individual deity sādhanā, see BL1217+
1238.58.S26 Samadhi
1238.58.T36 Tapas
Monasticism and monastic life. Ashram life
For works limited to a sect, see BL1272.152+
1238.72 General works. History
1238.74 General special
1238.76 Monastic discipline. Rules
By region or country
India
General works, see BL1238.72

Religion
History and principles of religions
Asian. Oriental
By religion
Hinduism
Practice. Forms of worship. Religious life
Religious life. Spiritual life. Discipline
Monasticism and monastic life. Ashram life
By region or country
India -- Continued
1238.78.A-Z Local, A-Z
1238.82.A-Z Other regions or countries, A-Z
Apply table at BL1108.7.A-Z
Pilgrims and pilgrimages
1239.32 General works
1239.34 General special
By region or country
India
General works, see BL1239.32
1239.36.A-Z Local, A-Z
1239.38.A-Z Other regions or countries, A-Z
Apply table at BL1108.7.A-Z
1239.5.A-Z Other special religious practice, A-Z
1239.5.A25 Acting
1239.5.A52 Ancestor worship
1239.5.A82 Asceticism
1239.5.G58 Giving
1239.5.H35 Hair. Haircutting
1239.5.H47 Hermitage life
Cf. BL1237.75, Āśramas
1239.5.S24 Salutations
1239.5.S37 Serpent worship
1239.5.T74 Tree planting
1239.5.T75 Tree worship
1239.5.W38 Wayfaring life
Festivals. Fasts and feasts. Days and seasons
Cf. BL1237.76, Fasting
Cf. GT4876, India
For works limited to a sect, see BL1272.152+
1239.72 General works
1239.74 General special
By region or country
India
General works, see BL1239.72
1239.76.A-Z Local, A-Z
1239.78.A-Z Other regions or countries, A-Z
Apply table at BL1108.7.A-Z
1239.82.A-Z Special, A-Z
1239.82.D37 Dasara

Religion
History and principles of religions
Asian. Oriental
By religion
Hinduism
Practice. Forms of worship. Religious life
Religious life. Spiritual life. Discipline
Festivals. Fasts and feasts. Days and seasons
Special, A-Z -- Continued
1239.82.D58 Divali (Dipavali)
1239.82.D87 Durgā-pūjā
1239.82.E36 Ekādaśī
1239.82.H65 Holī
1239.82.K85 Kumbha Melā
1239.82.M34 Malamāsa
Temple organization. Institution. Ministry. Priesthood. Government
Cf. BL1243.72+, Monasteries, temples, etc.
For works limited to a sect, see BL1272.152+
1241.32 General works
1241.34 General special
By region or country
India
General works, see BL1241.32
1241.36.A-Z Local, A-Z
1241.38.A-Z Other regions or countries, A-Z
Apply table at BL1108.7.A-Z
1241.42 Offices
Priesthood. Leadership. Sainthood. Holymen
Cf. BL1171, Biography of saints, gurus, leaders, etc.
1241.44 General works
Special groups
1241.46 Brahmans
1241.48 Guruship
1241.52 Rishis
1241.53 Sadhus
1241.54 Sannyasins
1241.56 Siddhas
1241.57 Yogis
1241.58 Membership
1241.62 Finance
1241.64 Education and training for the ministry and leadership
Preaching
1241.72 General works
1241.74 General special

Religion
History and principles of religions
Asian. Oriental
By religion
Hinduism
Practice. Forms of worship. Religious life
Temple organization.
Institution. Ministry.
Priesthood. Government
Preaching -- Continued
Sermons
For sermons on a particular subject, see the subject
Collections
1241.76 Several authors
1241.78 Individual authors
Missionary works
1243.32 General works
1243.34 General special
1243.36.A-Z By region or country, A-Z
Under each country:
.x *General*
.x2A-Z *Local, A-Z*
Benevolent work. Social work. Welfare work, etc.
1243.52 General works
1243.54 General special
1243.56.A-Z Work with special groups, A-Z
By region or country
India
General works, see BL1243.52
1243.57.A-Z Local, A-Z
1243.58.A-Z Other regions or countries, A-Z
Apply table at BL1108.7.A-Z
Monasteries. Temples. Shrines. Ashrams. Sacred sites, etc.
For works limited to a sect, see BL1272.152+
1243.72 Directories. India
1243.74 General works
By region or country
India
General works, see BL1243.74
1243.76.A-Z Local, A-Z
Under each:
.x *General works. Directories*
.x2A-Z *Individual, A-Z*

Religion
History and principles of religions
Asian. Oriental
By religion
Hinduism
Monasteries. Temples. Shrines. Ashrams. Sacred sites, etc.
By region or country -- Continued
1243.78.A-Z Other regions or countries, A-Z
Under each country:
.A1-.A29 General works. Directories
.A3-.Z Local, or by name if nonurban, A-Z
Under each city:
.x General
.x2 Individual
Modifications. Sects. Movements. Cults
1271.2 General works. India
1271.3 General special
Local of India, see BL1153.7.A+
Other regions and countries see BL1154.2+
Individual sects, movements, cults
Aghorīs, see BL1280.9+
1272.2-292 Akhilananda (Table BL5)
1272.5-592 Alakhiyas (Alakhgīrs) (Table BL5)
1272.7-792 Alekha (Table BL5)
1272.8-892 Ananda Marga (Table BL5)
Biography
1272.89 Collective
1272.892.A-Z Founders and most important leaders, A-Z
1272.892.A5 Ānandamūrti, 1923-1990 (Table BL4)
1273.2-292 Anuvrati Sangh (Table BL5)
1273.5-592 Arya-Samaj (Table BL5)
Biography
1273.59 Collective
1273.592.A-Z Founders and most important leaders, A-Z
1273.592.D38 Dayananda Sarvasti, Swami, 1824-1883 (Table BL4)
1273.8-892 Aurobindo Ashram (Table BL5)
Biography
1273.89 Collective
1273.892.A-Z Founders and most important leaders, A-Z
1273.892.G56 Ghose, Aurobindo, 1872-1950 (Table BL4)
1273.895-89592 Babburukamme (Table BL5)
1273.9-992 Balahāṛis. Balarāmīs (Table BL5)
Bauls, see BL1284.8+

	Religion
	History and principles of religions
	Asian. Oriental
	By religion
	Hinduism
	Modifications. Sects. Movements. Cults
	Individual sects, movements, cults -- Continued
	Bhagavatas, see BL1285.2+
1274.2-292	Brahmakumari (Table BL5)
	Biography
1274.29	Collective
1274.292.A-Z	Founders and most important leaders, A-Z
1274.292.L44	Lekharāja, Dada, 1876-1968 (Table BL4)
	Brahmanism, see BL1152.5, BL1212.52
1274.5-592	Brahma-samaj (Brahmosomaj) (Table BL5)
	Biography
1274.59	Collective
1274.592.A-Z	Founders and most important leaders, A-Z
1274.592.R36	Rammohun Roy, Raja, 1772?-1833 (Table BL4)
1274.592.S35	Sen, Keshub Chunder, 1838-1884 (Table BL4)
	Buddhism
	see subclass BQ
	Chaitanya, see BL1285.3+
	Dādūpanthīs, see BL1285.5+
1275.2-292	Daśnāmīs (Table BL5)
1275.5-592	Dattatreya (Table BL5)
1275.8-892	Dev-samaj (Table BL5)
	Biography
1275.89	Collective
1275.892.A-Z	Founders and most important leaders, A-Z
1275.892.S27	Satyanand Agnihotri, 1850-1929 (Table BL4)
1276.2-292	Dharmaṭhākura (Table BL5)
1276.3-392	Divine Life Society (Table BL5)
	Biography
1276.39	Collective
1276.392.A-Z	Founders and most important leaders, A-Z
1276.392.S59	Sivananda Swami (Table BL4)
1276.4-492	Garībadāsīs (Table BL5)
	Goraknāthīs, see BL1278.8+
1276.5-592	Gusains (Table BL5)
	Haridasas, see BL1285.7+
	International Society for Krishna, see BL1285.8+
	Jainism, see BL1300+

Religion
History and principles of religions
Asian. Oriental
By religion
Hinduism
Modifications. Sects. Movements. Cults
Individual sects, movements, cults -- Continued
Kabīrpanthīs, see BL2020.K3+
1276.8-892 Karthābhajā (Table BL5)
1277.2-292 Kaulas (Table BL5)
1277.5-592 Krama (Table BL5)
1277.6-692 Lāladāsī (Table BL5)
Biography
1277.69 Collective
1277.692.A-Z Founders and most important leaders, A-Z
1277.692.L34 Lāladāsa (Table BL4)
Mādhvas, see BL1286.2+
1277.8-892 Mahānubhāva (Table BL5)
Biography
1277.89 Collective
1277.892.A-Z Founders and most important leaders, A-Z
1277.892.C35 Cakradhara, 13th cent. (Table BL4)
1277.9-992 Mānava Sevā Saṅgha (Table BL5)
1278.2-292 Nagesh (Table BL5)
1278.5-592 Nāthas (Table BL5)
Biography
1278.59 Collective
1278.592.A-Z Founders and most important leaders, A-Z
1278.592.M38 Matsyendra (Table BL4)
1278.8-892 Kānphaṭas (Gorakhnāthīs, Kanaphātās) (Table BL5)
Biography
1278.89 Collective
1278.892.A-Z Founders and most important leaders, A-Z
1278.892.G67 Gorakhnāth (Goraksa) (Table BL4)
1278.895-89592 Navalapanthīs (Table BL5)
Nimbarka, see BL1286.5+
1279.2-292 Palatu (Table BL5)
Biography
1279.29 Collective
1279.292.A-Z Founders and most important leaders, A-Z
1279.292.P35 Palaṭū Sāhiba, fl. 1800 (Table BL4)
Pāñcarātra, see BL1286.8+
1279.5-592 Prāthanā Samāj (Table BL5)
Biography

Religion
History and principles of religions
Asian. Oriental
By religion
Hinduism
Modifications. Sects. Movements. Cults
Individual sects, movements, cults
Prāthanā Samāj
Biography -- Continued
1279.59 Collective
1279.592.A-Z Founders and most important leaders, A-Z
1279.592.A84 Atma Ram Pandurang (Table BL4)
1279.7-792 Premaprakāśis (Table BL5)
Rādhāvallabha, see BL1287.2+
1279.8-892 Rām Sanehīs (Table BL5)
Biography
1279.89 Collective
1279.892.A-Z Founders and most important leaders, A-Z
1279.892.D37 Dāsa, Rāma Ratana, 1908-1964 (Table BL4)
1280.2-292 Ramakrishna Mission (Table BL5)
Biography
1280.29 Collective
1280.292.A-Z Founders and most important leaders, A-Z
1280.292.R36 Ramakrishna, 1836-1886 (Table BL4)
1280.292.S27 Sarada Devi, 1853-1920 (Table BL4)
1280.292.V58 Vivekananda, 1863-1902 (Table BL4)
Rāmānandīs, see BL1287.5+
Rāmānuja, see BL1288.2+
1280.3-392 Sadhs (Table BL5)
Sahajiyā, see BL1287.8+
1280.5-592 Saivism (Table BL5)
Cf. BL1218+, Siva (Hindu deity)
1280.8-892 Kāpālikas (Table BL5)
1280.9-992 Aghorīs (Table BL5)
1281.15-1592 Kashmir Saivism (Table BL5)
Biography
1281.159 Collective
1281.1592.A-Z Founders and most important leaders, A-Z
1281.1592.V38 Vasugupta (Table BL4)
1281.2-292 Lingayats (Vīraśaivas) (Table BL5)
Biography
1281.29 Collective
1281.292.A-Z Founders and most important leaders, A-Z
1281.292.B37 Basava, fl. 1160 (Vasava) (Table BL4)
1281.292.R48 Rēvaṇasiddha, ca. 1075-ca. 1205 (Table BL4)

Religion
History and principles of religions
Asian. Oriental
By religion
Hinduism
Modifications. Sects. Movements. Cults
Individual sects, movements, cults
Saivism -- Continued

1281.5-592 Pāśupatas (Table BL5)
1281.8-892 Saiva Siddhānta (Table BL5)
1281.9-992 Saiva Siddhanta Church (Table BL5)
1282.2-292 Saktism (Table BL5)
Cf. BL1214.34, Śakti concept
1282.5-592 Samarasa Suddha Sanmarga Sathia Sangam (Table BL5)
Biography
1282.59 Collective
1282.592.A-Z Founders and most important leaders, A-Z
1282.592.R36 Ramalinga, 1823-1874 (Table BL4)
1282.8-892 Samartha Sampradaya (Table BL5)
1283.2-292 Śaktiviśiṣṭādvaitavedānta (Table BL5)
Sanaka, see BL1286.5+
1283.2924-292492 Satyaśodhaka Samāja (Table BL5)
1283.3-392 Shri Ram Chandra Mission (Table BL5)
1283.5-592 Śiva Nārāyanīs (Śrīnārāyanīs) (Table BL5)
Srīvaisnavas, see BL1288.2+
Swami-Narayanis, see BL1289.2+
1283.7-792 SYDA Foundation (Table BL5)
Biography
1283.79 Collective
1283.792.A-Z Founders and most important leaders, A-Z
1283.792.C45 Chidvilasananda, Gurumayi (Table BL4)
1283.792.M84 Muktananda, Swami (Table BL4)
1283.8-892 Tantrism (Table BL5)
Tenkalais, see BL1288.8+
Vandakalais, see BL1288.5+
1284.5-592 Vaishnavism (Table BL5)
1284.8-892 Bauls (Table BL5)
1285.2-292 Bhagavatas (Table BL5)
1285.3-392 Chaitanya (Table BL5)
Biography
1285.39 Collective
1285.392.A-Z Founders and most important leaders, A-Z
1285.392.C53 Chaitanya, 1486-1534 (Table BL4)
1285.5-592 Dādūpanthīs (Table BL5)
Biography
1285.59 Collective

Religion
History and principles of religions
Asian. Oriental
By religion
Hinduism
Modifications. Sects. Movements. Cults
Individual sects, movements, cults
Vaishnavism
Dādūpanthīs
Biography -- Continued

1285.592.A-Z Founders and most important leaders, A-Z

1285.592.D34 Dādūdayāla, 1544-1603 (Dadu) (Table BL4)

1285.7-792 Haridasas (Table BL5)

1285.8-892 International Society for Krishna Consciousness (Table BL5)

Biography

1285.89 Collective

1285.892.A-Z Founders and most important leaders, A-Z

1285.892.A28 A.C. Bhaktivedanta Swami, Prabhupāda, 1896-1977 (Table BL4)

1286.2-292 Mādhvas (Table BL5)

Biography

1286.29 Collective

1286.292.A-Z Founders and most important leaders, A-Z

1286.292.M34 Madhva, 13th cent. (Table BL4)

1286.5-592 Nimbarka (Nīmāvats, Nīmānandins, Sanaka) (Table BL5)

Biography

1286.59 Collective

1286.592.A-Z Founders and most important leaders, A-Z

1286.592.N55 Nimbārka (Table BL4)

1286.8-892 Pāñcarātra (Table BL5)

Biography

1286.89 Collective

1286.892.A-Z Founders and most important leaders, A-Z

1286.892.S36 Śāṇḍilya (Table BL4)

1287.2-292 Rādhāvallabha (Table BL5)

Biography

1287.29 Collective

1287.292.A-Z Founders and most important leaders, A-Z

1287.292.H58 Hita Harivaṃśa Gosvāmī, 1502-1552 (Table BL4)

1287.3-392 Rām Sanehīs (Table BL5)

Biography

1287.39 Collective

Religion
History and principles of religions
Asian. Oriental
By religion
Hinduism
Modifications. Sects. Movements. Cults
Individual sects, movements, cults
Vaishnavism
Rām Sanehīs
Biography -- Continued

1287.392.A-Z	Founders and most important leaders, A-Z
1287.392.R36	Rāmacaraṇa, Swami, 1719-1798 (Table BL4)
1287.5-592	Rāmānandīs (Rāmavats, Rāmānandins) (Table BL5)
	Biography
1287.59	Collective
1287.592.A-Z	Founders and most important leaders, A-Z
1287.592.R56	Rāmananda (Table BL4)
1287.6-692	Senāpanthīs (Table BL5)
	Biography
1287.69	Collective
1287.692.A-Z	Founders and most important leaders, A-Z
1287.692.S45	Senā, b. 1300 (Table BL4)
	Rāmānuja, see BL1288.2+
1287.8-892	Sahajiyā (Table BL5)
1288.2-292	Srīvaisnavas (Rāmānuja sect) (Table BL5)
	Biography
1288.29	Collective
1288.292.A-Z	Founders and most important leaders, A-Z
1288.292.M35	Maṇavāḷa Māmuṉi, 1370-1444 (Table BL4)
1288.292.R36	Rāmānuja (Table BL4)
1288.5-592	Vadakalais (Vadagalais, Northern Sect) (Table BL5)
	Biography
1288.59	Collective
1288.592.A-Z	Founders and most important leaders, A-Z
1288.592.V46	Veṅkaṭanātha, 1268-1369 (Deśika) (Table BL4)
1288.8-892	Tenkalais (Tengalais, Southern sect) (Table BL5)
1289.2-292	Swami-Narayanis (Svāmīnārāyaṇa) (Table BL5)
	Biography
1289.29	Collective
1289.292.A-Z	Founders and most important leaders

Religion
History and principles of religions
Asian. Oriental
By religion
Hinduism
Modifications. Sects. Movements. Cults
Individual sects, movements, cults
Vaishnavism
Swami-Narayanis (Svāmīnārāyaṇa)
Biography
Founders and most important leaders -- Continued
1289.292.S25 Sahajānanda, Swami, 1781-1830 (Table BL4)
1289.4-492 Vaikhanasas (Table BL5)
1289.5-592 Vallabha sect (Vallabhācāryas) (Table BL5)
Biography
1289.59 Collective
1289.592.A-Z Founders and most important leaders, A-Z
1289.592.V35 Vallabhācārya, 1479-1531? (Table BL4)
Vedism, see BL1152.3+, BL1212.52
1295.A-Z Other sects, movements, etc., A-Z
1295.M47-M4792 Meyvaḻi (Sect) (Table BL6 modified)
For individual biography other than founders and most important leaders see BL1175
For local or individual temples, etc., see BL1243.76+
1295.S23-S2392 Sakalamata (Sect) (Table BL6 modified)
For individual biography other than founders and most important leaders see BL1175
For local or individual temples, etc., see BL1243.76+
1295.S25-S2592 Sāṃīndātās (Table BL6 modified)
For individual biography other than founders and most important leaders see BL1175
For local or individual temples, etc., see BL1243.76+
Jainism
1300 Periodicals. Societies. Serials
1301 Congresses
1303 Dictionaries. Encyclopedias
1305 Collections (nonserial)
Museums. Exhibitions
1306 General works

	Religion
	History and principles of religions
	Asian. Oriental
	By religion
	Jainism
	Museums. Exhibitions -- Continued
1307.A-Z	By region or country, A-Z
	Each region or country subarranged by author
	Sacred books. Sources. Āgama (Siddhānta) literature
	Collections
	Original
1310	Comprehensive
1310.2	Selections. Anthologies
	Translations
1310.3.A-Z	Comprehensive. By language, A-Z
1310.32.A-Z	Selections. Anthologies. By language, A-Z
1310.4	General works. History and criticism
1310.5	General special
1310.6	Dictionaries
	Including terminology, indexes, concordances, etc.
	Biography. Characters in the Āgamas (Collective)
1310.7	General works
1310.72.A-Z	Special groups of characters, A-Z
1310.8.A-Z	Special topics, A-Z
1310.8.R57	Rites and ceremonies
	Special divisions and individual texts
	Angas
1312.2-29	General (Table BL1)
1312.3.A-Z	Individual texts. By title, A-Z
1312.3.A58-A589	Antagaḍadasāo (Antakṛtadaśa) (Table BL3)
1312.3.A59-A599	Anuttarovavāiyadasāo (Anuttaropapātikadaśa) (Table BL3)
1312.3.A93-A939	Āyāraṅga (Acārāṅga) (Table BL3)
1312.3.B53-B539	Bhagavaī (Bhagavatī) (Table BL3)
1312.3.D58-D589	Diṭṭhivāya (Dṛṣṭivāda) (Table BL3)
1312.3.N39-N399	Nāyādhammakahāo (Jñātādharmakathāṅga) (Table BL3)
1312.3.P35-P359	Paṇhāvāgaraṇa (Praśnavyākaraṇa) (Table BL3)
1312.3.S35-S359	Samavāyāṅga (Table BL3)
1312.3.S88-S889	Sūyagaḍa (Sūtrakṛtāṅga) (Table BL3)

Religion
History and principles of religions
Asian. Oriental
By religion
Jainism
Sacred books. Sources.
Āgama (Siddhānta) literature
Special divisions and individual texts
Angas
Individual texts.
By title, A-Z -- Continued

1312.3.T53-T539 Ṭhāṇāṅga (Sthānāṅga) (Table BL3)
1312.3.U83-U839 Uvāsagadasāo (Upāsakadaśā) (Table BL3)
1312.3.V58-V589 Vivāgasuya (Vipāka) (Table BL3)

Uvangas (Upāṅgas)

1312.5-59 General (Table BL1)
1312.6.A-Z Individual texts. By title, A-Z
1312.6.C35-C359 Candapannatti (Candraprajñapti) (Table BL3)
1312.6.J35-J359 Jambuddīvapannattī (Jambūdvīpaprajñapti) (Table BL3)
1312.6.J58-J589 Jīvābhigama (Table BL3)
1312.6.J62-J629 Jīvājīvābhigamasūtra (Table BL3)
1312.6.K36-K369 Kappāvadamsiāo (Kalpāvatamsikā) (Table BL3)
1312.6.N57-N579 Nirayāvaliyāo (Kalpikā) (Table BL3)
1312.6.P35-P359 Paṇṇāvanā (Prajñāpanā) (Table BL3)
1312.6.P85-P859 Pupphacūliāo (Puṣpacūlikā) (Table BL3)
1312.6.P87-P879 Pupphiāo (Puṣikā) (Table BL3)
1312.6.R38-R389 Rāyapaseṇiya (Rājapraśnīya) (Table BL3)
1312.6.S87-S879 Sūrapannatti (Sūriyapannatti) (Table BL3)
1312.6.U83-U839 Uvavāiya (Aupapātika) (Table BL3)
1312.6.V35-V359 Vaṇhidsāo (Vṛṣṇidaśā) (Table BL3)

Paiṇṇas (Prakīrṇas)

1312.8-89 General (Table BL1)
1312.9.A-Z Individual texts. By title, A-Z
1312.9.A56-A569 Angavijjā (Table BL3)
1312.9.C35-C359 Candāvejjhaya (Table BL3)
1312.9.D47-D479 Devindatthao (Table BL3)
1312.9.G35-G359 Gacchācāra (Table BL3)
1312.9.G37-G379 Gaṇividyā (Table BL3)
1312.9.M34-M349 Mahāpratyākhyāna (Table BL3)
1312.9.S25-S259 Saṃstāraka (Table BL3)

Religion
History and principles of religions
Asian. Oriental
By religion
Jainism
Sacred books. Sources.
Āgama (Siddhānta) literature
Special divisions and individual texts
Paiṇṇas (Prakīrṇas)
Individual texts.
By title, A-Z -- Continued
1312.9.T35-T359 Tandulaveyāliya (Tandulavaicārika) (Table BL3)
1312.9.V57-V579 Vīrastava (Table BL3)
Cheyasuttas (Chedasūtras)
1313.2-29 General (Table BL1)
1313.3.A-Z Individual texts. By title, A-Z
1313.3.A83-A839 Āyāradasāo (Ācāradaśā) (Table BL3)
1313.3.K36-K369 Kappa (Bṛhat-kalpa) (Table BL3)
1313.3.N58-N589 Nisīha (Niśītha) (Table BL3)
1313.3.V38-V389 Vavahāra (Vyavahāra) (Table BL3)
Cūlikasuttas
1313.5-59 General (Table BL1)
1313.6.A-Z Individual texts. By title, A-Z
1313.6.A58-A589 Aṇuogadāra (Anuyogadvāra) (Table BL3)
1313.6.N34-N349 Nandisutta (Nandīsūtra) (Table BL3)
Mūlasuttas (Mūlasūtras)
1313.8-89 General (Table BL1)
1313.9.A-Z Individual texts. By title, A-Z
1313.9.A83-A839 Āvassaya (Āvaśyaka) (Table BL3)
1313.9.D38-D389 Dasaveāliya (Daśavaikālika) (Table BL3)
1313.9.O53-O539 Ohanijjutti (Oghaniryukti) (Table BL3)
1313.9.U77-U779 Uttarajjhayaṇa (Uttarādhyayana) (Table BL3)
1314.2.A-Z Other individual texts. By title, A-Z
1314.2.J35-J359 Jambūdvīpasaṅgrahaṇī (Table BL3)
1314.2.T38-T389 Tattvārthadhigamasūtra (Table BL3)
Jain literature. Jain authors
Including devotional or theologico-philosophical works of Jain authors not limited specifically by subject. For works on specific subjects, regardless of authorship, see the subject
For sacred books, see BL1310+
Collections of several authors
1315 Two or more volumes
1315.5 Single volumes

Religion
History and principles of religions
Asian. Oriental
By religion
Jainism
Jain literature. Jain authors -- Continued
1316.A-Z Individual authors, A-Z
Including individual anonymous works
For biography, see BL1360+
For Mahāvīra, see BL1370+
Apply table at BL1146.A-Z
1317 History and criticism
1318 Study and teaching
1320 History
By region or country
India
General works, see BL1320
1324.A-Z By region or state, A-Z
1325.9.A-Z Local, A-Z
1327.A-Z Other regions or countries, A-Z
General works
1350 Through 1800
1351 1801-1950
1351.2 1951-2000
1351.3 2001-
1353 General special
1355 Addresses, essays, lectures
Fasts and feasts
1355.5 General works
1355.6.A-Z Special, A-Z
1355.6.P37 Paryuṣaṇā
Doctrine
1356 General works
1357.A-Z Special doctrines, A-Z
1357.A85 Atman
1357.K37 Karma
Philosophy, see B162.5
Relation to other religions, etc.
1358 General works
Special
Buddhism, see BQ4610.J3
1358.2 Hinduism
Biography
1360 Collective
Individual
Mahāvīra
1370 Works
1371 Biography, criticism, etc.
1373.A-Z Other, A-Z
1375.A-Z Special topics, A-Z
1375.A35 Ahimsa
1375.A75 Asceticism
1375.A8 Atonement

Religion
History and principles of religions
Asian. Oriental
By religion
Jainism
Special topics, A-Z -- Continued
1375.C3 Caste
1375.C44 Celibacy
1375.C45 Charity
1375.C6 Cosmogony. Cosmology
1375.D53 Dietary laws
1375.D73 Dreams
1375.F35 Family
1375.F37 Fate and fatalism
1375.F65 Food
1375.G58 Giving
1375.G87 Gurus
1375.H45 Hell
1375.L35 Language. Letters
Letters, see BL1375.L35
1375.P37 Parapsychology
1375.P4 Penance
1375.P64 Politics
1375.S26 Sallekhanā
1375.S3 Salvation
1375.S35 Science
1375.S4 Self
1375.S43 Self-realization
1375.S65 Soul
1375.S95 Suicide
1375.V44 Vegetarianism
1375.W65 Women
1375.Y63 Yoga
Jaina pantheon. Deities. Mythical characters
1375.3 General works. History
1375.4 General special
By region or country
India
General works, see BL1375.3
1375.5.A-Z Local, A-Z
1375.6.A-Z Other regions or countries, A-Z
Apply table at BL1108.7.A-Z
1375.7.A-Z Individual deities, A-Z
1375.7.M35 Maṇibhadra (Table BL7)
1375.7.N34 Nāgakumāra (Table BL7)
1375.7.P33 Padmāvatī (Table BL7)
1375.7.Y34 Yakṣas (Table BL7)
Forms of worship. Jain practice
1376 General works
Ceremonies and rituals
1377 General works
1377.3 Hymns, mantras, etc.
1377.5 Sermons

Religion
History and principles of religions
Asian. Oriental
By religion
Jainism
Forms of worship.
Jain practice -- Continued
Monasticism and monasteries
1378 General works
By region or country
India
General works, see BL1378
1378.2.A-Z By region or state, A-Z
1378.23.A-Z Local, A-Z
1378.3.A-Z Other regions or countries, A-Z
Under each country:
.x General works
.x2A-Z Special. By city, A-Z
Temples and shrines
1378.4 General works
1378.45.A-Z By region or country, A-Z
Apply table at BL1378.3.A-Z
Pilgrims and pilgrimages
1378.52 General works
By region or country
India
General works, see BL1378.52
1378.56 Local, A-Z
1378.58.A-Z Other regions or countries, A-Z
Apply table at BL1243.36.A-Z
1378.6 Devotion. Meditation. Prayer
1378.7 Devotional literature. Prayers
Mysticism
1378.8 General works
1378.85 Contemplation. Samadhi
Special modifications, schools, sects, etc.
1379 General works
1380.A-Z Individual, A-Z
1380.A55 Aṇuvrata
1380.D34 Dakshiṇa Bhārata Jaina Sabhā
1380.D53 Ḍigambara
1380.S8 Śvetāmbara
1380.T4 Terehpanth
Buddhism, see BQ1+
Zoroastrianism (Mazdeism). Parseeism
For Mithraism, see BL1585
For Parseeism, see BL1530
1500 Periodicals. Societies. Serials
1505 Collections (Nonserial)
Sacred books. Sources
1510 General
Avesta (or Zend-Avesta)
1515 Original text. By date

	Religion
	History and principles of religions
	Asian. Oriental
	By religion
	Zoroastrianism (Mazdeism). Parseeism
	Sacred books. Sources
	Avesta (or Zend-Avesta) -- Continued
1515.2.A-Z	Translations. By language, A-Z, and date
1515.4	Commentaries
	For philological commentaries, see subclass PK
1515.5.A-Z	Parts. By name or part, A-Z
	Husparam nask
1515.5.H8A2	Original text. By date
1515.5.H8A4-H8A49	Translations. By language and date
1515.5.H8A5-H8Z	Commentaries
	Khordah Avesta
1515.5.K5A2	Original text. By date
1515.5.K5A4-K5A49	Translations. By language and date
1515.5.K5A5-K5Z	Commentaries
	Vendidād
1515.5.V4A2	Original text. By date
1515.5.V4A4-V4A49	Translations. By language and date
1515.5.V4A5-V4Z	Commentaries
	Yashts
1515.5.Y28A2	Original text. By date
1515.5.Y28A4-.Y28A49	Translations. By language and date
1515.5.Y28A5-Y28Z	Commentaries
	Yasna
1515.5.Y3A2	Original text. By date
1515.5.Y3A4-Y3A49	Translations. By language and date
1515.5.Y3A5-Y3Z	Commentaries
1520.A-Z	Other, A-Z
	Dinkard
1520.D5A2	Original text. By date
1520.D5A4-D5A49	Translations. By language and date
1520.D5A5-D5Z	Commentaries
1525	History. Iran (Persia)
	By region or country
1530	India
	Iran (Persia), see BL1525
1535.A-Z	Other regions or countries, A-Z
	Biography
1550	Collective
	Individual
1555	Zoroaster
1560.A-Z	Other, A-Z
	Relation to other religions
1565	General works
1566.A-Z	Special religions, A-Z
	Buddhism, see BQ4610.Z6
1566.J8	Judaism
	General works

Religion
History and principles of religions
Asian. Oriental
By religion
Zoroastrianism (Mazdeism). Parseeism
General works -- Continued
1570 Early through 1950
1571 1951-2000
1572 2001-
1575 Addresses, essays, lectures
Special topics
1580 Mazda or Ormazd
1585 Mithras (God). Mithraism
1588 Sraosha (God)
1590.A-Z Other, A-Z
1590.F73 Fravashis
Government, see BL1590.S73
1590.H36 Haoma
1590.L58 Liturgy. Rites and ceremonies
1590.M9 Mysticism
Politics, see BL1590.S73
1590.P7 Prayers
1590.P85 Purity
1590.R5 Rider-gods
Rites and ceremonies, see BL1590.L58
1590.S73 State. Politics and government
1590.S95 Symbolism
1595 Yezidis
Semitic religions
For Islam, see BP1+
For Judaism, see BM1+
1600 General works
1605.A-Z Special topics, A-Z
1605.A5 Anat
1605.A7 Asherah
1605.B26 Baal
Cf. BL1671, Baal (Canaanite deity)
1605.G63 Gods
1605.I77 Išhara (Semitic goddess)
1605.I8 Ishtar
Including Astarte, Ashtoreth, etc.
1605.L55 Lilith
1605.M6 Moloch
1605.N3 Names (Semitic)
1605.N35 Navel
Ocean, see BL1605.W3
1605.P7 Prophets
1605.R5 Ritual
1605.S65 Spring
1605.T45 Theomachy
1605.W3 Water. Ocean
1610 Aramean
Sumerian

Religion
History and principles of religions
Asian. Oriental
By religion
Semitic religions
Sumerian -- Continued
1615 General works
1616.A-Z Special topics, A-Z
1616.E54 Enki (Sumerian deity)
1616.F87 Future life
1616.I5 Inanna (Sumerian deity)
1616.T45 Temples
Assyro-Babylonian
1620 General works
1625.A-Z Special topics, A-Z
1625.A35 Adapa
1625.A5 Anu (Deity)
1625.A8 Assur (Assyrian deity)
1625.C6 Cosmogony
Deities, see BL1625.G6
1625.D4 Deluge
1625.F35 Family religious life
1625.F8 Future life
1625.G6 Gods
Ishtar, see BL1605.I8
1625.M37 Marduk (Deity)
1625.M45 Memory
1625.M6 Monotheism
1625.N32 Nabu
1625.N37 Nergal
1625.N4 New Year
1625.O2 Oaths
1625.P3 Panbabylonism
1625.P7 Prophets
1625.S38 Shirkûtu
1625.S49 Sin (Deity)
1625.S5 Sin (Doctrine)
1625.T3 Tammuz
1625.T42 Temples
1630 Chaldean
1635 Harranian. Pseudo-Sabian
Syrian. Palestinian. Samaritan
Class here ancient religions only
Cf. BL2340+, Syria and Palestine
1640 General works
1645.A-Z Special topics, A-Z
1645.A53 Anat
1650 Hebrew
For Judaism, see BM1+
Phoenician, Carthaginian, etc.
1660 General works
1665.A-Z Special topics, A-Z
Astarte, see BL1605.I8

Religion
History and principles of religions
Asian. Oriental
By religion
Semitic religions
Phoenician, Carthaginian, etc.
Special topics, A-Z -- Continued
1665.B3 Baal Hammon
1665.S24 Sailors. Seafaring life
Seafaring life, see BL1665.S24
1665.T3 Tanit
Canaanite
1670 General works
Special topics
1671 Baal
1672.A-Z Other, A-Z
Ashtoreth, see BL1605.I8
1672.R47 Rešep
1675 Moabite. Philistine
1677 Nabataean
Arabian (except Islam)
1680 General works
1685 Pre-Islamic
Islam, see BP1+
1695 Druses
Cf. DS94.8.D8, Ethnography (Syria)
1710 Ethiopian
Other, see BL1750+
By region or country
Afghanistan
1750 General works
1750.7.A-Z By ethnic group, etc., A-Z
1750.7.K34 Kafirs
Arabia, see BL1680+
Armenia, see BL2330+
Assyria and Babylonia, see BL1620+
China
1790 Periodicals. Societies. Serials
General works
1800 Early through 1800
1801 1801-1950
1802 1951-2000
1803 2001-
1810 Addresses, essays, lectures
1812.A-Z Special topics, A-Z
Beijing, see BL1812.P45
1812.F87 Future life
1812.G63 Gods
Including individual deities not associated with any specific religion
1812.H44 Hell
1812.M68 Mountains
1812.M94 Mysticism

Religion
History and principles of religions
Asian. Oriental
By region or country
China
Special topics, A-Z -- Continued
1812.P45 Peking. Beijing
1812.R57 Rites and ceremonies
1812.S45 Shamanism
1812.S95 Symbolism
1812.Y55 Yin-yang cults
Special religions
Buddhism, see BQ1+
1825 Primitive religion of China
Confucianism
Cf. B127.C65, Confucian philosophy
Cf. B128.C8, Confucius
1830 Sources
1840 History. China
By region or country, A-Z
China, see BL1840
1842 Korea
1843 Japan
1844.A-Z Other, A-Z
General works
1850 Early through 1800
1851 1801-1950
1852 1951-2000
1853 2001-
1855 Addresses, essays, lectures
Practices of Confucianism
1857 Religious life
Ceremonies and rituals
1858 General works
1859.A-Z Special, A-Z
1859.M45 Memorial services
Biography
Confucius, see B128.C8
Mencius, see B128.M324
1875.A-Z Other, A-Z
Shrines
1880 General works
1882.A-Z By region or country, A-Z
Apply table at BL1108.7.A-Z
1883.A-Z Other special topics, A-Z
1883.E56 Emotions
1883.F35 Family
1883.H43 Heaven
Taoism
1899 Periodicals. Societies. Serials.
Collections

Religion
History and principles of religions
Asian. Oriental
By region or country
China
Special religions
Taoism -- Continued
Sacred books. Sources
For philological commentaries, see subclass PL

1900.A1 Collected works (nonserial). Selections
1900.A3-Z Individual works. By author when known
Under each work, unless otherwise indicated:

.x	*Original text. By date*
.x2A-Z	*Translations of original text. By language, A-Z, and date*
.x3	*Selections. By date*
.x4A-Z	*Translations of selections. By language, A-Z, and date*
.x5	*Criticism*
.x6	*Special topics (not A-Z)*
.x7	*Dictionaries, terminology, indexes, concordances*

e. g.
Chuang-tzu. Nan-hua ching (Zhuangzi. Nanhua jing)
Original text
1900.C45 General. By date
1900.C46A-Z Translations. By language, A-Z, and date
Selections
1900.C48 General. By date
1900.C5A-Z Translations. By language, A-Z, and date
1900.C576 Criticism
Laozi. Dao de jing
Original text
1900.L25 General. By date
1900.L26A-Z Translations. By language, A-Z, and date
Selections
1900.L28 General. By date
1900.L3A-Z Translations. By language, A-Z, and date
1900.L35 Criticism
1900.L36 Special topics (not A-Z)
1900.L37 Dictionaries, terminology, indexes, concordances
Zhuangzi. Nanhua jing, see BL1900.C45+
1908 Study and teaching. Research

Religion
History and principles of religions
Asian. Oriental
By region or country
China
Special religions
Taoism -- Continued
1910 History. China
By region or country
China, see BL1910
1912 Korea
1913 Japan
1914.A-Z Other, A-Z
1920 General works
1923 General special
1925 Addresses, essays, lectures
Biography
1929 Collective
1930 Laozi
1940.A-Z Other, A-Z
1940.4 Ceremonies and rituals
Temples. Shrines, etc.
1941 General works
By region or country
China
General works, see BL1941
1941.5.A-Z Local, A-Z
1942.A-Z Other regions or countries, A-Z
1942.8 Devotions. Meditations. Prayers
1942.85.A-Z Other special topics, A-Z
(1942.85.H75) Hsi Wang Mu (Deity)
see BL1942.85.X58
1942.85.T53 Tianfei (Deity)
1942.85.W45 Wenchang (Deity)
1942.85.W65 Wong Tai Sin (Deity)
1942.85.X58 Xi Wang Mu (Deity)
1943.A-Z Other religions in China, A-Z
Ba gua jiao, see BL1943.P34
Bon (Tibetan religion), see BQ7960+
1943.C5 Chen k'ung chiao. Zhen kong jiao
1943.C55 Ch'üan chen chiao. Quan zhen jiao
1943.H74 Hsien t'ien tao. Xian tian dao
1943.I35 I kuan tao. Yi guan dao
1943.P34 Pa kua chiao. Ba gua jiao
Quan zhen jiao, see BL1943.C55
Xian tian dao, see BL1943.H74
Yi guan dao, see BL1943.I35
Zhen kong jiao, see BL1943.C5
1945.A-Z By country division, A-Z
e. g.
1945.M6 Mongolia
Cf. BL2370.M7, Mongols
Cf. BQ7530+, Lamaism

Religion
History and principles of religions
Asian. Oriental
By region or country
China
By country division, A-Z -- Continued
1945.T5 Tibet
Cf. BQ7530+, Lamaism
Cf. BQ7960+, Bonpo (Sect)
1950.A-Z Chinese religions in countries other than China, A-Z
Cf. BL1842-BL1844, Confucianism in countries other than China
1950.S5 Singapore
(1950.T5) Tibet
see BL1945.T5
1950.U6 United States
1975 Taiwan
1977 Himalaya Mountains Region
India
General works
2000 Early through 1800
2001 1801-1950
2001.2 1951-2000
2001.3 2001-
2003 General special
By period
2005 Early through 1200
2006 1200-1765
1765-
2007 General works
2007.5 1765-1947
2007.7 1947-
2010 Addresses, essays, lectures
2015.A-Z Special topics, A-Z
2015.A6 Ancestor worship
2015.A65 Animals
2015.A8 Asceticism
2015.C65 Communication
2015.C67 Cosmogony. Cosmology
2015.F2 Fakirs
2015.F3 Fasts and feasts
2015.F55 Fire. Heat
2015.G6 Goddesses
Cf. BL2015.M68, Mother goddesses
2015.G63 Gods
2015.G85 Gurus
2015.I4 Idolatry
2015.I6 Immortality
2015.K3 Karma
2015.K5 Kings and rulers
2015.L38 Law
2015.M27 Mahāvrata

Religion
History and principles of religions
Asian. Oriental
By region or country
India
Special topics, A-Z -- Continued
2015.M3 Mandala
Cf. BL604.M36, Symbols
2015.M4 Meditation
2015.M47 Messianism. Messiah
2015.M64 Mokṣa
2015.M66 Monasticism and religious orders
2015.M68 Mother goddesses
Cf. BL2015.G6, Goddesses
2015.M9 Mysticism
2015.N26 Nationalism
2015.N3 Nativistic movements
2015.N64 Nonviolence
2015.P3 Pantheism
2015.P57 Politics and religions
2015.P6 Poverty (Virtue)
2015.R4 Reincarnation
2015.R44 Religious pluralism
2015.R46 Religious tolerance
2015.R48 Rites and ceremonies
2015.R5 Rivers
Rulers, see BL2015.K5
2015.S3 Saints
2015.S4 Serpent worship
Shrines, see BL2015.T4
2015.S6 Society and religion
2015.S72 State
2015.S86 Suffering
2015.S9 Sun. Sun worship
2015.T4 Temples and shrines
2015.T7 Trees. Tree worship
2015.V5 Visions
2015.W6 Women
2015.Y6 Yogis
2016.A-Z Local, A-Z
Individual religions
Buddhism, see BQ1+
Hinduism, see BL1100+
Jainism, see BL1300+
Islam, see BP1+
Parseeism, see BL1500+
Sikhism. Sikh religion
2017 Periodicals. Societies. Collections
2017.3 Dictionaries. Encyclopedias
2017.35 Study and teaching
Adi-Granth
Original texts
2017.4.A2 General. By date

Religion
History and principles of religions
Asian. Oriental
By region or country
India
Individual religions
Sikhism. Sikh religion
Adi-Granth
Original texts -- Continued
2017.4.A32 Selections. By date
Translations
2017.4.A4A-Z English. By translator, A-Z
2017.4.A7-Z Other languages, A-Z
Assign second Cutter number for translator
Special parts
Including texts and criticism
Introductory parts
2017.421 General
2017.422 Nānak's Japujī
2017.424 Nānak's Sidha gosati
The Rāgs
2017.427 General works
2017.428.A-Z Special authors of Rāgs, A-Z
2017.43.A-Z Special Rāgs, A-Z
2017.44 Arjun's Sukhamani
2017.45 General works. Criticism
Daswen Pādshāh kā Granth. Dasam Granth
2017.455 Texts
2017.456 Criticism
Sikh literature. Sikh authors
Including devotional or theologico-philosophical works of Sikh authors not limited specifically by subject
Cf. BJ1290.5, Sikh ethics
For Adi-Granth, see BL2017.4+
For biography, see BL2017.8+
For Daswen Pādshāh kā Granth (Dasam Granth), see BL2017.455+
For works by founders of special sects or movements, see BL2018.7.A+
For works on specific subjects, regardless of authorship, see the appropriate subjects
2017.46 Collections of several authors
2017.47.A-Z Individual authors, A-Z
Including individual anonymous works
Apply table at BL1146.A-Z
2017.48 History and criticism
2017.6 History
Biography

Religion
History and principles of religions
Asian. Oriental
By region or country
India
Individual religions
Sikhism. Sikh religion
Biography -- Continued
2017.8 Collective
Sikh Gurus (Ten Gurus)
2017.83 Collective
2017.85.A-Z Individual, A-Z
Subarrange each person by Table BL4
2017.9.A-Z Other individual, A-Z
2018 General works. Treatises
Cf. BL2017.46+, Devotional or theologico-philosophical works of Sikh authors not limited specifically by subject
2018.15 Relation to other religions, etc.
Christianity, see BR128.S6
Islam, see BP173.S5
Theology
2018.2 General works
2018.22 God
Cultus. Ritual. Worship
2018.3 General works
2018.32 Hymns
Temples and shrines
2018.35 General works
By region or country
India
General works, see BL2018.35
2018.36.A-Z Local, A-Z
Apply table at BL1109.5.A-Z
2018.367.A-Z Other regions or countries, A-Z
Under each country:
.A1-.A29 *General works*
.A3-.Z *Local, or by name if non-urban, A-Z*
Under each locality:
.x *General*
.x2 *Individual*
Sikh religious life (Descriptive works)
2018.37 General works
Devotional literature
2018.38 General works
2018.39.A-Z For special classes, A-Z
Devotion. Meditation. Prayer
2018.4 General works
2018.42 Devotions. Meditations. Prayers

Religion
History and principles of religions
Asian. Oriental
By region or country
India
Individual religions
Sikhism. Sikh religion
Cultus. Ritual. Worship -- Continued

2018.43	Mysticism
2018.5.A-Z	Special topics, A-Z
2018.5.A47	Amrit
2018.5.B4	Bangle
2018.5.B45	Bhakti
2018.5.C4	Charities
2018.5.D4	Death
2018.5.D5	Dietary laws
2018.5.E36	Economics
2018.5.F34	Faith and reason
2018.5.G85	Gurus
	For biography, see BL2017.8+
2018.5.H3	Hair. Haircutting
2018.5.M35	Man
2018.5.N37	Nature
2018.5.N65	Nonviolence
2018.5.P64	Politics and government
2018.5.P75	Psychology
2018.5.R44	Religious tolerance
2018.5.S3	Salvation
2018.5.S35	Science
2018.5.S84	Suffering
2018.5.W65	Women
2018.7.A-Z	Special sects, modifications, etc., A-Z
2018.7.A1	General works
2018.7.K44	Khalsa
2018.7.N34	Namdharis
2018.7.N57	Nirankaris
2018.7.N59	Nirmalas
	Sant Mat, see BP605.R335
2018.7.S48	Sevāpanthas
2018.7.U33	Udāsī (Sect)
2020.A-Z	Other, A-Z
2020.A4-A493	Ajivikas (Table BL6)
2020.D47-D4793	Ḍerā Saccā Saudā (Table BL6)
2020.D7-D793	Dravidian religion (Table BL6)
2020.K3-K393	Kabīrpanthīs (Table BL6)
	Founded by Kabir, 15th cent.
2020.M3-M393	Mahima Dharma (Table BL6)
2020.P7-P793	Prānnāthīs (Table BL6)
	Founded by Prānanātha
2020.S25-S2593	Sāhebadhanīs (Table BL6)
2020.V7-V793	Vratyas (Table BL6)

Religion
History and principles of religions
Asian. Oriental
By region or country
India -- Continued
2030.A-Z By country division, A-Z
Including former divisions
e. g.
(2030.B8) Burma
see BL2051-BL2053
(2030.C5) Sri Lanka
see BL2045-BL2047
2030.C6 Coorg
2030.M3 Malabar
2032.A-Z By ethnic group, etc., A-Z
2032.A2 Abors
2032.A35 Ahoms
2032.A63 Apatani
2032.B48 Bhils
2032.D37 Dard
2032.G6 Gonds
2032.K3 Kandhs
2032.K34 Karbis
2032.K43 Kharia
2032.K45 Khasis
2032.L87 Lushai
2032.M34 Mahars
2032.M4 Meitheis
2032.M5 Minas
2032.M84 Mundas
2032.O73 Oraons
2032.P38 Patidars
2032.R32 Rabaris
2032.R34 Rajputs
2032.R38 Rathvi
2032.S24 Santals
(2032.S45) Sherpas
see BL2034.5.S53
2032.S55 Sinhalese
2032.T3 Tamils
Nepal
2033 General works
2033.5.A-Z Special topics, A-Z
2033.5.S52 Shamanism
2034.3.A-Z Local, A-Z
2034.5.A-Z By ethnic group, A-Z
2034.5.D48 Dhimal
2034.5.K55 Kiranti
2034.5.L55 Limbus
2034.5.S53 Sherpas
Pakistan
2035 General works
2035.5.A-Z Special topics, A-Z

Religion
History and principles of religions
Asian. Oriental
By region or country
Pakistan -- Continued
2036.A-Z Local, A-Z
2036.5.A-Z By ethnic group, A-Z
2036.5.K34 Kalash
2040 Bangladesh. East Pakistan
Sri Lanka
2045 General works
2045.5.A-Z Special topics, A-Z
Planets, see BL2045.5.S73
2045.5.S73 Stars. Planets
2046.A-Z Local, A-Z
2047.A-Z By ethnic group, A-Z
Southeast Asia
2050 General works
By region or country
Burma
2051 General works
2052.A-Z Special topics, A-Z
2052.N37 Nats
2053.A-Z Local, A-Z
Vietnam
2055 General works
2057.A-Z Special topics, A-Z
2058.A-Z Local, A-Z
2060 Cambodia
2065 Cochin China
2067 Laos
2070 Tongking (Tonkin)
Thailand
2075 General works
2077.A-Z By state, region, etc., A-Z
2078.A-Z By ethnic group, A-Z
2078.L57 Lisu
Malaysia
2080 General works
2082.A-Z By state, region, etc., A-Z
2083.A-Z By ethnic group, A-Z
2083.B45 Berawan
2083.M34 Mah-Meri
2085 Singapore
Indonesia
2110 General works
2112 General special
2120.A-Z By island, etc., A-Z
e. g.
2120.B2 Bali (Island)
2120.B6 Borneo
2120.C4 Celebes
2120.F5 Flores

Religion
History and principles of religions
Asian. Oriental
By region or country
Southeast Asia
By region or country
Indonesia
By island, etc., A-Z -- Continued
2120.J3 Java
2120.M4 Mentawai Islands
2120.S8 Sumatra
2122.A-Z Special sects, cults, etc., A-Z
2122.P3 Paguyuban Sumarah
2122.P34 Pangestu (Organization)
2122.P36 Paseban Jati (Organization)
2122.S43 Sedulur Sejati (Organization)
2122.S52 Shamanism
2123.A-Z By ethnic group, A-Z
2123.A84 Asmat
2123.B38 Batak
2123.B83 Bugis
2123.D35 Dani
2123.D9 Dyaks
2123.K35 Karo-Batak
2123.N32 Nage
2123.N43 Ngaju
2123.T47 Tetum
2123.T62 Toba-Batak
2123.T67 Toraja
Philippines
2130 General works
2135.A-Z By ethnic group, A-Z
2135.B34 Bajau
2150.A-Z By ethnic group, A-Z
2150.H57 Hmong (Asian people)
2150.Y25 Yao
Japan
2195 Periodicals. Societies. Serials
General works
2200 Early through 1800
2201 1801-1950
2202 1951-2000
2202.3 2001-
2203 General special
By period
2204 Early through 592
2205 592-1185
2206 1185-1600
2207 1600-1868
2207.3 19th century
1868-
2207.5 General works
2208 1868-1912

Religion
History and principles of religions
Asian. Oriental
By region or country
Japan
By period
1868- -- Continued
2208.5 20th century
2209 1945-
2210 Addresses, essays, lectures
2210.5 Study and teaching
2211.A-Z Special topics, A-Z
2211.A5 Ancestor worship
2211.A6 Animal worship
2211.B56 Blood
2211.C67 Cosmogony
2211.D33 Daikokuten
2211.D35 Death and life
2211.D4 Demons and demonology
2211.D68 Dōsojin
2211.D73 Dreams
2211.E24 Ebisu
2211.E46 Emperor worship
2211.F34 Fans
2211.F37 Fasts and feasts
2211.F47 Fetishism
2211.F86 Funeral rites and ceremonies
2211.F87 Future life
2211.G6 Gods
Cf. BL2226+, Shinto deities
2211.H32 Healing gods
2211.H4 Hermits
2211.I5 Inari cult
2211.I53 Incantations
2211.K35 Kamagami
2211.K6 Kōshin cult
Life, see BL2211.D35
2211.M37 Masks
2211.M43 Meditation
2211.M57 Mother goddesses
2211.M59 Mountain gods
2211.M6 Mountains
2211.N37 Nature worship
2211.P48 Phallicism
2211.P5 Pilgrims and pilgrimages
Politics and government, see BL2211.S73
2211.P7 Prison
2211.R33 Rain gods
2211.R34 Rainmaking rite
2211.R44 Reward
2211.R47 Rice gods
2211.R5 Rites and ceremonies

Religion
History and principles of religions
Asian. Oriental
By region or country
Japan
Special topics, A-Z -- Continued
2211.S33 Sepulchral monuments
Cf. BQ5075.S4, Buddhist sepulchral monuments
2211.S34 Serpents
2211.S36 Seven gods of fortune
2211.S38 Shamanism
2211.S4 Shrines
Cf. BL2225+, Shinto shrines
2211.S73 State. Politics and government
2211.S76 Stone
2211.S84 Sun worship
2211.T3 Takamagahara
2211.T8 Tutelaries
2211.V6 Votive offerings
2211.W48 Wetlands
2211.W65 Women
2211.Y56 Yin-yang cults
2215.A-Z Local, A-Z
e. g.
2215.O4 Okinawa
Individual religions
For special Christian denominations and sects, see BX1+
Christianity, see BR1300+
Buddhism, see BQ670+
Shinto
2216 Periodicals. Societies. Serials
2216.1 Dictionaries. Encyclopedias
Collections. Collected works
For Shinto authors, see BL2217.6+
2216.2 Several authors
2216.3.A-Z Individual authors, A-Z
Sources. Sacred books
2217 General
Kojiki. Nihon shoki
Including studies of these works from the point of view of religion and mythology, and texts accompanied by such studies
For literary and linguistic studies of these works, see PL784.A+
For original texts, translations, and general and historical studies of these works, see DS855+
2217.2 General
2217.3 Kojiki
2217.4 Nihon shoki

Religion
History and principles of religions
Asian. Oriental
By region or country
Japan
Individual religions
Shinto
Sources. Sacred books
Kojiki. Nihon shoki -- Continued
2217.5.A-Z Other, A-Z
Kogo shūi (by Imbe, Hironari, fl. 808)
Complete texts
2217.5.K6 Original. By date
2217.5.K62A-Z Translations. By language, A-Z, and date
Selections
2217.5.K63 Original. By date
2217.5.K64A-Z Translations. By language, A-Z, and date
2217.5.K65 Criticism
Kujiki
Complete texts
2217.5.K8 Original. By date
2217.5.K82A-Z Translations. By language, A-Z, and date
Selections
2217.5.K83 Original. By date
2217.5.K84A-Z Translations. By language, A-Z, and date
2217.5.K85 Criticism
Uetsufumi
Complete texts
2217.5.U3 Original. By date
2217.5.U32A-Z Translations. By language, A-Z, and date
Selections
2217.5.U33 Original. By date
2217.5.U34A-Z Translations. By language, A-Z, and date
2217.5.U35 Criticism
Shinto literature. Shinto authors
Including devotional or theologico-philosophical works of Shinto authors not limited specifically by subject. For works on specific subjects, regardless of authorship, see the subject
For biography, see BL2219.7+
For sacred books, see BL2217+
For works by founders of special sects, see BL2222.A+

Religion
History and principles of religions
Asian. Oriental
By region or country
Japan
Individual religions
Shinto
Shinto literature.
Shinto authors -- Continued
2217.6.A-Z Individual authors, A-Z
Including individual anonymous works
Apply table at BL1146.A-Z
2217.8 History and criticism
2217.9 Study and teaching. Research
History. Japan (General)
2218 General works
2218.2 General special
By period
2218.3 Origins through 1868
2218.4 1868-1945
2218.5 1945-
By region or country
Japan
General works, see BL2218
2219.A-Z Local, A-Z
Other regions or countries
2219.6 General works
2219.65.A-Z Special regions or countries, A-Z
Biography
2219.7 Collective
2219.8.A-Z Individual, A-Z
2220 General works
2220.3 General special
2220.5 Addresses, essays, lectures
2220.6 Controversial works against Shinto
2220.7 Philosophical theology. The essence, genius, and nature of Shinto
Doctrines. Theology
2221 General works
2221.7 Creeds and catechisms. Questions and answers
2221.9.A-Z Special schools, A-Z
2221.9.I8 Ise Shintō
2221.9.S5 Shirakawa Shintō
2221.9.S9 Suika Shintō
2221.9.Y6 Yoshikawa Shintō
2221.9.Y67 Yuiitsu Shintō. Yoshida Shintō
2222.A-Z Individual sects, A-Z
2222.F88-F8893 Fusōkyō (Table BL6)
2222.H56-H5693 Hinomoto (Table BL6)
2222.H66-H6693 Honmiti (Table BL6)
2222.I99-I9993 Izumo Taisha (Table BL6)
2222.J55-J5593 Jikkōkyō (Table BL6)

Religion
History and principles of religions
Asian. Oriental
By region or country
Japan
Individual religions
Shinto
Individual sects, A-Z -- Continued

2222.K66-K6693	Konkōkyō (Table BL6)
2222.K88-K8893	Kurozumikyō (Table BL6)
	Maruyamakyō, see BL2228.M37+
2222.M57-M5793	Misogikyō (Table BL6)
2222.M58-M5893	Mitake (Table BL6)
2222.O65-O6593	Ōmoto (Table BL6)
2222.S45-S4593	Sekai Shintō (Table BL6)
2222.S54-S5493	Shinri (Table BL6)
2222.S55-S5593	Shinshu (Table BL6)
2222.S56-S5693	Shinto-Honkyoku (Table BL6)
2222.S57-S5793	Shintō Taiseikyō (Table BL6)
2222.S58-S5893	Shizensha (Table BL6)
2222.S59-S5993	Shūsei (Table BL6)
2222.T34-T3493	Taisei (Table BL6)
	Taisha, see BL2222.I99+
2222.T35-T3593	Taiwa Kyōdan (Table BL6)
2222.T45-T4593	Tennō (Table BL6)
2222.T46-T4693	Tenrikyō (Table BL6)
2222.Y35-Y3593	Yamakage (Table BL6)
	Relation to other religions, etc.
2222.2	General works
	Special
2222.23	Buddhism
	Christianity, see BR128.S5
	Judaism, see BM536.S5
2223.A-Z	Relation to other subjects, A-Z
2223.S8	State
2223.5	Apologetics
	Forms of worship. Shinto practice
2224	General works
	Ceremonies and rituals
2224.2	General works
2224.25.A-Z	Special, A-Z
2224.25.D34	Daijōsai (Ōnie no Matsuri)
2224.25.D4	Dedication services
(2224.25.D46)	Dengaku see PN2924.5.D45
2224.25.F8	Funeral rites
2224.25.H3	Harai
2224.25.K3	Kagura
2224.25.M57	Misogi
(2224.25.O5)	Ōnie no Matsuri (Daijō-sai) see BL2224.25.D34
2224.3	Devotional literature. Meditations. Prayers (Norito)

Religion
History and principles of religions
Asian. Oriental
By region or country
Japan
Individual religions
Shinto
Forms of worship.
Shinto practice -- Continued
Altars, liturgical objects, etc.
2224.35 General works
2224.38.A-Z Special, A-Z
2224.38.V47 Vestments
Ministry. Organization. Government
2224.4 General works
Priests. Priestesses
2224.5 General works
2224.55 Pastoral theology. Counseling
Shrine management
2224.6 General works
2224.63 Miyaza
Religious life
2224.7 General works
2224.73 Spiritual life. Meditation. Prayer
Shrines
Cf. BL2224.6+, Shrine management
Japan
2225.A1 General works
2225.A3-Z Local, A-Z, or individual, A-Z, if location is unnamed
Apply table at BL1102.5.A-Z
2225.3.A-Z Other regions or countries, A-Z
Under each country:
.A1-.A29 General works
.A3-.Z By city (or by name if non-urban)
Special deities. Shinto mythology
2226 General works
2226.2.A-Z Individual deities, A-Z
2226.2.A5 Amaterasu Ōmikami
2226.2.H3 Hachiman
2226.2.O48 Ōkuninushi no kami
2226.2.S27 Sarutahiko no Kami
2226.2.S84 Sugawara Michizane as Tenjin
2226.2.S94 Susanoo no Mikoto
2227.8.A-Z Topics not otherwise provided for, A-Z
2227.8.A45 Amulets, talismans, charms, etc.
2227.8.A5 Antiquities
2227.8.M54 Mikoshi
2227.8.P7 Psychical research
2228.A-Z Other, A-Z
2228.B92-B9293 Byakkō Shinkōkai (Table BL6)

Religion
History and principles of religions
Asian. Oriental
By region or country
Japan
Individual religions
Other, A-Z -- Continued
2228.E55-E5593 Ennōkyō (Table BL6)
2228.F85-F8593 Fujidō (Table BL6)
2228.I35-I3593 Ijun Mitto (Table BL6)
2228.K98-K9893 Kyūseishukyō (Table BL6)
2228.M37-M3793 Maruyamakyō (Table BL6)
2228.P23-P2393 PL Kyōdan (Table BL6)
2228.S45-S4593 Seichō no Ie (Table BL6)
Including biographies of its founder Masaharu Taniguchi
2228.S55-S5593 Sekai Kyūseikyō (Table BL6)
2228.S56-S5693 Shinri Jikkōkai (Table BL6)
2228.S57-S5793 Shūyōdan (Table BL6)
2228.S5796-S579693 Shūyōdan Hōseikai (Table BL6)
2228.S58-S5893 Sūkyō Mahikari (Table BL6)
2228.T42-T4293 Tengenkyō (Table BL6)
2228.T45-T4593 Tenshō Kōtai Jingūkyō (Table BL6)
Korea
2230 General works
2231 General special
By period
2232 Early to 1864
2233 1864-1945
2233.5 1945-
2234 Addresses, essays, lectures
2236.A-Z Special topics, A-Z
2236.A53 Ancestor worship
2236.C6 Cults
2236.G62 Goddesses
2236.G63 Gods
2236.M68 Mountains
2236.P54 Pilgrims and pilgrimages
2236.R58 Rites and ceremonies
2236.S5 Shamanism
2236.S54 Shrines
2236.S76 Stone
2236.T35 Tan'gun
2236.Y55 Yin-yang cults
2238.A-Z Local, A-Z
2240.A-Z Individual religions, A-Z
Buddhism, see BQ1+
2240.C5-C593 Ch'ŏndogyo (Table BL6)
2240.C6 Ch'ŏnji Taean'gyo
2240.C63 Ch'ŏnjin'gyo
Confucianism, see BL1842
2240.H36-H3693 Hanŏlgyo (Table BL6)
2240.T33-T3393 Taejonggyo (Table BL6)

Religion
History and principles of religions
Asian. Oriental
By region or country
Korea
Individual religions, A-Z -- Continued
2240.T34-T3493 Taesun Chillihoe (Table BL6)
2240.Y64 Yonghwagyo
2250 Media. Magi
Iran
2270 General works
Individual religions
Zoroastrianism, see BL1500+
2280.A-Z Other, A-Z
2290 Phrygia
2300 Russia in Asia. Siberia
2320 Turkey in Asia. Asia Minor
For Islam, see BP1+
For Semitic religions, see BL1600+
2325 Cyprus
Armenia
2330 General works
2335.A-Z Special deities and topics, A-Z
2335.A52 Anahit (Goddess)
2335.V34 Vahagn
Syria and Palestine
Cf. BL1640+, Ancient religions
2340 General works
2345.A-Z By province, region, city, etc., A-Z
e. g.
2345.H3 Hauran
2350.A-Z Other, A-Z
e. g.
2350.I7 Iraq
2350.M7 Mosul
2370.A-Z Other special, A-Z
2370.A5 Ainu
2370.A52 Altais
2370.B87 Buriats
2370.C5 Circassians
2370.H5 Hittites
2370.K53 Khanty
2370.K57 Kirghiz
2370.K8 Kurds
2370.M34 Mansi
2370.M7 Mongols
2370.S25 Saka
2370.S3 Samoyeds
2370.S5 Shamanism
2370.S53 Shans
2370.T19 Tajiks
2370.T23 Tamang (Nepalese people)
2370.T25 Tamils

Religion
History and principles of religions
Asian. Oriental
Other special, A-Z -- Continued
2370.T3 Tatars
2370.T8 Tunguses
2370.T84 Turks (General)
2370.Y34 Yakuts
African
2390 Periodicals. Societies. Serials
2400 General works
2410 Hamitic
Egyptian
General works
2420 Early through 1800
2421 1801-1950
2422 1951-2000
2423 2001-
Ancient Egypt
Cf. DT68+, Religious antiquities of ancient Egypt
2428 Dictionaries. Encyclopedias
2430 Sacred books. Sources
For philological commentaries, see subclass PJ
General works
2440 Early through 1800
2441 1801-1950
2441.2 1951-2000
2441.3 2001-
2443 General special
2445 Addresses, essays, lectures
2450.A-Z Special deities and topics, A-Z
2450.A45 Amon
2450.A54 Animals
2450.A6 Animism
2450.A62 Anubis
2450.A64 Apedemak
2450.A83 Aten
2450.A89 Atum
2450.B2 Ba
Birth, see BL2450.C65
2450.C3 Camephis
2450.C62 Cobras
2450.C65 Conception. Birth
2450.C67 Cosmogony
2450.C69 Cows
2450.C74 Creation
2450.D43 Death
2450.E8 Eschatology
Eternity, see BL2450.T55
2450.F28 Fasts and feasts
2450.F3 Fate and fatalism

Religion
History and principles of religions
African
Egyptian
Ancient Egypt
Special deities
and topics, A-Z -- Continued

2450.F5 Fish
2450.F55 Flowers
2450.F8 Funeral rites
2450.F83 Future life
2450.F84 Future punishment
2450.G42 Gems
2450.G58 Goddesses
2450.G6 Gods
2450.H3 Hathor
2450.H35 Heaven
2450.H5 Hippopotamus
2450.H6 Horus
2450.I44 Imiut
2450.I5 Immortality
2450.I7 Isis
2450.K3 Ka
2450.L5 Lions
2450.M33 Maat
2450.M4 Mert-seger. Mr.t
2450.M55 Min
2450.M9 Mysteries
2450.N3 Navel
2450.N45 Neith
2450.O7 Osiris
2450.P3 Palms
2450.P69 Priests
2450.P7 Ptah
2450.Q44 Queens
2450.R2 Ra
2450.R25 Renenet
2450.R3 Reshpu
2450.R4 Resurrection
2450.S23 Sacrifice
2450.S34 Sekhmet
2450.S37 Serapis
2450.S4 Seth (Set)
2450.S55 Shadows
2450.S56 Shai
2450.S6 Shu
2450.S65 Sky
2450.S72 Sokar
2450.S75 Sopdu
2450.T37 Tatenen
2450.T42 Temple seas
2450.T43 Temples
2450.T5 Thoth

Religion
History and principles of religions
African
Egyptian
Ancient Egypt
Special deities
and topics, A-Z -- Continued
2450.T55 Time. Eternity
2450.W55 Wine
2455 Greco-Roman period
Including from Alexander's conquest to the Islamic conquest
For special topics that are survivals from the ancient period, see BL2450.A+
2460 Modern Egypt
By region or country
2462 North Africa
2462.5 Sub-Saharan Africa
2463 Southern Africa
2464 East Africa
2465 West Africa
2466 Central Africa
2470.A-Z Other regions or countries, A-Z
e. g.
Benin, see BL2470.D3
2470.D3 Dahomey. Benin
Egypt, see BL2420+
2470.G6 Gold Coast. Ghana
2470.G8 Guinea
2470.M3 Madagascar
2470.M6 Morocco
2470.N5 Nigeria
2480.A-Z By ethnic group, etc., A-Z
2480.A3 Abidji
2480.A33 Acoli
2480.A4 Akans
2480.A47 Angas
2480.A5 Anlo
2480.A8 Ashantis
2480.A88 Atuot
2480.B22 Bachama
2480.B225 Baganda
2480.B23 Bakoko
2480.B244 Bakossi
2480.B25 Baluba
2480.B26 Bambara
2480.B27 Bamileke
2480.B3 Bantus
2480.B32 Banum
2480.B33 Baoulé
2480.B337 Basa
2480.B34 Basakata

Religion
History and principles of religions
African
By ethnic group, etc., A-Z -- Continued

(2480.B35) Basuto
see BL2480.S67
2480.B37 Batetela
2480.B4 Bembas
2480.B47 Beti
2480.B49 Betsimisaraka
2480.B5 Birifor
2480.B64 Bobo
2480.B84 Builsa
Bushmen, see BL2480.S24
2480.C43 Chaga
2480.C45 Chamba
2480.C48 Chiga
2480.C49 Chokọssi
2480.C5 Chokwe
2480.D3 Dagaaba
2480.D36 Dangaleat
2480.D5 Dinka
2480.D53 Diola
2480.D6 Dogons
2480.E96 Ewe
2480.F3 Fang
2480.F65 Fon
2480.G3 Gã
2480.G32 Gabbra
2480.G34 Gallas
2480.G36 Gbaya
2480.G57 Giryama
2480.H28 Hadjerai
2480.H3 Hausas
2480.H4 Hereros
Hottentots, see BL2480.K45
Ibo, see BL2480.I2
2480.I2 Igbo
2480.I53 Ingassana
2480.K32 Kabre
2480.K35 Kalenjin
2480.K45 Khoikhoi
2480.K54 Kikuyu
2480.K56 Kinga
2480.K6 Kono
Kossi, see BL2480.B244
2480.K72 Kpelle
2480.K74 Kposo
2480.K85 Kuria
2480.L76 Lugbara
2480.L8 Luo
2480.M22 Mambila
2480.M25 Manala

Religion
History and principles of religions
African
By ethnic group, etc., A-Z -- Continued

2480.M28 Mandari
2480.M3 Mashona
Matabele, see BL2480.N33
2480.M32 Mawri
2480.M33 Mbala
2480.M35 Mbundu
2480.M4 Mende
2480.M43 Meru
2480.M63 Moba
2480.M67 Mossi
2480.N33 Ndebele
2480.N35 Ndembu
2480.N45 Ngbaba-Ma'bo
2480.N458 Nika
2480.N7 Nuer
2480.N8 Nupe
2480.N9 Nzima
2480.O77 Ovambo
2480.O8 Owegbe Society
2480.S23 Sakalava (Malagasy people)
2480.S24 San
2480.S25 Sara
2480.S44 Senufo
2480.S45 Serer
2480.S63 Sobo
2480.S65 Songhai
2480.S67 Sotho
2480.S78 Suk
2480.S8 Suku
Tabeles, see BL2480.N33
2480.T25 Tagbana
2480.T27 Taita
2480.T3 Tallensi
Tebeles, see BL2480.N33
2480.T5 Tivi
2480.T76 Tswana
2480.T87 Turkana
2480.U38 Uduk
2480.X55 Xhosa
2480.Y32 Yaka
2480.Y34 Yanzi
2480.Y6 Yorubas
2480.Z37 Zela
2480.Z4 Zezuru
2480.Z56 Zinza
2480.Z75 Zulgo
2480.Z8 Zulus

Religion
History and principles of religions
African -- Continued
2490 Survival of African religions in America
Including voodooism in general
For works limited to individual cults, religious movements, see BL2532, BL2592
American
For religion of American Indians, see E-F
2500 General works
2510 Pre-Columbian
North America
2520 General works
By region or country
United States
2525 General works
2527.A-Z Local, A-Z
2530.A-Z Other regions or countries, A-Z
2532.A-Z Special cults, religious movements, etc. A-Z
Including special cults and religious movements of the West Indies and Caribbean Area
Afro-Caribbean cults (General), see BL2565+
2532.E86 Espiritualistas Trinitarios Marianos
2532.G33 Gagá
2532.I33 Ifa
2532.K85 Kumina
2532.O23 Obeah
2532.P83 Puerto Rican Spiritualism
2532.R37 Rastafarians
2532.S3 Santeria. Lucumí
2532.S5 Shango
2540 Latin America
Central America
2550 General works
2560.A-Z By country, etc., A-Z
e. g.
2560.G8 Guatemala
2560.M3 Mayas
West Indies
Including the Carribbean Area (General)
For special cults, religious movements, etc., see BL2532.A+
2565 General works
2566.A-Z By country, etc., A-Z
South American
2580 General works
2590.A-Z By country, etc., A-Z
e. g.
2590.B7 Brazil
Including Afro-Brazilian cults (General)
2590.P4 Peru. Incas
2592.A-Z Special cults, religious movements, etc., A-Z

Religion
History and principles of religions
American
South America
Special cults, religious movements, etc., A-Z -- Continued
Afro-Brazilian cults (General), see BL2590.B7
2592.B3 Batuque
2592.B45 Benito
2592.C34 Campanha do Quilo
2592.C35 Candomblé
2592.C38 Catimbó
2592.F73 Fraternidade Eclética Espiritualista Universal
2592.I35 Iemanjá
2592.I75 Irmandade da Santa Cruz
2592.L4 Legião da Boa Vontade
2592.L56 Litolatria
2592.M23 Macumba
2592.M3 Malê
2592.M35 María Lionza
2592.P45 Peregrinos
2592.Q54 Quimbanda
2592.S25 Santo Daime
Umbanda
2592.U4 Museums. Exhibitions
2592.U5 General works. History
2592.U512 Dictionaries
2592.U513 Doctrine. Rituals
2592.U514A-Z Special topics, A-Z
2592.U514G6 Gods
2592.U514P55 Plants. Trees. Flowers
2592.W56 Winti
2592.X36 Xangô
Pacific Ocean islands. Oceania
2600 General works
By country or island group
2610 Australia
2615 New Zealand
Including Maoris
2620.A-Z Other, A-Z
e. g.
2620.A4 Admiralty Islands
2620.H3 Hawaii
2620.M4 Melanesia
2620.N45 New Guinea
2620.P6 Polynesia
2620.T8 Tuamotu Islands
2630.A-Z By ethnic group, etc., A-Z
2630.A68 Ananda
2630.A72 Arapesh
2630.H38 Hawaiians
2630.H82 Hua

Religion
History and principles of religions
Pacific Ocean islands. Pacific Area
By ethnic group, etc., A-Z -- Continued
2630.K85 Kwaio
2630.M87 Murngin
2630.P3 Papuans
2630.T64 Tolai
2630.W35 Wampar
Arctic regions
2670 General works
Eskimos, see E99.E7
Local
see BL875.F5, Finland; BL980.L3, Lapland; BL2530, North America; etc.
2680 Developing countries
Religions of preliterate peoples (General), see GN470+
Gypsies, see DX151
Rationalism
Including agnosticism, deism, free thought, atheism, secularism, etc.
Cf. B808.A+, Agnosticism in philosophy
Cf. B833.A1+, Rationalism in philosophy
Cf. B837.A1+, Skepticism in philosophy
Cf. BR128.A8, Christianity and atheism
Cf. BR160.3, Early ancient writers against Christianity
Cf. BT1095+, Apologetics
2700 Periodicals. Societies. Serials
2703 Congresses
2705 Dictionaries. Encyclopedias
Collected works
2710 Several authors
Individual authors
Cf. BL2773+, Individual works except those of Ingersoll and Paine
2715 A - Ingersoll
e. g.
2715.D4 Denton, William
2715.I3 I͡Aroslavskiĭ, Emel'i͡an
Ingersoll, Robert Green
Cf. AC8, Collected works (General)
Works on religious subjects
Collected works
English
2720.A2 General
2720.A4 Other
2720.A5-Z Other languages
2725.A-Z Individual works, A-Z
e. g.
2725.A3 About the Holy Bible
2725.L5 Liberty of man, woman, and child
2725.S6 Some mistakes of Moses

Rationalism
Collected works
Individual authors
Ingersoll, Robert Green
Works on religious subjects
Individual works, A-Z -- Continued
2725.W4 What must we do to be saved?
2727 Controversial works against Ingersoll
2728 Controversial works in favor of Ingersoll
2730 Ingersoll - Paine
e. g.
2730.M5 Mills, Benjamin Fay
Paine, Thomas
Cf. JC177+, Works on political theory
Works on religious subjects
2735 Collected works
Individual works
Age of reason
English
2740.A1 Editions. By date
2740.A2 Special parts. By number and date
2740.A3 French
2740.A4 German
2740.A5A-Z Other languages, A-Z
2740.A7 Collections of criticisms
2740.A8-Z History and criticism
2741.A-Z Other works, A-Z
2742 Controversial works against Paine
2745 Paine - Z
2747 General works
Special theories
For special regions or countries, see BL2760+
2747.2 Agnosticism
2747.3 Atheism
2747.4 Deism
2747.5 Free thought
2747.6 Humanism
2747.7 Rationalism
2747.8 Secularism
History
General works
2749 Early through 1800
2750 1801-1950
2751 1951-2000
2752 2001-
2755 Other
By period
2756 Early and medieval
Modern
2757 General works
2758 16th-18th centuries
2759 19th-20th centuries
By region or country

Rationalism
History
By region or country -- Continued
2760 United States
2765.A-Z Other regions or countries, A-Z
Works by agnostics, atheists, freethinkers, etc.
For collected works, see BL2715+
General works
2773 Early through 1800
2775 1801-1950
2775.2 1951-2000
2775.3 2001-
2776 General special
2777.A-Z Special topics, A-Z
2777.B8 Burial services for freethinkers
2777.P7 Prayers
2777.R4 Religious training of children
2777.R5 Ritual, hymns, etc. for freethinker meetings
2778 Joint debates and discussions
2780 Addresses, essays, lectures
Works against deists, see BT1180
Works against agnostics, atheists, etc , see BT1209+
Biography
2785 Collective
2790.A-Z Individual, A-Z
e. g.
2790.C5 Chubb, Thomas
2790.I6 Ingersoll, Robert Green
Cf. BL2727, Controversial works against Ingersoll
Cf. BL2728, Controversial works in favor of Ingersoll
Paine, Thomas, see JC178.V5

	Judaism
	For works on Jewish history, see DS101+
	For Biblical texts and exegesis, see Subclass BS
1	Periodicals. Societies. Serials
11	Yearbooks
21	Societies
30	Congresses. Conferences
	Collected works
40	Several authors
42	Addresses, essays, lectures
43	Extracts from several authors
44	Pamphlet collections
45	Individual authors
50	Dictionaries. Encyclopedias
51	Questions and answers
52	Pictorial works
	Directories
55	General
	By region or country
60	United States
65.A-Z	Other regions or countries, A-Z
66	Information services
67	Computer network resources
	Including the Internet
	Study and teaching
70	General works
	Cf. BM570, Manuals of religious instruction
71	General special
	By region or country
	United States
75	General works
77.A-W	By state, A-W
80.A-Z	By city, A-Z
85.A-Z	Other regions or countries, A-Z
	Biography
88	Collective
	Individual, see BM755.A+
	By school
90.A-Z	American (United States), A-Z
95.A-Z	Other, A-Z
	Religious education of the young. Sabbath schools
100	Periodicals. Societies. Serials
101	Congresses. Conferences
102.A-Z	Biography, A-Z
103	General works
105	Textbooks
107	Stories, etc.
108	Teacher training
109.A-Z	Special types of schools, A-Z
	For general education, see LC720+
109.C6	Congregational Hebrew School
109.H4	Heder
109.T3	Talmud Torah

Study and teaching
Religious education of
the young. Sabbath schools -- Continued
110.A-Z Individual schools. By place, A-Z
Entertainments, exercises, etc.
125 General works
127.A-Z Special days, A-Z
135 Social life, recreation, etc., in the synagogue. Camps
History
General works
150 Early through 1800
155 1801-1950
155.2 1951-2000
155.3 2001-
156 Handbooks, manuals, etc.
157 General special
160 Addresses, essays, lectures
By period
Ancient
165 General works
170 General special
173 Addresses, essays, lectures
175.A-Z Individual sects, parties, etc., A-Z
Including the tenets of each
175.A1 General works
175.A2 Unidentified sects
175.E8 Essenes
175.H36 Hasideans
175.P4 Pharisees
175.Q6 Qumran community
175.S2 Sadducees
Samaritans, see BM900+
175.T5 Therapeutae
175.Z3 Zadokites
175.Z4 Zealots (Party)
Religion of the Old Testament, see BM165+, BS1192.5
176 Last centuries before Christian Era
Including period between Old and New Testaments, Hellenistic movements, etc.
177 Judaism in the early centuries of the Christian Era
Including the influence of Philo, etc.
Cf. BM504.3, Theology of the Talmud
178 Other
e.g. Ancestor worship
Medieval
180 General works
182 Ashkenazim. Sephardim
The Ashkenazim are treated as standard Judaism. Class here works dealing with the Sephardim alone or in relation to the Ashkenazim

History
By period
Medieval -- Continued
Karaites
Including tenets
185 General works
Liturgy and ritual
185.3 General works
185.4.A-Z Special liturgical books. By title, A-Z
Hagadah
185.4.H35 Texts. By date
185.4.H353A-Z Criticism. By author
Seder berakhot le-khol ha-shanah
185.4.S43 Texts. By date
185.4.S433A-Z Criticism. By author
Sidur
185.4.S53 Texts. By date
185.4.S533A-Z Criticism. By author
Modern
190 General works
By period
193 16th-18th centuries
194 Haskalah
195 19th-20th centuries
Special movements
Including the tenets of each
196 General works
197 Reform movements
For individual congregations, see BM225.A+
197.5 Conservative Judaism
197.7 Reconstructionist Judaism
197.8 Humanistic Judaism
Hasidism. Hasidim
Cf. BM532, Hasidic tales and legends
For comprehensive works on Jewish mysticism, see BM723+
General works
198 Through 1994
198.2 1995-
198.3 History
198.4.A-Z By region or country, A-Z
By sect
198.5 Belz
198.52 Bratslav
198.53 Guardian-of-the-Faithful
198.54 Habad. Lubavitch
198.55 Satmar
198.56.A-Z Other sects, A-Z
198.56.G87 Gur
198.56.Z35 Zanz
Hasideans, see BM175.H36
Biography, see BM750+
198.8 Mitnaggedim

History
By period
Modern
Special movements -- Continued
199.A-Z Other, A-Z
e.g.
199.S3 Sabbathaians
By region or country
Including history of individual synagogues
201 America
North America
203 General works
United States
205 General works
By region
208 New England
211 South
214 Central
218 West
221 Pacific coast
223.A-W By state, A-W
225.A-Z By city, A-Z
Subarrange each city by Table BM2
Canada
227 General works
228.A-Z By province, A-Z
229.A-Z By city, A-Z
Subarrange each city by Table BM2
Mexico
230 General works
231.A-Z By state, A-Z
232.A-Z By city, A-Z
Subarrange each city by Table BM2
Central America
233 General works
Belize
234 General works
235.A-Z Local, A-Z
Subarrange each locality by Table BM2
Costa Rica
236 General works
237.A-Z Local, A-Z
Subarrange each locality by Table BM2
El Salvador, see BM246+
Guatemala
238 General works
239.A-Z Local, A-Z
Subarrange each locality by Table BM2
Honduras
240 General works
241.A-Z Local, A-Z
Subarrange each locality by Table BM2
Nicaragua

History
By region or country
Central America
Nicaragua -- Continued
242 General works
243.A-Z Local, A-Z
Subarrange each locality by Table BM2
Panama
244 General works
245.A-Z Local, A-Z
Subarrange each locality by Table BM2
Salvador. El Salvador
246 General works
247.A-Z Local, A-Z
Subarrange each locality by Table BM2
West Indies
248 General works
Bahamas
250 General works
251.A-Z Local, A-Z
Subarrange each locality by Table BM2
Cuba
252 General works
253.A-Z Local, A-Z
Subarrange each locality by Table BM2
Haiti
254 General works
255.A-Z Local, A-Z
Subarrange each locality by Table BM2
Jamaica
256 General works
257.A-Z Local, A-Z
Subarrange each locality by Table BM2
Puerto Rico
258 General works
259.A-Z Local, A-Z
Subarrange each locality by Table BM2
260.A-Z Other islands, A-Z
South America
261 General works
Argentina
262 General works
263.A-Z Local, A-Z
Subarrange each locality by Table BM2
Bolivia
264 General works
265.A-Z Local, A-Z
Subarrange each locality by Table BM2
Brazil
266 General works
267.A-Z Local, A-Z
Subarrange each locality by Table BM2
Chile

History
By region or country
South America
Chile -- Continued
268 General works
269.A-Z Local, A-Z
Subarrange each locality by Table BM2
Colombia
270 General works
271.A-Z Local, A-Z
Subarrange each locality by Table BM2
Ecuador
272 General works
273.A-Z Local, A-Z
Subarrange each locality by Table BM2
Guianas
274 General works
Guyana
276 General works
277.A-Z Local, A-Z
Subarrange each locality by Table BM2
Surinam
278 General works
279.A-Z Local, A-Z
Subarrange each locality by Table BM2
French Guiana
280 General works
281.A-Z Local, A-Z
Subarrange each locality by Table BM2
Paraguay
282 General works
283.A-Z Local, A-Z
Subarrange each locality by Table BM2
Peru
284 General works
285.A-Z Local, A-Z
Subarrange each locality by Table BM2
Uruguay
286 General works
287.A-Z Local, A-Z
Subarrange each locality by Table BM2
Venezuela
288 General works
289.A-Z Local, A-Z
Subarrange each locality by Table BM2
Europe
290 General works
Great Britain. England
292 General works
294.A-Z By English county, A-Z
By English city, A-Z
London
294.8 General works

History
By region or country
Europe
Great Britain. England
By English city, A-Z
London -- Continued
295.A-Z Individual synagogues or congregations, A-Z
296.A-Z Other, A-Z
Subarrange each city by Table BM2
Scotland
297 General works
298.A-Z By political division, A-Z
299.A-Z By city, A-Z
Subarrange each city by Table BM2
Ireland
300 General works
301.A-Z By political division, A-Z
302.A-Z By city, A-Z
Subarrange each city by Table BM2
Wales
303 General works
304.A-Z By political division, A-Z
305.A-Z By city, A-Z
Subarrange each city by Table BM2
Austria
307 General works
308.A-Z By political division, A-Z
309.A-Z By city, A-Z
Subarrange each city by Table BM2
Belgium
310 General works
311.A-Z By political division, A-Z
312.A-Z By city, A-Z
Subarrange each city by Table BM2
France
313 General works
314.A-Z By political division, A-Z
315.A-Z By city, A-Z
Subarrange each city by Table BM2
Germany
316 General works
317.A-Z By political division, A-Z
318.A-Z By city, A-Z
Subarrange each city by Table BM2
Greece
319 General works
320.A-Z By political division, A-Z
321.A-Z By city, A-Z
Subarrange each city by Table BM2
Italy
322 General works
323.A-Z By political division, A-Z

History
By region or country
Europe
Italy -- Continued
324.A-Z By city, A-Z
Subarrange each city by Table BM2
Netherlands
325 General works
326.A-Z By political division, A-Z
327.A-Z By city, A-Z
Subarrange each city by Table BM2
Portugal
328 General works
329.A-Z By political division, A-Z
330.A-Z By city, A-Z
Subarrange each city by Table BM2
Russia
331 General works
332.A-Z By political division, A-Z
333.A-Z By city, A-Z
Subarrange each city by Table BM2
Finland
334 General works
335A-335.Z By political division, A-Z
336.A-Z By city, A-Z
Subarrange each city by Table BM2
Poland
337 General works
338.A-Z By political division, A-Z
339.A-Z By city, A-Z
Subarrange each city by Table BM2
Scandinavia
340 General works
Denmark
342 General works
343.A-Z By political division, A-Z
344.A-Z By city, A-Z
Subarrange each city by Table BM2
Iceland
345 General works
346.A-Z By political division, A-Z
347.A-Z By city, A-Z
Subarrange each city by Table BM2
Norway
348 General works
349.A-Z By political division, A-Z
350.A-Z By city, A-Z
Subarrange each city by Table BM2
Sweden
351 General works
352.A-Z By political division, A-Z
353.A-Z By city, A-Z
Subarrange each city by Table BM2

History
By region or country
Europe -- Continued
Spain
354 General works
355.A-Z By political division, A-Z
356.A-Z By city, A-Z
Subarrange each city by Table BM2
Switzerland
357 General works
358.A-Z By political division, A-Z
359.A-Z By city, A-Z
Subarrange each city by Table BM2
Turkey
360 General works
361.A-Z By political division, A-Z
362.A-Z By city, A-Z
Subarrange each city by Table BM2
Other Balkan states
363 General works
Bulgaria
364 General works
365.A-Z By political division, A-Z
366.A-Z By city, A-Z
Subarrange each city by Table BM2
Romania
370 General works
371.A-Z By political division, A-Z
372.A-Z By city, A-Z
Subarrange each city by Table BM2
Yugoslavia
373 General works
374.A-Z By political division, A-Z
375.A-Z By city, A-Z
Subarrange each city by Table BM2
376.A-Z Other European countries, A-Z
Under each:
.x *General works*
.x2A-Z *Individual synagogues or congregations. By place, A-Z*
Asia
377 General works
Southwestern Asia
379 General works
Turkey in Asia
381 General works
382.A-Z By Turkish vilayet, region, etc., A-Z
383.A-Z By city, A-Z
Subarrange each city by Table BM2
Armenia
384 General works
385.A-Z By political division, A-Z

History
By region or country
Asia
Southwestern Asia
Armenia -- Continued
386.A-Z By city, A-Z
Subarrange each city by Table BM2
Mesopotamia. Iraq
386.4 General works
386.5.A-Z By political division, A-Z
386.6.A-Z By city, A-Z
Subarrange each city by Table BM2
Syria. Palestine
Cf. BM165+, Ancient history of Judaism
387 General works
388.A-Z By political division, A-Z
389.A-Z By city, A-Z
Subarrange each city by Table BM2
Israel (The modern state)
390 General works
391.A-Z By political division, A-Z
392.A-Z By city, A-Z
Subarrange each city by Table BM2
Arabia
393 General works
394.A-384.Z By political division, A-Z
395.A-Z By city, A-Z
Subarrange each city by Table BM2
Iran
396 General works
397.A-Z By political division, A-Z
398.A-Z By city, A-Z
Subarrange each city by Table BM2
Central Asia
399 General works
400 Afghanistan
402 Bokhara (Bukhara)
403 Khiva. Khorezm
404.A-Z Other, A-Z
Southern Asia
405 General works
India
406 General works
407 Burma
408 Sri Lanka
409.A-Z By political division, A-Z
410.A-Z By city, A-Z
Subarrange each city by Table BM2
Indochina. Malay Peninsula
Including Cambodia, Cochin China, Malaya, Thailand, Vietnam, etc.
411 General works
412.A-Z By political division, A-Z

History
By region or country
Asia
Southern Asia
Indochina. Malay Peninsula -- Continued
413.A-Z By city, A-Z
Subarrange each city by Table BM2
Indonesia. Malay Archipelago
414 General works
Indonesia
415 General works
416.A-Z By political division, A-Z
417.A-Z By city, A-Z
Subarrange each city by Table BM2
Philippines
418 General works
419.A-Z By political division, A-Z
420.A-Z By city, A-Z
Subarrange each city by Table BM2
Eastern Asia
422 General works
China
423 General works
424.A-Z By political division, A-Z
425.A-Z By city, A-Z
Subarrange each city by Table BM2
Japan
426 General works
427.A-Z By political division, A-Z
428.A-Z By city, A-Z
Subarrange each city by Table BM2
Northern Asia. Siberia
429 General works
430.A-Z By political division, A-Z
431.A-Z By city, A-Z
Subarrange each city by Table BM2
Africa
432 General works
Egypt
434 General works
435.A-Z By political division, A-Z
436.A-Z By city, A-Z
Subarrange each city by Table BM2
437 South Africa
440.A-Z Other political divisions, A-Z
Australia and New Zealand
443 General works
444.A-Z By political division, A-Z
445.A-Z By city, A-Z
Subarrange each city by Table BM2
Pacific islands
447 General works

History
By region or country
Pacific islands -- Continued
449.A-Z By individual island or group of islands, A-Z
Subarrange each island by Table BM2
Pre-Talmudic Jewish literature (non-Biblical)
480 Collections
485 History and criticism
Special texts or groups of texts
For Apocrypha and apocryphal books, see BS1691+
For Aristeas' epistle, see BS744.A7
Dead Sea scrolls
Texts
487.A05 Facsimiles. By date
487.A1 Original language. By date
Translations
487.A2 Hebrew. By date
487.A3 English. By date
487.A4 French. By date
487.A5 German. By date
487.A6A-Z Other languages. By language, A-Z, and date
487.A62A-Z Periodicals
487.A7-Z History and criticism
Language, see PJ4901+
488.A-Z Individual scrolls, A-Z
For Biblical texts, see Subclass BS
488.C6 Copper Scroll (Table BM3)
Genesis Apocryphon, see BS1830.G4+
Habakkuk commentary, see BS1635.H26+
488.M3 Manual of discipline (Table BM3)
488.N48 New Jerusalem Scroll (Table BM3)
488.R85 Rule of the congregation (Table BM3)
488.S47 Serekh shirot olat ha-Shabbat (Table BM3)
Songs of the Sabbath sacrifice, see BM488.S47
488.T44 Temple scroll (Table BM3)
488.T5 Thanksgiving Psalms. Thanksgiving scroll (Table BM3)
488.W3 War of the Sons of Light against the Sons of Darkness (Table BM3)
Selections of scrolls from individual caves
Cave 4
Texts
488.5.A05 Facsimiles. By date
488.5.A1 Original language. By date
Translations
488.5.A2 Hebrew. By date
488.5.A3 English. By date
488.5.A4 French. By date
488.5.A5 German. By date
488.5.A6A-Z Other languages. By language, A-Z, and date
488.5.A7-Z History and criticism
Cave 11

Pre-Talmudic Jewish literature (non-Biblical)
Special texts or groups of texts
Dead Sea scrolls
Selections of scrolls from individual caves
Cave 11 -- Continued
Texts

488.8.A05	Facsimiles. By date
488.8.A1	Original language. By date
	Translations
488.8.A2	Hebrew. By date
488.8.A3	English. By date
488.8.A4	French. By date
488.8.A5	German. By date
488.8.A6A-Z	Other languages. By language, A-Z, and date
488.8.A7-Z	History and criticism
	Elephantine papyri, see PJ5208.E4+
	Sources of Jewish religion. Rabbinical literature
	Including Bible. Mishnah, Palestinian Talmud, Babylonian Talmud, Baraita, Tosefta, Midrash
	Collections. Selections. Extracts, quotations, etc.
495	Several authors
495.5	Individual authors
	Works about the sources
496.A1	Periodicals. Societies. Serials
	Treatises
496.A4-Z	Early through 1900
496.5	1901-
496.8	Publication and distribution
496.9.A-Z	Special topics in rabbinical literature, A-Z
	Cf. BM518.A+, Special topics in the Midrash
496.9.B63	Boethusians
496.9.C45	Census
496.9.C76	Crown of God
496.9.D73	Dream interpretation
496.9.E4	Elijah, the prophet
496.9.E9	Evil eye
496.9.H4	Hell. Gehenna
496.9.H85	Humanism
496.9.I5	Image of God
496.9.I53	Incense
496.9.J67	Jordan
496.9.K5	Kings and rulers
496.9.M47	Messiah
496.9.M87	Mysticism
496.9.P64	Politics
496.9.P75	Prophets
496.9.R33	Rain
496.9.R66	Rome
496.9.S38	Saul, King of Israel
496.9.S43	Scapegoat
496.9.S48	Sex
496.9.S93	Suffering of God

BM	JUDAISM BM

Sources of Jewish religion. Rabbinical literature
  Special topics in rabbinical
    literature, A-Z -- Continued

496.9.S95	Supererogation
	Bible, see BS701+
	Talmudic literature
	The bulk of Talmudic literature is devoted to the Babylonian Talmud. The classification for the Babylonian Talmud BM499-BM504.7, is therefore carried out in detail and is to be used for all Talmudic material unless any work is limited to the Mishnah or the Palestinian Talmud
	Mishnah
	Original language (Hebrew and Aramaic)
497	Complete texts. By date
497.2	Selections. Miscellaneous tractates. By editor or date
497.5.A-Z	Translations. By language, A-Z
	Under each language:
(1)	*Complete texts. By date*
(2)	*Selections. Miscellaneous tractates. By editor or date*
	Works about the Mishnah
497.7	Early through 1900
497.8	1901-
(497.9)	Gemara
	Palestinian Talmud
	Original language (Hebrew and Aramaic)
498	Complete texts. By date
498.2	Selections. Miscellaneous tractates. By editor or date
498.5.A-Z	Translations. By language, A-Z
	Apply table at BM497.5.A-Z
	Works about the Palestinian Talmud
498.7	Early through 1900
498.8	1901-
	Babylonian Talmud
	Original language (Hebrew and Aramaic)
499	Complete texts. By date
499.2	Selections. Miscellaneous tractates. By editor or date
499.5.A-Z	Translations. By language, A-Z
	Under each language:
.x	*Complete texts. By date*
.x2	*Selections. Miscellaneous tractates. By editor or date*
	Works about the Babylonian Talmud
	Including the Palestinian Talmud, if necessary
500	Periodicals. Societies. Serials
500.2	Collections. Collected works
	Including addresses, essays, etc.
500.5	Concordances. Subject dictionaries. Indexes, etc.

Sources of Jewish religion. Rabbinical literature
Talmudic literature
Babylonian Talmud
Works about the Babylonian Talmud -- Continued
Language, see PJ4901+, PJ5201+, PJ5251+, PJ5301+
Language dictionaries, see PJ4935+
501 General works
Development of the Talmud
501.15 Collective biography of Talmudists (General)
Under each group of Talmudists include collective biography
For the biography of individual Talmudists, see BM755.A+
For the evaluation of individual Talmudists, see BM502.3.A+
501.17 Soferim
501.2 Tannaim
501.25 Beth Hillel and Beth Shammai
501.3 Amoraim
For Baraita, see BM507+
For Tosefta, see BM508+
501.4 Saboraim
501.5 Geonim
501.6 "Rishonim" (Early authorities)
501.7 North African and Spanish scholars
Cf. BM545+, Maimonides
501.8 French and German scholars
e.g. Rashi, 1040-1105 and his school; Tosafists
501.9 "Aharonim" (Later authorities, 16th century to date)
502 Talmudic academies in Babylonia and Palestine (through 11th century)
502.3.A-Z Criticism and evaluation of individual Talmudists, A-Z
For biography, see BM755.A+
502.3.A2 Abba Arika, called Rab, d. 247
502.3.A36 Akiba ben Joseph, ca. 50-ca. 132
502.3.E38 Eleazar ben Azariah
502.3.E4 Eliezer ben Hyrcanus
502.3.G35 Gamaliel II, fl. 80-110
502.3.H35 Ḥanina, Segan ha-Kohanim, lst cent.
502.3.H55 Hillel, lst cent. B.C./lst cent.
502.3.I8 Ishmael ben Elisha, 2nd cent.
502.3.J67 Jose the Galilean
502.3.J68 Joshua ben Ḥananiah, lst cent.
502.3.M44 Meir, 2nd cent.
502.3.P36 Papa
502.3.R3 Rabbah bar Bar Ḥana, 3rd cent.
Rav, 3rd cent., see BM502.3.A2
502.3.S34 Samuel ben Naḥman, 3rd/4th cent.
502.3.S37 Samuel of Nehardea, ca. 177-257
502.3.S5 Simeon bar Yoḥai, 2nd cent.

Sources of Jewish religion. Rabbinical literature
Talmudic literature
Babylonian Talmud
Works about the Babylonian Talmud
Criticism and evaluation of individual Talmudists -- Continued

502.3.T37 Tarfon
502.3.U44 Ulla I, 3rd cent.
Study and teaching
502.5 General works
502.7 Hadranim
Individual institutions, see BM90+
503 Authority. Tradition. Oral tradition
Cf. BM529, Jewish tradition
503.3 Apologetics
Cf. BM648, Judaism
For "Anti-Talmud", see BM585+
503.5 Introductions
Methodology
503.6 General works
503.7 Hermeneutics
503.8 Pilpul
503.9 Textual criticism
Commentaries
504 General works
504.2 Novellae (Hidushim)
504.3 Theology
504.5 Addresses, essays, lectures
504.7 Juvenile works
Cf. BM530+, Jewish myths, legends, and traditions
Aggada, see BM516+
506.A-Z Special orders and tractates of the Mishnah and the Palestinian and Babylonian Talmuds, A-Z (Table BM1)
e.g.
506.S2-S23 Sanhedrin
Minor tractates (Not part of the Mishnah)
506.2 Collections
506.3 Works on the minor Tractates
506.4.A-Z Special tractates, A-Z
Abadim (Avadim)
506.4.A15 Original texts (Hebrew or Aramaic). By date
506.4.A15A-Z Translations. By language, A-Z
506.4.A16 Selections. By date
506.4.A17 Criticism. Commentaries, etc.
Avadim, see BM506.4.A15+
Avot de-Rabbi Nathan
506.4.A94 Original texts (Hebrew or Aramaic). By date
506.4.A94A-Z Translations. By language, A-Z
506.4.A942 Selections. By date
506.4.A943 Criticism. Commentaries, etc.
Derekh ereẓ

Sources of Jewish religion. Rabbinical literature
Talmudic literature
Minor tractates (Not part of the Mishnah)
Special tractates, A-Z
Derekh ereẓ -- Continued

506.4.D4	Original texts (Hebrew or Aramaic). By date
506.4.D4A-Z	Translations. By language, A-Z
506.4.D5	Selections. By date
506.4.D6	Criticism. Commentaries, etc.
	Evel, see BM506.4.S4+
	Gerim
506.4.G4	Original texts (Hebrew or Aramaic). By date
506.4.G4A-Z	Translations. By language, A-Z
506.4.G42	Selections. By date
506.4.G43	Criticism. Commentaries, etc.
	Kallah
506.4.K3	Original texts (Hebrew or Aramaic). By date
506.4.K3A-Z	Translations. By language, A-Z
506.4.K32	Selections. By date
506.4.K33	Criticism. Commentaries, etc.
	Kallah rabbati
506.4.K35	Original texts (Hebrew or Aramaic). By date
506.4.K35A-Z	Translations. By language, A-Z
506.4.K352	Selections. By date
506.4.K353	Criticism. Commentaries, etc.
	Kutim
506.4.K8	Original texts (Hebrew or Aramaic). By date
506.4.K8A-Z	Translations. By language, A-Z
506.4.K82	Selections. By date
506.4.K83	Criticism. Commentaries, etc.
	Mezuzah
506.4.M48	Original texts (Hebrew or Aramaic). By date
506.4.M48A-Z	Translations. By language, A-Z
506.4.M482	Selections. By date
506.4.M483	Criticism. Commentaries, etc.
	Semaḥot. Evel
506.4.S4	Original texts (Hebrew or Aramaic). By date
506.4.S4A-Z	Translations. By language, A-Z
506.4.S42	Selections. By date
506.4.S43	Criticism. Commentaries, etc.
	Soferim
506.4.S6	Original texts (Hebrew or Aramaic). By date
506.4.S6A-Z	Translations. By language, A-Z
506.4.S62	Selections. By date
506.4.S63	Criticism. Commentaries, etc.
	Tsitsit, see BM506.4.Z5+
	Ẓiẓit
506.4.Z5	Original texts (Hebrew or Aramaic). By date
506.4.Z5A-Z	Translations. By language, A-Z
506.4.Z52	Selections. By date
506.4.Z53	Criticism. Commentaries, etc.
	Baraita
507	Collections

Sources of Jewish religion. Rabbinical literature
Talmudic literature
Baraita -- Continued
507.2 Works on the Baraita
507.5.A-Z Special Baraitot, A-Z
Baraita on the Aboth (Abot)
507.5.A2 Original texts (Hebrew or Aramaic). By date
507.5.A2A-Z Translations. By language, A-Z
507.5.A3 Selections. By date
507.5.A4 Criticism. Commentaries, etc.
Baraita of Rabbi Ada
507.5.A5 Original texts (Hebrew or Aramaic). By date
507.5.A5A-Z Translations. By language, A-Z
507.5.A6 Selections. By date
507.5.A7 Criticism. Commentaries, etc.
Baraita of Rabbi Eliezer, see BM517.P7+
Baraita on the Erection of the tabernacle
507.5.E6 Original texts (Hebrew or Aramaic). By date
507.5.E6A-Z Translations. By language, A-Z
507.5.E7 Selections. By date
507.5.E8 Criticism. Commentaries, etc.
Baraita of the Forty-nine rules
507.5.F5 Original texts (Hebrew or Aramaic). By date
507.5.F5A-Z Translations. By language, A-Z
507.5.F6 Selections. By date
507.5.F7 Criticism. Commentaries, etc.
Baraita of Rabbi Ishmael (Yishma'el)
507.5.I7 Original texts (Hebrew or Aramaic). By date
507.5.I7A-Z Translations. By language, A-Z
507.5.I8 Selections. By date
507.5.I9 Criticism. Commentaries, etc.
Baraita de-Melekhet ha-Mishkan, see BM507.5.E6+
Baraita of the Mystery of the calculation of the calendar
507.5.M7 Original texts (Hebrew or Aramaic). By date
507.5.M7A-Z Translations. By language, A-Z
507.5.M8 Selections. By date
507.5.M9 Criticism. Commentaries, etc.
Baraita de-Niddah
507.5.N4 Original texts (Hebrew or Aramaic). By date
507.5.N4A-Z Translations. By language, A-Z
507.5.N5 Selections. By date
507.5.N6 Criticism. Commentaries, etc.
Baraita of Rabbi Phinehas ben Jair
Including sayings on Messianic times and on Sotah IX.15
507.5.P4 Original texts (Hebrew or Aramaic). By date
507.5.P4A-Z Translations. By language, A-Z
507.5.P5 Selections. By date
507.5.P6 Criticism. Commentaries, etc.
Baraita of Rabbi Phinehas ben Jair (Genesis), see BM517.T3+
Baraita on Salvation

Sources of Jewish religion. Rabbinical literature
Talmudic literature
Baraita
Special Baraitot, A-Z
Baraita on Salvation -- Continued
507.5.S2 Original texts (Hebrew or Aramaic). By date
507.5.S2A-Z Translations. By language, A-Z
507.5.S3 Selections. By date
507.5.S4 Criticism. Commentaries, etc.
Baraita of Samuel
507.5.S6 Original texts (Hebrew or Aramaic). By date
507.5.S6A-Z Translations. By language, A-Z
507.5.S7 Selections. By date
507.5.S8 Criticism. Commentaries, etc.
Baraita of the Thirty-two rules
507.5.T4 Original texts (Hebrew or Aramaic). By date
507.5.T4A-Z Translations. By language, A-Z
507.5.T5 Selections. By date
507.5.T6 Criticism. Commentaries, etc.
Tosefta
508.A-Z Editions. By editor, A-Z
508.12 Selections. Miscellaneous tractates. By editor or date
508.13.A-Z Translations. By language, A-Z
Apply table at BM497.5.A-Z
508.15 Concordances. Subject dictionaries, indexes, etc.
508.2 Works on the Tosefta
508.5.A-Z Special Orders and Tractates, A-Z (Table BM1)
509.A-Z Special topics in Talmudic literature (not otherwise provided for), A-Z
509.A48 Angels
509.A5 Animals
509.A7 Astrology
509.A72 Astronomy
509.B6 Botany
509.C3 Caesarean section
509.C4 Ceramics
509.C5 Christians
509.C67 Creation
509.D5 Dialectic
509.E27 Economics
509.E3 Education
509.E8 Eschatology
509.G4 Geography
509.G63 Gods
509.H4 Hermaphroditism
509.H54 Hides and skins
509.H84 Human anatomy
509.I6 Iran
509.J48 Jews
509.L2 Labor. Working class
509.M3 Mathematics
509.M4 Messiah

Sources of Jewish religion. Rabbinical literature
Talmudic literature
Special topics in Talmudic literature (not otherwise provided for), A-Z -- Continued
509.M6 Mnemonic devices
509.N3 Names
509.N4 Natural history
509.P3 Palestine
Plants, see BM509.B6
509.P8 Psychology
509.S34 Science
509.S55 Ships
Skins, see BM509.H54
509.T5 Titus, emperor of Rome
509.W4 Weights and measures
509.W7 Women
Midrash
510 Original language (Hebrew or Aramaic)
Translations
511 English
512 Selections
513.A-Z Other languages, A-Z
514 Works about the Midrash
515 Halacha in the Midrash
Aggada
Including Talmudic Aggada
516.A-Z Texts. By author or title, A-Z
Under each:
.x *Original. By date*
.x2A-Z *Translations. By language, A-Z, and date*
.x3 *Criticism, commentaries, etc.*
516.5 Works about the Aggada
517.A-Z Special Midrashim, A-Z
Abba Guryon
517.A1 Original texts (Hebrew or Aramaic). By date
517.A1A-Z Translations. By language, A-Z
517.A12 Selections. By date
517.A13 Criticism. Commentaries, etc.
Abkir (Avkir)
517.A2 Original texts (Hebrew or Aramaic). By date
517.A2A-Z Translations. By language, A-Z
517.A22 Selections. By date
517.A23 Criticism. Commentaries, etc.
Aggadat Bereshit
517.A3 Original texts (Hebrew or Aramaic). By date
517.A3A-Z Translations. By language, A-Z
517.A32 Selections. By date
517.A33 Criticism. Commentaries, etc.
Agadat Ester
517.A34 Original texts (Hebrew or Aramaic). By date
517.A34A-Z Translations. By language, A-Z

Sources of Jewish religion. Rabbinical literature
Midrash
Special Midrashim, A-Z
Agadat Ester -- Continued
517.A35 Selections. By date
517.A36 Criticism. Commentaries, etc.
Al yithalel
517.A4 Original texts (Hebrew or Aramaic). By date
517.A4A-Z Translations. By language, A-Z
517.A5 Selections. By date
517.A6 Criticism. Commentaries, etc.
Alef bet, see BM517.A63+
Alef bet de-Rabbi Akiva, see BM517.O8+
Aleph beth
517.A63 Original texts (Hebrew or Aramaic). By date
517.A63A-Z Translations. By language, A-Z
517.A632 Selections. By date
517.A633 Criticism. Commentaries, etc.
'Aśeret ha-dibrot
517.A7 Original texts (Hebrew or Aramaic). By date
517.A7A-Z Translations. By language, A-Z
517.A8 Selections. By date
517.A9 Criticism. Commentaries, etc.
Avkir, see BM517.A2+
Bamidbar rabbah, see BM517.M68+
Baraita of Rabbi Eliezer, see BM517.P7+
Baraita of Rabbi Phinehas ben Jair (Genesis), see BM517.T3+
Bereshit rabati
517.B7 Original texts (Hebrew or Aramaic). By date
517.B7A-Z Translations. By language, A-Z
517.B72 Selections. By date
517.B73 Criticism. Commentaries, etc.
Bereshit rabbah, see BM517.M65+
Bereshit zuta
517.B8 Original texts (Hebrew or Aramaic). By date
517.B8A-Z Translations. By language, A-Z
517.B82 Selections. By date
517.B83 Criticism. Commentaries, etc.
Devarim rabbah, see BM517.M69+
Devarim zuta
517.D4 Original texts (Hebrew or Aramaic). By date
517.D4A-Z Translations. By language, A-Z
517.D42 Selections. By date
517.D43 Criticism. Commentaries, etc.
Divrei ha-yamim shel Moshe
517.D5 Original texts (Hebrew or Aramaic). By date
517.D5A-Z Translations. By language, A-Z
517.D6 Selections. By date
517.D7 Criticism. Commentaries, etc.
Eikhah rabbah, see BM517.M74+
Eleh ezkerah. Ma'aśeh 'aśarah haruge malkhut
517.E5 Original texts (Hebrew or Aramaic). By date

Sources of Jewish religion. Rabbinical literature
Midrash
Special Midrashim, A-Z
Eleh ezkerah. Ma'aśeh 'aśarah haruge malkhut -- Continued

517.E5A-Z Translations. By language, A-Z
517.E52 Selections. By date
517.E53 Criticism. Commentaries, etc.

Eser galuyyot
517.E6 Original texts (Hebrew or Aramaic). By date
517.E6A-Z Translations. By language, A-Z
517.E62 Selections. By date
517.E63 Criticism. Commentaries, etc.

Esfah
517.E7 Original texts (Hebrew or Aramaic). By date
517.E7A-Z Translations. By language, A-Z
517.E72 Selections. By date
517.E73 Criticism. Commentaries, etc.

Esther rabbah, see BM517.M76+
Midrash ha-gadol, see BM517.M5+
Ḥamesh Megillot, see BM517.M7+
Ḥaserot vi-yeterot, see BM517.T2+

Iyov
517.I7 Original texts (Hebrew or Aramaic). By date
517.I7A-Z Translations. By language, A-Z
517.I8 Selections. By date
517.I9 Criticism. Commentaries, etc.

Kohelet
517.K5 Original texts (Hebrew or Aramaic). By date
517.K5A-Z Translations. By language, A-Z
517.K6 Selections. By date
517.K7 Criticism. Commentaries, etc.

Kohelet rabbah, see BM517.M75+

Konen
517.K8 Original texts (Hebrew or Aramaic). By date
517.K8A-Z Translations. By language, A-Z
517.K82 Selections. By date
517.K83 Criticism. Commentaries, etc.

Ma'aśeh 'aśarah haruge malkhut, see BM517.E5+

Ma'aśeh Torah
517.M2 Original texts (Hebrew or Aramaic). By date
517.M2A-Z Translations. By language, A-Z
517.M22 Selections. By date
517.M23 Criticism. Commentaries, etc.

Mekhilta of Rabbi Ishmael
517.M4 Original texts (Hebrew or Aramaic). By date
517.M4A-Z Translations. By language, A-Z
517.M42 Selections. By date
517.M43 Criticism. Commentaries, etc.

Mekhilta of Rabbi Simeon ben Yoḥai
517.M45 Original texts (Hebrew or Aramaic). By date
517.M45A-Z Translations. By language, A-Z
517.M46 Selections. By date

	Sources of Jewish religion. Rabbinical literature
	Midrash
	Special Midrashim, A-Z
	Mekhilta of Rabbi Simeon ben Yoḥai -- Continued
517.M47	Criticism. Commentaries, etc.
	Midrash ha-gadol
517.M5	Original texts (Hebrew or Aramaic). By date
517.M5A-Z	Translations. By language, A-Z
517.M52	Selections. By date
517.M53	Criticism. Commentaries, etc.
	Special parts
	Genesis
517.M55	Texts. By date
	Translations
517.M55A3	English. By date
517.M55A32-M55A49	Other languages, alphabetically. By date
517.M55A5-M55Z	Criticism. Commentaries, etc.
	Exodus
517.M56	Texts. By date
	Translations
517.M56A3	English. By date
517.M56A32-M56A49	Other languages, alphabetically. By date
517.M56A5-M56Z	Criticism. Commentaries, etc.
	Leviticus
517.M57	Texts. By date
	Translations
517.M57A3	English. By date
517.M57A32-M57A49	Other languages, alphabetically. By date
517.M57A5-M57Z	Criticism. Commentaries, etc.
	Numbers
517.M58	Texts. By date
	Translations
517.M58A3	English. By date
517.M58A32-M58A49	Other languages, alphabetically. By date
517.M58A5-M58Z	Criticism. Commentaries, etc.
	Deuteronomy
517.M59	Texts. By date
	Translations
517.M59A3	English. By date
517.M59A32-M59A49	Other languages, alphabetically. By date
517.M59A5-M59Z	Criticism. Commentaries, etc.
	Midrash rabbah
517.M6	Original texts (Hebrew or Aramaic). By date
517.M6A-Z	Translations. By language, A-Z
517.M62	Selections. By date
517.M63	Criticism. Commentaries, etc.
	Special parts
	Pentateuch
517.M64	Texts. By date
	Translations
517.M64A3	English. By date
517.M64A32-M64A49	Other languages, alphabetically. By date
517.M64A5-M64Z	Criticism. Commentaries, etc.

Sources of Jewish religion. Rabbinical literature
Midrash
Special Midrashim, A-Z
Midrash rabbah
Special parts
Pentateuch -- Continued
Genesis. Bereshit rabbah
517.M65 Texts. By date
Translations
517.M65A3 English. By date
517.M65A32-M65A49 Other languages, alphabetically. By date
517.M65A5-M65Z Criticism. Commentaries, etc.
Exodus. Shemot rabbah
517.M66 Texts. By date
Translations
517.M66A3 English. By date
517.M66A32-M66A49 Other languages, alphabetically. By date
517.M66A5-M66Z Criticism. Commentaries, etc.
Leviticus. Vayikra rabbah
517.M67 Texts. By date
Translations
517.M67A3 English. By date
517.M67A32-M67A49 Other languages, alphabetically. By date
517.M67A5-M67Z Criticism. Commentaries, etc.
Numbers. Bamidbar rabbah
517.M68 Texts. By date
Translations
517.M68A3 English. By date
517.M68A32-M68A49 Other languages, alphabetically. By date
517.M68A5-M68Z Criticism. Commentaries, etc.
Deuteronomy. Devarim rabbah
517.M69 Texts. By date
Translations
517.M69A3 English. By date
517.M69A32-M69A49 Other languages, alphabetically. By date
517.M69A5-M69Z Criticism. Commentaries, etc.
Five Scrolls. Ḥamesh Megillot
517.M7 Texts. By date
Translations
517.M7A3 English. By date
517.M7A32-M7A49 Other languages, alphabetically. By date
517.M7A5-M7Z Criticism. Commentaries, etc.
Song of Solomon. Shir ha-shirim rabbah
517.M72 Texts. By date
Translations
517.M72A3 English. By date
517.M72A32-M72A49 Other languages, alphabetically. By date

	Sources of Jewish religion. Rabbinical literature
	Midrash
	Special Midrashim, A-Z
	Midrash rabbah
	Special parts
	Five Scrolls. Ḥamesh Megillot
	Song of Solomon.
	Shir ha-shirim rabbah -- Continued
517.M72A5-M72Z	Criticism. Commentaries, etc.
	Ruth. Ruth rabbah
517.M73	Texts. By date
	Translations
517.M73A3	English. By date
517.M73A32-M73A49	Other languages, alphabetically. By date
517.M73A5-M73Z	Criticism. Commentaries, etc.
	Lamentations. Eikhah rabbah
517.M74	Texts. By date
	Translations
517.M74A3	English. By date
517.M74A32-M74A49	Other languages, alphabetically. By date
517.M74A5-M74Z	Criticism. Commentaries, etc.
	Ecclesiastes. Kohelet rabbah
517.M75	Texts. By date
	Translations
517.M75A3	English. By date
517.M75A32-M75A49	Other languages, alphabetically. By date
517.M75A5-M75Z	Criticism. Commentaries, etc.
	Esther. Esther rabbah
517.M76	Texts. By date
	Translations
517.M76A3	English. By date
517.M76A32-M76A49	Other languages, alphabetically. By date
517.M76A5-M76Z	Criticism. Commentaries, etc.
	Mishle. Proverbs
517.M77	Original texts (Hebrew or Aramaic). By date
517.M77A-Z	Translations. By language, A-Z
517.M78	Selections. By date
517.M79	Criticism. Commentaries, etc.
	Otiyyot de-Rabbi Akiva
517.O8	Original texts (Hebrew or Aramaic). By date
517.O8A-Z	Translations. By language, A-Z
517.O82	Selections. By date
517.O83	Criticism. Commentaries, etc.
	Panim aḥerim le-Esther
517.P1	Original texts (Hebrew or Aramaic). By date
517.P1A-Z	Translations. By language, A-Z
517.P12	Selections. By date
517.P13	Criticism. Commentaries, etc.
	Peli'ah

Sources of Jewish religion. Rabbinical literature
Midrash
Special Midrashim, A-Z
Peli'ah -- Continued
517.P2 Original texts (Hebrew or Aramaic). By date
517.P2A-Z Translations. By language, A-Z
517.P22 Selections. By date
517.P23 Criticism. Commentaries, etc.
Pesikta
517.P3 Original texts (Hebrew or Aramaic). By date
517.P3A-Z Translations. By language, A-Z
517.P32 Selections. By date
517.P33 Criticism. Commentaries, etc.
Pesikta de-Rav Kahana
517.P34 Original texts (Hebrew or Aramaic). By date
517.P34A-Z Translations. By language, A-Z
517.P35 Selections. By date
517.P36 Criticism. Commentaries, etc.
Pesikta rabbati
517.P4 Original texts (Hebrew or Aramaic). By date
517.P4A-Z Translations. By language, A-Z
517.P42 Selections. By date
517.P43 Criticism. Commentaries, etc.
Peṭirat Aharon
517.P5 Original texts (Hebrew or Aramaic). By date
517.P5A-Z Translations. By language, A-Z
517.P52 Selections. By date
517.P53 Criticism. Commentaries, etc.
Peṭirat Mosheh
517.P6 Original texts (Hebrew or Aramaic). By date
517.P6A-Z Translations. By language, A-Z
517.P62 Selections. By date
517.P63 Criticism. Commentaries, etc.
Pirkei de-Rabbi Eliezer
517.P7 Original texts (Hebrew or Aramaic). By date
517.P7A-Z Translations. By language, A-Z
517.P72 Selections. By date
517.P73 Criticism. Commentaries, etc.
Proverbs, see BM517.M77+
Midrash rabbah, see BM517.M6+
Ruth rabbah, see BM517.M73+
Samuel, see BM517.S4+
Shemot rabbah, see BM517.M66+
Shemu'el. Samuel
517.S4 Original texts (Hebrew or Aramaic). By date
517.S4A-Z Translations. By language, A-Z
517.S42 Selections. By date
517.S43 Criticism. Commentaries, etc.
Shir ha-shirim
517.S45 Original texts (Hebrew or Aramaic). By date
517.S45A-Z Translations. By language, A-Z
517.S46 Selections. By date
517.S47 Criticism. Commentaries, etc.

	Sources of Jewish religion. Rabbinical literature
	Midrash
	Special Midrashim, A-Z -- Continued
	Shir ha-shirim rabbah, see BM517.M72+
	Shoḥer ṭov, see BM517.M77+, BM517.S4+, BM517.T5+
	Sifra. Torat Kohanim
517.S6	Original texts (Hebrew or Aramaic). By date
517.S6A-Z	Translations. By language, A-Z
517.S62	Selections. By date
517.S63	Criticism. Commentaries, etc.
	Sifrei
517.S7	Original texts (Hebrew or Aramaic). By date
517.S7A-Z	Translations. By language, A-Z
517.S72	Selections. By date
517.S73	Criticism. Commentaries, etc.
	Special parts
	Numbers
517.S74	Texts. By date
	Translations
517.S74A3	English. By date
517.S74A32-S74A49	Other languages, alphabetically. By date
517.S74A5-S74Z	Criticism. Commentaries, etc.
	Deuteronomy
517.S75	Texts. By date
	Translations
517.S75A3	English. By date
517.S75A32-S75A49	Other languages, alphabetically. By date
517.S75A5-S75Z	Criticism. Commentaries, etc.
	Sifrei zuta
517.S85	Original texts (Hebrew or Aramaic). By date
517.S85A-Z	Translations. By language, A-Z
517.S86	Selections. By date
517.S87	Criticism. Commentaries, etc.
	Ta'ame ḥaserot vi-yeterot
517.T2	Original texts (Hebrew or Aramaic). By date
517.T2A-Z	Translations. By language, A-Z
517.T22	Selections. By date
517.T23	Criticism. Commentaries, etc.
	Tadshe
517.T3	Original texts (Hebrew or Aramaic). By date
517.T3A-Z	Translations. By language, A-Z
517.T32	Selections. By date
517.T33	Criticism. Commentaries, etc.
	Tanḥuma. Yelammedenu
517.T35	Original texts (Hebrew or Aramaic). By date
517.T35A-Z	Translations. By language, A-Z
517.T36	Selections. By date
517.T37	Criticism. Commentaries, etc.
	Tanna de-vei Eliyahu
	In two parts: (1) Seder Eliyahu rabbah; (2) Seder Eliyahu zuta
517.T4	Original texts (Hebrew or Aramaic). By date
517.T4A-Z	Translations. By language, A-Z

Sources of Jewish religion. Rabbinical literature
Midrash
Special Midrashim, A-Z
Tanna de-vei Eliyahu -- Continued
517.T42 Selections. By date
517.T43 Criticism. Commentaries, etc.
Tehillim
517.T5 Original texts (Hebrew or Aramaic). By date
517.T5A-Z Translations. By language, A-Z
517.T52 Selections. By date
517.T53 Criticism. Commentaries, etc.
Temurah
517.T6 Original texts (Hebrew or Aramaic). By date
517.T6A-Z Translations. By language, A-Z
517.T7 Selections. By date
517.T8 Criticism. Commentaries, etc.
Torat Kohanim, see BM517.S6+
Va-yekhullu
517.V2 Original texts (Hebrew or Aramaic). By date
517.V2A-Z Translations. By language, A-Z
517.V22 Selections. By date
517.V23 Criticism. Commentaries, etc.
Va-yikra rabah, see BM517.M67+
Va-yissa'u
517.V4 Original texts (Hebrew or Aramaic). By date
517.V4A-Z Translations. By language, A-Z
517.V42 Selections. By date
517.V43 Criticism. Commentaries, etc.
Va-yosha'
517.V5 Original texts (Hebrew or Aramaic). By date
517.V5A-Z Translations. By language, A-Z
517.V52 Selections. By date
517.V53 Criticism. Commentaries, etc.
Vayikra rabbah, see BM517.M67+
Ve-hizhir
517.V6 Original texts (Hebrew or Aramaic). By date
517.V6A-Z Translations. By language, A-Z
517.V7 Selections. By date
517.V8 Criticism. Commentaries, etc.
Yalkut ha-Makhiri
517.Y2 Original texts (Hebrew or Aramaic). By date
517.Y2A-Z Translations. By language, A-Z
517.Y22 Selections. By date
517.Y23 Criticism. Commentaries, etc.
Yalkut Shimoni
517.Y3 Original texts (Hebrew or Aramaic). By date
517.Y3A-Z Translations. By language, A-Z
517.Y32 Selections. By date
517.Y33 Criticism. Commentaries, etc.
Yelammedenu, see BM517.T35+
Yesha'yah
517.Y4 Original texts (Hebrew or Aramaic). By date
517.Y4A-Z Translations. By language, A-Z

Sources of Jewish religion. Rabbinical literature
Midrash
Special Midrashim, A-Z
Yesha'yah -- Continued
517.Y5 Selections. By date
517.Y6 Criticism. Commentaries, etc.
Yonah
517.Y7 Original texts (Hebrew or Aramaic). By date
517.Y7A-Z Translations. By language, A-Z
517.Y8 Selections. By date
517.Y9 Criticism. Commentaries, etc.
Midrash zuta
517.Z8 Original texts (Hebrew or Aramaic). By date
517.Z8A-Z Translations. By language, A-Z
517.Z82 Selections. By date
517.Z83 Criticism. Commentaries, etc.
518.A-Z Special topics in the Midrash, A-Z
Cf. BM496.9.A+, Special topics in rabbinical literature
518.A2 Abraham
518.A4 Adam
518.A45 Allegory
518.B87 Burning bush
518.C34 Cain
518.C5 Circumcision
518.H35 Haman
518.I8 Isaac
518.J4 Jerusalem
518.K5 Kings and rulers
518.L32 Laban
518.M6 Moses
518.P25 Palestine
518.P3 Parables
518.S24 Sabbath
518.T5 Titus, emperor of Rome
Halacha
520 Periodicals. Societies. Serials
Collected works
520.2 Several authors
520.3 Individual authors
520.4 Dictionaries
520.5 History
520.6 Philosophy
520.65 Sources. Halakic portions of the Bible, Talmudic literature, and Midrash
Cf. BM515, Halacha in the Midrash
Commandments
520.7 General works
520.73 Noahide Laws
Cf. BP605.N63, Noahides. Noachide movement
520.75 Ten commandments
520.8 Six hundred and thirteen commandments
Codes (Poskim)

Sources of Jewish religion. Rabbinical literature
Halacha
Codes (Posḳim) -- Continued

520.82	Alfasi, Isaac ben Jacob, 1013-1103. Halakhot
520.82.A2	Original texts. By date
520.82.A21-A219	Translations. By language. Subarrange by translator
520.82.A3-Z	Criticisms, commentaries, etc.
520.84	Maimonides, Moses, 1135-1204 (Moses ben Maimon). Mishneh Torah
520.84.A2	Original texts. By date
520.84.A21-A219	Translations. By language. Subarrange by translator
520.84.A3-Z	Criticism, commentaries, etc.
520.86	Jacob ben Asher, ca. 1269-ca. 1340. Arba'ah ṭurim
520.86.A2	Original texts. By date
520.86.A3-A39	Original selections. By date
520.86.A4-A49	Translations. By language, alphabetically. Subarrange by translator
	Special parts
	Oraḥ ḥayim
520.86.A52	Texts
520.86.A53	Criticism, commentaries, etc.
	Yoreh de'ah
520.86.A54	Texts
520.86.A55	Criticism, commentaries, etc.
	Even ha-'ezer
520.86.A56	Texts
520.86.A57	Criticism, commentaries, etc.
	Ḥoshen mishpaṭ
520.86.A58	Texts
520.86.A59	Criticism, commentaries, etc.
520.86.A6-Z	Criticism, commentaries, etc.
520.88	Karo, Joseph ben Ephraim, 1488-1575 (Caro, Joseph). Shulḥan 'arukh
520.88.A2	Original texts. By date
520.88.A3-A39	Original selections. By date
520.88.A4-A49	Translations. By language, alphabetically. Subarrange by translator
	Special parts
	Oraḥ ḥayim
520.88.A52	Texts
520.88.A53	Criticism, commentaries, etc.
	Yoreh de'ah
520.88.A54	Texts
520.88.A55	Criticism, commentaries, etc.
	Even ha-'ezer
520.88.A56	Texts
520.88.A57	Criticism, commentaries, etc.
	Ḥoshen mishpaṭ
520.88.A58	Texts
520.88.A59	Criticism, commentaries, etc.

Sources of Jewish religion. Rabbinical literature
Halacha
Codes (Posḳim)
Karo, Joseph ben Ephraim, 1488-1575 (Caro, Joseph).
Shulḥan 'arukh -- Continued

520.88.A6-Z Criticism, commentaries, etc.
520.9 Other codes
521 General works
Responsa
522.A1 Several authors
Individual authors, A-Z
Special numbers are assigned to forenames. However, if a forename has become a family name, Cutter numbers are assigned as usual for family names.
522.17 Aa-Aaron
Cutter number for author is based on third letter in the name
522.18 Aaron (Forename)
Cutter number for author is based on name following the forename, disregarding "ben," i. e., son of ...
522.19 Aaron, A-Abraham
Cutter number for author is based on second letter in the name
522.2 Abraham (Forename)
Cutter number for author is based on name following the forename, disregarding "ben," i. e., son of ...
522.21 Abraham, A-Aryeh Loeb
Cutter number for author is based on second letter in the name
522.22 Aryeh Loeb (Forename)
Cutter number for author is based on name following the forename, disregarding "ben," i. e., son of ...
522.23 Aryeh Loeb, A-Az
Cutter number for author is based on second letter in the name
522.24 Ba-Baruch
Cutter number for author is based on third letter in the name
522.25 Baruch (Forename)
Cutter number for author is based on name following the forename, disregarding "ben," i. e., son of ...
522.26 Baruch, A-Bz
Cutter number for author is based on second letter in the name
522.27 C
Cutter number for author is based on second letter in the name

Sources of Jewish religion. Rabbinical literature
Halacha
Responsa
Individual authors, A-Z
C -- Continued

522.27.O8 Covo, Joseph, 17th cent.

522.28 Da-David
Cutter number for author is based on third letter in the name

522.29 David (Forename)
Cutter number for author is based on name following the forename, disregarding "ben," i. e., son of ...

522.3 David, A-Dz
Cutter number for author is based on second letter in the name

522.31 Ea-Eliezer
Cutter number for author is based on second letter in the name

522.32 Eliezer (Forename)
Cutter number for author is based on name following the forename, disregarding "ben," i. e., son of ...

522.33 Eliezer, A-Elijah
Cutter number for author is based on fourth letter in the name

522.34 Elijah (Forename)
Cutter number for author is based on name following the forename, disregarding "ben," i. e., son of ...

522.35 Elijah, A-Ez
Cutter number for author is based on second letter in the name

Eliyahu ben Avraham Yuzpa, me-ʻir Pulav, see BM522.6.E715

522.36 F
Cutter number for author is based on second letter in the name

522.37 Ga-Gabriel
Cutter number for author is based on third letter in the name

522.38 Gabriel (Forename)
Cutter number for author is based on name following the forename, disregarding "ben," i. e., son of ...

522.39 Gabriel, A-Gz
Cutter number for author is based on second letter in the name

522.39.R3 Graubert, Issachar Berish, 1847-1913

522.39.R38 Greenblatt, Ephraim

Grinblaṭ, Efrayim, see BM522.39.R38

Sources of Jewish religion. Rabbinical literature
Halacha
Responsa
Individual authors, A-Z -- Continued

522.4 Ha-Ḥayyim
Cutter number for author is based on third letter in the name
Hadayah, Ovadiah, ca. 1890-1969, see BM522.42.D3

522.41 Ḥayyim (Forename)
Cutter number for author is based on name following the forename, disregarding "ben," i. e., son of ...

522.42 Ḥayyim, A-Hz
Cutter number for author is based on second letter in the name

522.42.D3 Hdaya, Obadia, 1890-

522.43 Ia-Isaac
Cutter number for author is based on second letter in the name
Ibn Shang'i, Yitsḥaḳ ben Eliyahu, d. 1761, see BM522.85.H37

522.44 Isaac (Forename)
Cutter number for author is based on name following the forename, disregarding "ben," i. e., son of ...

522.44.A23 Isaac Abraham ben Dob Berush, ha-Kohen, 18th cent.

522.45 Isaac, A-Israel
Cutter number for author is based on third letter in the name

522.46 Israel (Forename)
Cutter number for author is based on name following the forename, disregarding "ben," i. e., son of ...

522.47 Israel, A-Iz
Cutter number for author is based on second letter in the name

522.48 Ja-Jacob
Cutter number for author is based on third letter in the name

522.49 Jacob (Forename)
Cutter number for author is based on name following the forename, disregarding "ben," i. e., son of ...

522.5 Jacob, A-Jehiel
Cutter number for author is based on second letter in the name

522.51 Jehiel (Forename)
Cutter number for author is based on name following the forename, disregarding "ben," i. e., son of ...

Sources of Jewish religion. Rabbinical literature
Halacha
Responsa
Individual authors, A-Z -- Continued

522.52 Jehiel, A-Joseph
Cutter number for author is based on second letter in the name

522.53 Joseph (Forename)
Cutter number for author is based on name following the forename, disregarding "ben," i. e., son of ...

522.54 Joseph, A-Joshua
Cutter number for author is based on fourth letter in the name

522.55 Joshua (Forename)
Cutter number for author is based on name following the forename, disregarding "ben," i. e., son of ...

522.56 Joshua, A-Judah
Cutter number for author is based on second letter in the name

522.57 Judah (Forename)
Cutter number for author is based on name following the forename, disregarding "ben," i. e., son of ...

522.58 Judah, A-Jz
Cutter number for author is based on second letter in the name

522.59 K
Cutter number for author is based on second letter in the name

Ḳovo, Yosef, d. 1727, see BM522.27.O8

522.59.R34 Krausz, Solomon

Ḳroiz, Shalom, see BM522.59.R34

522.6 L
Cutter number for author is based on second letter in the name

522.6.E715 Lermann, Elijah

522.61 Ma-Meir
Cutter number for author is based on second letter in the name

522.62 Meir (Forename)
Cutter number for author is based on name following the forename, disregarding "ben," i. e., son of ...

522.63 Meir, A-Menahem
Cutter number for author is based on third letter in the name

522.64 Menahem (Forename)
Cutter number for author is based on name following the forename, disregarding "ben," i. e., son of ...

Sources of Jewish religion. Rabbinical literature
Halacha
Responsa
Individual authors, A-Z -- Continued

522.65 Menahem, A-Meshullam
Cutter number for author is based on third letter in the name

522.66 Meshullam (Forename)
Cutter number for author is based on name following the forename, disregarding "ben," i. e., son of ...

522.67 Meshullam, A-Mordecai
Cutter number for author is based on second letter in the name

Mintz, Mose, ca. 1750-1831, see BM522.71.U3

522.68 Mordecai (Forename)
Cutter number for author is based on name following the forename, disregarding "ben," i. e., son of ...

522.69 Mordecai, A-Moses
Cutter number for author is based on third letter in the name

522.7 Moses (Forename)
Cutter number for author is based on name following the forename, disregarding "ben," i. e., son of ...

522.71 Moses, A-Mz
Cutter number for author is based on second letter in the name

522.71.U3 Münz, Moses, ca. 1750-1831

522.72 Na-Nathan
Cutter number for author is based on third letter in the name

522.72.B56 Nabon, Benjamin Mordecai

522.73 Nathan (Forename)
Cutter number for author is based on name following the forename, disregarding "ben," i. e., son of ...

522.74 Nathan, A-Nz
Cutter number for author is based on second letter in the name

Navon, Benjamin Mordecai ben Ephraim, 1788-1851, see BM522.72.B56

522.75 O
Cutter number for author is based on second letter in the name

522.76 P
Cutter number for author is based on second letter in the name

522.77 Q
Cutter number for author is based on second letter in the name

Sources of Jewish religion. Rabbinical literature
Halacha
Responsa
Individual authors, A-Z -- Continued

522.78 Ra-Raphael
Cutter number for author is based on third letter in the name

522.79 Raphael (Forename)
Cutter number for author is based on name following the forename, disregarding "ben," i. e., son of ...

522.8 Raphael, A-Rz
Cutter number for author is based on second letter in the name

522.8.I3 Ridbaz, Jacob David, 1845-1913

522.81 Sa-Samson
Cutter number for author is based on third letter in the name

522.82 Samson (Forename)
Cutter number for author is based on name following the forename, disregarding "ben," i. e., son of ...

522.83 Samson, A-Samuel
Cutter number for author is based on fourth letter in the name

522.84 Samuel (Forename)
Cutter number for author is based on name following the forename, disregarding "ben," i. e., son of ...

522.85 Samuel, A-Solomon
Cutter number for author is based on second letter in the name

522.85.C47 Schapiro, Abraham Duber, 1870-1943

522.85.C493 Schreiber, Moses, 1762-1839

522.85.H37 Shangi, Isaac

Shapira, Avraham Duber Kahana, 1870-1943, see BM522.85.C47

Shperber, Daṿid, see BM522.87.P4

Shṭern, Betsal'el, see BM522.87.T38

Shṭern, Mosheh, see BM522.87.T3872

Shṭernberg, Ḥayim Eliy. (Ḥayim Eliyahu), see BM522.87.T388

Sofer, Moses, 1762-1839, see BM522.85.C493

522.86 Solomon (Forename)
Cutter number for author is based on name following the forename, disregarding "ben," i. e., son of ...

522.87 Solomon, A-Sz
Cutter number for author is based on second letter in the name

522.87.P4 Sperber, David

522.87.T38 Stern, Bezalel

522.87.T3872 Stern, Moses

Sources of Jewish religion. Rabbinical literature
Halacha
Responsa
Individual authors, A-Z
Solomon, A-Sz -- Continued
522.87.T388 Sternberg, Chaim Elijah
522.88 T
Cutter number for author is based on second letter in the name
522.89 U
Cutter number for author is based on second letter in the name
522.9 V
Cutter number for author is based on second letter in the name
Ṿaldenberg, Eli'ezer Yehudah, see BM522.91.A357
Ṿolner, Mosheh Dov, see BM522.91.O44
Ṿozner, Shemu'el, ha-Leṿi, 1913- , see BM522.91.O85
522.91 W
Cutter number for author is based on second letter in the name
522.91.A354 Waingarten Joab Joshua
522.91.A357 Waldenberg, Eliezer Judah
Weingarten, Joab Joshua, 1847-1922, see BM522.91.A354
Willowski, Jacob David ben Ze'ev, 1845-1913, see BM522.8.I3
522.91.O44 Wolner, M. D.
522.91.O85 Wosner, Shmuel Halewi, 1913-
522.92 X
Cutter number for author is based on second letter in the name
522.93 Y
Cutter number for author is based on second letter in the name
Yiśakhar Berish, a.b.d. ḳ. Bendin ṿeha-galil, 1847-1913, see BM522.39.R3
Yitsḥaḳ Avraham ben Dov Berush, 18th cent , see BM522.44.A23
522.94 Za-Ze'ev
Cutter number for author is based on second letter in the name
522.95 Ze'ev (Forename)
Cutter number for author is based on name following the forename, disregarding "ben," i. e., son of ...
522.96 Ze'ev, A-Zevi
Cutter number for author is based on third letter in the name

Sources of Jewish religion. Rabbinical literature
Halacha
Responsa
Individual authors, A-Z -- Continued
522.97 Zevi (Forename)
Cutter number for author is based on name following the forename, disregarding "ben," i. e., son of ...
522.98 Zevi, A-Zz
Cutter number for author is based on second letter in the name
523 Works on Responsa. History. Criticism
Oraḥ ḥayim law
523.2 General works
523.3.A-Z Special topics, A-Z
523.3.B4 Benedictions
Festivals, see BM690+
(523.3.F7) Fringes
See BM657.F7
523.3.I5 International date line
(523.3.P5) Phylacteries
See BM657.P5
523.3.P7 Prohibited work
Sabbath, see BM685
Synagogue, see BM653+
523.3.T9 Twilight
Work, see BM523.3.P7
Yoreh de'ah law
523.4 General works
523.5.A-Z Special topics, A-Z
523.5.B4 Benevolence (Gemilut ḥasadim)
Circumcision, see BM705
Dietary laws, see BM710
523.5.H3 Hallah
523.5.I3 Idolatry
523.5.I5 Interest
Mourning, see BM712
Purity, see BM702+
Redemption of the firstborn, see BM720.R4
523.5.R4 Respect to parents and teachers
523.5.S5 Shaatnez
523.5.S53 Shaving
Slaughter of animals, see BM720.S6+
Visiting the sick, see BM729.V5
523.5.W5 Wine and wine making
Even ha-'ezer law
523.6 General works
523.7.A-Z Special topics, A-Z
Agunah
See Class K
Common law marriage
See Class K
Divorce

	Sources of Jewish religion. Rabbinical literature
	Halacha
	Even ha-‘ezer law
	Special topics, A-Z
	Divorce -- Continued
	Civil aspects
	See class K
	Religious aspects, see BM713.5
	Marriage
	Civil aspects
	See class K
	Religious aspects, see BM713
523.7.P3	Parent and child
	Ḥoshen mishpaṭ law
	See Class K
	Cabala
	Including ancient and medieval mystical works
	Cf. BF1585+, Cabala and magic
	For comprehensive works on Jewish mysticism, see BM723+
	Sources
525.A2	Collections
	Individual texts
525.A3-A319	Bahir (Table BM4)
525.A36-A3619	Book of Raziel (Table BM4)
	Book of temunah, see BM525.A39+
	Ḥarba de-Mosheh, see BM525.A43+
525.A364-A3649	Heikhalot rabbati (Table BM5)
525.A365-A3659	Heikhalot zutrati (Table BM5)
525.A367-A3679	Ma‘aśeh merkavah (Table BM5)
	Sefer ha-bahir, see BM525.A3+
	Sefer ha-Raziel, see BM525.A36+
525.A37-A3719	Sefer ha-razim (Table BM4)
525.A39-A3919	Sefer ha-temunah (Table BM4)
525.A4-A419	Sefer Yeẓirah (Table BM4)
525.A42-A4219	Shi‘ur komah (Table BM4)
525.A426-A4269	Sod ha-egoz (Table BM5)
525.A43-A4319	Sword of Moses (Table BM4)
525.A5-A59	Zohar (Table BM5)
	Zohar supplements
525.A6A2-A6A29	Collections
525.A6A3-A6Z	Individual
	Subarrange each like BM525.A6T5-BM525.A6T579
525.A6H4-A6H479	Hekhalot. Hebrew book of Enoch
525.A6I22-A6I2279	Idra de-mashkena
525.A6I3-A6I379	Idra rabba
525.A6I5-A6I579	Idra zuta
525.A6M5-A6M579	Midrash ha-ne‘lam
	Including Tapuḥe zahav (Midrash ha-ne‘lam to the Book of Ruth)
525.A6R2-A6R279	Ra‘aya mehemana
525.A6S5-A6S579	Sifra di-tseni‘uta

	Sources of Jewish religion. Rabbinical literature
	Calala
	Sources
	Individual texts
	Zohar supplements
	Individual -- Continued
	Tapuḥe zahav, see BM525.A6M5+
525.A6T5-A6T579	Tikkunei Zohar. Tiḳune ha-Zohar
525.A6T5	Aramaic original. By date
525.A6T52-A6T529	English, alphabetically by translator
525.A6T53-A6T539	French, alphabetically by translator
525.A6T54-A6T549	German, alphabetically by translator
525.A6T55-A6T559	Hebrew, alphabetically by translator
525.A6T56-A6T569	Other languages, alphabetically by language
525.A6T57-A6T579	Criticism, alphabetically by critic
525.A6Z6-A6Z679	Zohar ḥadash
525.A7-Z	Modern Cabalistic works. By author, A-Z
	e.g.
	Luria, Isaac ben Solomon
525.L83	Works
525.L835	History and criticism
	Including biography of Luria as a cabalist
526	History and criticism
529	Jewish tradition
	Myths and legends
	Cf. PN6120.95.J5, Jewish legends and tales
530	General works
531	Golem
532	Hasidic tales and legends
	Relation of Judaism to special subject fields
	Ethics, see BJ1279+
	Religions
534	General works
535	Christianity. Jews and Christianity
	Cf. BM590, Jewish works against Christianity
	Cf. BM620, Jewish attitude toward Jesus Christ
	Cf. BT93+, Judaism (Christian theology)
	Cf. BT590.J34, Attitude of Jesus Christ to Jewish law
	Cf. BT590.J8, Relation of Jesus Christ to Judaism
	Cf. BV2619+, Christian missions among Jews
	Judaism and Evangelicalism, see BR1641.J83
	Judaism and Mormonism, see BX8643.J84
	Judaism and Islam, see BP173.J8
536.A-Z	Other religions, A-Z
536.A8	Assyro-Babylonian
	Buddhism, see BQ4610.J8
536.E3	Egyptian
536.G54	Gnosticism
536.G7	Greek

Relation of Judaism to special subject fields
Religions
Other religions, A-Z -- Continued
536.H5 Hinduism
536.P5 Phoenician
536.S5 Shinto
Zoroastrianism, see BL1566.J8
537 Civilization
Including influence of Judaism
538.A-Z Other, A-Z
538.A4 Agriculture
538.A7 Art
Cf. N7414.75+, Jewish art
538.A75 Astronautics
538.A8 Atomic warfare
Communism, see HX550.J4
Conscientious objectors, see BM538.P3
538.E8 Evolution
538.H43 Health. Medicine
538.H85 Human ecology
538.H87 Humanism
538.I58 Internet
538.L34 Language and languages
Medicine, see BM538.H43
538.P2 Parapsychology
538.P3 Peace and war, violence and nonviolence, conscientious objectors
Philosophy, see B154+
538.P68 Psychoanalysis. Psychology
538.S3 Science (General)
Socialism, see HX550.J4
538.S7 State and society
Cf. HN40.J5, Social history and the Jews
538.S8 Superstition
538.T85 Twelve-step programs
538.V43 Vegetarianism
Violence and nonviolence, see BM538.P3
War and peace, see BM538.P3
540.A-Z Relation of Judaism to special classes, groups, etc., A-Z
540.A35 Aged
540.H35 Handicapped
540.Y6 Youth
General works on the principles of Judaism
Cf. B154+, Ancient Jewish philosophy
Cf. B755+, Medieval Jewish philosophy
Early to 1800
Maimonides. Moses ben Maimon
Cf. B759.M3, Maimonides as philosopher
For Mishneh Torah, see BM520.84
Collected works
545.A2 Original. By date
545.A212-A219 Translations. By language and date
Selected works

	General works on the principles of Judaism
	Early to 1800
	Maimonides. Moses ben Maimon
	Selected works -- Continued
545.A25	Original. By date
545.A2512-A2519	Translations. By language and date
545.A3-Z	Separate works. By title
	Dalālat al-ḥā'irīn
545.D33	Original text
	Translations
545.D3312	Hebrew
545.D3313	English
545.D3314-D3319	Other languages
545.D34	Selections
	Translations
545.D3412	Hebrew
545.D3413	English
545.D3414-D3419	Other languages
545.D35	Criticism
546	Criticism
550.A-Z	Other early writers, A-Z
	e.g.
	Caro, Joseph, see BM520.88
550.J79	Judah, ha-Levi, 12th cent.
550.S25	Saadiah ben Joseph, 882-942
	Modern works
560	1801-1950
561	1951-2000
562	2001-
565	General special
570	Manuals of religious instruction
573	Juvenile works
	Cf. BM105, Textbooks
580	Addresses, essays, lectures
582	Other
	Controversial works against the Jews
	Cf. BT1120, Christian apologetics
585	General works
585.2	Blood accusation cases
585.4	Host desecration accusation
590	Jewish works against Christianity
590.A1	Collections
591	Jewish works against Islam
591.A1	Collections
	Dogmatic Judaism
	For early works, see BM545+
	General works
	Cf. BM150+, History of Judaism
600	Early through 1950
601	1951-2000
602	2001-
603	History of theology
	Theology of the Old Testament, see BS1192.5

	Dogmatic Judaism -- Continued
607	Thirteen articles of faith
610	Conception of God
612	Revelation on Sinai
612.5	Covenants. Covenant theology
612.7	Holy Spirit
	Mission of Israel. Election. Chosen people
613	General works
613.5	The diaspora in relation to Israel's election
	Messiah
	Cf. BS680.M4, Biblical conception of Messiah
615	General works
620	Attitude toward Jesus Christ
621	Attitude toward Virgin Mary
	Messianic era
625	General works
625.5	The State of Israel in relation to the Messianic era
627	Man
630	Sin
	Eschatology. Future life
635	General works
635.4	Death
635.7	Transmigration
645.A-Z	Other topics, A-Z
645.A6	Angels
645.A8	Atonement
645.C6	Conversion
645.C73	Creative ability
	Determinism, see BM645.F69
645.E9	Exodus, The
645.F4	Fear
645.F69	Free will and determinism
645.F7	Freedom
645.F73	Freedom of speech
645.H43	Heaven
645.H58	Holiness
645.H6	Holocaust
645.H64	Hope
645.H85	Human rights
645.I5	Immortality
645.J67	Joy
645.J8	Justice
	Kings and rulers, see BM645.P64
645.L54	Light
	For candles and lights in worship, see BM657.C3
645.M34	Martyrdom
645.M37	Mediation
645.M4	Merit
645.P64	Politics. Kings and rulers
645.P67	Prophecy
645.P7	Providence and government of God
645.R3	Race
645.R4	Redemption

Dogmatic Judaism
Other topics, A-Z -- Continued
645.R45 Repentance
645.R47 Resurrection
645.R5 Revelation
645.R55 Reward
645.S6 Soul
645.S9 Suffering
646 Heresy, heresies, heretics, etc.
Cf. BM720.H5, Treatment of heretics, etc.
648 Apologetics
Including the history of apologetics
Practical Judaism
650 General works
Priests, rabbis, etc.
651 History
Cf. BS1199.P7, Priests in the Old Testament
652 Office of the rabbi
Including ordination, etc.; also rabbi's work, if included
Work of the rabbi
652.3 General works
652.4 Professional development, study, etc.
652.5 Psychology and psychiatry for the rabbi. Counseling
652.6 Conduct of services, meetings, etc.
Cf. BM676, Rabbinical manuals
652.7 Participation in community affairs, interfaith movements, etc.
Congregations. Synagogues
653 Organization and administration
653.2 Synagogue seating. Mixed pews. Mehitsah. Separation of sexes
653.3 Management of financial affairs
653.5 Management of subsidiary organizations
Including sisterhoods, men's clubs, etc.
653.7 Management of educational activities and youth work
654 The tabernacle
Including history, structure, etc.
Cf. BS680.T32, Tabernacle (Typology)
The temple
Including function, purpose, etc.
Cf. BS649.J4, Jerusalem Temple (Prophecy)
Cf. BS680.T4, Temple of God (Symbolism)
Cf. DS109.3, History of the temple
Cf. NA243, Architecture of the temple
655 General works
655.4 The Sanhedrin
Cf. BM506.S2+, Tractate Sanhedrin
655.45 The Nasi
655.5 French Sanhedrin under Napoleon
655.6 Proposals for restoration

Practical Judaism -- Continued
Forms of worship
656 General works
657.A-Z Special objects and instruments, A-Z
657.A1 Collective
657.A5 Altars
657.A8 Ark of the covenant
657.A85 Ark of the law
657.B7 Breastplate of the High Priest (Ḥoshen)
657.C3 Candles and lights
For light as a theological topic, see BM645.L54
657.C5 Citron. Etrog
657.E7 Ephod
Etrog, see BM657.C5
657.F68 Four species (Sukkot)
657.F7 Fringes. Zizith
Cf. BM657.T44, Tekhelet (Dye)
657.H3 Hanukkah lamp
657.K53 Kiddush cups
Lights, see BM657.C3
657.L8 Lulav. Lulab
657.M35 Menorah
657.M4 Mezuzah
657.P5 Phylacteries. Tefillin
657.S5 Shofar (Shophar)
657.S64 Spice boxes
Tefillin, see BM657.P5
657.T44 Tekhelet (Dye)
Cf. BM657.F7, Fringes. Zizith
657.T59 Torah cases
657.T6 Torah scrolls
657.U7 Urim and Thummim
Zizith, see BM657.F7
Symbols and symbolism
Cf. N7414.75+, Jewish art
657.2 General works
657.5.A-Z Special symbols, A-Z
657.5.M3 Magen David
Music in Jewish worship
Cf. ML3195, Jewish sacred vocal music
658 General works
658.2 Cantors
For biography, see BM750+
659.A-Z Other religious functionaries, A-Z
659.G3 Gabai
659.M3 Magid (Preacher)
Mohel, see BM705
659.S3 Scribe (Sofer)
659.S5 Shamesh (Sexton)
Shochet, see BM720.S6+
Liturgy and ritual
660 General works
663 Reading of the Bible

Practical Judaism
Liturgy and ritual -- Continued
General and miscellaneous prayer and service books
General collections
665.A2 By title where editor, compiler, or translator is unknown
665.A3A-Z Local. By synagogue, A-Z
Cf. BM673.A+, Liturgy and ritual of special places
665.A4-Z By editor, etc.
Works for special classes
666 Children
667.A-Z Other classes, A-Z
667.A35 Aged
Armed Forces, see BM667.S6
667.G5 Girls
667.M45 Men
667.S4 School prayers
667.S55 Sick
667.S6 Soldiers. Armed Forces
667.W6 Women
669 General works on prayer
670.A-Z Special elements of the liturgy, A-Z
Including individual prayers
Cf. BM674.2+, Special liturgical books
670.A42 Akdamut millin (Table BM6)
670.A44 Aleinu le-shabbe'aḥ (Table BM6)
670.A64 Amen (Table BM6)
Amidah, see BM670.S5
670.A69 Ashmorot (Table BM6)
670.A73 Avodah (Yom Kippur liturgy) (Table BM6)
670.A8 Azharot (Table BM6)
Birkat kohanim, see BM670.P74
670.B57 Birkat She-heḥeyanu (Table BM6)
Blessing of the moon, see BM675.N45
670.C64 Confession of sins. Ṿidui (Table BM6)
670.E32 Eḥad mi yode'a (Table BM6)
670.H28 Ḥad gadya (Table BM6)
670.H3 Haftarot (Table BM6)
670.H35 Hallel (Table BM6)
670.H67 Hoshanot (Table BM6)
670.K3 Kaddish (Table BM6)
670.K39 Kavvanot (Cabala) (Table BM6)
670.K52 Kiddush (Table BM6)
670.K6 Kol nidrei (Table BM6)
670.M33 Mah tovu (Table BM6)
670.M34 Malkhuyyot (Table BM6)
670.P47 Pataḥ Eliyahu (Table BM6)
670.P5 Piyutim (Table BM6)
For criticism and biography, see BM678.A+
670.P74 Priestly blessing. Birkat kohanim (Table BM6)
670.S4 Seder Haḳafot (Table BM6)
670.S42 Seder Tashlikh (Table BM6)

Practical Judaism
Liturgy and ritual
Special elements of the liturgy, A-Z -- Continued

670.S45	Shema (Table BM6)
670.S5	Shemoneh 'esreh (Table BM6)
670.S55	Shir ha-yiḥud (Table BM6)
670.T35	Taḥanun (Table BM6)
	Tashlikh, see BM670.S42
670.U25	U-netanneh tokef (Table BM6)
	Ṿidui, see BM670.C64
670.Y69	Yoẓerot (Table BM6)
672.A-Z	Special rites, A-Z
	For special liturgical books, see BM674.2+
672.A8	Ashkenazic. Mitnaggedic
672.A82	Hasidic
672.F3	Falasha
	Karaite, see BM185+
672.S4	Sephardic
672.Y4	Yemenite
672.Z36	Zanz
673.A-Z	Special places, A-Z
	Cf. BM665.A3A+, General collections by synagogue
	For special liturgical books, see BM674.2+
	Special liturgical books
	Siddur (Daily prayers)
	Texts
	Ashkenazi or unspecified rite
	Hebrew only
674.2.A3	By date (if editor is unknown)
674.2.A5-Z	By editor
674.23	Manuscripts in facsimile. By name of manuscript or by name of artist or calligrapher
	Translations. By date (if editor is unknown)
674.242	Polyglot. By editor or translator
674.243	English. By editor or translator
674.244	French. By editor or translator
674.245	German. By editor or translator
674.246	Russian. By editor or translator
674.247	Spanish. By editor or translator
674.248	Yiddish. By editor or translator
674.249.A-Z	Other languages, A-Z
	Subarrange by editor or translator
	Other traditional rites
674.27	Sephardic. By editor
674.28	Ari. By editor
674.29	Hasidic. By editor
674.293	Other. By rite as given in uniform title
	Non-traditional rites
674.32	Conservative. By editor or institution given in uniform title

Practical Judaism
Liturgy and ritual
Special liturgical books
Siddur (Daily prayers)
Texts
Non-traditional rites -- Continued

674.33 Reconstructionist. By editor or institution given in uniform title

674.34 Reform. By editor or institution given in uniform title
Including European liberal

674.35 Other. By editor or institution given in uniform title

674.36 Adaptations for children. By editor or institution given in uniform title or added entry

674.39 Criticism

Maḥzor (Festival prayers)
Texts
Ashkenazi or unspecified rite
Hebrew only

674.4.A3 By date (if editor is unknown)

674.4.A5-Z By editor

674.43 Manuscripts in facsimile. By name

Translations. By date (if editor is unknown)

674.442 Polyglot. By editor or translator

674.443 English. By editor or translator

674.444 French. By editor or translator

674.445 German. By editor or translator

674.446 Russian. By editor or translator

674.447 Spanish. By editor or translator

674.448 Yiddish. By editor or translator

674.449.A-Z Other languages, A-Z
Subarrange by editor or translator

Other traditional rites

674.47 Sephardic. By editor

674.48 Ari. By editor

674.49 Hasidic. By editor

674.493 Other. By rite as given in uniform title

Non-traditional rites

674.52 Conservative. By editor or institution given in uniform title

674.53 Reconstructionist. By editor or institution given in uniform title

674.54 Reform. By editor or institution given in uniform title
Including European liberal

674.55 Other. By editor or institution given in uniform title

674.56 Adaptations for children. By editor or institution given in uniform title or added entry

Practical Judaism
Liturgy and ritual
Special liturgical books
Maḥzor (Festival prayers) -- Continued
674.59 Criticism
Haggadah
Texts
Ashkenazi or unspecified rite
Hebrew only
674.6.A3 By date (if editor is unknown)
674.6.A5-Z By editor
674.63 Manuscripts in facsimile. By name
Translations. By date (if editor is unknown)
674.642 Polyglot. By editor or translator
674.643 English. By editor or translator
674.644 French. By editor or translator
674.645 German. By editor or translator
674.646 Russian. By editor or translator
674.647 Spanish. By editor or translator
674.648 Yiddish. By editor or translator
674.649.A-Z Other languages, A-Z
Subarrange by editor or translator
Other traditional rites
674.67 Sephardic. By editor
674.68 Ari. By editor
674.69 Hasidic. By editor
674.693 Other. By rite as given in uniform title
Non-traditional rites
674.72 Conservative. By editor or institution given in uniform title
674.73 Reconstructionist. By editor or institution given in uniform title
674.74 Reform. By editor or institution given in uniform title
Including European liberal
674.75 Other. By editor or institution given in uniform title
674.76 Adaptations for children. By editor or institution given in uniform title or added entry
674.79 Criticism
674.795 Miscellaneous adaptations
675.A-Z Other liturgical books, A-Z
675.A78 Arvit (Table BM7)
Arvit (Sabbath), see BM675.S35
Atonement. Kol nidre, see BM675.Y58
Ayelet ha-shaḥar, see BM675.R412
675.B4 Benedictions (Table BM7)
Birkat ha-ḥamah, see BM675.B53
675.B48 Birkat ha-ilanot (Table BM7)
675.B53 Blessing of the sun (Table BM7)

Practical Judaism
Liturgy and ritual
Special liturgical books
Other liturgical books, A-Z -- Continued

(675.D3) Daily prayers
See BM674.2-39
Day of Atonement prayers, see BM675.Y58
675.F3 Fast-day prayers (Table BM7)
(675.F45) Festival prayers
See BM674.4-59
Friday evening service, see BM675.S35
675.G7 Grace at meals (Table BM7)
Haggadah, see BM674.6+
675.H33 Hanukkah prayers (Table BM7)
675.H35 Hatarat nedarim (Table BM7)
675.H5 High Holiday prayers (Table BM7)
675.H55 Holocaust Remembrance Day prayers (Table BM7)
675.H6 Hoshana Rabba prayers (Table BM7)
675.I87 Israel Independence Day prayers (Table BM7)
675.K5 Kinot. Ninth of Av prayers (Table BM7)
Liḳuṭe Tsevi, see BM675.R42
Ma'amadot, see BM675.R44
675.M4 Memorial services (Table BM7)
675.M7 Mourners' prayers (Table BM7)
Including Book of life, etc.
675.N45 New moon prayers (Table BM7)
New Year prayers, see BM675.R67
Ninth of Av prayers, see BM675.K5
675.O25 Occasional prayers (Table BM7)
675.P3 Passover (Table BM7)
Cf. BV199.P25, Christian observance
(675.P4) Haggadah
See BM674.6-79
675.P5 Pentecost. Shavuot (Table BM7)
Pereḳ shirah, see BM675.P6
675.P59 Pilgrim Festival prayers (Table BM7)
675.P6 Pirḳe shirah. Pereḳ shirah (Table BM7)
675.P8 Purim prayers (Table BM7)
675.R4 Readings (Table BM7)
675.R412 Ayelet ha-shaḥar (Table BM7)
675.R42 Liḳuṭe Tsevi (Table BM7)
675.R44 Ma'amadot (Table BM7)
675.R46 Sha'are Tsiyon (Table BM7)
675.R48 Tiḳun (General) (Table BM7)
675.R67 Rosh ha-Shanah (New Year) prayers (Table BM7)
675.S3 Sabbath prayers (Table BM7)
675.S35 Friday evening service. Arvit (Sabbath) (Table BM7)
675.S4 Seliḥot (Table BM7)
Sha'are Tsiyon, see BM675.R46
675.S44 Shaḥarit (Table BM7)
675.S45 Shaḥarit (Sabbath) (Table BM7)
Shavuot, see BM675.P5

Practical Judaism
Liturgy and ritual
Special liturgical books
Other liturgical books, A-Z -- Continued
Siddur, see BM674.2+
675.S5 Simḥat Torah prayers (Table BM7)
Sukkot, see BM675.T2
675.S9 Synagogue dedication services (Table BM7)
675.T2 Tabernacle service. Sukkot (Table BM7)
675.T38 Tefilat ha-derekh (Table BM7)
675.T4 Tehinnot (Table BM7)
Tikkun (General), see BM675.R48
675.T5 Tikkun ḥaẓot (Table BM7)
Tikkun leil Hoshana Rabba, see BM675.H6
Tikkun leil Shavuot (Pentecost), see BM675.P5
Tiḳun (General), see BM675.R48
675.T52 Tiḳun shovavim (Table BM7)
Tishʻah be-Av, see BM675.K5
675.T82 Tu bi-Shevat prayers (Table BM7)
675.Y55 Yom ha-zikaron prayers (Table BM7)
675.Y58 Yom Kippur (Day of Atonement, Kol nidre) prayers (Table BM7)
675.Y6 Yom Kippur Katan prayers (Table BM7)
675.Z4 Zemirot (Table BM7)
676 Selections for the use of rabbis, etc. Rabbinical manuals
Hymns
Cf. BM670.P5, Piyutim
History and criticism
Including Piyutim
678.A1 Periodicals. Societies. Serials
678.A3-Z General works
Biography
Including authors of Piyutim
678.4 Collective
678.5.A-Z Individual, A-Z
679.A-Z By language, A-Z
685 The Sabbath
685.5 Shabbat ha-gadol
Festivals and fasts
Cf. BM125+, Sabbath school exercises
690 General works
693.A-Z Special groups, A-Z
693.A32 Adar
693.E48 Elul
693.H5 High Holidays (High Holy Days)
693.H64 Hol ha-Moed
693.P5 Pilgrim Festivals
Three Festivals, see BM693.P5
693.T6 Tishri
695.A-Z Individual festivals and fasts, A-Z
695.A8 Atonement, Day of (Yom Kippur)
695.H3 Hanukkah (Feast of Lights)

Practical Judaism
Festivals and fasts
Individual festivals and fasts, A-Z -- Continued
695.L3 Lag b'Omer
695.N4 New moon. Rosh Hodesh
695.N5 New Year (Rosh ha-Shanah)
Cf. BS1199.R6, Old Testament
Ninth of Av, see BM695.T57
Passover
Cf. BS680.P33, Passover in the Bible
Cf. BV199.P25, Christian liturgy and ritual
695.P3 General works
695.P35 Ritual ceremonies
Pentecost, see BM695.S5
695.P8 Purim (Feast of Esther)
Rosh ha-Shanah, see BM695.N5
Rosh Hodesh, see BM695.N4
695.S4 Sefirah period
695.S43 Seged
695.S5 Shavuot. Pentecost
695.S53 Shemini Atzeret
695.S6 Simḥat Torah
695.S8 Sukkot (Sukkoth)
695.T4 Three Weeks (Jewish mourning period)
695.T57 Tish'ah be-Av. Ninth of Av
695.T9 Tu bi-Shevat
Yom Kippur, see BM695.A8
Rites and customs
For halacha, see BM523.2+
700 General works
Ritual purity. Purification
702 General works
703 Ritual baths. Mikveh. Baptism
704 Hand washing
705 Berit milah (Circumcision)
706 Brit bat
Bar mitzvah. Bat mitzvah. Confirmation
707 General works
707.2 Instruction and study. Manuals
707.3 Sermons. Addresses, essays, etc.
707.4 Services, etc.
710 Dietary laws
Cf. BM720.S6+, Slaughter of animals
Cf. TX724, Jewish cookery
712 Funeral rites. Mourning customs
Cf. BM675.M7, Mourners' prayers
713 Marriage
For Jewish law on marriage, see class K
713.5 Divorce
For Jewish law on marriage, see class K
715 Sacrifices
720.A-Z Other, A-Z
Aliens, see BM720.N6

Practical Judaism
Rites and customs
Other, A-Z -- Continued

720.C6	Clothing and dress
720.C65	Cohanim
720.D2	Dancing, Religious
720.E9	Excommunication. Ḥerem
720.F3	Fasting
720.F4	Fellowship
	Gentiles, see BM720.N6
	Goyim, see BM720.N6
720.H3	Ḥalitsah
	Heathen, see BM720.N6
	Ḥerem, see BM720.E9
720.H5	Heretics, apostates, etc. (Treatment) Cf. BM646, Heresy, heresies, heretics (Dogmatic Judaism) Cf. BM720.M3, Treatment of Maranos
720.H6	Hospitality
720.I6	Incense
720.K3	Karaites (Treatment)
720.K5	Kissing
720.M3	Maranos (Treatment)
720.N3	Nazarite
720.N6	Non-Jews (Aliens, Goyim, Gentiles, Heathen), Position of
720.O3	Oaths
720.R3	Rain. Prayers for rain
720.R4	Redemption of the firstborn
720.S2	Sabbatical year. Shemiṭah
720.S23	Special observances e.g. Reading of Deuteronomy
720.S4	Sex
	Shehitah, see BM720.S6+
	Shemiṭah, see BM720.S2
	Slaughter of animals
720.S6A1-S6A4	Societies. Organisations, boards, etc.
720.S6A5-S6Z	Ritual. Procedure
720.S62	History. Politics
720.S63	Humanitarian aspects
720.T4	Tithes. Terumah
720.T7	Travel
	Jewish way of life. Spiritual life. Mysticism.
	Personal religion
	For Cabala, including ancient and medieval mystical works, see BM525+
	For Hasidism, see BM198+
723	General works
723.5	Admonition
723.7	Confession
724	Devotional works. Meditations
	Religious duties
725	General, and men

Practical Judaism
Jewish way of life.
Spiritual life. Mysticism.
Personal religion
Religious duties -- Continued
725.5 Duties of fathers and children
726 Women. Motherhood
727 Children and youth. Students
727.5 Soldiers
728 Moral theology
Cf. BJ1279+, Jewish ethics
For Halacha, see BM523.4+
729.A-Z Other special topics, A-Z
729.A34 Alcohol
729.A4 Amulets. Talismans
729.A5 Animals (Protection and treatment)
Cf. BM509.A5, Animals in Talmudic literature
729.C4 Censorship
729.C6 Consolation
729.D92 Dybbuk
729.E45 Electric apparatus and appliances
729.F3 Faith
729.F57 Fire
Gays, see BM729.H65
729.H35 Handicraft
729.H65 Homosexuality. Gays. Lesbians
729.J4 Jewish science (Applied psychology: health, happiness, etc.)
Lesbians, see BM729.H65
729.N3 Name (Jew, Israel, Hebrew)
Cf. CS3010, Jewish personal names
Nonviolence, see BM538.P3
729.P3 Palestine. Jerusalem, etc.
729.P35 Parchment
(729.P4) Peace, pacifism, conscientious objectors, nonviolence
see BM538.P3
729.P65 Printing
729.P7 Proselytes and proselyting
729.S6 Social ideals
729.S7 Social service
729.S85 Summer
Talismans, see BM729.A4
729.T55 Time
729.T7 Trust in God
729.V5 Visiting the sick
729.W38 Water
729.W6 Women
Preaching. Homiletics
730.A1 Periodicals. Societies. Serials
730.A2 Collections. Collected works
History
730.A3 General works

Practical Judaism
Preaching. Homiletics
History -- Continued

730.A4A-Z	By country, A-Z
730.A5-Z	General works
731	Addresses, essays, lectures
732	Outlines, texts, etc.
733	Illustrations for sermons
	Sermons. Addresses, etc.
735	Collective
	Individual authors
740	Works through 1950
740.2	1951-2000
740.3	2001-
742	To the young
743	To children
	Occasional sermons. Special sermons
744	General works
744.3	Funeral sermons. Memorial sermons
744.5	Wedding sermons
	Bar mitzvah sermons, see BM707.3
744.6	Dedication sermons
744.7	Installation and ordination sermons of rabbis
744.8	Installation sermons of synagogue officials
	Festival day sermons
	For sermons discussing the weekly Torah portion, see BS1225
745	General works
746	High Holiday sermons
746.5	Pilgrim Festival sermons (Three Festivals)
747.A-Z	Individual festivals, A-Z
747.H3	Hanukkah
747.J47	Jerusalem Day
747.P3	Passover sermons
747.P8	Purim sermons
747.R6	Rosh ha-Shanah sermons
747.S53	Shavuot sermons
747.S84	Sukkot sermons
747.Y65	Yom Kippur sermons
	Reform movements, see BM197
	Biography
	Cf. BM88+, Religious educators
	Cf. BM102.A+, Sabbath school teachers
	Cf. DS151.A+, Zionist biography
750	Collective
752	Pseudo-Messiahs
753	Women
755.A-Z	Individual, A-Z
	e.g.
755.A115	Aaron of Belz, 1880-1957
755.A2	Abba Arika, called Rab
	Abi-Ḥasira, Jacob ben Masoud, 1808-1880, see BM755.A87

Biography
Individual, A-Z -- Continued

755.A25 Abravanel, Isaac, 1437-1508
755.A28 Abulafia, Abraham ben Samuel, 1240-ca. 1292
Aharon ben Yiśakhar Dov, a.b.d. ḳ. Belza, 1880-1957, see BM755.A115
755.A87 Aviḥatsira, Jacob, 1808-1880
Ba'al Shem Ṭov, ca. 1700-1760, see BM755.I8
Bar Cocheba, see DS122.9
Bar Kokba, see DS122.9
755.C28 Caro, Joseph, 1488-1575
755.E6 Elijah ben Solomon, gaon of Vilna, 1720-1797
755.G4 Geiger, Abraham, 1810-1874
755.H73 Horowitz, Jacob Isaac, 1745-1815
755.H76 Horowitz, Naphtali Zebi, 1760-1827
755.I8 Israel ben Eliezer, Ba'al-Shem-Tob, called Beshṭ
Israel Meir, ha-Kohen, 1838-1933, see BM755.K25
Jacob Isaac, ha-Ḥozeh, mi-Lublin, 1745-1815, see BM755.H73
755.J8 Judah Löw ben Bezaleel, ca. 1525-1609
755.K25 Kahan, Israel Meir, 1838-1933
Karo, Joseph ben Ephraim, 1488-1575, see BM755.C28
755.L45 Levinsohn, Isaac Baer, 1788-1860
755.L54 Lipkin, Israel, 1810-1883
755.L8 Luzzatto, Samuel David, 1800-1865
Maimonides, Moses, 1135-1204, see BM755.M6
755.M6 Moses ben Maimon, 1135-1204
755.M62 Moses ben Naḥman, ca. 1195-ca. 1270
Naḥman, of Bratslav, 1722-1811, see BM755.N25
755.N25 Naḥman ben Simḥah, of Bratzlav, 1722-1811
Naḥmanides, ca. 1195-ca. 1270, see BM755.M62
Ouziel, Ben-Zion Meir Ḥai, 1880-1953, see BM755.U72
755.R15 Rabinowitz, Elijah David, 1845-1905
Rabinowitz-Teomin, Elijah David ben Benjamin, 1845-1905, see BM755.R15
Rashi, 1040-1105, see BM755.S6
Ropshitser, Naphtali Ẓevi, 1760-1827, see BM755.H76
755.R6 Rosenzweig, Franz, 1886-1929
755.S2 Saadiah ben Joseph, gaon, 882-942
Salanter, Israel, 1810-1883, see BM755.L54
755.S256 Schapiro, Joshua Isaac ben Jehiel, 1801-1873
755.S33 Schreiber, Moses, 1762-1839
755.S45 Shabbethai Tzevi, 1626-1676
Shapira, Joshua Isaac ben Jehiel, 1801-1873, see BM755.S256
755.S525 Shneor Zalman ben Baruch, 1747-1813
Shneur Zalman, of Lyady, 1745-1813, see BM755.S525
Sofer, Moses, 1762-1839, see BM755.S33
755.S6 Solomon ben Isaac, called Rashi, 1040-1105
755.U72 Usiel, Ben-Zion Meir Hai, 1880-1953
755.W5 Wise, Isaac Mayer, 1819-1900
755.Z8 Zunz, Leopold, 1794-1886

Samaritans

Samaritans -- Continued
900 Periodicals. Serials
903 Societies
Collections
905 Collective authors
907 Individual authors
History
910 General works
913.A-Z Special sects, etc., A-Z
915 Relation to Judaism
Sources of Samaritan religion
917 General works
Samaritan Pentateuch
Original texts
920 Printed texts. By date of printing
922 Manuscripts. History and criticism of manuscripts
923 Facsimiles
924 Samaritan and Hebrew versions paralleled. By editor
924.5 Samaritan and Latin versions paralleled. By editor
925.A-Z Translations. By language, A-Z
927 History and criticism
Including comparison with Masoretic Pentateuch
Samaritan Targum
930 General
933 Samaritan-Arabic version of Targum
935 General works
940 General special
945 Dogmas
Practical religion
950 Priesthood
Liturgy and ritual
960 General works
960.3.A-Z Special liturgical books. By title, A-Z
Under each:
.*x* *Texts. By date*
.*x3* *Criticism*
960.3.D33-D333 ha-Daftar
960.3.S52-S523 Shabat ḥol-mo'ed Sukot
960.3.S53-S533 Shemini 'atseret
970 Festivals and fasts
980 Rites and ceremonies
982 Ritual purity
Biography
990.A1 Collective
990.A3-Z Individual, A3-Z

Islam. Bahai Faith. Theosophy, etc.
Islam
Cf. DS35.3 +, The Islamic world
1 Periodicals
9 Yearbooks
10 Societies. Conferences. Clubs
15 Congresses
Collected works
20 Several authors
25 Individual authors
40 Dictionaries. Encyclopedias
Study and teaching. Research
Including general and advanced
Cf. BP130.77 +, Koran
42 General works
43.A-Z Individual regions and countries, A-Z
Under each (using two successive Cutter numbers):
.x General works
.x2A-Z Individual schools, A-Z
Religious education of the young
44 General. Organization, method, etc.
45 Textbooks. Stories, catechisms, etc.
48.A-Z Individual schools, A-Z
Historiography
49 General works
49.5.A-Z Biography of students and historians
Class here mainly non-Muslim scholars and specialists writing from outside Islam
For Muslim scholars (Ulama, theologians, etc.) writing from within Islam, as Muslims, see BP70, BP80.A+
49.5.A1 Collective
49.5.A2-Z Individual, A-Z
History
50 General works
52 General special
52.5 Muslims in non-Muslim countries
53 Addresses, essays, etc.
By period
55 Origins. Early through 1800
60 1801-
62.A-Z By race, ethnic group, tribe, etc., A-Z
Prefer country, region, etc.
62.B56 Blacks. African Americans
Cf. BP221 +, Black Muslims
Negroes, see BP62.B56
By continent and country
Asia
63.A1 General works

Islam
History
By continent and country
Asia -- Continued
63.A3A-Z By ethnic group, etc., A-Z
Prefer country, region, etc.
By region
63.A32 Arab countries (Collectively)
63.A33 Caucasus
63.A34 Central Asia. Soviet Central Asia
Former Soviet republics
see BP63.A33, BP63.A34, BP63.R8, BP65.R8
63.A35 Middle East. Near East
63.A37 South Asia
63.A38 Southeastern Asia
63.A4A-Z Other regions, A-Z
63.A5-Z By country, A-Z
Under each:
.x *General works*
.x2A-Z *Local, A-Z*
e. g.
63.A54 Afghanistan
63.I5 Indonesia
63.R8 Russia in Asia
Including former Soviet republics collectively
Cf. BP63.A33, Caucasus
Cf. BP63.A34, Central Asia
(63.S65) Soviet Union
see BP63.R8, BP65.R8
63.T8 Turkey
Africa
64.A1 General works
64.A3A-Z By ethnic group, etc., A-Z
Prefer country, region, etc.
By region
64.A32 East Africa
64.A34 North Africa
64.A36 Northeast Africa
64.A37 Sub-Saharan Africa
64.A38 West Africa
64.A4A-Z Other regions, A-Z
64.A5-Z By country, A-Z
Apply table at BP63.A5-Z
e. g.
64.A5 Algeria
64.E3 Egypt
Europe
65.A1 General works
65.A3A-Z By ethnic group, etc., A-Z
Prefer country, region, etc.
65.A4A-Z By region, A-Z

Islam
History
By continent and country
Europe
By region, A-Z -- Continued
Former Soviet republics
see BP63.A33, BP63.A34, BP63.R8, BP65.R8
65.A5-Z By country, A-Z
Apply table at BP63.A5-Z
e. g.
65.R8 Russia (Federation)
Cf. BP63.A33, Caucasus
Cf. BP63.R8, Russia in Asia
(65.S65) Soviet Union
see BP63.R8, BP65.R8
65.S7 Spain
66 Australia
66.5 Pacific Islands
America. North America
67.A1 General works
67.A3A-Z By ethnic group, etc., A-Z
Prefer country, region, etc.
67.A5-Z By country, A-Z
Apply table at BP63.A5-Z
South America
68.A1 General works
68.A5-Z By country, A-Z
Apply table at BP63.A5-Z
Biography
70 Collective
Cf. BP75.5, Companions of Muḥammad (Ṣaḥābah)
For Hadith transmitters, see BP136.46, BP136.47, BP136.48
Saints, see BP189.4+
Shiites, see BP192.8
Sufism, see BP189.4+
Non-Muslim scholars and specialists, see BP49.5.A1
Local, see BP63+
72 Martyrs
73 Women
Individual
Muḥammad, Prophet, d. 632
Cf. BP133.7.M84, Muḥammad in the Koran
Cf. BP135.8.M85, Hadith literature
Cf. BP166.5+, Muḥammad in Islamic theology
By language
Translations class with the new language, not the original work
75 English
75.13 French
75.16 German
75.2 Arabic

Islam
Biography
Individual
Muḥammad, Prophet, d. 632
By language -- Continued
75.22 Bengali
75.24 Indonesian
75.26 Persian
75.27 Turkish
75.28 Urdu
75.29.A-Z Other, A-Z
75.3 Historiography
Including history and criticism of biographies
Biographers of Muḥammad
75.4 Collective
Individual, see BP80.A+
Companions (Ṣaḥābah)
For Companions as transmitters of Hadith, see BP136.46
75.5 Collective
Individual, see BP80.A+
Special topics
75.6 Illiteracy
75.8 Miracles
Cf. BP166.65, Islamic theology
75.84 Language
75.9 Relics
Mission, see BP166.55
76.2 Panegyrics
Teachings, see BP132+
Special doctrines, see BP166.2+
76.3 Attitude toward paganism
76.4 Relations with Jews
76.45 Relations with Hinduism. Hindu interpretations of Muḥammad
76.7 Domestic life
76.8 Family. Wives and daughters
76.9 Friends and associates. Companions
For biography of the Companions, see BP75.5+
For the Companions as authorities for the Hadith, see BP136.46
Special events
77.2 Birth and childhood
Period at Mecca
77.4 General works
77.43 Call and early revelations
77.47 Public appearance. Persecution and emigration of his followers to Abyssinia
77.5 Hijrah. Flight to Medina
Period at Medina
77.6 General works
77.63 Attempted assassination
77.65 Escape to Mt. Thaur

Islam
Biography
Individual
Muḥammad, Prophet, d. 632
Special events
Period at Medina -- Continued
77.67 Return to Medina as ruler of the city
77.68 Farewell pilgrimage. Ḥajjat al-wadāʻ
77.69 Political career
77.7 Military campaigns. Truce with the Meccans
77.75 Death
80.A-Z Other individual, A-Z
For non-Muslim scholars and specialists, see BP49.5.A2+
e.g.
80.G3 al-Ghazzālī
Cf. B753.G3, al-Ghazzālī as philosopher
80.H23 Ḥājj ʻUmar ibn Saʻīd al-Fūtī, 1794?-1864
80.H279 Hamzah Fansuri, 16th/17th cent.
For general biography and criticism, see PL5139.H3
80.I6 Iqbal, Muhammad, Sir, 1877-1938
Cf. B5129.I57+, Iqbal as a philosopher
Islamic literature. Islamic authors
Including devotional or theologico-philosophical works of Islamic authors not limited specifically by subject
Cf. B740+, Islamic philosophy
For works on specific subjects, regardless of authorship, see the appropriate subject
Sacred books, see BP100+
Biography, see BP70+
Collections of several authors
87 Two or more volumes
87.5 Single volumes
88.A-Z Individual authors, A-Z
Including individual anonymous works
Under each author, using two successive Cutter numbers:
.xA1-.xA3 *Collected works*
.xA1 *Original texts. By date*
.xA2 *Partial editions, selections, etc. By date*
.xA3-.xA39 *Translations. By language, alphabetically*
.xA4-.xZ *Separate works, A-Z*
.x2 *General works. Criticism, interpretation, etc.*
89 History and criticism
Sacred books
Koran
Texts. By language
Arabic

Islam
Sacred books
Koran
Texts. By language
Arabic -- Continued
100 Texts. By date
100.3 Works on manuscripts
100.5 Facsimiles of manuscripts
101 Selections. By date
History and criticism, see BP130+
Philological works, see PJ6696.A6+
Other Asian languages
Turkish
102 Complete text. By date
103 Selections. By date
History and criticism, see BP130+
Hebrew
104 Complete text. By date
104.2 Selections. By date
History and criticism, see BP130+
Chinese
104.3 Complete text. By date
104.32 Selections. By date
History and criticism, see BP130+
Indonesian
104.4 Complete text. By date
104.42 Selections. By date
History and criticism, see BP130+
Marathi
104.47 Complete text. By date
104.472 Selections. By date
History and criticism, see BP130+
Pahlavi
104.5 Complete text. By date
104.52 Selections. By date
History and criticism, see BP130+
Persian
104.6 Complete text. By date
104.62 Selections. By date
History and criticism, see BP130+
Sanskrit
104.67 Complete text. By date
104.672 Selections. By date
History and criticism, see BP130+
Sundanese
104.7 Complete text. By date
104.72 Selections. By date
History and criticism, see BP130+
Urdu
104.8 Complete text. By date
104.82 Selections. By date
History and criticism, see BP130+
Bengali

Islam
Sacred books
Koran
Texts. By language
Other Asian languages
Bengali -- Continued
104.9 Complete text. By date
104.92 Selections. By date
History and criticism, see BP130+
105.A-Z Other languages. By language, A-Z and date
105.5.A-Z Oceanic, African, American, and artificial languages. By language, A-Z, and date
European languages
Dutch
106 Complete text. By date
107 Selections. By date
History and criticism, see BP130+
English
109 Complete text. By date
110 Selections. By date
History and criticism, see BP130+
French
112 Complete text. By date
113 Selections. By date
History and criticism, see BP130+
German
115 Complete text. By date
116 Selections. By date
History and criticism, see BP130+
Italian
118 Complete text. By date
119 Selections. By date
History and criticism, see BP130+
Scandinavian
121 Complete text. By date
122 Selections. By date
History and criticism, see BP130+
Spanish and Portuguese
124 Complete text. By date
125 Selections. By date
History and criticism, see BP130+
127.A-Z Other languages. By language, A-Z, and date
Special parts and chapters
128.15 Juz' al-Ḥamd (Pt. I) (Table BP1)
128.16 Sūrat al-Fātiḥah (Chap. 1) (Table BP1)
128.17 Sūrat al-Baqarah (Chap. 2) (Table BP1)
128.18 Juz' Sa-yaqūl (Pt. II) (Table BP1)
128.19 Juz' Tilka al-rusul (Pt. III) (Table BP1)
128.2 Sūrat Āl 'Imrān (Chap. 3) (Table BP1)
128.22 Juz' Kull al-ṭa'ām (Pt. IV) (Table BP1)
128.23 Sūrat al-Nisā' (Chap. 4) (Table BP1)
128.24 Juz' Wa-al-muḥṣanāt (Pt. V) (Table BP1)
128.25 Juz' Lā yuḥibb (Pt. VI) (Table BP1)

Islam
Sacred books
Koran
Special parts and chapters
Juz' Lā yuḥibb (Pt. VI) -- Continued
128.26 Sūrat al-Mā'idah (Chap. 5) (Table BP1)
128.27 Juz' La-tajidanna (Pt. VII) (Table BP1)
128.28 Sūrat al-An'ām (Chap. 6) (Table BP1)
128.29 Juz' Wa-law annanā (Pt. VIII) (Table BP1)
128.3 Sūrat al-A'rāf (Chap. 7) (Table BP1)
128.32 Juz' Qāla al-mala' (Pt. IX) (Table BP1)
128.33 Sūrat al-Anfāl (Chap. 8) (Table BP1)
128.34 Juz' Wa-i 'lamū (Pt. X) (Table BP1)
128.35 Sūrat al-Tawbah (Chap. 9) (Table BP1)
128.36 Juz' Innamā al-sabīl (Pt. XI) (Table BP1)
128.37 Sūrat Yūnus (Chap. 10) (Table BP1)
128.38 Sūrat Hūd (Chap. 11) (Table BP1)
128.39 Juz' Wa-mā min dābbah (Pt. XII) (Table BP1)
128.4 Sūrat Yūsuf (Chap. 12) (Table BP1)
128.42 Juz' Wa-mā ubarri' (Pt. XIII) (Table BP1)
128.43 Sūrat al-Ra'd (Chap. 13) (Table BP1)
128.44 Sūrat Ibrāhīm (Chap. 14) (Table BP1)
128.45 Sūrat al-Ḥijr (Chap. 15) (Table BP1)
128.46 Juz' Alif-lām-rā' (Pt. XIV) (Table BP1)
128.47 Sūrat al-Naḥl (Chap. 16) (Table BP1)
128.48 Juz' Subḥān (Pt. XV) (Table BP1)
128.49 Sūrat al-Isrā' (Chap. 17) (Table BP1)
128.5 Sūrat al-Kahf (Chap. 18) (Table BP1)
128.52 Juz' Qāla a-lam aqul (Pt. XVI) (Table BP1)
128.53 Sūrat Maryam (Chap. 19) (Table BP1)
128.54 Sūrat Ṭā-hā (Chap. 20) (Table BP1)
128.55 Juz' Iqtarab (Pt. XVII) (Table BP1)
128.56 Sūrat al-Anbiyā' (Chap. 21) (Table BP1)
128.57 Sūrat al-Ḥajj (Chap. 22) (Table BP1)
128.58 Juz' Qad aflaḥ (Pt. XVIII) (Table BP1)
128.59 Sūrat al-Mu'minūn (Chap. 23) (Table BP1)
128.6 Sūrat al-Nūr (Chap. 24) (Table BP1)
128.62 Sūrat al-Furqān (Chap. 25) (Table BP1)
128.63 Juz' Wa-qāla alladhīna (Pt. XIX) (Table BP1)
128.64 Sūrat al-Shu'arā' (Chap. 26) (Table BP1)
128.65 Sūrat al-Naml (Chap. 27) (Table BP1)
128.66 Juz' Fa-mā kān (Pt. XX) (Table BP1)
128.67 Sūrat al-Qaṣaṣ (Chap. 28) (Table BP1)
128.68 Sūrat al-'Ankabūt (Chap. 29) (Table BP1)
128.69 Juz' Wa-lā tujādilū (Pt. XXI) (Table BP1)
128.7 Sūrat al-Rūm (Chap. 30) (Table BP1)
128.72 Sūrat Luqmān (Chap. 31) (Table BP1)
128.73 Sūrat al-Sajdah (Chap. 32) (Table BP1)
128.74 Sūrat al-Aḥzāb (Chap. 33) (Table BP1)
128.75 Juz' Wa-man yaqnut (Pt. XXII) (Table BP1)
128.76 Sūrat Saba' (Chap. 34) (Table BP1)
128.77 Sūrat Fāṭir (Chap. 35) (Table BP1)
128.78 Sūrat Yā-sīn (Chap. 36) (Table BP1)

Islam
Sacred books
Koran
Special parts and chapters -- Continued

128.79 Juz' Wa-mā anzalnā (Pt. XXIII) (Table BP1)
128.8 Sūrat al-Ṣāffāt (Chap. 37) (Table BP1)
128.82 Sūrat Ṣād (Chap. 38) (Table BP1)
128.83 Sūrat al-Zumar (Chap. 39) (Table BP1)
128.84 Juz' Fa-man aẓlam (Pt. XXIV) (Table BP1)
128.85 Sūrat Ghāfir (Chap. 40) (Table BP1)
128.86 Sūrat Fuṣṣilat (Chap. 41) (Table BP1)
128.87 Juz' Ilayh (Pt. XXV) (Table BP1)
128.88 Sūrat al-Shūrá (Chap. 42) (Table BP1)
128.89 Sūrat al-Zukhruf (Chap. 43) (Table BP1)
128.9 Sūrat al-Dukhān (Chap. 44) (Table BP1)
128.92 Sūrat al-Jāthiyah (Chap. 45) (Table BP1)
128.93 Juz' Ḥā'-mīm (Pt. XXVI) (Table BP1)
128.94 Sūrat al-Aḥqaf (Chap. 46) (Table BP1)
128.95 Sūrat Muḥammad (Chap. 47) (Table BP1)
128.96 Sūrat al-Fatḥ (Chap. 48) (Table BP1)
128.97 Sūrat al-Ḥujurāt (Chap. 49) (Table BP1)
128.98 Sūrat Qāf (Chap. 50) (Table BP1)
128.99 Sūrat al-Dhāriyāt (Chap. 51) (Table BP1)
129 Juz' Qāla fa-mā khaṭbukum (Pt. XXVII) (Table BP1)
129.12 Sūrat al-Ṭūr (Chap. 52) (Table BP1)
129.13 Sūrat al-Najm (Chap. 53) (Table BP1)
129.14 Sūrat al-Qamar (Chap. 54) (Table BP1)
129.15 Sūrat al-Raḥmān (Chap. 55) (Table BP1)
129.16 Sūrat al-Wāqi'ah (Chap. 56) (Table BP1)
129.17 Sūrat al-Ḥadīd (Chap. 57) (Table BP1)
129.18 Juz' Qad sami' (Pt. XXVIII) (Table BP1)
129.19 Sūrat al-Mujādalah (Chap. 58) (Table BP1)
129.2 Sūrat al-Ḥashr (Chap. 59) (Table BP1)
129.22 Sūrat al-Mumtaḥinah (Chap. 60) (Table BP1)
129.23 Sūrat al-Ṣaff (Chap. 61) (Table BP1)
129.24 Sūrat al-Jumu'ah (Chap. 62) (Table BP1)
129.25 Sūrat al-Munāfiqūn (Chap. 63) (Table BP1)
129.26 Sūrat al-Taghābun (Chap. 64) (Table BP1)
129.27 Sūrat al-Ṭalāq (Chap. 65) (Table BP1)
129.28 Sūrat al-Taḥrīm (Chap. 66) (Table BP1)
129.29 Juz' Tabārak (Pt. XXIX) (Table BP1)
129.3 Sūrat al-Mulk (Chap. 67) (Table BP1)
129.32 Sūrat al-Qalam (Chap. 68) (Table BP1)
129.33 Sūrat al-Ḥāqqah (Chap. 69) (Table BP1)
129.34 Sūrat al-Ma'ārij (Chap. 70) (Table BP1)
129.35 Sūrat Nūḥ (Chap. 71) (Table BP1)
129.36 Sūrat al-Jinn (Chap. 72) (Table BP1)
129.37 Sūrat al-Muzammil (Chap. 73) (Table BP1)
129.38 Sūrat al-Muddaththir (Chap. 74) (Table BP1)
129.39 Sūrat al-Qiyāmah (Chap. 75) (Table BP1)
129.4 Sūrat al-Dahr (Sūrat al-Insān) (Chap. 76) (Table BP1)

Islam
Sacred books
Koran
Special parts and chapters
Juz' Tabārak (Pt. XXIX) -- Continued
129.41 Sūrat al-Mursalāt (Chap. 77) (Table BP1)
129.42 Juz' 'Amma (Pt. XXX) (Table BP1)
129.43 Sūrat al-Naba' (Chap. 78) (Table BP1)
129.44 Sūrat al-Nāzi'āt (Chap. 79) (Table BP1)
129.45 Sūrat 'Abas (Chap. 80) (Table BP1)
129.46 Sūrat al-Takwīr (Chap. 81) (Table BP1)
129.47 Sūrat al-Infiṭār (Chap. 82) (Table BP1)
129.48 Sūrat al-Muṭaffifīn (Chap. 83) (Table BP1)
129.49 Sūrat al-Inshiqāq (Chap. 84) (Table BP1)
129.5 Sūrat al-Burūj (Chap. 85) (Table BP1)
129.52 Sūrat al-Ṭāriq (Chap. 86) (Table BP1)
129.53 Sūrat al-A'lá (Chap. 87) (Table BP1)
129.54 Sūrat al-Ghāshiyah (Chap. 88) (Table BP1)
129.55 Sūrat al-Fajr (Chap. 89) (Table BP1)
129.56 Sūrat al-Balad (Chap. 90) (Table BP1)
129.57 Sūrat al-Shams (Chap. 91) (Table BP1)
129.58 Sūrat al-Layl (Chap. 92) (Table BP1)
129.59 Sūrat al-Ḍuḥá (Chap. 93) (Table BP1)
129.6 Sūrat al-Sharḥ (Chap. 94) (Table BP1)
129.62 Sūrat al-Tīn (Chap. 95) (Table BP1)
129.63 Sūrat al-'Alaq (Chap. 96) (Table BP1)
129.64 Sūrat al-Qadr (Chap. 97) (Table BP1)
129.65 Sūrat al-Bayyinah (Chap. 98) (Table BP1)
129.66 Sūrat al-Zalzalah (Chap. 99) (Table BP1)
129.67 Sūrat al-'Ādiyāt (Chap. 100) (Table BP1)
129.68 Sūrat al-Qāri'ah (Chap. 101) (Table BP1)
129.69 Sūrat al-Takāthur (Chap. 102) (Table BP1)
129.7 Sūrat al-'Aṣr (Chap. 103) (Table BP1)
129.72 Sūrat al-Humazah (Chap. 104) (Table BP1)
129.73 Sūrat al-Fīl (Chap. 105) (Table BP1)
129.74 Sūrat Quraysh (Chap. 106) (Table BP1)
129.75 Sūrat al-Mā'ūn (Chap. 107) (Table BP1)
129.76 Sūrat al-Kawthar (Chap. 108) (Table BP1)
129.77 Sūrat al-Kāfirūn (Chap. 109) (Table BP1)
129.78 Sūrat al-Naṣr (Chap. 110) (Table BP1)
129.79 Sūrat al-Masad (Chap. 111) (Table BP1)
129.8 Sūrat al-Ikhlāṣ (Chap. 112) (Table BP1)
129.82 Sūrat al-Falaq (Chap. 113) (Table BP1)
129.83 Sūrat al-Nās (Chap. 114) (Table BP1)
Works about the Koran
For languages of the Koran, including glossaries, vocabularies, etc., see PJ6696.A6+
130 General works
130.1 Criticism
Principles of criticism. Hermeneutics
130.2 General works

Islam
Sacred books
Koran
Works about the Koran
Criticism
Principles of criticism.
Hermeneutics -- Continued
130.3 Abrogator and abrogated verses. Nāsikh wa-al-mansūkh
130.32 Asbāb al-nuzūl
Hadith and hermeneutics, see BP136.38
130.38 Data processing
130.4 Commentaries. Exegesis. Interpretation
130.45 History of criticism and exegesis
130.5 History of events in the Koran
130.58 Koran stories
130.6 Addresses, essays, lectures
Appreciation. Excellence. Inspiration. Authority. Credibility
130.7 General works
130.73 I'jāz. Inimitability
130.74 Createdness. Khalq al-Qur'ān
Study and teaching. Koran studies. 'Ulūm al-Qur'ān
130.77 History
130.78.A-Z By region or country, A-Z
Including collective biography of commentators and scholars
For individual biography, see BP80.A+
General works
130.79 Early through 1800
130.8 1801-
Textbooks
130.82 General
130.84 Advanced
130.86 Juvenile. Catechisms
History of the Koran
131 General works
131.13 Translating the Koran. Theory, methods, problems, etc.
131.14 History of translations of the Koran
131.15.A-Z Special languages, A-Z
Publication and distribution
131.18.A1 General works
131.18.A2-Z By region or country, A-Z
131.2 Geography
Language, see PJ6696.A6+
131.3 Metaphors
131.4 Peculiar dialectal words
131.5 Readings (Qirā'āt)
131.6 Recitation. Melodic reading. Tajwīd
Koran as literature
131.8 General works

Islam
Sacred books
Koran
Works about the Koran
Koran as literature -- Continued
131.85 Proverbs
Theology. Teachings of the Koran
132 General works
132.5 Symbols. Symbolism
133 Concordances. Dictionaries. Indexes, etc.
Men, women, and children of the Koran
Biography
Collective
133.5 General works
133.6.A-Z Special groups, A-Z
133.6.E5 Enemies of Muḥammad
133.6.W6 Women
133.7.A-Z Individual, A-Z
133.7.A27 Abraham (Biblical patriarch). Ibrāhīm
133.7.A3 Adam (Biblical figure). Ādam
133.7.A42 Alexander, the Great. Dhū al-Qarnayn
133.7.A44 ʻAlī ibn Abī Ṭālib, Caliph, 600 (ca.) - 661
133.7.D38 David, King of Israel. Dāwūd
Dhū al-Qarnayn. Alexander the Great, see BP133.7.A42
Ibrāhīm, see BP133.7.A27
133.7.I85 Ishmael (Biblical figure). Ismāʻīl
133.7.J33 Jacob (Biblical patriarch). Yaʻqūb
133.7.J65 John the Baptist. Yaḥyá
133.7.J67 Joseph (Son of Jacob). Yūsuf
133.7.L84 Luqmān
133.7.M37 Mary, Blessed Virgin, Saint. Maryam
Maryam, see BP133.7.M37
133.7.M67 Moses (Biblical leader). Mūsá
133.7.M84 Muḥammad, Prophet, d. 632
Mūsá, see BP133.7.M67
133.7.N63 Noah (Biblical figure). Nūḥ
Nūḥ, see BP133.7.N63
133.7.S64 Solomon, King of Israel. Sulaymān
Yaḥyá, see BP133.7.J65
Yaʻqūb, see BP133.7.J33
Yūsuf, see BP133.7.J67
134.A-Z Special topics, A-Z
134.A38 Aesthetics
134.A5 Angels
Animals, see BP134.N3
134.A8 Astronomy
134.B4 Bible and the Koran
134.B5 Bible characters in the Koran
134.C45 Christianity
134.C56 Communication
134.C6 Cosmogony. Cosmology. Creation

Islam
Sacred books
Koran
Works about the Koran
Special topics, A-Z -- Continued

134.D35	Death
134.D4	Demonology
134.D43	Devil. Shayṭān. Iblīs
134.E25	Economics
134.E38	Education
134.E5	Egypt
134.E55	Emigration and immigration
134.E7	Eschatology
134.E8	Ethics
	Evil, see BP134.G65
134.F23	Faith
134.F25	Family. Family relations
134.F3	Fasting
134.F58	Food
134.F6	Forgiveness of sin
134.F8	Future life
134.G6	God
134.G65	Good and evil
134.H5	Historiography
134.H57	History
134.H85	Human rights
	Immigration, see BP134.E55
	Intellect, see BP134.R33
134.I72	Iran. Iranians
134.J37	Jesus Christ
134.J4	Jews. Judaism
134.J45	Jihad
134.J52	Jinn
134.K6	Knowledge. Theory of knowledge
134.L34	Labor. Work ethic
134.L54	Life
134.L67	Love
134.M24	Malicious accusation
134.M3	Man
134.M47	Mercy
	Mind, see BP134.R33
134.M86	Munāfiqūn
134.N3	Nature. Natural history
134.O27	Oaths
134.P5	Philosophy. Koran and philosophy
134.P55	Plants
134.P6	Political science
134.P7	Prayer
134.P74	Prophecies
134.P745	Prophets. Pre-Islamic prophets
134.P747	Psychology
134.P8	Punishment
134.R33	Reason. Intellect. Mind

	Islam
	Sacred books
	Koran
	Works about the Koran
	Special topics, A-Z -- Continued
134.R35	Religious life
134.R4	Resurrection
134.S3	Science
134.S6	Social teachings
134.S67	Soul
134.S7	Spirit
134.S94	Supernatural
134.W37	Water
134.W6	Women (Attitude toward)
	Work ethic, see BP134.L34
	Hadith literature. Traditions. Sunna
	Cf. BP193.25+, Shiite Hadith literature
	Canonical collections
135.A1	General
	Special. By compiler
	Bukhārī, Muḥammad ibn Ismā'īl, 810-870
135.A12	Texts
135.A122	Selections. By date
135.A124A-Z	Translations. By language, A-Z
	Including selections under each
135.A126	Concordances. Dictionaries. Indexes, etc.
135.A128	Commentaries. Criticism
	Abū Dā'ūd Sulaymān ibn al-Ash'ath al-Sijistānī, 817 or 18-889
135.A13	Texts
135.A132	Selections. By date
135.A134A-Z	Translations. By language, A-Z
	Including selections under each
135.A136	Concordances. Dictionaries. Indexes, etc.
135.A138	Commentaries. Criticism
	Muslim ibn al-Ḥajjāj al-Qushayrī, ca. 821-875
135.A14	Texts
135.A142	Selections. By date
135.A144A-Z	Translations. By language, A-Z
	Including selections under each
135.A146	Concordances. Dictionaries. Indexes, etc.
135.A148	Commentaries. Criticism
	Tirmidhī, Muḥammad ibn 'Īsá, d. 892
135.A15	Texts
135.A152	Selections. By date
135.A154A-Z	Translations. By language, A-Z
	Including selections under each
135.A156	Concordances. Dictionaries. Indexes, etc.
135.A158	Commentaries. Criticism
	Nasā'ī, Aḥmad ibn Shu'ayb, 830 or 31-915
135.A16	Texts
135.A162	Selections. By date

Islam
Sacred books
Hadith literature. Traditions. Sunna
Canonical collections
Special. By compiler
Nasā'ī, Aḥmad ibn
Shu'ayb, 830 or 31-915 -- Continued
135.A164A-Z Translations. By language, A-Z
Including selections under each
135.A166 Concordances. Dictionaries. Indexes, etc.
135.A168 Commentaries. Criticism
Ibn Mājah, Muḥammad ibn Yazīd, d. 887
135.A17 Texts
135.A172 Selections. By date
135.A174A-Z Translations. By language, A-Z
Including selections under each
135.A176 Concordances. Dictionaries. Indexes, etc.
135.A178 Commentaries. Criticism
135.A2 Other compilations
Subarranged by author
135.A3 Selections. Extracts, etc.
Subarranged by author
135.A4-Z General works
135.2 Concordances. Dictionaries. Indexes, etc.
Language, including glossaries, vocabularies, etc., see PJ6697.A6+
Study and teaching. Hadith studies. 'Ilm al-Ḥadīth
135.6 History
135.62.A-Z By region or country, A-Z
Including collective biography of commentators and scholars
For individual biography, see BP80.A+
General works
135.65 Early through 1800
135.66 1801-
135.68 Textbooks
135.8.A-Z Special topics, A-Z
135.8.A28 Abū Bakr, Caliph, d. 634
135.8.A54 Animals
135.8.A7 Arabs
135.8.C35 Caliphs
135.8.E28 Economics
135.8.E3 Education. Knowledge
135.8.E64 Epithets
135.8.F35 Faith
135.8.F37 Fasting
135.8.F67 Forgiveness of sin
135.8.I65 Intention
135.8.I67 Interpersonal relations
135.8.I7 Iran
135.8.J47 Jerusalem
135.8.J48 Jews

Islam
Sacred books
Hadith literature. Traditions. Sunna
Special topics, A-Z -- Continued
135.8.J54 Jihad
Knowledge, see BP135.8.E3
135.8.M43 Medicine
135.8.M45 Medina (Saudi Arabia)
135.8.M85 Muḥammad, Prophet, d. 632
135.8.P37 Parents
135.8.P66 Prayer
135.8.P7 Predestination
135.8.P75 Proverbs
135.8.P87 Purity, Ritual
135.8.R3 Ramadan
135.8.R4 Religious life
Ritual purity, see BP135.8.P87
135.8.S24 Salvation
135.8.S95 Syria
135.8.T87 Turkic peoples
135.8.U85 ʻUthmān ibn ʻAffān, Caliph, d. 656
135.8.W6 Women
135.8.Y46 Yemen
History
136 General works
136.2 Origin
Organization of Hadith
136.3 General works
136.33 Ascription and chain of transmission (Isnād)
136.36 Subject matter (Matn)
136.38 Relation to the Koran
Appreciation. Excellence. Inspiration. Authority. Credibility
136.4 General works
Transmission. Transmitters
136.42 Establishment of authoritativeness of transmitters
136.44 Ascription to Muḥammad or a companion
136.46 Companions of Muḥammad (Ṣaḥābah)
Class here works on the Companions as Hadith transmitters only
For general biography of the Companions, see BP75.5+
For individual biography, see BP80.A+
136.47 Followers (al-Tābiʻīn)
Guarantors. Reporters. Transmitters
136.48 General works
136.485 Women transmitters
136.5 Quality of the transmission of the tradition into "sound, fair, or weak" transmission
136.6 Methods of testing the transmission of a tradition by "wounding, impugning, interpolating"

	Islam
	Sacred books
	Hadith literature.
	Traditions. Sunna -- Continued
	Special critical problems
136.7	General works
136.72	Interpolation
136.74	Forgery
136.76	Misconstruction
136.78	Abrogating and abrogated Hadith
136.8	Commentaries on the Hadith
136.9	Hadith stories. Retelling of the Hadith
	Teaching, theology, see BP160+
	Koranic and other Islamic legends
	Including Biblical legends
137	General works
137.5.A-Z	Individual legends, A-Z
137.5.D3	David, King of Israel
137.5.K5	Khiḍr. Khaḍir
(140-157)	Islamic law (Fiqh)
	For ceremonial and religious law, see special topics in Subclass BP
	For civil, criminal, and other law, see Class K
	General works on Islam. Treatises
	Cf. B740+, Islamic philosophy
	Cf. BP87+ , Devotional or theologico-philosophical works of Islamic authors not limited specifically by subject
160	Early through 1800
161	1801-1950
161.2	1951-2000
161.3	2001-
163	General special
165	Addresses, essays, lectures
165.5	Dogma (ʻAqā'id)
165.7	Authority. Taqlīd. Bidʻah
	Theology (Kalām)
	Including Sunnite theology
166	General works
166.1	History of theology
166.14.A-Z	Special schools, movements, etc., A-Z
	For branches, sects, modifications, see BP191+
	For Shīʻah, see BP194+
	For Sufism, see BP189.26+
166.14.A84	Asharites. Ashʻarīyah
166.14.B37	Bareelly School
166.14.D4	Deoband School
166.14.F85	Fundamentalism. Usūlīyah. Integrism
166.14.H2	Hanafite
166.14.H3	Hanbalite
	Integrism, see BP166.14.F85
166.14.M3	Malikite
166.14.S4	Shafiite

	Islam
	Theology (Kalām)
	Special schools, movements, etc., A-Z -- Continued
	Usūlīyah, see BP166.14.F85
	Special doctrines
166.2	God. Unity of God
166.22	Polytheism. Shirk
166.23	Creation. Cosmology. Cosmogony
166.25	Atomism
	Fatalism. Determinism. Predestination
166.3	General works
166.33	Merit
	Prophets. Prophecy
166.38	General works
166.4	Prophets prior to Muḥammad
	Muḥammad, Prophet, d. 632, see BP166.5+
	Muḥammad, Prophet, d. 632
166.5	General works
166.55	Mission
166.57	Mi'rāj. Ascension. Isrā'. Night journey to Jerusalem
	Revelation
166.6	General works
166.65	Miracles Cf. BP75.8, Muḥammad, the Prophet
	Man
166.7	General works
166.72	Health and sickness. Islam and medicine
166.73	Soul
166.75	Sin
166.76	Mediation between God and man. Shafā'ah
	Salvation
166.77	General works
	Faith. Faith and works
166.78	General works
166.783	Intention. Sincerity. Nīyah. Ikhlāṣ
166.785	Kufr. Unbelief
166.79	Repentance. Tawbah
166.793	Forgiveness of sin
	Eschatology. Future life
166.8	General works
166.815	Death
166.82	Intermediate state
166.825	Intercession
166.83	Resurrection
166.84	Antichrist. Dajjāl
166.85	Judgment
166.87	Paradise
166.88	Hell
166.89	Spirit world: Angels, demons, jinn, devil Cf. BP134.A5, Angels (Koran)
	Other

Islam
Theology (Kalām)
Special doctrines
Other -- Continued
166.9 Caliphate
166.93 Mahdism
166.94 Imamate
Ethics, see BJ1291
167 Addresses, essays, lectures. Pamphlets, etc.
167.3 Blasphemy
167.5 Heresy, heresies, heretics
Including the charge of heresy
168 Apostasy from Islam
169 Works against Islam and the Koran
Cf. BM591, Jewish works against Islam
Cf. BT1170, Christian works against Islam
170 Works in defense of Islam. Islamic apologetics
170.2 Benevolent work. Social work. Welfare work, etc.
170.25 Waqf. Awqāf. Charities. Endowments
For legal aspects, see Class K
170.3 Missionary work of Islam
Cf. BV2625+, Christian missions to Muslims
170.5 Converts to Islam
Cf. BV2626.3+, Converts to Christianity from Islam
170.5.A1 Collective
170.5.A3-Z Individual, A-Z
170.8 Universality of Islam
170.82 Unity of Islam
170.85 Da'wah. Mission of Islam. Summons, invitation, etc.
Cf. BP166.55, Mission of Muḥammad
Relation of Islam to other religions
Cf. BP170.3, Missionary work of Islam
171 General works
171.5 Toleration
Relation to Christianity
Cf. BT1170, Apologetics
172 General works
172.5.A-Z Special denominations, sects, A-Z
e.g.
172.5.C6 Coptic Church
173.A-Z Other, A-Z
173.B9 Buddhism
173.C65 Confucianism
173.H5 Hinduism
Cf. BP76.45, Muḥammad's relations with Hinduism
Special sects, etc.
173.H58 Vaishnavism
173.J8 Judaism
Cf. BP76.4, Muḥammad's relations with Jews
Cf. BP134.J4, Judaism in the Koran
173.S5 Sikhism

Islam
Relation of Islam to other religions
Other, A-Z -- Continued
173.S92 Subud
173.T45 Theosophy
173.2 Sources of Islam
Islamic sociology
For Islam and social problems, see HN40.M6
For Islam and socialism and communism, see HX550.I8
173.25 General works
173.3 Children
173.33 Orphans
173.4 Women
173.43 Social justice. Theology of justice
173.44 Civil rights. Theology of civil rights
173.45 Equality
Cf. BP190.5.R3, Race
173.5 Islam and world politics
173.55 Islam and nationalism
173.6 Islam and the state
Cf. JC49, Political science
173.65 Islam and religious liberty
173.66 Islam and freedom of speech
173.7 Islam and politics
Cf. BP134.P6, Political science in the Koran
173.75 Islam and economics
Islam and labor, see HD6338.4
173.77 Islam and work
The practice of Islam
174 General works
175 Psychology of Islam
Including the psychology of religious experience
The five duties of a Moslem. Pillars of Islam
176 General works
177 Profession of faith
Cf. BP166.2, God
Cf. BP166.5+, Muḥammad, Prophet, d. 632
178 Prayer
Cf. BP183.3, Prayers
Cf. BP184.3, Prayer, the call to prayer
179 Fasting
Cf. BP184.5, Mode of fasting
Cf. BP186+, Fast days
180 Alms (Zakat)
181 Pilgrimage to Mecca
Cf. BP184.7, Pilgrimages in general
Cf. BP187.3, Descriptive works of the pilgrimage to Mecca
Cf. DS248.M4, Mecca
182 Jihad (Holy War)
The Jihad is on a par with the five duties among the Kharijites

Islam
The practice of Islam -- Continued
Symbols and symbolism
Cf. N6260+, Islamic art
182.5 General works
182.6.A-Z Special symbols, A-Z
The formularies of worship, texts, etc.
183 General works
183.3 Prayers, invocations, quatrains, praises, religious preludes
183.4 Calls to prayer
183.5 Hymns, songs
183.6 Sermons
Sermons for special days, seasons, etc.
183.63 ‘Āshūrā (The tenth of Muḥarram)
183.634 Mawlid al-Nabī
183.636 Laylat al-Mi‘rāj
183.638 Laylat al-Barā’ah (Berat gecesi) Night of mid-Sha‘bān
183.64 Ramadan
183.643 Laylat al-Qadr
183.645 ‘Īd al-Fiṭr. Fast-breaking at the end of Ramadan
183.66 ‘Īd al-Aḍḥā (Day of sacrifice)
183.7.A-Z Other, A-Z
183.7.B3 Basmalah
Tasmiyah, see BP183.7.B3
Religious ceremonies, rites, actions, customs, etc.
184 General works
184.2 Public worship
Including mode and manner
184.25 Preaching. Homiletics
184.27 Communication
184.3 Prayer
Including the call to prayer, the hours of prayer, the manner of prayer
184.4 Purifications and ablutions
184.5 Fasting
For special days, see BP186+
184.6 Sacrifices
For special days, see BP186+
184.7 Pilgrimages
For special places, see BP187+
184.8 Circumcision
184.9.A-Z Other, A-Z
184.9.B5 Blood as food or medicine
184.9.D5 Dietary laws
184.9.F8 Funeral rites and ceremonies
184.9.M68 Mourning
184.9.T73 Travel
Minbar, liturgical objects, ornaments, memorials, etc.
184.95 General works

Islam
The practice of Islam
Minbar, liturgical objects, ornaments, memorials, etc. -- Continued
184.96.A-Z Special objects, A-Z
184.96.R66 Rosaries
Religious functionaries. Polity. Government.
Ulama
Including mosque officials
185 General works
185.3 Muezzin
185.4 Imam
185.5.A-Z Other, A-Z
185.5.S53 Shaykh al-Islām
Mass media and telecommunication in Islam
185.7 General works
185.72 Advertising. Publicity. Public relations
Religious broadcasting
185.74 General works
185.75.A-Z By region or country, A-Z
185.76 Radio broadcasting
185.77 Television broadcasting
Special days and seasons, fasts, feasts, festivals, etc.
Cf. BP194.5.A+, Shiite festivals, etc.
186 General works
186.15 Fridays. al-Jum'ah
186.2 New Year's Day (The first of Muḥarram)
186.3 'Āshūrā (The tenth of Muḥarram)
For Shiite Tenth of Muḥarram, see BP194.5.T4
186.34 Mawlid al-Nabī
186.36 Laylat al-Mi'rāj
186.38 Laylat al-Barā'ah (Berat gecesi). Night of mid-Sha'bān
186.4 Ramadan
186.43 Laylat al-Qadr
186.45 'Īd al-Fiṭr. Fast-breaking at the end of Ramadan
186.6 'Īd al-Aḍḥā (Day of sacrifice)
186.9.A-Z Other, A-Z
186.97 Relics. Veneration, etc.
Cf. BP75.9, Relics of Muḥammad
Shrines, sacred places, etc.
187 General works
Mecca
187.2 General works
187.3 Pilgrimages to Mecca. Hajj
187.4 Ka'bah
187.45 Qiblah. Direction of prayer
187.48 Zamzam Well
Non-Meccan shrines, sanctuaries, etc.
For Shiite shrines, sacred places, etc., see BP194.6.A2+

Islam
The practice of Islam
Shrines, sacred places, etc.
Non-Meccan shrines, sanctuaries, etc. -- Continued
187.52 General works
187.55.A-Z By region or country, A-Z
Subarrange each country by Table BP2
Mosques. Monasteries
Cf. BJ2019.5.I8, Islamic etiquette. Mosque etiquette
Cf. BP185+, Mosque officials
For mosques on Temple Mount, Jerusalem, see DS109.32.A+
187.62 General works
187.65.A-Z By region or country, A-Z
Subarrange each country by Table BP2
187.9.A-Z Other, A-Z
Islamic religious life (Descriptive works)
188 General works
Sins. Vices
188.13 General works
188.14.A-Z Individual sins, A-Z
188.14.A92 Avarice
188.14.B75 Bribery
188.14.E58 Envy
188.14.F3 Falsehood
188.14.G35 Gambling
188.14.H65 Homosexuality
188.14.H94 Hypocrisy
188.14.O4 Omens
188.14.P74 Pride
188.14.S55 Slander
Virtues
188.15 General works
188.16.A-Z Individual virtues, A-Z
188.16.C47 Chivalry
188.16.G45 Generosity. Karam
188.16.G7 Gratitude
188.16.H67 Hospitality
188.16.J88 Justice
Karam, see BP188.16.G45
188.16.K56 Kindness
188.16.L68 Love
188.16.M3 Magnanimity
188.16.M59 Moderation. Tawāzun
188.16.M6 Modesty. Naẓar
Naẓar, see BP188.16.M6
188.16.P37 Patience. Ṣabr
188.16.P74 Promises
Ṣabr, see BP188.16.P37
Tawāzun, see BP188.16.M59
188.16.T78 Truthfulness

Islam
The practice of Islam
Islamic religious life
(Descriptive works) -- Continued

188.18.A-Z	Special classes of persons, A-Z
188.18.F35	Families
188.18.G57	Girls
188.18.P45	Physicians
188.18.S53	Sick
188.18.W65	Women
188.18.Y68	Youth
	Devotional literature
188.2	General works
188.3.A-Z	For special classes, A-Z
188.3.C5	Children
188.3.C64	College students
188.3.F3	Families
188.3.K55	Kings. Rulers. Princes
188.3.M3	Married people
	Princes, see BP188.3.K55
188.3.P7	Prisoners
	Rulers, see BP188.3.K55
188.3.S5	Sick
188.3.S6	Soldiers
188.3.W6	Women
188.3.Y6	Youth
188.4	History and criticism of devotional literature
	Sufism. Mysticism. Dervishes
188.45	Periodicals. Societies. Congresses
188.48	Dictionaries and encyclopedias
	History
188.5	General works
188.55	Addresses, essays, lectures
	By period
188.6	Through 1900
188.7	1901-
188.8.A-Z	By region or country, A-Z *Under each country:* *.x* *General works* *.x2A-Z* *Local, A-Z*
	General works
188.9	Early works through 1900
189	1901-
189.2	General special
189.23	Addresses, essays, lectures
	Doctrine
189.26	Early works through 1900
189.3	1901-
	Special topics
189.33	Sainthood
	Other special topics, see BP166.2+
189.36	Controversial works about the sect. Polemics
	Biography

Islam
The practice of Islam
Islamic religious life (Descriptive works)
Sufism. Mysticism. Dervishes
Biography -- Continued
Collective (Saints, etc.)
For biography of individual orders, see BP189.7.A+
For collective biography of individual regions, countries, cities, see BP188.8.A+
189.4 General works
189.43 History and criticism. Historiography. Hagiography
Individual, see BP80.A+
Shrines, sacred places, etc , see BP187.52+
Sufi practice
189.5 General works
Special topics
189.52 Asceticism
189.55 Formularies of worship, texts, etc.
Ceremonies, rites, actions, etc.
e.g. Recital of the Names of God, etc.
189.58 General works
189.585 Saint worship
For shrines of saints, see BP187.52+
For the doctrine of sainthood, see BP189.33
Religious life
189.6 General works
189.62 Devotional literature
189.65.A-Z Other special topics, A-Z
189.65.A47 Alphabet. Symbolism and numeric value of letters
189.65.D36 Dancing
189.65.F35 Faith-cure. Spiritual healing
Letters, Symbolism and numeric value of, see BP189.65.A47
189.65.L68 Love
189.65.M87 Music. Singing. Sam'
189.65.P78 Psychology
Sam, see BP189.65.M87
Singing, see BP189.65.M87
Spiritual healing, see BP189.65.F35
Monasticism. Sufi orders. Brotherhoods
189.68 General works
189.7.A-Z Individual orders, A-Z
189.7.B3-B32 Badawiyah. Ahmadiyya (Table BP3)
189.7.B4-B42 Bektashi (Table BP3)
189.7.C47-C472 Cerrahiye (Table BP3)
189.7.C49-C492 Chishtīyah (Table BP3)
189.7.H3-H32 Haddāwā (Table BP3)
Halvetiyye, see BP189.7.K44+

Islam
The practice of Islam
Islamic religious life (Descriptive works)
Sufism. Mysticism. Dervishes
Monasticism. Sufi orders. Brotherhoods
Individual orders, A-Z -- Continued

189.7.H34-H342 Ḥamadsha (Table BP3)
189.7.I7-I72 ʻĪsāwīyah (Table BP3)
189.7.I74-I742 Ishrāqīyah (Table BP3)
189.7.K44-K442 Khalwatīyah. Halvetiyye (Table BP3)
189.7.K46-K462 Khānaqāh-i Niʻmat Allāhī. Niʻmat Allāhī Order (Table BP3)
189.7.K5-K52 Khatmīyah (Table BP3)
189.7.M26-M262 Mahdiyah (Table BP3)
189.7.M28-M282 Maktab Tarighe Oveyssi Shahmaghsoudi. Oveyssi School (Table BP3)
189.7.M3-M32 Malāmatīyah (Table BP3)
189.7.M4-M42 Mevleviyeh (Table BP3)
189.7.M5-M52 Mīrghanīyah (Table BP3)
189.7.N35-N352 Naqshabandīyah (Table BP3)
Niʻmat Allāhī Order, see BP189.7.K46+
189.7.Q3-Q32 Qādirīyah (Table BP3)
189.7.R5-R52 Rifāʻīyah (Table BP3)
189.7.S4-S42 Senussites (Sanūsīyah) (Table BP3)
189.7.S5-S52 Shādhilīyah (Table BP3)
189.7.T5-T52 Tijānīyah (Table BP3)
190 Communal religious activities
For asylums, see RC443+
For benevolent and welfare societies, see HS1556+
For hospitals, see RA960+
For orphanages, see HV959+
For Red Crescent, see HV560+, RT108, UH535+
For religious corporations; religious endowments, property, waqfs, see Class K
190.5.A-Z Topics not otherwise provided, A-Z
ʻAlmānīyah, see BP190.5.S35
190.5.A5 Amulets. Talismans
190.5.A55 Amusements
190.5.A6 Animism
190.5.A66 Arabian Peninsula
190.5.A67 Arabs in Islam
Including Arab contributions to Islam, Islam as an Arab religion, and Arab status in Islam
190.5.A7 Art. Images. Photography
190.5.A75 Asceticism
For Sufi asceticism, see BP189.52
190.5.A8 Astronautics
190.5.B3 Barakah
Beard, see BP190.5.H3
Bereavement, see BP190.5.C57

Islam
Topics not otherwise provided, A-Z -- Continued

190.5.B63 Body, Human
190.5.B72 Breast feeding
190.5.B74 Brotherliness. Brotherhood
190.5.C54 Civilization
190.5.C56 Conflict management
190.5.C57 Consolation. Bereavement
190.5.C6 Costume. Clothing and dress
190.5.C75 Crime
190.5.D45 Democracy
190.5.D53 Dialogue
190.5.D65 Dogs
190.5.D73 Dreams
Ecology, see BP190.5.N38
190.5.E86 Evolution
190.5.F42 Fear
190.5.F7 Freedom
190.5.F73 Friendship
190.5.H3 Hair. Haircutting. Beard
190.5.H34 Happiness
190.5.H5 History
(190.5.H7) Homosexuality
See BP188.14.H65
190.5.H8 Humor in Islam
190.5.H85 Hunger
Images, see BP190.5.A7
190.5.I57 Interpersonal relations
Jerusalem, see BP190.5.P3
190.5.L4 Leadership
190.5.L47 Light
190.5.M25 Magic
190.5.M3 Martyrdom
190.5.M34 Mathematics
190.5.M67 Motherhood
190.5.M8 Music
190.5.N38 Nature. Ecology
190.5.N54 Nile River
Nonviolence, see BP190.5.V56
190.5.P3 Palestine. Jerusalem, etc.
190.5.P34 Peace
190.5.P4 Performing arts
Photography, see BP190.5.A7
190.5.P56 Poetry
190.5.P57 Pollution
190.5.P6 Poverty
190.5.P63 Power
190.5.P74 Promises
190.5.P79 Psychotherapy
190.5.R3 Race. Race problems
190.5.R4 Reason
190.5.S3 Science
190.5.S35 Secularism. ʻAlmānīyah

Islam
Topics not otherwise provided, A-Z -- Continued
190.5.S4 Sex
190.5.S5 Shu'ūbīyah
190.5.S57 Social security
190.5.S6 Solitude
Talismans, see BP190.5.A5
190.5.T54 Time
190.5.T73 Travel
190.5.V3 Values
190.5.V56 Violence. Nonviolence
190.5.V63 Voting
190.5.W35 War
190.5.W37 Water
190.5.W4 Wealth
Branches, sects, and modifications
Cf. BP63+, By country
191 General works
Sunnites, see BP166+
Shiites
History
192 General works
192.2 General special
192.3 Addresses, essays, lectures
By period
192.4 661-1502
192.5 1502-1900
192.6 1901-
192.7.A-Z By region, country, city, etc., A-Z
Biography
192.8 Collective
Imams
193 Collective
Individual
193.1 1st, 'Alī ibn Abī Ṭālib, Caliph, 600 (ca.)-661 (Table BP4)
193.12 2nd, Ḥasan ibn 'Alī, d. ca. 669 (Table BP4)
193.13 3rd, Ḥusayn ibn 'Alī, d. 680 (Table BP4)
193.14 4th, Zayn al-'Ābidīn 'Alī ibn al-Ḥusayn, d. 710? (Table BP4)
193.15 5th, Muḥammad al-Bāqir ibn 'Alī Zayn al-'Ābidīn, d. 731 or 2 (Table BP4)
193.16 6th, Ja'far al-Ṣādiq, 702?-765 or 6 (Table BP4)
Ismā'īl ibn Ja'far, see BP195.I8+
193.17 7th, Mūsá al-Kāẓim ibn Ja'far, 745?-799 (Table BP4)
193.18 8th, 'Alī al-Riḍā ibn Mūsá, d. 818 or 19 (Table BP4)
193.19 9th, Muḥammad al-Jawād ibn 'Alī al-Riḍā, 810 or 11-835 or 6 (Table BP4)

Islam
Branches, sects, and modifications
Shiites
Biography
Imams
Individual -- Continued
193.2 10th, 'Alī al-Hādī ibn Muḥammad, 827-868 (Table BP4)
193.21 11th, 'Askarī, al-Ḥasan ibn 'Alī, d. 874 (Table BP4)
193.22 12th, Mahdī, Muḥammad ibn al-Ḥasan, b. 869 (Table BP4)
Other individual, see BP80.A+
Hadith literature. Traditions
Class here the collective sayings, etc., of the Imams and Muḥammad, the Prophet
For the Hadith of individual Imams, see BP193.1+
For the Hadith of Muḥammad, the Prophet, see BP135+
193.25.A-Z Collections. By compiler, A-Z
193.26.A-Z Selections. Extracts, etc. By compiler, A-Z
193.27 General works
For works on the science of Hadith, see BP136.3+
193.275 Concordances. Dictionaries. Indexes, etc.
193.28 Authorities. Transmitters
Class here only Shiite authorities
General works
193.3 Early works through 1800
193.5 1801-
193.7 Addresses, essays, etc.
Theology. Doctrine
194 General works
Special topics, see BP166+
194.1 Controversial literature, apologetics, etc.
Relation to other religious and philosophical systems
194.15 General works
194.16 Relation to Sunnites
194.17 Relation to Sufism
194.18.A-Z Other, A-Z
194.185 Shī'ah and politics
Shiite practice
194.2 General works
194.3 Formularies of worship, texts, etc.
194.4 Ceremonies, rites, actions, etc.
194.5.A-Z Special days and seasons, fasts, feasts, festivals, etc.
194.5.G45 Ghadīr. 'Id al-Ghadīr
194.5.T4 Tenth of Muḥarram
Shrines, sacred places, etc.
194.6.A2 Collective

Islam
Branches, sects, and modifications
Shiites
Shiite practice
Shrines, sacred places, etc. -- Continued
194.6.A3-Z Individual. By place, A-Z
For shrines, tombs, etc. related to an individual Imam, see BP193.1+
194.7 Shiite religious life
Including devotional literature
194.9.A-Z Other special topics, A-Z
194.9.E3 Education. Religious education
194.9.G68 Government. Polity. Religious functionaries
194.9.H34 Health. Hygiene
Hygiene, see BP194.9.H34
Polity, see BP194.9.G68
194.9.P7 Prayer. Prayers
Religious education, see BP194.9.E3
Religious functionaries, see BP194.9.G68
Branches, sects, and modifications of the Shiites, see BP195.A+
195.A-Z Other (to 1900), A-Z
195.A3-A32 Ahl-i Ḥadīth (Table BP3)
195.A4-A42 Ahl-i Ḥaqq (Table BP3)
195.A5-A6 Ahmadiyya. Qādiyānī (Table BP3)
Founded by Aḥmad, G̲h̲ulām, Hazrat Mirza, 1839?-1908
195.A8-A82 Assassins (Table BP3)
195.A84-A85 Azraqites (Azāriqah) (Table BP3)
Babism, Bahai Faith, see BP300+
195.B3-B32 Batinites (Table BP3)
195.D5-D52 Dīn-i Ilāhī (Table BP3)
Founded by Akbar, Emperor of Hindustan, 1542-1605
Druses, see BL1695
195.H3-H32 Ḥashwīya (Table BP3)
195.H8-H82 Hurufis (Table BP3)
195.I3-I32 Ibadites (Table BP3)
195.I8-I82 Ismailites (Table BP3)
195.J3-J32 Jahmīyah (Table BP3)
195.K3-K32 Karmathians (Table BP3)
195.K35-K36 Karramites. Karrāmīyah (Table BP3)
195.K38-K382 Kaysāniyah (Table BP3)
195.K4-K42 Kharijites (Table BP3)
Khojahs, see BP195.N58+
195.M6-M62 Motazilites (Table BP3)
195.M66-M67 Murīdīyah. Murids (Table BP3)
195.M7-M72 Murjites (Table BP3)
195.N58-N582 Nizārīs. Khojas (Table BP3)
195.N7-N72 Nosairians (Table BP3)
Qādiyānī, see BP195.A5+
195.S18-S182 Salafīyah (Table BP3)
195.S2-S22 Sālimīyah (Table BP3)

	Islam
	Branches, sects, and modifications
	Other (to 1900), A-Z -- Continued
195.S5-S52	Shabak (Table BP3)
195.S55-S56	Shaykhī (Table BP3)
195.S6-S62	Sifatites (Table BP3)
195.W2-W22	Wahhabis. Wahhābīyah (Table BP3)
	Yezidis, see BL1595
195.Z18-Z182	Zahirites. Ẓāhirīyah (Table BP3)
195.Z2-Z22	Zaidites (Table BP3)
195.Z54-Z542	Ẕikrī (Table BP3)
	Other, 1900-
212	Ansaru Allah Community
	Black Muslims
221.A1	Periodicals
	History
221.A4-Z3	General works
221.Z5A-Z	Local, A-Z
222	General works
223.A-Z5	Doctrines, ritual, government
223.Z6	Sermons
	Biography
223.Z8A1-Z8A5	Collective
223.Z8A6-Z8Z	Individual, A-Z
223.Z8L57	Little, Malcolm, 1925-1965
	X, Malcolm, 1925-1965, see BP223.Z8L57
232	Moorish Science Temple of America
	Nurculuk
251.A1	Periodicals
	History
251.A4-Z3	General works
251.Z5A-Z	Local, A-Z
252	General works
253.A-Z5	Doctrines, ritual, government
253.Z6	Sermons
	Biography
253.Z8A1-Z8A5	Collective
253.Z8A6-Z8Z	Individual, A-Z
	Bahai Faith
300	Periodicals
310	Societies. Institutions
	Collections. Collected works
320	Several authors
325	Individual authors
327	Dictionaries. Encyclopedias
	History
330	General works
340	Babism
	By region or country
	United States
350	General works
352.A-W	By state, A-W

Bahai Faith
History
By region or country -- Continued
355.A-Z Other regions or countries, A-Z
e.g.
Iran, see BP330
Scriptures
360 Collections and selections by more than one author
361-364 By author
Under each:
.A2 *Collected or selected works. By date*
.A3-.A4 *Translations*
.A3A-Z *English. By translator or editor, A-Z*
.A4A-Z *Other languages. By language, A-Z, and date*
.A5-.Z *Separate works, A-Z*
361 Works by the Báb
362 Works by Bahá'u'lláh
363 Works by 'Abdu'l-Bahá
364 Works of interpretation by Shoghi Effendi
365 General works
370 General special
375 Addresses, essays, etc.
377 Miscellaneous
380 Devotions. Directions, etc.
382 Messages of the Universal House of Justice
Festivals. Fasts and feasts. Days and seasons
385 General works
387.A-Z Special, A-Z
387.N38 Nawrúz
387.R53 Riḍván
388.A-Z Special topics, A-Z
388.E36 Ecology
388.E94 Evolution
388.H43 Heaven
388.J87 Justice
388.M37 Marriage
388.P73 Prayer
Biography
390 Collective
Individual
391 'Alī Muḥammad Shīrāzī, called Bāb, 1819-1850
392 Bahá'u'lláh, 1817-1892
393 'Abdu'l-Bahá
395.A-Z Other, A-Z
Temples and shrines
420 General works
420.5.A-Z By region or country, A-Z
Under each country:
.x *General works*
.x2A-Z *Special. By city, A-Z*
Theosophy
500 Periodicals

Theosophy -- Continued
509 Yearbooks
510 Societies. Institutions
e.g.
510.T52 Theosophical Society, Covina, California
Collections
520 Several authors
525 Individual authors
527 Dictionaries. Encyclopedias
528 Study and teaching. Schools
History
530 General works
By region or country
540 United States
545 Great Britain
550.A-Z Other regions or countries, A-Z
e.g.
India, see BP530
General works
Works by Helene Petrovna Blavatsky
561.A1 Collected works
561.A5-Z Individual works. By title, A-Z
563 Works by Annie Wood Besant. By title, A-Z
565.A-Z Works by other writers. By author and title, A-Z
567 General special
570 Addresses, essays, etc.
Special topics, A-Z
573.A5 Angels. Angelic communion
573.A55 Animals
573.A7 Astral body
573.A8 Aura
573.B5 Blood
573.B7 Breath
573.C2 Causal body
573.C5 Chakras
573.C7 Concentration
573.D4 Death
573.D5 Discipleship
573.E7 Etheric double
573.E8 Evolution
573.E9 Extrasensory perception
573.F46 Feminism
573.F8 Future life
573.G4 Gems
573.G6 God
573.H4 Health. Mental healing
573.H5 Hierarchies
573.H8 Human body
573.I5 Immortality
573.K3 Karma
573.M3 Man
573.M4 Memory
573.N5 Nirvana

Theosophy
Special topics, A-Z -- Continued
573.P3 Peace
573.P4 Periodicity
Philosophy of science, see BP573.S35
573.P7 Political science
573.R5 Reincarnation
573.S35 Science. Philosophy of science
573.S4 Self-preparation
573.S47 Seven rays
573.S6 Sociology
573.S95 Sun
573.T5 Thought
573.W56 Whole and parts (Philosophy)
575 Works against the Theosophists
Biography
580 Collective
585.A-Z Individual, A-Z
585.B3 Besant, Annie Wood
585.B6 Blavatsky, Helena Petrovna
585.K7 Krishnamurti, Jiddu
585.T5 Tingley, Katherine Augusta Westcott
Anthroposophy
595.A1 Periodicals. Societies. Yearbooks. Collections
595.A2 Dictionaries. Encyclopedias
History
595.A25 General works
595.A26A-Z By region or country, A-Z
595.A3-Z General works
Works by and about Rudolf Steiner
595.S894 Works. By title
Cf. B3333, Philosophical works
595.S895 Biography and criticism
596.A-Z Special topics, A-Z
596.A36 Adolescence
Astrology, see BP596.Z6
596.B47 Bereavement
596.B56 Biography (as a concept)
596.C37 Change
596.C4 Christmas. Christmas trees
596.C68 Council of Constantinople (869-870)
596.E25 Economics
Eurythmy, see BP596.R5
596.F37 Fasts and feasts. Seasonal festivals
596.F67 Forgiveness
596.F85 Future life
596.G7 Grail
596.H57 History and anthroposophy
596.I57 Interpersonal relations
596.J4 Jesus Christ
596.L67 Love
596.M37 Marxism and anthroposophy
Medicine, see RZ409.7

Anthroposophy
Special topics, A-Z -- Continued
596.M52 Middle East
596.N43 Near-death experiences
596.O73 Organic farming
596.P47 Physiology
596.R44 Reincarnation
596.R45 Religion. Religions
596.R5 Rhythm. Eurythmy
Seasonal festivals, see BP596.F37
596.S4 Second Advent
596.S54 Silica
596.S63 Soul
596.S65 Spirits
596.S66 Spiritual life
596.V5 Virtues
596.W38 Water
596.Z6 Zodiac. Astrology
596.Z66 Zoology
Biography
597.A1 Collective
597.A3-Z Individual, A-Z
e.g.
597.B3 Bauer, Michael
Steiner, Rudolf, see BP595.S895
Other beliefs and movements
Cf. BF1995+, Other beliefs and movements occult in nature
Cf. BX9998, Other beliefs and movements akin to Christianity
600 Periodicals
601 Dictionaries
602 Directories. Yearbooks
603 General works
Anti-cult movements
604 General works
604.2.A-Z By region or country, A-Z
605.A-Z Works. By movement, A-Z
605.A2 Abrahamites (Bohemia)
605.A25 Actualism
605.A33 Aetherius Society
Founded by George King, 1919-
605.A4 Ametsuchi no Kai
Ananda Cooperative Village, see BP605.S38A52
605.A617 Aquarian Educational Group
605.A62 Aquarian Foundation (Brother XII)
605.A67 Arete Truth Center
605.A7 Arica Institute
605.A77 Association for Research and Enlightenment, Virginia Beach, Va.
605.A8 Astara
Grail movement
605.B4-B49 Works by Bernhardt

	Other beliefs and movements
	Works. By movement, A-Z
	Grail movement -- Continued
605.B5	Works by other adherents
605.B52	General works. History
	Biography
605.B53	Collective
605.B54A-Z	Individual, A-Z
	e.g.
605.B54B4	Bernhardt, Oscar Ernst (Abd-ru-shin)
	Bhagwan Shree Rajneesh, see BP605.R34
605.B63	Black Hebrew Israelite Nation. African Hebrew Israelite Nation of Jerusalem
605.B64	Black Hebrews (General)
	For individual groups see the number for the group, e. g. BP605.B63, Black Hebrew Israelite Nation
605.B72	Branch Davidians
605.C38	Children of God (Movement). Family of Love
605.C42	Christ Foundation
605.C43	Christ Ministry Foundation
	Founded by Eleanore Mary Thedick, 1883-1973
605.C45	Christengemeinschaft (Friedrich Rittelmeyer)
605.C5	Christward Ministry (Newhouse)
605.C53	Church of Creative Bio-dynamics
605.C534	Church of God Unlimited
605.C54	Church of Religious Research
	Church of Religious Science, see BP605.U53
605.C55	Church of the Creator
605.C557	Church of the Path
605.C56	Church of the Truth
	Church Universal and Triumphant, see BP605.S73
605.C57	Círculo Esotérico da Comunhão do Pensamento
	Course in Miracles (Movement). Foundation for Inner Peace
605.C67	Course in miracles (Text)
605.C68	General works, commentaries, criticism, etc.
605.C74	Creative Initiative Foundation
	Dawn Horse Communion, see BP610.B8+
605.D48	Deutschgläubige Gemeinschaft
	Dianetics, see BP605.S2
605.D58	Divine Light Mission
	Divine-Love, International Society of, see BP605.I55
605.D59	Divine Revelation (Organization)
605.E27	Echerian Church
605.E3	Eckankar
605.E4	Emissaries of Divine Light
605.E57	Entity Mission
605.E73	EREVNA (Organization)
605.E84	Ethical culture movement
	Family of Love, see BP605.C38
605.F34	Faithists. John Ballou Newbrough. Oahspe
605.F44	Fellowship of Isis

Other beliefs and movements
Works. By movement, A-Z -- Continued
605.F5 Findhorn Community
Foundation for Inner Peace, see BP605.C67+
605.G44 Gentle Wind Retreat
Including the Brotherhood (Brothers and Sisters of the Inner World)
605.G68 Great White Brotherhood
Greater Community Way of Knowledge, Society for, see BP605.S58
Gurdjieff movement. Gurdjieff Foundation, "the Fourth Way," "the Work," etc.
605.G8A-Z Works by Gurdgieff. By title, A-Z
605.G9A-Z Works by other adherents, followers, etc., A-Z
605.G92 General works. History
Biography
605.G93 Collective
605.G94A-Z Individual, A-Z
e.g.
Bennett, John Godolphin, see BP610.B46+
605.G94G87 Gurdjieff, Georges Ivanovitch, 1872-1949
605.G94U75 Uspenskiĭ, P. D., 1878-1947
605.H36 Heaven's Gate
605.H4 Heimholungswerk Jesu Christi
Founded by Gabriele Wittek, 1933-
605.H5 Ḥikmati-i nuvīn
605.H58 Hohm Community
605.H6 Holy Order of Mans
605.H64 Holyearth Foundation
605.H85 Human-etisk forbund (Norway)
605.I18 I AM Religious Activity. I AM Movement
Including the Saint Germain Foundation
Institute for Research in Human Happiness, see BP605.K55
605.I44 Institute for the Development of the Harmonious Human Being
605.I45 International Community of Christ
605.I5 International Friends
605.I55 International Society of Divine-Love
605.I8 Ittōen
Founded by Nishida, Tenkō, 1872-1968
Keepers of the Flame (Fraternity), see BP605.S73
605.K55 Kōfuku no Kagaku (Organization) (The Institute for Research in Human Happiness)
605.K6 Koreshanity
Founded by Cyrus Reed Teed, 1838-1908
605.K63 Kosumomeito
605.L53 Light Institute
Founded by Chris Griscom, 1942-
605.L56 Lindisfarne Association
605.M37 Mazdaznan
605.M44 Melchizedek Synthesis Light Academy
605.M68 Movement of Spiritual Inner Awareness

Other beliefs and movements
Works. By movement, A-Z -- Continued
605.N3 Naropa Institute
605.N44 Neo-American Church
605.N46 Neo-paganism
Cf. BL432, Paganism
605.N48 New Age movement
Cf. BR128.N48, Relation of Christianity to New Age movement
New Universal Union, see BP605.H5
Newbrough, John Ballou, see BP605.F34
Noachide movement, see BP605.N63
605.N63 Noahides. Noachide movement
Cf. BM520.73, Noahide Laws
Oahspe, see BP605.F34
605.O65 Order of the Lily and the Eagle
605.O7 Ordo Arcanorum Gradalis
605.O73 Ordo Novi Templi
605.O77 Ordre du temple solaire
605.O88 Oumu Shinrikyō. Asahara, Shōkō
605.P46 Peoples Temple
Founded by Jim Jones, 1931-1978
605.P68 The Power (Society)
605.P8 Pure Life Society
Radhasoami Satsang
Including Radhasoami Satsang (Agra); Radhasoami Satsang (Beas); Radhasoami Satsang (Dayalbagh); Radhasoami Satsang (Soamibagh)
605.R33 General works
Biography
605.R333 Collective
605.R334.A-Z Individual, A-Z
605.R335 Sant Mat
Rajneesh Foundation (International). Bhagwan Shree Rajneesh
605.R34 Works by Osho (Rajneesh, Bhagwan Shree)
605.R342 General works
Biography
605.R343 Collective
605.R344A-Z Individual, A-Z
605.R35 Ramala Centre
605.R37 Ramtha School for Enlightenment
Religious Science International, see BP605.U53
605.R56 Risen Christ Foundation
605.R85 Ruhani Satsang
Founded by Kirpal Singh, 1896-1974
Including Kirpal Ruhani Satsang (Kensington, Calif.), led by Master Thakar Singh; Sant Bani Ashram (Sanbornton, N.H.), led by Sant Ajaib Singh; Sawan Kirpal Ruhani Mission, (Alexander, Va.) which recognized Sant Darshan Singh, son of Kirpal Singh, as his successor
605.S113 Sabian Assembly

	Other beliefs and movements
	Works. By movement, A-Z -- Continued
	Saint Germain Foundation, see BP605.I18
605.S116	Sangreal Sodality
605.S12	Sant Nirankari Mandal
605.S18	Le Scarabée (Association)
605.S2	Scientology. Dianetics
	Founded by L. Ron Hubbard, 1911-
	Self-Realization movement
605.S35	Periodicals
	Societies
605.S36	Self-Realization Fellowship. Yogoda. Sat-sanga Society
605.S37A-Z	Local organization, A-Z
605.S38A-Z	Other, A-Z
605.S38A52	Ananda Cooperative Village
605.S38D63	Doctrine of Truth Foundation
605.S39	History
605.S4	General works
	Cf. B132.Y6, Yoga
	Biography
605.S42	Collective
605.S43A-Z	Individual, A-Z
605.S43L9	Lynn, James Jesse
605.S43Y6	Yogananda, Paramhansa, 1893-1952
605.S49	Share International Foundation
605.S53	Shikōkai
605.S55	Shinri no Kai
	Shree Rajneesh Ashram, Pune, India, see BP605.R34+
605.S58	Society for the Greater Community Way of Knowledge
605.S6	Sōgōgaku Gakuin
605.S65	Solar Quest (Organization)
605.S66	Spiritual Frontiers Fellowship
	Spiritual Inner Awareness Movement, see BP605.M68
605.S7	Subud
605.S73	Summit Lighthouse (Group). Church Universal and Triumphant. Mark L. and Elizabeth Clare Prophet
	Including Keepers of the Flame (Fraternity)
605.S74	Sunburst Communities
	Swami Order of America
605.S8	Periodicals
605.S82-S829	Works by Swami Premananda
605.S83	Works by other adherents
605.S84	General works. History
605.S85A-Z	Local organizations, A-Z
605.S85W3	Washington, D.C. Self-Revelation Church of Absolute Monism
	Biography
605.S86	Collective
605.S87A-Z	Individual, A-Z
605.T69	True Life Foundation
605.T78	Truth Consciousness
	Founded by Swami Amar Jyoti in 1974

	Other beliefs and movements
	Works. By movement, A-Z -- Continued
605.U52	Unarius Educational Foundation. Unarius Academy of Science
605.U53	United Church of Religious Science. Religious Science International
605.U536	Universal Great Brotherhood
	Urantia Brotherhood
605.U7	Periodicals
605.U71	Official documents, governing boards, conferences
605.U72	Study and teaching
605.U73	History
	The Urantia Book
605.U74	Text
605.U75	Commentary, criticism, theology
605.U76A-Z	Topics, A-Z
605.U76S3	Science
605.U77	General works
605.U78A-Z	Local organizations, A-Z
	Biography
605.U79A1-U79A19	Collective
605.U79A2-U79Z	Individual, A-Z
605.V44	Velikoe beloe bratstvo
605.V47	Veritat Foundation
605.W48	White Brotherhood
605.W49	White Eagle Lodge
605.W67	Word Foundation
	Founded by Harold W. Percival
605.Y64	Yoga Association for Self Analysis
610	Works. By author (where name of movement cannot be determined)
610.A32-A322	Abubabaji (Table BP5)
610.A35-A352	Aïvanhov, Omraam Mikhaël (Table BP5)
	Les Amitiés spirituelles, see BP610.S43+
610.A54-A542	Andrews, Lynn V. (Table BP5)
610.B46-B462	Bennett, John Godolphin (Table BP5)
610.B8-B82	Bubba Free John, 1939- (Table BP5)
(610.C48-C482)	Chidvilasananda, Gurumayi see BL1283.792.C45
	Da Free John, see BP610.B8+
	Da Love-Ananda, Avadhoota, see BP610.B8+
610.D65-D652	Dōrizas, Dionysēs (Table BP5)
610.G37-G372	Gaskin, Stephen (Table BP5)
610.G64-G642	Goldsmith, Joel (Table BP5)
610.H35-H352	Hansadutta, Swami, 1941- (Table BP5)
	John, Bubba Free. John, Da Free, see BP610.B8+
610.K8-K82	Kushi, Michio (Table BP5)
610.L67-L672	Lorber, Jakob, 1800-1864 (Table BP5)
610.M42-M422	Meera, Mother, 1960- (Table BP5)
610.M43-M432	Meher Baba, 1894-1969 (Table BP5)
610.M65-M652	Monro, Kiyo Sasaki, 1941- (Table BP5)
	Osho, 1931-1990, see BP605.R34

	Other beliefs and movements
	Works. By author (where name or movement cannot be determined) -- Continued
610.S43-S432	Sédir, Paul, 1871-1926. Les Amitiés spirituelles (Table BP5)
610.S5-S52	Sherman, Ingrid, 1919- (Table BP5)
610.S54-S542	Shiloh, the Lightbringer, 1937- (Table BP5)
610.S75-S752	Stone, Hal (Table BP5)
610.V6-V62	Voorthuyzen, Louwrens (the man and his following) (Table BP5)
610.Y34-Y342	Yahweh Ben Yahweh (Table BP5)

Buddhism
Periodicals (General)
For works limited to a particular country, see BQ251+
For works limited to a sect, see BQ7001+
1 Polyglot
2 English
3 Chinese
4 French
5 German
6 Japanese
8.A-Z Other languages, A-Z
10 Yearbooks (General)
Societies, councils, associations, clubs, etc.
For works limited to a sect, see BQ7530
International (General)
12 General works. History
14 Young Buddhist associations
16 Young men's associations
18 Women's associations
20.A-Z Individual associations, councils, etc., A-Z
Under each:
.x *Periodicals. Yearbooks*
.x2 *Congresses. Conferences. Documents. By date*
.x3 *Directories*
.x4 *General works. History*
.x5 *Biography (Collective)*
.x6A-Z *National branches. By country, A-Z*
20.A74-A746 Asian Buddhist Conference for Peace
20.E8-E86 European Congress
20.I58-I586 International Buddhist Conference (International Brotherhood Association)
20.W5-W56 World Buddhist Sangha Council
Headquarters in Colombo, Sri Lanka
20.W6-W66 World Buddhist Union
Headquarters in Seoul, Korea
20.W7-W76 World Fellowship of Buddhists
Headquarters in Bangkok, Thailand
By region or country
Asia
India
21 General works. History
22.A-Z Local, A-Z
23.A-Z Individual societies, A-Z
Sri Lanka
24 General works. History
25.A-Z Local, A-Z
26.A-Z Individual societies, A-Z
Burma
27 General works. History
28.A-Z Local, A-Z
29.A-Z Individual societies, A-Z
Thailand

Societies, councils, associations, clubs, etc.
By region or country
Asia
Thailand -- Continued
31 General works. History
32.A-Z Local, A-Z
33.A-Z Individual societies, A-Z
Vietnam
34 General works. History
35.A-Z Local, A-Z
36.A-Z Individual societies, A-Z
Malaysia
37 General works. History
38.A-Z Local, A-Z
39.A-Z Individual societies, A-Z
Indonesia
41 General works. History
42.A-Z Local, A-Z
43.A-Z Individual societies, A-Z
China
44 General works. History
45.A-Z Local, A-Z
46.A-Z Individual societies, A-Z
Korea
47 General works. History
48.A-Z Local, A-Z
49.A-Z Individual societies, A-Z
Japan
50 General works. History
51.A-Z Local, A-Z
52.A-Z Individual societies, A-Z
53.A-Z Other Asian countries, A-Z
Under each country:
.x *General works*
.x2A-Z *Local, A-Z*
.x3A-Z *Individual societies, A-Z*
Europe
Great Britain
Including Sangha Sabhā (Council) of the United Kingdom
54 General works. History
55.A-Z Local, A-Z
56.A-Z Individual societies, A-Z
Belgium
57 General works. History
58.A-Z Local, A-Z
59.A-Z Individual societies, A-Z
France
61 General works. History
62.A-Z Local, A-Z
63.A-Z Individual societies, A-Z
Germany
64 General works. History

	Societies, councils, associations, clubs, etc.
	By region or country
	Europe
	Germany -- Continued
65.A-Z	Local, A-Z
66.A-Z	Individual societies, A-Z
	Netherlands
67	General works. History
68.A-Z	Local, A-Z
69.A-Z	Individual societies, A-Z
	Sweden
71	General works. History
72.A-Z	Local, A-Z
73.A-Z	Individual societies, A-Z
	Russia
74	General works. History
75.A-Z	Local, A-Z
76.A-Z	Individual societies, A-Z
77.A-Z	Other European countries, A-Z
	Apply table at BQ53.A-Z
78	Africa
78.A1	General works. History
78.A2A-Z	Local, A-Z
78.A3-Z	Individual societies, A-Z
	America
	United States
	Including Hawaii and Alaska
81	General works. History
82.A-Z	Local, A-Z
83.A-Z	Individual societies, A-Z
	Canada
84	General works. History
85.A-Z	Local, A-Z
86.A-Z	Individual societies, A-Z
	Brazil
87	General works. History
88.A-Z	Local, A-Z
89.A-Z	Individual societies, A-Z
90.A-Z	Other American countries, A-Z
	Apply table at BQ53.A-Z
91	Australia
91.A1	General works. History
91.A2A-Z	Local, A-Z
91.A3-Z	Individual societies, A-Z
92	New Zealand
92.A1	General works. History
92.A2A-Z	Local, A-Z
92.A3-Z	Individual societies, A-Z
93	Pacific islands
	For works dealing with Hawaii, see BQ81+
93.A1	General works. History
93.A2A-Z	Local, A-Z
93.A3-Z	Individual societies, A-Z

Financial institutions. Trusts
96 General works. History
98 General special
99.A-Z By country, A-Z
Under each country:
.x *General works. History*
.x2A-Z *Local, A-Z*
.x3A-Z *Individual, A-Z*
Bibliography, see Z7860+
Congresses. Conferences (General)
For works limited to a sect, see BQ7001+
For councils of a specific period, see the period in BQ286+
100 General works
102 Organization, methods, etc.
Directories (General)
For directories limited to a sect, see BQ7001+
For individual associations, see BQ12+
104 International
105.A-Z By region or country, A-Z
Under each country:
.x *General*
.x2A-Z *Local, A-Z*
Museums. Exhibitions
107 General works
109.A-Z By region or country, A-Z
Under each country:
.x *General works*
.x2-.x3 *By city*
.x2 *General*
.x3A-Z *Individual museums, A-Z*
General collections. Collected works
Several authors
Comprehensive volumes
115 Early works through 1800
118 1801-
120 Minor collections. Collected essays. Festschriften
122 Selections. Excerpts
124-126 Individual authors
For individual works of Pali and Sanskrit writers in the Tripiṭaka, see BQ1170+
For works by founders (original and local) and other important leaders of sects, see BQ7001+
For individual works other than Pāli and Sanskrit originals, see the subject
Under each:
.x *Collected works. By date*
.xA-Z *Translations. By language, A-Z*
.x2A-Z *Addresses, essays, etc. By title, A-Z*
124 Authors through 1800
126 1801-
128 Encyclopedias (General)
For encyclopedias limited to a sect, see BQ7001+

130 Dictionaries (General)
For dictionaries limited to a sect, see BQ7001+
133 Terminology
135 Questions and answers. Maxims (General)
For works limited to a sect, see BQ7001+
Religious education (General)
Cf. BQ5251+, Education for the ministry (General)
Cf. BQ7001+, Works limited to a sect
Cf. LC921+, General education managed by Buddhist institutions
Periodicals. Yearbooks. Societies
141 Polyglot
142 English
143 Chinese
144 French
145 German
146 Japanese
148.A-Z Other languages, A-Z
150 Conventions, conferences, etc.
152 Collections
154 Encyclopedias. Dictionaries
156 Theory, philosophy, etc.
158 Methods of study and teaching
158.5 Aids and devices
160 History (General)
162.A-Z By region or country, A-Z
Under each country:
.x *General works. History*
.x2A-Z *Local, A-Z*
164 Biography (Collective)
General works
166 Early works through 1945
167 1946-
168 General special
169 Addresses, essays, lectures, etc.
Religious education of the young. Sunday schools, etc.
For works limited to a sect, see BQ7001+
Periodicals. Societies. Serials
171 Polyglot
172 English
173 Chinese
174 French
175 German
176 Japanese
178.A-Z Other languages, A-Z
180 Congresses
182 History
184 General works
186 General special
188 Methods of teaching, organization
190 Aids and devices
192 Textbooks for children

Religious education (General)
Religious education of
the young. Sunday schools, etc. -- Continued
194 Teachers' manuals
196 Stories, catechisms, etc.
198 Teacher training
199.A-Z By region or country, A-Z
Under each country:
.x *General works. History*
.x2A-Z *Local, A-Z*
.x3A-Z *Individual schools, including monasteries and temples, A-Z*
Religious education in the home
200 General works
202 General special
204 History
209.A-Z By region or country, A-Z
Apply table at BQ162.A-Z
Research
Class here works limited to methodology and programs
210 General works. International
219.A-Z By region or country, A-Z
Apply table at BQ162.A-Z
Antiquities. Archaeology
Class here works limited to religious points of view only
For descriptive works, see Subclass DS
Periodicals. Societies. Collections
221 Polyglot
222 English
223 Chinese
224 French
225 German
226 Japanese
228.A-Z Other languages, A-Z
230 Dictionaries
232 General works. Methodology
236 General special
239.A-Z By region or country, A-Z
Under each country:
.x *General works. History*
.x2A-Z *By province, A-Z*
.x3A-Z *By city, A-Z*
Literary discoveries
240 General works. History and criticism
242 General special

Antiquities. Archaeology
Literary discoveries -- Continued
244.A-Z Individual, A-Z
Under each:
.x *Collections*
.x2 *Original texts (including facsimiles). By date*
.x35A-Z *Translations (with or without original text). By language, A-Z, and date*
.x4 *General works. Criticism, etc.*
Dunhuang manuscripts, see BQ244.T8+
244.G35-G354 Gandhara manuscripts
244.G5-G54 Gilgit manuscripts
244.T8-T84 Tun-huang (Dunhuang) manuscripts
Inscriptions, etc.
Class here works limited to religious points of view only
For Aśoka inscriptions, see PK1480+
For philological works, see Subclasses PK and PL
246 General works. History and criticism
248 General special
249.A-Z By region or country, A-Z
Under each country:
.x *General works*
.x2A-Z *Local, A-Z*
.x3A-Z *Individual inscriptions, A-Z*
History
Periodicals. Societies. Serials
251 Polyglot
252 English
253 Chinese
254 French
255 German
256 Japanese
258.A-Z Other languages, A-Z
260 Collections. Collected works. Sources
For works limited to a sect, see BQ7001+
General works
262 Early works through 1800
Including history written by Bu-ston
264 1801-1945
266 1946-
270 General special
272 Textbooks, compends, etc.
274 Outlines, syllabi, chronological tables, etc.
276 Popular works
277 Juvenile works
278 Addresses, essays, lectures, etc.
280 Historiography
282 Philosophy
284 Biography of historians (Collective)
By period

History
By period -- Continued
286 Early and medieval (Early to ca. 1200 A.D.)
Including Buddhist history of India to ca. 1200 A.D.
287 Early to rise of Mahayana Buddhism (ca. 100 A.D.)
288 Origin of Buddhism
289 Ca. 486 B.C.-ca. 100 A.D. (Early Buddhism and Hinayana Abhidharma to the rise of Mahayana Buddhism)
Early Councils
290 General works
291 First Council (Rājagṛha) ca. 486 B.C.
292 Second Council (Vaiśālī) ca. 380 B.C.
293 Third Council (Pāṭaliputra) ca. 246 B.C.
Fourth Council (Kaśmīra), see BQ304
295 Aśoka, Mauryan king, ca. 264-227 B.C., and Buddhism
For biography, see DS451.5
296 First missionaries to foreign lands (General)
By country, see BQ365, etc.
Inscriptions, see BQ246+
298 Menander, Indo-Greek king, fl. 150 B.C. and Buddhism
Cf. BQ2610+, Milindapañhā
300 Ca. 100-ca. 550 A.D. (Development of Mahayana Buddhism and the introduction of Buddhism to other parts of Asia
Kaniṣka, Kushan emperor, ca. 144-170, and Buddhism
302 General works
304 Fourth Council (Kaśmīra) ca. 150
306 Ca. 550-ca. 1200 (Rise of Tantric Buddhism and the decline of Buddhism in India)
308 Harṣavardhana, King of Thānesar and Kanauj, fl. 606-647, and Buddhism
Modern (ca. 1200-)
310 General works
312 ca. 1200-1850
1850-1945
314 General works
315 Fifth Council (Mandalay) 1868-1871
1945-
316 General works
317 Sixth Council (Rangoon) 1954-1956
By region or country
Asia
General, see BQ251+
South Asia
320 Periodicals. Collections, etc. Sources
General works
Early through 1800, see BQ262

History
By region or country
Asia
South Asia
General works -- Continued
322 1801-
325 General special
327 Addresses, essays, lectures, etc.
328 Biography (Collective)
Special regions or countries
India
330 Periodicals. Collections, etc. Sources
General works
332 Early works through 1800
334 1801-1946
336 1947-
339 General special
340 Addresses, essays, lectures
342 Biography (Collective)
By period
Early to 1203 A.D , see BQ286+
344 1204-1761 (Muslim era)
345 1761-1947 (British era)
346 1947-
349.A-Z Local, A-Z
e.g.
349.J35 Jammu and Kashmir
349.L27 Ladākh
349.S57 Sikkim
Sri Lanka
350 Periodicals. Collections, etc. Sources
General works
352 Early works through 1800
Cf. BQ2570+, Dāthāvaṃsa
Cf. BQ2580+, Dīpavaṃsa
Cf. BQ2600+, Mahāvaṃsa
354 1801-1947
356 1948-
359 General special
360 Addresses, essays, lectures
362 Biography (Collective)
By period
364 Early to 1153, the end of Cholas rule
365 First missionaries to Sri Lanka, 3rd century, B.C.
366 Buddhaghosa and his activities
367 Cholas invasion, 1073
Including Cholas rule
369 1153-1505 (Restoration of Buddhism)
372 1505-1850 (European era)
374 1850-1948 (Buddhist revival)
376 1948-
379.A-Z Local, A-Z

History
By region or country
Asia
South Asia
Special regions or countries -- Continued
Nepal
380 Periodicals. Societies. Serials
382 General works
384 General special
386 Addresses, essays, lectures
388 Biography (Collective)
By period
390 Early to 1846
392 1846-1951 (Rana period)
394 1951-
396.A-Z Local, A-Z
400.A-Z Other regions or countries, A-Z
Subarrange each country by Table BQ10
400.A5-A55 Afghanistan (Table BQ10)
400.B3-B35 Bangladesh (Table BQ10)
400.B5-B55 Bhutan (Table BQ10)
400.H542 Himalaya region
(400.K37) Kashmir
see BQ349.J35
(400.L33) Ladākh
see BQ349.L27
400.P3-P35 Pakistan (Table BQ10)
For history to 1946, see BQ330+
(400.S5) Sikkim
see BQ349.S57
Southeast Asia
402 Periodicals. Collections, etc. Sources
General works
406 Early works through 1800
408 1801-
410 General special
412 Addresses, essays, lectures
414 Biography (Collective)
Special regions or countries
Burma
416 Periodicals. Collections, etc. Sources
418 General works
420 General special
422 Addresses, essays, lectures
424 Biography (Collective)
By period
426 Early to 1044
428 1044-1287 (Pegan dynasty to Mongol invasion)
430 1287-1486 (Shan period)
432 1486-1752 (Toungoo dynasty)
434 1752-1885 (Alaungpaya dynasty)
436 1885-1948 (British era)

History
By region or country
Asia
Southeast Asia
Special regions or countries
Burma
By period -- Continued
438 1948-
439.A-Z Local, A-Z
Indochina
440 Periodicals. Collections, etc. Sources
442 General works
444 General special
446 Addresses, essays, lectures
448 Biography (Collective)
Special regions or countries
Cambodia
450 Periodicals. Collections, etc. Sources
452 General works
454 General special
456 Addresses, essays, lectures
458 Biography (Collective)
By period
460 Early to 1432
Including Khmer era
462 1432-1864 (Thai era)
464 1864-1949 (French era)
466 1949-
469.A-Z Local, A-Z
Laos
470 Periodicals. Collections, etc. Sources
472 General works
474 General special
476 Addresses, essays, lectures
478 Biography (Collective)
By period
480 Early to 1885
482 1885-1946 (French era)
484 1946-
489.A-Z Local, A-Z
Vietnam
Including the former South Vietnam
For material concerned with the former North Vietnam, see BQ509.N6
490 Periodicals. Collections, etc. Sources
492 General works
494 General special
496 Addresses, essays, lectures
498 Biography (Collective)
By period
500 Early to 939 (Chinese era)
502 939-1787
504 1787-1945 (French era)

History
By region or country
Asia
Southeast Asia
Special regions or countries
Indochina
Special regions or countries
Vietnam
By period -- Continued
506 1945-
509.A-Z Local, A-Z
e.g.
509.N6 North Vietnam
Indonesia
510 Periodicals. Collections, etc. Sources
512 General works
514 General special
516 Addresses, essays, lectures
518 Biography (Collective)
By region
Bali
520 Periodicals. Collections, etc. Sources
522 General works
524 General special
526 Biography (Collective)
Java
530 Periodicals. Collections, etc. Sources
532 General works
534 General special
536 Biography (Collective)
538.A-Z Local, A-Z
539.A-Z Other local, A-Z
Malaysia. Malaya
540 Periodicals. Collections, etc. Sources
542 General works
544 General special
546 Addresses, essays, lectures
548 Biography (Collective)
549.A-Z Local, A-Z
For material concerned with Singapore, see BQ569.S5+
Thailand (Siam)
550 Periodicals. Collections, etc. Sources
552 General works
554 General special
555 Addresses, essays, lectures
556 Biography (Collective)
By period
558 Early to 1238
560 1238-1350 (Sukhōthai period)
562 1350-1782 ('Ayutthayā period)
Including Thonburī period 1767-1782
564 1782-1932 (Rattanakōsin (Bangkok) period)

History
By region or country
Asia
Southeast Asia
Special regions or countries
Thailand (Siam)
By period -- Continued
566 1932-
568.A-Z Local, A-Z
569.A-Z Other regions or countries, A-Z
Subarrange each country by Table BQ10
569.M342 Malay Archipelago
569.P5-P55 Philippine Islands (Table BQ10)
569.S5-S55 Singapore (Table BQ10)
Central Asia
570 Periodicals. Collections, etc. Sources
572 General works
574 General special
576 Addresses, essays, lectures
579 Biography (Collective)
Special regions or countries
Mongolia. Mongolian People's Republic. Outer Mongolia
580 Periodicals. Collections, etc. Sources
582 General works
584 General special
586 Addresses, essays, lectures
588 Biography (Collective)
By period
590 Early to 1260
591 1260-1578
593 1578-1750
595 1750-1924
597 1924-
599.A-Z Local, A-Z
For material concerned with Inner Mongolia, see BQ649.I7
Tibet, see BQ7530+
609.A-Z Other regions or countries, A-Z
Including ancient kingdoms of Central Asia
Subarrange each country by Table BQ10
609.K52 Khotan
609.K8 Kucha
609.L6 Lou-lan
609.S6 Soviet Central Asia
Far East
610 Periodicals. Collections, etc. Sources
General works
612 Early works through 1800
614 1801-
616 General special
618 Addresses, essays, lectures
619 Biography (Collective)

History
By region or country
Asia
Far East -- Continued
Special countries
China
620 Periodicals. Collections, etc. Sources
General works
622 Early works through 1800
624 1801-1948
626 1949-
628 General special
630.A-Z Special topics, A-Z
630.K8 Ku-i Buddhism
632 Addresses, essays, lectures
634 Biography (Collective)
By period
636 Early to 581 A.D.
638 581-960 (Sui, Tang and Five dynasties)
640 960-1368 (Song and Yuan dynasties)
641 1368-1644 (Ming dynasty)
643 1644-1912 (Manchu (Qing) dynasty)
645 1912-1949
647 1949-
649.A-Z Local, A-Z
Dunhuang, see BQ649.T86
Formosa, see BQ649.T32
649.H6 Hong Kong
649.I7 Inner Mongolia
649.M3 Manchuria
649.T32 Taiwan. Formosa
649.T86 Tun-huang. Dunhuang
Korea. South Korea
650 Periodicals. Collections, etc. Sources
General works
652 Early works through 1800
654 1801-1945
656 1946-
658 General special
659 Addresses, essays, lectures
660 Biography (Collective)
By period
661 Early to 935 A.D.
Including Silla Kingdom
662 935-1392 (Koryŏ (Koryu) period)
664 1392-1910 (I (Yi) dynasty)
665 1910-1945 (Chōsen. Japanese era)
667 1945-
669.A-Z Local, A-Z
e.g.
669.N6 North Korea
Japan
670 Periodicals. Collections, etc. Sources

History
By region or country
Asia
Far East
Special countries
Japan -- Continued
General works
672 Early works through 1800
674 1801-1945
676 1946-
678 General special
680.A-Z Special topics, A-Z
680.H6 Honji Suijaku
Cf. BL2222.23, Relations to Shinto
680.W65 Women
682 Addresses, essays, lectures
683 Biography (Collective)
By period
684 Early to 794 A.D.
685 794-1185 (Heian period)
687 1185-1600 (Kamakura through Momoyama period)
689 1600-1868 (Tokugawa period)
1868-
691 General
693 1868-1912
20th century
695 General
697 1945-
699.A-Z Local, A-Z
Europe
700 Periodicals. Collections, etc. Sources
702 General works
704 General special
706 Addresses, essays, lectures
708 Biography (Collective)
709.A-Z By region or country, A-Z
Subarrange each country by Table BQ10
Africa
710 Periodicals. Collections, etc. Sources
712 General works. History
714 General special
716 Addresses, essays, lectures
718 Biography (Collective)
719.A-Z By region or country, A-Z
Subarrange each country by Table BQ10
America
Including both North and South America
720 Periodicals. Collections, etc. Sources
722 General works
724 General special
726 Addresses, essays, lectures
728 Biography (Collective)

History
By region or country
America -- Continued
Special countries
United States
730 Periodicals. Collections, etc. Sources
732 General works
734 General special
736 Addresses, essays, lectures
738 Biography (Collective)
739.A-Z By region or state, A-Z
e.g.
Subarrange each state by Table BQ10
739.C2-C25 California (Table BQ10)
739.H2-H25 Hawaii (Table BQ10)
Canada
740 Periodicals. Collections, etc. Sources
742 General works
744 General special
746 Addresses, essays, lectures
748 Biography (Collective)
749.A-Z By region or province, A-Z
Subarrange each province by Table BQ10
Brazil
750 Periodicals. Collections, etc. Sources
752 General works
754 General special
756 Addresses, essays, lectures
758 Biography (Collective)
759.A-Z By region or state, A-Z
Subarrange each state by Table BQ10
760.A-Z Other American regions or countries, A-Z
Subarrange each country by Table BQ10
Australia
770 Periodicals. Collections, etc. Sources
772 General works
774 General special
776 Addresses, essays, lectures
778 Biography (Collective)
779.A-Z By state or territory, A-Z
Subarrange each state or territory by Table BQ10
New Zealand
780 Periodicals. Collections, etc. Sources
782 General works
784 General special
786 Addresses, essays, lectures
788 Biography (Collective)
789.A-Z By island or district, A-Z
Subarrange each island or district by Table BQ10
Pacific islands
790 Periodicals. Collections, etc. Sources
792 General works
794 General special

History
By region or country
Pacific islands -- Continued
796 Addresses, essays, lectures
798 Biography (Collective)
799.A-Z By island groups, A-Z
Subarrange each island group by Table BQ10
Persecutions
For classification with individual modifications, schools, etc., see BQ7001+
800 Collections
810 General works
815 General special
820 History
829.A-Z By region or country, A-Z
Apply table at BQ162.A-Z
Biography
Collective
Cf. BQ164, Educators
Cf. BQ284, Historians
Cf. BQ900+, Gautama Buddha's disciples
Cf. BQ7920+, Lamaists
For special modifications, sects, etc., see BQ7001+
840 General works
843 Monks. Priests. Novices. Bhikṣu. Bhikkhu
Laymen, see BQ840
846 Upāsaka (Men believers)
Women
850 General works
855 Nuns. Bhikṣunī. Bhikkunī
858 Upāsikā (Women believers)
Individual
Gautama Buddha
General works
For Buddhakāya, see BQ4180
For Sakyamuni Buddha, see BQ4690.S3+
860 Early works through 1200
For Avadānas, see BQ1530+
For Jātakas, see BQ1460+
Gautama Buddha in the Tripiṭaka
865 History and criticism
Individual texts, see BQ1300.A+
868 1201-1800
1801-1945
871 Polyglot
872 English
873 Chinese
874 French
875 German
876 Japanese
878.A-Z Other languages, A-Z
1946-
881 Polyglot

Biography
Individual
Gautama Buddha
General works
1946- -- Continued
882 English
883 Chinese
884 French
885 German
886 Japanese
888.A-Z Other languages, A-Z
890 Pictorial works
892 Juvenile works
893 Popular works
894 General special
895 Addresses, essays, lectures
897 Historiography
899 Chronology
Disciples. Friends and associates
900 Collective
905.A-Z Individual, A-Z
905.N2 Nanda
e.g.
905.N2A7 Saundarananda (by Aśvaghoṣa)
910 His attitude toward contemporary religions or philosophies
912 Sermons about the life of Gautama Buddha
915 Selections of his sayings and teachings. Parables
Class here descriptive works only
For doctrinal works on his teachings, see BQ4061+
918.A-Z Special topics, A-Z
918.G6 God
Cultus
920 General works
Special topics
922 Footprints
923 Iconography. Physical attributes
Class here works limited to religious points of view only
Cf. N8193.2, Gautama Buddha in art
924 Relics
925 Stūpas
Including descriptive works on Stūpa worship
Cf. BQ6460+, Sacred shrines in India, etc.
For works concerned with the meaning of the Stūpa, see BQ5125.S8
927 Symbolism
929.A-Z Other, A-Z
929.P7 Prophecies
Special events

Biography
Individual
Gautama Buddha
Special events -- Continued
930 Former lives (mythological)
932 Birth. Youth. Married life
933 Family
934 Renunciation and ascetic life
935 Enlightenment
937 First sermon and deliverance of teachings
Including life with followers
For works limited to doctrines, see BQ4180+
938 Last years. Last illness. Death (Pari-nirvana). Cremation
939.A-Z Other, A-Z
Other individuals
The number for the individual is determined by the letter following the letter or letters for which each class number stands
For works limited to the disciples of Gautama Buddha, see BQ900+
For works limited to founders and important persons of individual sects, see the sect
940 A
942 B
944 Ca - Cg
946 Ch
948 Ci - Cz
950 D
952 E
954 Fa - Ft
956 Fu
958 Fv - Fz
960 G
962 H
964 I
966 J
968 K
970 L
972 M
974 N
976 O
978 P
980 Q
982 R
984 Sa - Sg
986 Sh
988 Si - Sz
990 T
992 U
994 V
995 Wa
996 Wb - Wz

Biography
Individual
Other individuals -- Continued
997 X
998 Y
999 Z
Buddhist literature
For devotional literature, see BQ5535+
For works limited to a particular sect, see BQ7001+
Periodicals. Societies. Serials
1001 Polyglot
1002 English
1003 Chinese
1004 French
1005 German
1006 Japanese
1008.A-Z Other languages, A-Z
1010 Dictionaries
Collections. Collected works
1011 Polyglot
1012 English
1013 Chinese
1014 French
1015 German
1016 Japanese
1018.A-Z Other languages, A-Z
Individual works, see BQ4000+
1020 History and criticism
1029.A-Z By region or country, A-Z
Under each country:
.x *Collections*
.x2 *History and criticism*
Juvenile works
Collections
1031 Polyglot
1032 English
1033 Chinese
1034 French
1035 German
1036 Japanese
1038.A-Z Other languages, A-Z
Individual works
See the subject, especially the special numbers for juvenile works, e.g., BQ4032
1040 History and criticism
1045.A-Z By region or country, A-Z
Apply table at BQ1029.A-Z

Tripiṭaka (Canonical literature)
Class here texts originally transmitted (though not necessarily extant) in Pali, Sanskrit, or Prakrit (including translations and commentaries) as well as anonymous sutras originally written in Tibetan, Chinese, etc.
This classification schedule does not reflect the internal organization of any one version or edition, but it is rather a practical working synthesis

1100 Collections. Collected works
1105 General works
1107 General special
1110 Introductions. Popular works
1112 Addresses, essays, lectures, etc.
1113 Origins and development. History
1115 Philological studies
1115.5 Hermeneutics. Exegetics. Principles of interpretation
History of publication
1117 General works
1118 General special
1119.A-Z By region or country, A-Z
History of translation
1120 General works
Bibliography, see Z7862+
1122.A-Z By region or country, A-Z
1124.A-Z By language, A-Z
Preservation of manuscripts, books, etc. Kyōzō
1126 General works
1128 General special
e.g. Mainōkyō, kyōzuka, kyōzutsu
1129.A-Z By region or country, A-Z
Under each country:
.x *General works*
.x2A-Z *Local, A-Z*
1130 Dictionaries, indexes, etc.
Biography in the Tripiṭaka (Collective)
1132.A1 Dictionaries
1132.A2-Z General works. Sermons on characters
1133.A-Z Special classes, groups, etc., A-Z
1133.W6 Women
1136.A-Z Special topics, A-Z
1136.C6 Copying
1136.N38 Natural history
1136.P35 Parables
1136.P56 Plants
1138 General collections or selections from the Tripiṭaka not related to a special piṭaka or version
By piṭaka
Class here general editions, commentaries, etc., covering more than one version
1140-1149 Sūtrapiṭaka (Table BQ1)
1150-1159 Vinayapiṭaka (Table BQ1)

Tripiṭaka (Canonical literature)
By piṭaka -- Continued
1160-1169 Abhidharmapiṭaka (Table BQ1)
By version
1170-1179 Pali version (Tipiṭaka) (Table BQ1)
1180-1189 Vinayapiṭaka (Table BQ1)
1190-1199 Suttapiṭaka (Table BQ1)
1200-1209 Abhidhammapiṭaka (Table BQ1)
1210-1219 Chinese version (Da zang jing) (Table BQ1)
Including those works composed in Korea and Japan
1220-1229 Jing zang (Sūtrapiṭaka) (Table BQ1)
1230-1239 Lü zang (Vinayapiṭaka) (Table BQ1)
1240-1249 Lun zang (Abhidharmapiṭaka) (Table BQ1)
1250-1259 Tibetan version (Table BQ1)
1260-1269 Kanjur. Bkaḥ-ḥgyur (Table BQ1)
1270-1279 Tanjur. Bstan-ḥgyur (Table BQ1)
Divisions not limited to a particular linguistic version
Sūtrapiṭaka
1280-1289 Early Buddhist suttas (Table BQ1)
Class here the five Nikāyas or four Āgamas which include the nine or twelve Aṅgas
The originals are mainly in Pali. As this classification is based on the Pali version, individual texts in the Chinese version should be converted according to the catalog by Akanuma, Chizen: Kan-Pa shibu shiagon goshōroku. The comparative catalog of Chinese Āgamas and Pāli Nikāyas.
1290-1299 Dīghanikāya (Table BQ1)
1295 Early commentaries
e.g. Sumaṅgalavilāsinī (by Buddhaghosa)
1295.5.A-Z Major divisions, A-Z
Mahāvagga, see BQ2370+
1295.5.P35-P359 Pāṭikavagga (Table BQ3)
1295.5.S65-S659 Sīlakkhandha (Table BQ3)
1300.A-Z Individual suttas, A-Z
1300.A35-A359 Aggaññasutta (Table BQ3)
1300.A45-A459 Ambaṭṭha sutta (Table BQ3)
1300.B73-B739 Brahmajālasutta (Table BQ3)
1300.C35-C359 Catuṣapariṣatsūtra (Table BQ3)
1300.M33-M339 Mahānidānasutta (Table BQ3)
1300.M34-M349 Mahāpadānasutta (Table BQ3)
1300.M35-M359 Mahāparinibbānasutta (Table BQ3)
1300.M36-M369 Mahāsatipaṭṭhānasutta (Table BQ3)
1300.M37-M379 Mahāsudassanasutta (Table BQ3)
1300.M38-M389 Mahātaṇhāsaṅkhayasutta (Table BQ3)
1300.P68-P689 Poṭṭhapādasutta (Table BQ3)
1300.S25-S259 Sāmaññaphalasutta (Table BQ3)
1300.S27-S279 Sampasādaniyasutta (Table BQ3)
1300.S56-S569 Siṅgalovadāsutta (Table BQ3)
1310-1319 Majjhimanikāya (Table BQ1)

	Tripiṭaka (Canonical literature)
	By version
	Divisions not limited to a particular linguistic version
	Sūtrapiṭaka
	Early Buddhist suttas
	Majjhimanikāya -- Continued
1319.5.A-Z	Major divisions, A-Z
1319.5.M34-M349	Majjhimapaṇṇāsa (Table BQ3)
1319.5.M84-M849	Mūlapaṇṇāsa (Table BQ3)
1319.5.U62-U629	Uparipaṇṇāsa (Table BQ3)
1320.A-Z	Individual suttas, A-Z
1320.A42-A429	Alagaddūpama Sutta (Table BQ3)
1320.A48-A489	Ānāpānasatisutta (Table BQ3)
1320.A53-A539	Aṅgulimāla Sutta (Table BQ3)
1320.C85-C859	Cūlamālunkyasuttanta (Table BQ3)
1320.I53-I539	Indriyabhāvanāsutta (Table BQ3)
1320.M34-M349	Mahācattārisakasutta (Table BQ3)
1320.S25-S259	Satipaṭṭhānasutta (Table BQ3)
1320.U63-U639	Upālisutta (Table BQ3)
1320.V35-V359	Vammīkasutta (Table BQ3)
1330-1339	Saṃyuttanikāya (Table BQ1)
1339.3.A-Z	Major divisions, A-Z
1339.3.S4-S49	Saḷāytanavagga (Table BQ3)
1339.5.A-Z	Individual suttas, A-Z
1339.5.A52-A529	Anattalakkhaṇasutta (Table BQ3)
1339.5.B54-B549	Bhārasutta (Table BQ3)
1339.5.B72-B729	Brahmāsutta (Table BQ3)
1339.5.D45-D459	Dhammacakkapavattana Sutta (Table BQ3)
1339.5.V45-V459	Verahaccānisutta (Table BQ3)
1340-1349	Anguttaranikāya (Table BQ1)
1349.5.A-Z	Individual suttas, A-Z
1349.5.G57-G579	Girimānanda Sutta (Table BQ3)
1349.5.K35-K359	Kālakārāma Sutta (Table BQ3)
1349.5.M43-M439	Mettāsutta (Table BQ3)
1350-1359	Khuddakanikāya (Table BQ1)
1360-1369	Khuddakapāṭha (Table BQ1)
1369.5.A-Z	Individual suttas, A-Z
1369.5.M35-M359	Maṅgalasutta (Table BQ3)
1369.5.N48-N489	Netti (Table BQ3)
1370-1379	Dhammapada (Table BQ1)
1375	Early commentaries e.g. Dhammapadaṭṭhakathā
1380-1389	Udānavarga (by Dharmatrāta) (Table BQ1)
1389.5.A-Z	Other versions, A-Z
1389.5.F32-F329	Fa ju pi yu jing (Table BQ3)
1390-1399	Udāna (Table BQ1)
1400-1409	Itivuttaka (Table BQ1)
1410-1419	Suttanipāta (Table BQ1)
1419.5.A-Z	Individual suttas, A-Z
1419.5.A45-A459	Āḷavakasutta (Table BQ3)
1419.5.A86-A869	Aṭṭhakavagga (Table BQ3)

Tripiṭaka (Canonical literature)
By version
Divisions not limited to a particular linguistic version
Sūtrapiṭaka
Early Buddhist suttas
Khuddakanikāya
Suttanipāta
Individual suttas, A-Z -- Continued
1419.5.H45-H459 Hemavatasutta (Table BQ3)
1419.5.K48-K489 Khaggavisāṇasutta (Table BQ3)
1419.5.P36-P369 Pārāyanasutta (Table BQ3)
1419.5.U72-U729 Uragasutta (Table BQ3)
1420-1429 Vimānavatthu (Table BQ1)
1430-1439 Petavatthu (Table BQ1)
1440-1449 Theragāthā (Table BQ1)
1450-1459 Therīgāthā (Table BQ1)
1460-1469 Jātakas (Table BQ1)
Including Jātakamāla (by Āryaśūra)
1470.A-Z Individual Jātakas. By title, A-Z
1470.C34-C349 Candakumārajātaka (Table BQ3)
1470.D35-D359 Dasarathajātaka (Table BQ3)
1470.G53-G539 Ghāsī Vimaladattajātaka (Table BQ3)
1470.K33-K339 Kacchapajātaka (Table BQ3)
1470.M35-M359 Mahā Ummagga Jātaka (Table BQ3)
1470.M3594-M35949 Mahājanakajātaka (Table BQ3)
1470.M362-M3629 Mahākapijātaka (Table BQ3)
1470.M365-M3659 Mahāsutasomajātaka (Table BQ3)
1470.M367-M3679 Makhādevajātaka (Table BQ3)
1470.M38-M389 Maṇicūḍajātaka (Table BQ3)
1470.N53-N539 Nidānakathā (Table BQ3)
1470.N55-N559 Nigrodhamigajātaka (Table BQ3)
1470.P35-P359 Paññāsajātaka (Table BQ3)
1470.R63-R639 Rohinījātaka (Table BQ3)
1470.S26-S269 Sarvānanda (Table BQ3)
1470.S27-S279 Sasajātaka (Table BQ3)
1470.S65-S659 Sonanandajātaka (Table BQ3)
1470.S93-S939 Sudhābhojanajātaka (Table BQ3)
1470.S94-S949 Supriyasārthavāhajātaka (Table BQ3)
1470.U45-U459 Ummaggajātaka (Table BQ3)
1470.V48-V489 Vessantarājātaka (Table BQ3)
1480-1489 Niddesa (Table BQ1)
1490-1499 Paṭisaṁbhidāmagga (Table BQ1)
1495 Early commentaries
e.g. Saddhammapakāsinī
1500-1509 Apadāna (Table BQ1)
1510-1519 Buddhavaṃsa (Table BQ1)
1520-1529 Cariyāpiṭaka (Table BQ1)
1529.5.A-Z Other miscellaneous suttas, A-Z
Including non-Pali sutras
Ba da ren jue jing, see BQ1529.5.P34+
1529.5.C55-C559 Chih ch'an ping pi yao fa. Zhi chan bing bi yao fa (Table BQ3)

	Tripiṭaka (Canonical literature)
	By version
	Divisions not limited to a particular linguistic version
	Sūtrapiṭaka
	Early Buddhist suttas
	Other miscellaneous suttas, A-Z -- Continued
1529.5.P34-P349	Pa ta jen chüeh ching. Ba da ren jue jing (Table BQ3)
1529.5.P35-P359	Paritta (Table BQ3)
	Zhi chan bing bi yao fa, see BQ1529.5.C55+
1530-1539	Avadānas (Table BQ1)
	The originals are mainly in Sanskrit
1540-1549	Aśokāvadāna (Table BQ1)
1550-1559	Avadānaśataka (Table BQ1)
1560-1569	Divyāvadāna (Table BQ1)
1570-1579	Karmaśataka (Table BQ1)
1580-1589	Lalitavistara (Table BQ1)
1590-1599	Mahāvastu (Table BQ1)
1600.A-Z	Other, A-Z
1600.A23-A239	Abhiniṣkramaṇasūtra (Table BQ3)
	Guo qu xian zai yin guo jing, see BQ1600.K85+
1600.H74-H749	Hsien yü yin yüan ching. Xian yu yin yuan jing (Table BQ3)
1600.K85-K859	Kuo ch'ü hsien tsai yin kuo ching. Guo qu xian zai yin guo jing (Table BQ3)
1600.M34-M349	Mahajjātakamālā (Table BQ3)
1600.P72-P729	Pratītyasamutpādāvadāna (Table BQ3)
1600.S94-S949	Sumāgadhāvadāna (Table BQ3)
1600.S96-S969	Suvarṇavarṇāvadāna (Table BQ3)
1600.T73-T739	Tsa pao tsang ching. Za bao zang jing (Table BQ3)
1600.V56-V569	Vimalāvatīavadāna (Table BQ3)
	Xian yu yin yuan jing, see BQ1600.H74+
	Za bao zang jing, see BQ1600.T73+
	Poems, etc., on the life of Gautama Buddha
1603	Collections. Selections
1606.A-Z	Individual. By title, A-Z
1606.B83-B839	Buddhacarita (by Aśvaghoṣa) (Table BQ3)
1606.J53-J539	Jinacarita (by Vanaratna Medhaṃkara) (Table BQ3)
	History and criticism, see BQ865+
1610-1619	Mahayana Buddhist sūtras (Table BQ1)
1620-1629	Avataṃsakasūtra. Buddhāvataṃsakamahāvaipulyasūtra (Table BQ1)
	Including the 40, 60, and 80 volume Avataṃsakasūtras
1630-1639	Daśabhūmīśvara (Table BQ1)

	Tripiṭaka (Canonical literature)
	By version
	Divisions not limited to a particular linguistic version
	Sūtrapiṭaka
	Mahayana Buddhist sūtras
	Avataṃsakasūtra. Buddhāvatamsakamahāvaipulyasūtra
	Daśabhūmīśvara -- Continued
1635	Early commentaries
	e.g. Daśabhumivibhāṣāśāstra (by Nāgārjuna)
1640-1649	Gaṇḍavyūha (Table BQ1)
	Including Samantabhadracaryāpraṇidhānarāja
1660-1669	Dhāraṇīs (Table BQ1)
1670.A-Z	Individual dhāraṇīs, A-Z
1670.A63-A639	Aparimitāyur dhāraṇī. Aparimitāyurjñananāmamahāyānasūtra (Table BQ3)
	Ba ji ku nan tuo lo ni jing, see BQ1670.P29+
1670.J52-J529	Jñānolkanāmadhāraṇīsarvagatipariś-dhanī (Table BQ3)
1670.K85-K859	Kuntīdevīdhāraṇī (Table BQ3)
1670.M35-M359	Mahākāruṇikacittadhāraṇi (Table BQ3)
1670.M36-M369	Mahāsannipātaratnaketudhāraṇī (Table BQ3)
1670.N35-N359	Nakṣatramātṛkānāmadhāraṇī (Table BQ3)
1670.P29-P299	Pa chi k'u nan t'o lo ni ching. Ba ji ku nan tuo lo ni jing (Table BQ3)
1670.P35-P359	Pañcarakṣā (Table BQ3)
1670.P37-P379	Parnasabaridhāraṇī (Table BQ3)
1670.R37-R379	Raśmivimalaviśuddhaprabhānāmadhāra-ṇī (Table BQ3)
1670.S27-S279	Sarvatathāgatādhiṣṭhānahṛdayaguhy adhātukaraṇḍmudrādhāraṇī (Table BQ3)
1670.T35-T359	Tathāgatoṣṇīsaṣitātapatrāparāji tamahāpratyaṅgiratparmasiddhanāmadh-ārani (Table BQ3)
1680-1689	Fo yi jiao jing (Table BQ1)
1690-1699	Fu mu en zhong jing (Table BQ1)
1700-1709	Karuṇāpuṇḍarīka (Table BQ1)
1710-1719	Kṣitigarbhapraṇidhānasūtra
1720-1729	Laṅkāvatārasūtra (Table BQ1)
1730-1739	Mahāmāyūrīvidyārājñī. Mahāmāyūrī (Table BQ1)

	Tripiṭaka (Canonical literature)
	By version
	Divisions not limited to a particular linguistic version
	Sūtrapiṭaka
	Mahayana Buddhist sūtras -- Continued
1740-1749	Mahāparinirvāṇasūtra (Table BQ1)
1750-1759	Mahāratnakūṭasūtra (Table BQ1)
1760-1769	Kāśyapaparivarta (Table BQ1)
1770-1779	Rāṣṭrapālaparipṛcchā (Table BQ1)
1780-1789	Ratnārāśisūtra (Table BQ1)
1790-1799	Śrīmālādevīsiṃhanādasūtra (Śrīmālāsūtra) (Table BQ1)
1800.A-Z	Other parts, A-Z
1800.B45-B459	Bhadramāyākāravyākaraṇa (Table BQ3)
1800.B63-B639	Bodhisattvapiṭakasūtra (Table BQ3)
	Sukhāvatīvyūha (Larger), see BQ2030+
	Sukhāvatīvyūha (Smaller), see BQ2040+
1810-1819	Mahāsaṃnipātasūtra (Table BQ1)
1820-1829	Candragarbha (Table BQ1)
1830-1839	Pratyutpannasūtra. Bhadrapāla (Table BQ1)
1840-1849	Ratnadhvaja (Table BQ1)
1850-1859	Sūryagarbha (Table BQ1)
1860.A-Z	Other parts, A-Z
1870-1879	Mahāvairocanasūtra (Table BQ1)
1880-1889	Prajñāpāramitās (Table BQ1)
1890-1899	Adhyardhaśatikā (Table BQ1)
1900-1909	Aṣṭādaśasāhasrikā (Table BQ1)
1910-1919	Aṣṭasāhasrikā (Table BQ1)
1915	Early commentaries
	e.g. Prajñāparāmitāpiṇḍārtha (by Dignāga); Abhisamayālaṅkārāloka (by Haribhadra)
1920-1929	Prajñāpāramitāratnaguṇasamcayagatha (Table BQ1)
1930-1939	Jen wang po je ching. Ren wang bo re jing (Table BQ1)
1940-1949	Mahāprajñāpāramitāsūtra (Table BQ1)
1950-1959	Pañcaviṃśatisāhasrikā (Table BQ1)
1955	Early commentaries
	e.g. Abhisamayālaṅkāra (by Asaṅga); Mahāprajñapāramitāśāstra (by Nāgārjuna)
1960-1969	Prajñāpāramitāhṛdayasūtra (Table BQ1)
	Ren wang bo re jing, see BQ1930+
1970-1979	Śatasāhasrikā (Table BQ1)
1980-1989	Suvikrāntavikrāmiparipṛcchā (Table BQ1)
1990-1999	Vajracchedikā (Table BQ1)
2000.A-Z	Other Prajñāpāramitā sūtras, A-Z
2000.D37-D379	Daśasāhasrikā (Table BQ3)

Tripiṭaka (Canonical literature)
By version
Divisions not limited to a particular linguistic version
Sūtrapiṭaka
Mahayana Buddhist sūtras
Prajñāpāramitās
Other Prajñāpāramitā sūtras, A-Z -- Continued

2000.E53-E539	Ekaviṃśatistotra (Table BQ3)
2000.S24-S249	Sañcayagāthā (Table BQ3)
2000.S36-S369	Saptaśatikā (Table BQ3)
2010-2019	Pure Land sūtras (Table BQ1) Including Jing tu san bu jing (Jōdo sambukyō)
2020-2029	Guan wu liang shou jing (Amitāyurdhyānasūtra) (Table BQ1)
2030-2039	Sukhāvatīvyūha (Larger) (Table BQ1)
2035	Early commentaries e.g. Sukhāvatīvyūhopadeśa (by Vasubandhu)
2040-2049	Sukhāvatīvyūha (Smaller) (Table BQ1)
2049.5.A-Z	Other Pure Land sūtras, A-Z
2049.5.A63-A639	Aparamitāyurjñānadhrdaya (Table BQ3)
2050-2059	Saddharmapuṇḍarīkasūtra (Table BQ1)
2060-2069	Avalokiteśvarasamantamukhaparivarta (Table BQ1)
2070-2079	Amitārthasūtra (Wu liang yi jing) (Table BQ1)
2080-2089	Samādhirājasūtra (Table BQ1)
2090-2099	Saṃdhinirmocanasūtra (Table BQ1)
2100-2109	Shan e yin guo jing (Table BQ1)
2110-2119	Ṣi shi er zhang jing (Table BQ1)
2120-2129	Śūraṅgamasamādhisūtra. Sūraṅgamasūtra (Table BQ1)
2130-2139	Suvarṇaprabhāsasūtra (Table BQ1)
2140-2149	Tantras (Table BQ1)
2150-2159	Guhyasamājatantra (Table BQ1)
2160-2169	Hevajratantra (Table BQ1)
2170-2179	Kālacakramūlatantra. Kālacakratantra (Table BQ1)
2180.A-Z	Other individual tantras, A-Z
2180.A24-A249	Abhidhānottaratantra (Table BQ3)
2180.B53-B539	Bie xing jing (Table BQ3)
2180.C35-C359	Cakrasamvāratantra (Table BQ3)
2180.D74-D749	Dri ma med pa'i bśags rgyud (Table BQ3)
2180.G93-G939	Guhyagarbhatantra (Guhyamūlatantra) (Table BQ3)
2180.J54-J549	Jñānodayatantra (Table BQ3)
2180.K54-K549	Kīlayadvāśatantramahāyanasūtra (Table BQ3)
2180.M32-M329	Mahākālatantra (Table BQ3)
2180.M34-M349	Mañjuśrīmūlakalpa (Table BQ3)

Tripiṭaka (Canonical literature)
By version
Divisions not limited to a particular linguistic version
Sūtrapiṭaka
Mahayana Buddhist sūtras
Tantras
Other individual tantras, A-Z -- Continued

2180.S24-S249 Samvarodayatantra (Table BQ3)
2180.S25-S259 Sarvadharmamahāśāntibodhicittakulayarāja (Table BQ3)
2180.S26-S269 Sarvadurgatipariśodhanatantra (Table BQ3)
2180.S28-S289 Sarvatathāgatatattvasaṅgraha (Vajraśekharasūtra) (Table BQ3)
2180.S44-S449 Sekoddeśa (Table BQ3)
2180.S94-S949 Svarodaya (Table BQ3)
2180.T35-T359 Tārātantra (Table BQ3)
2180.V34-V349 Vajrabhairavatantra (Table BQ3)
2180.V3496-V34969 Vajraśekharavimānasarvayogayogisūtra (Table BQ3)
2180.V35-V359 Vajravidāraṇānāmadhāraṇī (Table BQ3)
2180.Y83-Y839 Yuddhavijayatantra (Table BQ3)
2190-2199 Tathāgatagarbhasūtra (Table BQ1)
(2200-2209) Vajraśekharasūtra (Sarvatathāgatatattvasaṅgraha) see BQ2180.S28-S289
2210-2219 Vimalakīrtinirdeśa (Table BQ1)
2220-2229 Yu lan pen jing (Table BQ1)
2230-2239 Yuan jue jing (Mahāvaipulyapūrnabuddhasūtraprasannārthsūtra) (Table BQ1)
2240.A-Z Other individual Mahayana sūtras, A-Z
2240.A24-A249 Adbhutadharmaparyāya (Table BQ3)
2240.A33-A339 Akṣayamatinirdeśasūtra (Table BQ3)
2240.A35-A359 Akṣobhyatathāgatavyūha (Table BQ3)
2240.A54-A549 Anityātasutra (Table BQ3)
2240.A58-A589 Anūnatvāpūrṇatvanirdeśaparivarta (Table BQ3)
2240.A77-A779 Arthaviniścayasūtra (Table BQ3)
2240.A85-A859 Aśōkarājasūtra (Table BQ3)
2240.B49-B499 Bhadrakalpikasūtra (Table BQ3)
2240.B53-B539 Bhaiṣajyaguruvaidūryaprabharājasūtra (Table BQ3)
2240.B82-B829 Buddhabhūmisūtra (Table BQ3)
2240.B83-B839 Buddhapiṭakaduḥśīlanigraha (Table BQ3)
2240.C35-C359 Candraprabhakumārasūtra (Table BQ3)
2240.C39-C399 Chan ch'a shan o yeh pao ching. Zhan cha shan e ye bao jing (Table BQ3)

Tripiṭaka (Canonical literature)
By version
Divisions not limited to a particular linguistic version
Sūtrapiṭaka
Mahayana Buddhist sūtras
Other individual Mahayana sūtras, A-Z -- Continued

2240.C43-C439 Chang shou mieh tsui hu chu t'ung tzu t'o lo ni ching. Zhang shou mie zui hu zhu tong zi tuo ni jing (Table BQ3)
2240.C45-C459 Chu fen shuo jing (Table BQ3)
Da fang bian fo bao en jing, see BQ2240.T313+
Da sheng li qu liu bo lo mi jing, see BQ2240.T32+
2240.D33-D339 Damamūkanidānasūtra (Table BQ3)
2240.D35-D359 Daśacakrakṣitigarbha (Table BQ3)
2240.D36-D369 Daśadigandhakāravidhvamsana (Table BQ3)
2240.D53-D539 Dharmasamuccaya (Table BQ3)
2240.D54-D549 Dharmaśarīrasūtra (Table BQ3)
2240.D56-D569 Dharmatrātadhyānasūtra (Table BQ3)
2240.D58-D589 Dīrghāgama (Table BQ3)
2240.D78-D789 Drumakinnararājaparipṛcchāsūtra (Table BQ3)
2240.F32-F329 Fa mie jin jing (Table BQ3)
2240.G52-G529 Ghaṇavyūhasūtra (Table BQ3)
2240.H76-H769 Hsiao tzu ching. Xiao zi jing (Table BQ3)
2240.I55-I559 Insadi-sūtra (Table BQ3)
Jin gang san mei jing, see BQ2240.V35+
2240.K34-K349 Kāraṇḍavyūhasūtra (Table BQ3)
2240.K36-K369 Karmavibhaṅga (Table BQ3)
2240.K42-K429 Kha mchu nag po źi bar byed pa źes bya ba theg pa chen po'i mdo (Table BQ3)
2240.K93-K939 Kujō shakujōkyo (Table BQ3)
2240.M27-M279 Mahābalasūtra (Table BQ3)
2240.M33-M339 Mahāmokṣasūtra (Table BQ3)
2240.M343-M3439 Maitreyavyākaraṇa (Table BQ3)
2240.M35-M359 Mañjuśrīnāmasaṅgīti (Table BQ3)
2240.M84-M849 Mulian jing (Table BQ3)
2240.P73-P739 Pratyutpannabuddhasammukhāvasthitasamādhisūtra (Table BQ3)
2240.P87-P879 Pūrṇapramukhāvadānaśataka (Table BQ3)
2240.R38-R389 Ratnajāliparipṛcchānāmamahāyānasūtra (Table BQ3)
2240.S33-S339 Saddharmasmṛtyupasthānasūtra (Table BQ3)
2240.S35-S359 Śālistambasūtra (Table BQ3)
2240.S36-S369 San shi yin guo jing (Table BQ3)
2240.S3695-S36959 Saṅghāṭasūtra (Table BQ3)
2240.S37-S379 Saptatathāgatapūrvapraṇidhānaviśeṣavistaranāmamahāyānasūtra (Table BQ3)

Tripiṭaka (Canonical literature)
By version
Divisions not limited to a particular linguistic version
Sūtrapiṭaka
Mahayana Buddhist sūtras
Other individual
Mahayana sūtras, A-Z -- Continued

2240.S3793-S37939 Śārdūlakarṇāvadāna (Table BQ3)
2240.S3795-S37959 Sarvabuddhaviṣayāvatārajñānālokālaṅkārasūtra (Table BQ3)
2240.S38-S389 Sarvapuṇyasamuccayasamādhisūtra (Table BQ3)
2240.S54-S549 Śīlasamyuktasūtra (Table BQ3)
2240.S85-S859 Su yao jing (Table BQ3)
2240.T313-T3139 Ta fang pien fo pao en ching. Da fang bian fo bao en jing (Table BQ3)
2240.T32-T329 Ta sheng li ch'ü liu po lo mi ching. Da sheng li qu liu bo lo mi jing (Table BQ3)
2240.T37-T379 Tārābhaṭṭārikānāmāṣṭaśataka (Table BQ3)
2240.T74-T749 Triratnānusmṛtisūtra (Table BQ3)
2240.V33-V339 Vaipulyasūtra (Table BQ3)
2240.V35-V359 Vajrasamādhisūtra. Jin gang san mei jing (Table BQ3)
2240.V55-V559 Viśeṣacintabrahmaparipṛcchāsūtra (Table BQ3)
Xiao zi jing, see BQ2240.H76+
Zhan cha shan e ye bao jing, see BQ2240.C39+
Zhang shou mie zui hu zhu tong zi tuo ni jing, see BQ2240.C43+

Vinayapiṭaka
2250-2259 Sarvāstivāda School Vinaya (Table BQ1)
2255 Early commentaries
e.g. Ḥdul-baḥi mdo (by Guṇaprabha)
2260-2269 Karmavācanā (Table BQ1)
2270-2279 Prātimokṣa (Table BQ1)
2280-2289 Bhikṣuprātimokṣa (Table BQ1)
2290-2299 Bhikṣuṇīprātimokṣa (Table BQ1)
2300-2309 Skanda (Table BQ1)
2309.5.A-Z Other individual texts. By title, A-Z
2309.5.A7-A79 Āryamūlasarvāstivādiśrāmaṇerakārikā (by Nāgārjuna)
2310-2319 Theravāda School Vinaya (Pali originals) (Table BQ1)
2315 Early commentaries
e.g. Samantapāsādikā (by Buddhaghosa); Vinayaninicca (by Buddhaghosa)
2320-2320.9 Pātimokkha (Table BQ2)
2322-2322.9 Bhikkupātimokkha (Table BQ2)
2324-2324.9 Bhikkuṇīpātimokkha (Table BQ2)

Tripiṭaka (Canonical literature)
By version
Divisions not limited to a particular linguistic version
Vinayapiṭaka
Theravāda School
Vinaya (Pali originals) -- Continued

2330-2339 Suttavibhaṅga (Table BQ1)
2340-2349 Mahāvibhaṅga (Table BQ1)
2350-2359 Bhikkhuṇīvibhaṅga (Table BQ1)
2360-2369 Khandhaka (Table BQ1)
2370-2379 Mahāvagga (Table BQ1)
2380-2389 Cullavagga (Table BQ1)
2390-2399 Parivāra (Table BQ1)
2400-2409 Dharmagupta School Vinaya (Table BQ1)
Cf. BQ8780+, Ritsu (Lü) Sect
2410.A-Z Individual texts. By title, A-Z
2420-2429 Mahāsāṃghika School Vinaya (Table BQ1)
2429.8.A-Z Individual texts. By title, A-Z
2429.8.A32-A329 Abhisamācārikā (Table BQ3)
2429.8.B48-B489 Bhiksunivinaya (Table BQ3)
2429.8.S75-S759 Śrīghanācārasaṅgraha (Table BQ3)
2429.8.V52-V529 Vinayakārikā (Table BQ3)
2430-2439 Mahīśāsaka School Vinaya (Table BQ1)
2439.8.A-Z Individual texts. By title, A-Z
2440.A-Z Vinaya of other special schools. By school, A-Z
2450-2459 Mahāyāna Bodhisattva Vinaya (Table BQ1)
For Bodhisattvaprātimokṣa, see BQ3060+
For works on the discipline, see BQ7442
2460-2469 Fan wang jing (Table BQ1)
2470-2479 Pu sa ying lo ben ye jing (Table BQ1)
2480.A-Z Other Mahāyāna Vinaya texts, A-Z
2480.U57-U579 Upālipariprcchāsūtra (Table BQ3)
2480.U62-U629 Upāsakaśīlasūtra (Table BQ3)

Abhidharmapiṭaka

2490-2499 Theravāda Abhidhamma texts (Pali originals) (Table BQ1)
2495 Early commentaries
e.g. Abhidhammatthasaṅgaha (by Anuruddha)
2500-2509 Dhammasaṅgaṇi (Table BQ1)
2505 Early commentaries (Table BQ1)
e.g. Aṭṭhasālinī (by Buddhaghosa)
2510-2519 Vibhaṅga (Table BQ1)
2515 Early commentaries
e.g. Sammohavinodanī (by Buddhaghosa)
2520-2529 Dhātukathā (Table BQ1)
2525 Early commentaries
e.g. Pañcappakaraṇāṭṭhakathā (by Buddhaghosa)
2530-2539 Puggalapaññatti (Table BQ1)
2540-2549 Kathāvatthu (Table BQ1)

	Tripiṭaka (Canonical literature)
	By version
	Divisions not limited to a particular linguistic version
	Abhidharmapiṭaka
	Theravāda Abhidhamma texts (Pali originals)
	Kathāvatthu -- Continued
2545	Early commentaries e.g. Kathāvatthuppakaraṇāṭṭhakathā (by Buddhaghosa)
2550-2550	Yamaka (Table BQ1)
2560-2569	Paṭṭhāna (Table BQ1)
	Other miscellaneous Pali texts
2570-2579	Dāṭhāvaṃsa (Table BQ1)
2580-2589	Dīpavaṃsa (Table BQ1)
2590-2599	Mahābodhivaṃsa (by Upatissa) (Table BQ1)
2600-2609	Mahāvaṃsa (by Mahānāma) (Table BQ1)
2610-2619	Milindapañhā (Table BQ1)
2620-2629	Vimuttimagga (by Upatissa) (Table BQ1)
2630-2639	Visuddhimagga (by Buddhaghosa) (Table BQ1)
2635	Early commentaries e.g. Paramatthamañjusā (by Dhammapāla)
2640.A-Z	Other texts, A-Z
2640.C85-C859	Cūlavaṃśa (Table BQ3)
2640.D37-D379	Dasabodhisattuppattikathā (Table BQ3)
2640.D48-D489	Dhammanīti (Table BQ3)
2640.N45-N459	Nettipakaraṇa (Table BQ3)
2640.T45-T459	Thūpavaṃsa (by Vācissara) (Table BQ3)
2650-2659	Hinayana Abhidharma texts (non-Pali originals) (Table BQ1) Including the works of the Mahāsāṅghika School, the Sarvāstivāda (Vaibhāṣika) School, the Sautrāntika School, etc. For works on the Abhidharma philosophy, see BQ4195+
2660-2669	Abhidharmadīpa (Table BQ1)
2670-2679	Abhidharmajñānaprasthānaśāstra (by Kātyāyanīputra) (Table BQ1)
2680-2689	Abhidharmakośa. Kārikā and bhāṣya (by Vasubandhu) (Table BQ1)
2685	Early commentaries e.g. Sphuṭārthā abhidharmakośavyākhyā (by Yaśomitra)
2690-2699	Abhidharmamahāvibhāṣaśāstra (Table BQ1)
2700-2709	Abhidharmanyāyānusārīśāstra (Table BQ1)
2710-2719	Samayabhedoparacanacakra (by Vasumitra) (Table BQ1)
2720-2729	Satyasiddhiśāstra (by Harivarman) (Table BQ1)
2730.A-Z	Other texts, A-Z
2730.A35-A359	Abhidharmahṛdayaśāstra (by Dharmaśreṣṭhi) (Table BQ3)
2730.A36-A369	Abhidharmāmṛtarasaśāstra (Table BQ3)

Tripiṭaka (Canonical literature)
By version
Divisions not limited to a particular linguistic version
Abhidharmapiṭaka
Hinayana Abhidharma texts (non-Pali originals)
Other texts, A-Z -- Continued

2730.A3697-A36979 Abhidharmaprakaraṇabhāsya (Table BQ3)
2730.A37-A379 Abhidharmaprakaraṇapāda (by Vasumitra) (Table BQ3)
2730.A39-A399 Abhidharmasaṃgītiparyāyapāda. Samgītiparyaya (by Mahākauṣṭhila) (Table BQ3)
2730.A44-A449 Abhidharmāvatāraśāstra (by Skandhila) (Table BQ3)
2730.A46-A469 Abhidharmavijñānakāyapāda (Table BQ3)
2730.D43-D439 Dharmaskandha (Table BQ3)
2730.L52-L529 Li shi a Pi tan lun (Table BQ3)
2730.N83-N839 Nyāyānusāra (by Saṅghabhadra) (Table BQ3)
2740-2749 Mahayana doctrinal texts (Table BQ1)
2750-2759 Mādhyamika School texts (Table BQ1)
Including the works of the Prāsaṅgika School and the Svātantrika School
Class here works by individual authors. By title.
2760-2769 Catuḥśatakaśāstra (by Āryadeva) (Table BQ1)
2770-2779 Dharmasaṅgrahaḥ (by Nāgārjuna) (Table BQ1)
2780-2789 Dvādaśanikāyaśāstra (by Nāgārjuna) (Table BQ1)
2790-2799 Madhyamakakārikā (by Nāgārjuna) (Table BQ1)
2800-2809 Akutobhaya mūlamadhyamakavṛtti (by Nāgārjuna) (Table BQ1)
2810-2819 Mādhyamakaśāstra (by Piṅgala) (Table BQ1)
2820-2829 Madhyāntānugamaśāstra (by Asaṅga) (Table BQ1)
2830-2839 Mahāyānamadhyamakaśāstravyākhyā (by Sthiramati) (Table BQ1)
2840-2849 Mūlamadhyamakavṛtti (by Buddhapālita) (Table BQ1)
2850-2859 Prajñāpradīpamūlamadhyamakavṛtti (by Bhāvaviveka) (Table BQ1)
2860-2869 Prasannapadā (by Candrakīrti) (Table BQ1)
2870-2879 Ratnāvalī (by Nāgārjuna) (Table BQ1)
2880-2889 Śataśāstra (by Āryadeva) (Table BQ1)
2890-2899 Vajrasūcī (by Aśvaghoṣa) (Table BQ1)

Tripiṭaka (Canonical literature)
By version
Divisions not limited to a particular linguistic version
Abhidharmapiṭaka
Mahayana doctrinal texts
Mādhyamika School texts -- Continued

2900-2909 Vigrahavyāvarttanī (by Nāgārjuna) (Table BQ1)

2910.A-Z Other texts, A-Z

2910.C38-C389 Catuḥstava (by Nāgārjuna) (Table BQ3)

2910.D48-D489 Dharmadhātustava (by Nāgārjuna) (Table BQ3)

2910.H38-H389 Hastavālanāmprakaraṇavṛtti (by Āryadeva) (Table BQ3)

2910.M34-M349 Madhyamakahṛdayakārikā (by Bhāvaviveka) (Table BQ3)

2910.M345 Early commentaries

e.g. Madhyamakahṛdayavṛttitarkajvālā. Tarkajvāla (by Bhāvaviveka)

2910.M35-M359 Madhyamakaratnapradīpa (by Bhāvaviveka) (Table BQ3)

2910.M36-M369 Madhyamakāvatāra (by Candrakīrti) (Table BQ3)

2910.M42-M429 Mahāyānaviṃśaka (by Nāgārjuna) (Table BQ3)

2910.N56-N569 Nītiśāstrajantupoṣaṇabindu (by Nāgārjuna) (Table BQ3)

2910.P69-P699 Prajñādaṇḍa (by Nāgārjuna) (Table BQ3)

2910.P72-P729 Prajñāśataka (by Nāgārjuna) (Table BQ3)

2910.P73-P739 Pratītyasamutpādahṛdayakārikā (by Nāgārjuna) (Table BQ3)

2910.S94-S949 Śūnyatāsaptatikārikā (by Nāgārjuna) (Table BQ3)

2910.T35-T359 Talāntāntarakaśāstra (by Bhāvaviveka) (Table BQ3)

2910.V34-V349 Vaidalyasūtra (by Nāgārjuna) (Table BQ3)

2910.Y84-Y849 Yuktiṣaṣṭikākarika (by Nāgārjuna) (Table BQ3)

2920-2929 Yogācāra School texts (Table BQ1)

Class here works by individual authors. By title

Including the works of the Anākāra School and the Sākāra School

2930-2939 Ālambanaparīkṣā (by Dignāga) (Table BQ1)

2940-2949 Buddhagotraśāstra (by Vasubandhu) (Table BQ1)

Tripiṭaka (Canonical literature)
By version
Divisions not limited to a particular linguistic version
Abhidharmapiṭaka
Mahayana doctrinal texts
Yogācāra School texts -- Continued

2950-2959 Karmasiddhiprakaraṇa (by Vasubandhu) (Table BQ1)

2960-2969 Madhyāntavibhāgasūtra (by Maitreyanātha) (Table BQ1)

2965 Early commentaries
e.g. Madhyāntavibhāgabhāṣya (by Vasubandhu); Madhyāntavibhāgaṭīkā (by Sthiramati)

2980-2989 Mahāyānasaṅgraha (by Asaṅga) (Table BQ1)

2990-2999 Mahāyānaśraddhotpādaśāstra (by Aśvaghoṣa) (Table BQ1)

3000-3009 Mahāyānasūtrālaṅkāra (by Asaṅga) (Table BQ1)

3010-3019 Mahāyānottaratantrāsāstra (Table BQ1)

3020-3029 Ratnagotravibhāga (Table BQ1)

3030-3039 Triṃśikāvijñaptimātratāsiddhi (by Vasubandhu) (Table BQ1)

3035 Early commentaries
e.g. Vijñaptimātratāsiddhiśāstra (by Dharmapāla); Triṃśikāvijñaptimātratāsiddhibh āṣya (by Sthiramati)

3040-3049 Viṃśatikāvijñaptimātratāsiddhi (by Vasubandhu) (Table BQ1)

3050-3059 Yogācārabhūmi (Table BQ1)

3060-3069 Bodhisattvabhūmi (Table BQ1)
Including Bodhisattvaprātimokṣa

3070.A-Z Other parts, A-Z

3070.S7-S79 Śrāvakabhūmi (Table BQ3)

3080.A-Z Other texts, A-Z

3080.A25-A259 Abhidharmasamuccaya. Mahāyānābhidharmasamuccaya (by Asaṇga) (Table BQ3)

3080.A255 Early commentaries
e.g. Abhidharmasamuccayavyākhyā (by Sthiramati)

3080.D53-D539 Dharmadharmatāvibhaṅga (by Maitreyanātha) (Table BQ3)

3080.G37-G379 Gāthāsaṅgraha (by Vasubandhu) (Table BQ3)

3080.M34-M349 Maitreyapraṇidhāna (by Sthiramati) (Table BQ3)

3080.P73-P739 Pratītyasamutpādavyākhyā (by Vasubandhu) (Table BQ3)

Tripiṭaka (Canonical literature)
By version
Divisions not limited to a particular linguistic version
Abhidharmapiṭaka
Mahayana doctrinal texts
Yogācāra School texts
Other texts, A-Z -- Continued

3080.S55-S559 Śīlaparikathā (by Vasubandhu) (Table BQ3)

3080.S97-S979 Sūtrālamkāra (by Maitreyanātha) (Table BQ3)

3080.T75-T759 Trisvabhāvanirdeśa (by Vasubandhu) (Table BQ3)

3090-3099 Later (5th-12th century) Indian texts (Table BQ1)

Including those works of the Mādhyamika-Yogācāra School, and Buddhist logic (Hetu-vidyā, Pramāṇa, Nyāya, etc.)

Class here works by individual authors. By title.

For general works on Buddhist logic, see BC25+

3100-3109 Antaryāptisamarthana (by Ratnākaraśanti) (Table BQ1)

3110-3119 Apohasiddhi (by Ratnakīrti) (Table BQ1)

3120-3129 Avayavinirākaraṇa (by Paṇḍita Aśoka) (Table BQ1)

3130-3139 Bhāvanākrama, Parts I-III (by Kamalaśīla) (Table BQ1)

3140-3149 Bodhicaryāvatāra (by Śāntideva) (Table BQ1)

3150-3159 Hetubindu (by Dharmakīrti) (Table BQ1)

3160-3169 Hetutattvopadeśa (by Jitāri) (Table BQ1)

3170-3179 Jātinirākṛti (by Jitāri) (Table BQ1)

3180-3189 Madhyamakālaṅkāra (by Śātarakṣita) (Table BQ1)

3190-3199 Nyāyabindu (by Dharmakīrti) (Table BQ1)

3195 Early commentaries

e.g. Nyāyabinduṭīkā (by Dharmottara); Nyāyabinduṭīkā (by Vinītadeva)

3200-3209 Nyāyapraveśa (by Śaṅkarasvāmin) (Table BQ1)

3210-3219 Pramānāntarbhāva (Table BQ1)

3220-3229 Pramāṇasamuccaya (by Dignāga) (Table BQ1)

3230-3239 Pramāṇavārttika (by Dharmakīrti) (Table BQ1)

3240-3249 Śikṣāsamuccaya (by Śāntideva) (Table BQ1)

Tripiṭaka (Canonical literature)
By version
Divisions not limited to a particular linguistic version
Abhidharmapiṭaka
Mahayana doctrinal texts
Later (5th-12th century) Indian texts -- Continued

3250-3259 Sūtrasamuccaya (by Śāntideva) (Table BQ1)
3260-3269 Tarkabhāṣā (by Mokṣākaragupta) (Table BQ1)
3270-3279 Tarkasōpāna (by Vidyākaraśānti) (Table BQ1)
3280-3289 Tattvasaṅgraha (by Śāntarakṣita) (Table BQ1)
3290-3299 Vādanyāya (by Dharmakīrti) (Table BQ1)
3300.A-Z Other texts, A-Z
3300.B62-B629 Bodhisattvamaṇyāvali (by Atīśa) (Table BQ3)
3300.C47-C479 Chan yao jing (Table BQ3)
3300.G35-G359 Gaṇḍīstotragāthā (Table BQ3)
3300.H47-H479 Hetucakranirnaya (by Dignāga) (Table BQ3)
3300.K73-K739 Kṣaṇabhangasiddhi (by Ratnakīrti) (Table BQ3)
3300.L34-L349 Laghuprāmāṇyaparīkṣā (by Dharmottara) (Table BQ3)
3300.N93-N939 Nyāyamukha (by Dignāga) (Table BQ3)
3300.P37-P379 Pāramitāsmāsa (by Āryaśūra) (Table BQ3)
3300.P73-P739 Pramāṇaviniścaya (by Dharmakīrti) (Table BQ3)
3300.S22-S229 Sāmānyadūṣaṇādikprasāritā (by Paṇḍita Aśoka) (Table BQ3)
3300.S24-S249 Sambandhaparīkṣā (by Dharmakīrti) (Table BQ3)
3300.S26-S269 Santānāntarasiddhi (by Dharmakīrti) (Table BQ3)
3300.S74-S749 Śrījñānaguṇabhadranāmastuti (by Vajravarman) (Table BQ3)
3300.T37-T379 Tarkarahasyam (Table BQ3)
3300.T75-T759 Trikālaparīksā (by Dignāga) (Table BQ3)
3300.T77-T779 Trisaṃvaraprabhāmālā (by Vibhūticandra) (Table BQ3)
3300.V37-V379 Varṇārhavarṇastotra (by Mātṛceṭa) (Table BQ3)
3300.V57-V579 Viśeṣastava (by Mtho-btsun-grub-rje) (Table BQ3)
3320-3329 Tantric Buddhist texts (Sanskrit originals only) (Table BQ1)
3340.A-Z Individual texts, A-Z

Tripiṭaka (Canonical literature)
By version
Divisions not limited to a particular linguistic version
Abhidharmapiṭaka
Mahayana doctrinal texts
Tantric Buddhist texts (Sanskrit originals only)
Individual texts, A-Z -- Continued

3340.A24-A249 Abhisamayamañjarī (by Śubhākaragupta) (Table BQ3)

3340.A25-A259 Ācāryakriyāsamuccaya (by Jagaddarpana) (Table BQ3)

3340.A34-A349 Advayasiddhi (by Lakṣmīṅkarā) (Table BQ3)

3340.A55-A559 Ajñāsaṃyakpramāṇa-nāma-ḍākinyupadeśa (by Tillopāda) (Table BQ3)

3340.B63-B639 Bodhicittavivaraṇa (by Nāgārjuna, 9th cent.) (Table BQ3)

3340.C35-C359 Caṇḍamahāroṣana (Table BQ3)

3340.C55-C559 Cittaviśuddhiprakaraṇa (by Āryadeva) (Table BQ3)

3340.D34-D349 Ḍākinījālasaṃvararahasya (by Anaṅgayogī) (Table BQ3)

3340.G85-G859 Gunavatī Mahāmāya (Table BQ3)

3340.G87-G879 Gurupañcāśikā (by Aśvaghoṣa) (Table BQ3)

3340.H38-H389 Hastapūjāvidhi (by Śāśvatavajra) (Table BQ3)

3340.J65-J659 Jñānasiddhi (by Indrabhūti) (Table BQ3)

3340.K33-K339 Kakṣapuṭa (by Nāgārjuna, Siddha) (Table BQ3)

3340.K35-K359 Kālacakrāvatāra (by Abhayākaragupta) (Table BQ3)

3340.K75-K759 Kriyāsaṅgraha (by Kuladatta) (Table BQ3)

3340.L33-L339 Laghukālacakratantra (by Mañjuśrīyaśa) (Table BQ3)

3340.N57-N579 Niṣpannayogāvali (by Abhayākaragupta) (Table BQ3)

3340.P74-P749 Prajñopāyaviniścayasiddhi (by Anaṅgavajra) (Table BQ3)

3340.P75-P759 Pratipattisāraśataka (by Āryadeva) (Table BQ3)

3340.S34-S349 Sādhanamālā (Table BQ3)

3340.S35-S359 Sahajasiddhi (by Dombī-heruka) (Table BQ3)

3340.S93-S939 Subhāṣitaratnakaraṇḍakakathā (by Āryaśūra) (Table BQ3)

Tripiṭaka (Canonical literature)
By version
Divisions not limited to a particular linguistic version
Abhidharmapiṭaka
Mahayana doctrinal texts
Tantric Buddhist texts (Sanskrit originals only)
Individual texts, A-Z -- Continued
3340.V33-V339 Vajraśekharayogānuttarasamyaksambodhicittopādaśāstra (Table BQ3)
3340.V35-V359 Vajrāvalī (Table BQ3)
Modern continuations of the canon
Modern continuations of the canon are to be developed as needed
General works
4000 Early through 1800
4005 1801-1945
1946-
4011 Polyglot
4012 English
4013 Chinese
4014 French
4015 German
4016 Japanese
4018.A-Z Other languages, A-Z
Introductions, see BQ4021+
4020 Textbooks. Compends. Manuals, outlines, syllabi, etc.
Popular works. Introductions
4021 Polyglot
4022 English
4023 Chinese
4024 French
4025 German
4026 Japanese
4028.A-Z Other languages, A-Z
4030 Pictorial works
4032 Juvenile works
4034 General special
4036 Essence, genius, and nature
4040 Philosophy of Buddhism. Philosophy and Buddhism
Cf. B162, Buddhist philosophy
4045 Controversial works against Buddhism
Cf. BQ7001+, Special modifications, schools, sects, etc.
4050 Apologetic works
Cf. BQ7001+, Special modifications, schools, sects, etc.
4055 Addresses, essays, lectures
4060 Miscellanea. Anecdotes, etc.
Doctrinal and systematic Buddhism
Periodicals. Societies. Serials

Doctrinal and systematic Buddhism
Periodicals. Societies. Serials -- Continued
4061 Polyglot
4062 English
4063 Chinese
4064 French
4065 German
4066 Japanese
4068.A-Z Other languages, A-Z
Collections. Collected works. Festschriften
4070 Several authors
4075 Individual authors
General works, see BQ4131+
History
Including history of doctrinal controversies
For works limited to a particular country, see BQ251+
For works limited to a particular sect, see BQ7001+
General works
4080 Early works through 1800
4085 1801-1945
4090 1946-
4095 General special
By period
Early Buddhism (Primitive Buddhism)
Including Original Buddhism (Gautama Buddha era) through to the split of the Hinayana schools
Cf. BQ915, Sayings of Gautama Buddha
4100 Collections. Collected works
General works
4105 Early works through 1800
4110 1801-1945
4115 1946-
4120 General special
4125 Addresses, essays, lectures
Hinayana Sthavira schools era, see BQ7100+
Mahayana Buddhism, see BQ7300+
Tantric Buddhism era (Vajrayāna Buddhism), see BQ8900+
By region or country, see BQ286+
Introductions
4131 Polyglot
4132 English
4133 Chinese
4134 French
4135 German
4136 Japanese
4138.A-Z Other languages, A-Z
Formal treatises
4140 Early works through 1800
4145 1801-1945
4150 1946-
4155 Handbooks, manuals, etc.

Doctrinal and systematic Buddhism -- Continued
4160 General special
4165 Addresses, essays, lectures
4170 Creeds and catechisms. Questions and answers
Systematization of Buddhist teachings. Methodology of classification of doctrines
4175 General works. History
For works limited to individual modifications, schools, sects, etc., see BQ7001+
Special doctrines
4180 Buddha. Tathāgata. Threefold Buddhakāya
Including the development of the concept of Buddha
4185 Worlds of Buddhas
For Sukhāvatī, see BQ4535+
Individual Buddhas, see BQ4690.A+
4190 Dharma and dharmas
Abhidharma. Abhidhamma
4195 General works
4200 General special
4205.A-Z Special subjects, A-Z
4205.T5 Time
Dharmatā. Dharmadhatu. Tathatā, etc.
4210 General works
4215 General special
4220 Two realms in Tantric Buddhism (Garbhakośa and Vajrakosá)
Cf. BQ5125.M3, Mandala
Four Noble Truths
4230 General works
4235 Suffering. Pain. Unsatisfactory quality of existence. Duḥkha (Dukkha)
Causes of suffering, see BQ4425+
Cessation of suffering, see BQ4263
Eightfold Path, see BQ4320
Pratītyasamutpāda. Causation. Relativity
4240 General works
4245 General special
4250.A-Z Special, A-Z
4250.D5 Dharmadhātu Origination
4250.S6 Six Great Origination (in Tantric Buddhism)
4250.T9 Twelve-linked Chain of Dependent Origination
4255 Truth. Paramārtha-satya. Saṃvṛti-satya
Seal of Three Laws
4260 Anitya. Impermanence
4262 Anātman. Non-self
4263 Nirvana. Vimokṣa. Cessation of suffering
Cf. BQ4398+, Enlightenment
Cf. BQ4570.I5, Immortality
4270 Absolute mind
4275 Sunyata. Emptiness. Non-attachment
4280 Madhyamā pratipad. Middle Way
Gotra. Religious instinct
4285 General works

Doctrinal and systematic Buddhism
Special doctrines
Gotra. Religious instinct -- Continued
Śrāvaka
4287 General works
4289 Arhat
4290 Pratyekabuddha
4293 Bodhisattva
Including the development of the concept of Bodhisattva
For individual Bodhisattvas, see BQ4710.A+
4297 Icchantika
Religious life. Religious practice. Perfection
For works limited to practice, see BQ5360+
General works
4301 Polyglot
4302 English
4303 Chinese
4304 French
4305 German
4306 Japanese
4308.A-Z Other languages, A-Z
4310 General special
4315 Awakening
4320 Eightfold Path
4324 Four pairs of stages in Hinayana Buddhism
Cf. BQ4195+, Abhidharma
Cf. BQ5595+, Meditation
4327 Nirodhasamāpatti
Ten stages in Mahayana Buddhism. Bodhisattva stages
4330 General works
4336 Six paramitas
Cf. BJ1289, Buddhist ethics
For individual virtues, see BQ4420.A+
Faith. Śraddhā. Prasāda. Adhimukti. Bhakti, etc.
4340 General works
4345 General special
4350 Threefold Refuges (Buddha, Dharma, and Saṃgha)
For confirmation of faith in Buddhism, see BQ5005
For general works on the Three Jewels, see BQ4000+, BQ4131+
For Triratna ceremony, see BQ5000
4355 Praṇidhāna. Vows
4358 Reward. Blessings in the present life
For prayer for temporal benefits, rewards, blessings, etc., see BQ5633.T4
4359 Love
Cf. BQ4570.L6, Love (nondoctrinal)

Doctrinal and systematic Buddhism
  Special doctrines
    Religious life. Religious practice. Perfection -- Continued
4360 Karunā. Maitrī (Mettā). Compassion. Loving kindness
4363 Guṇa. Merit
4365 Parināma. Merit transference
4370 Upāya
4375 No-mind (principally in Zen Buddhism)
      Wisdom. Jñāna. Prajñā. Mati
        Cf. BQ4336, Six paramitas
4380 General works
4385 General special
4394 Four types of wisdom (principally in Yogācāra Buddhism)
          Including Five Wisdoms in Trantic Buddhism
      Bodhi. Enlightenment
        Cf. BQ4263, Nirvana
        Cf. BQ9288, Satori
4398 General works
4398.5 Bodhicitta
4399 Thirty-seven requisites (Bodhipakkhiyadhammas) to enlightenment
    Virtues and vices
        Cf. BJ1289, Buddhist ethics
      General works
4401 Polyglot
4402 English
4403 Chinese
4404 French
4405 German
4406 Japanese
4408.A-Z Other languages, A-Z
4410 Ten cardinal virtues and ten capital vices
      Virtues
4415 General works
4420.A-Z Individual virtues, A-Z
4420.G6 Giving (dāna). Buddhist stewardship
            Cf. BQ5136+, Temple finance
4420.M6 Moderation
      Kleśa. Vices. Illlusions, etc.
4425 General works
        Ten capital vices, see BQ4410
4430.A-Z Individual vices, A-Z
4435 Karma
4440 Theory of knowledge. Buddhist epistemology
4443 Three Svabhāva theory (in Yogācāra Buddhism)
4445 Citta. Bīja. Vijñāna. Ālayavijñāna. Vijñaptimātratā
4450 Buddhatā. Buddhahood. Tathāgatagarbha
    Salvation. Other Power (principally in Pure Land Buddhist doctrines)

Doctrinal and systematic Buddhism
Special doctrines
Salvation. Other Power (principally in Pure Land Buddhist doctrines) -- Continued
4453 General works
4455 Original vow of Dharmākara Bodhisattva. Forty-eight Vows
4460 Nembutsu. Myōgō
For practice of Nembutsu, see BQ5630.N4
4465 Nine grades of life
Eschatology
4475 General works
4480 Saddharmavipralopa. End of the world
Transmigration. Reincarnation. Rebirth, etc. Saṃsāra
4485 General works
4487 Death
4490 Intermediate existence
Ten worlds
Including the worlds of Buddhas, Bodhisattvas, Pratyekabuddhas, Śrāvakas, and Six gatis
4500 General works
Six worlds (gatis)
4506 General works
Including works dealing with two or more worlds
Individual worlds
4508 Deva-gati. Heaven. World of devas
Cf. BQ4735+, Devas
4510 Manuṣya-gati. Sahā. World of men. This world
Including the relationship with the other shore, the ideal land
4513 Asura-gati. World of Asuras
Cf. BQ4790+, Asuras
4515 Tiryañ-gati. World of animals
4520 Preta-gati. World of hungry spirits
For Ullambana ceremony, see BQ5720.U6
4525 Naraka-gati. Hell
Including the eight kinds of hells, and Yamma, the King of Hell
Future life
4530 General works
Sukhāvatī. Western Paradise. Pure Land (Amitābha Buddha's Land)
4535 General works
4540 Rebirth in Western Paradise (Pure Land)
Saṃgha
Class here works limited to doctrinal points of view only
4545 General works
Bhikṣu and Bhikṣunī

Doctrinal and systematic Buddhism
Special doctrines
Saṃgha
Bhikṣu and Bhikṣuṇī -- Continued
4550 General works
4555 Meaning of renunciation
Upāsaka and Upāsikā
4560 General works
4565 Lay Buddhism
4570.A-Z Special topics (nondoctrinal) and relations to special subjects, A-Z
4570.A35 Agriculture
4570.A37 AIDS (Disease)
Amṛta, see BQ4570.I5
4570.A4 Amulets. Charms. Talismans
4570.A5 Ancestor worship
4570.A53 Animals. Speciesism
Cf. BQ4515, World of animals
4570.A54 Animism
4570.A7 Art
4570.A72 The arts
Astrology, see BF1714.B7
4570.B86 Business
4570.C3 Caste. Social classes
4570.C45 Charities
4570.C47 Children
4570.C58 Clairvoyance
4570.C6 Cosmogony. Cosmology
Including Jambu-dvīpa and Mt. Smeru
4570.C8 Culture. Civilization
4570.E23 Ecology. Human ecology
4570.E25 Economics. Labor
4570.F3 Faith cure. Spiritual healing
4570.F56 Flowers
4570.F6 Food
4570.F7 Freedom
4570.F74 Friendship
4570.H5 History
Class here general works on the three periods in the Buddhist doctrine
For works concerned with the end of the world or the third period (Saddharmavipralopa), see BQ4480
4570.H65 Homosexuality
Human ecology, see BQ4570.E23
4570.H78 Human rights
4570.H8 Humanism
4570.H85 Humor
4570.I5 Immortality. Amṛta
Cf. BQ4263, Nirvana
4570.I55 Information technology
4570.K5 King (Buddhist concept). Cakravartin

Doctrinal and systematic Buddhism
Special topics (nondoctrinal) and relations to special subjects, A-Z -- Continued

4570.L3 Language. Letters. Siddhām (a style of Sanskrit letters)
Cf. BQ5125.B5, Bijas
4570.L37 Law
4570.L5 Life, Meaning of
4570.L6 Love
Cf. BQ4359, Love (doctrinal)
4570.M3 Magic
4570.M34 Man. Pudgala. Buddhist anthropology
For gotra (religious instinct), see BQ4285+
For manuṣya-gati (world of man), see BQ4510
4570.M36 Marriage
4570.M37 Matter. Atoms
4570.M4 Medicine. Nursing. Health. Hygiene
4570.M45 Metaphor
4570.M5 Miracles
4570.M97 Music
4570.N3 Natural history. Nature
4570.O3 Occult sciences. Spiritualism
Cf. BQ4900+, Spirits, angels, demons, etc.
4570.P4 Peace
Popular faith, see BQ5633.T4
4570.P7 Prophecies. Prophets
Cf. BQ929.P7, Gautama Buddha
4570.P75 Psychical research. Parapsychology
4570.P76 Psychology. Consciousness. Status of religious experiences, etc.
Cf. BQ4195+, Abhidharma
Cf. BQ4445, Citta. Bīja. Vijñāma, etc.
4570.R3 Race
4570.R4 Reform and renewal
4570.S3 Science
4570.S48 Sex
4570.S5 Shamanism
4570.S55 Siddhas
Social problems, see HN40.B8
4570.S6 Sociology
Speciesism, see BQ4570.A53
Spiritual healing, see BQ4570.F3
4570.S7 State. Politics and government
Stūpa worship, see BQ925
4570.S9 Superstition
4570.T42 Technology
4570.T5 Time and space
4570.T6 Tolerance
4570.V43 Vegetarianism
4570.V5 Violence and nonviolence
4570.V6 Votive offerings
4570.W3 War

Doctrinal and systematic Buddhism
Special topics (nondoctrinal) and relations to special subjects, A-Z -- Continued
4570.W4 Wealth
4570.W6 Woman
4570.W64 World. Buddhism and the world
Relation of Buddhism to other religious and philosophical systems
4600 General works
Including comparative studies of Buddhism and other religious and philosophical systems
For works limited to a particular sect, see BQ7001+
4605 General special
4610.A-Z Special, A-Z
Bon, see BQ7654
4610.B7 Brahmanism
4610.C3 Cao Daism (Vietnam)
Christianity, see BR128.B8
4610.C6 Confucianism
4610.H6 Hinduism
Islam, see BP173.B9
4610.J3 Jainism
4610.J8 Judaism
Shinto, see BL2222.23
4610.T3 Taoism
4610.T46 Theosophy
4610.Z6 Zoroastrianism
Buddhist pantheon
4620 Dictionaries
4625 Collections
4630 General works
Class here descriptive works on the natures, representations, etc. of the pantheon
4635 General special
e.g. Comparative studies with deities of other religions
4640 Popular works. Introductions
4645 Juvenile works
4648 Addresses, essays, lectures
4650 Doctrinal development of Buddhist deities
Cultus
4655 General works. History
4660.A-Z By region or country, A-Z
Special deities
Buddhas. Tathāgatas
For doctrinal works on Buddhas, see BQ4180
4670 General descriptive works on various Buddhas
Cultus
4680 General works
4685.A-Z By region or country, A-Z
4690.A-Z Individual Buddhas, A-Z
4690.A6-A64 Akṣobhya (Table BQ11)

Buddhist pantheon
Special deities
Buddhas. Tathāgatas
Individual Buddhas, A-Z -- Continued
4690.A7-A74 Amitābha. Amitāyus (Table BQ11)
Cf. BQ4453+, Pure Land Buddhist doctrines
4690.B5-B54 Bhaiṣajyaguru (Table BQ11)
4690.D5-D54 Dīpaṃkara (Table BQ11)
4690.M3-M34 Maitreya (Metteyya) (Table BQ11)
4690.M36-M364 Man Núóng (Table BQ11)
4690.R3-R34 Ratnasambhava (Table BQ11)
4690.S3-S34 Śākyamuni (Table BQ11)
4690.U75-U754 Uṣṇiṣavijayā (Table BQ11)
4690.V3-V34 Vairocana (Table BQ11)
Bodhisattvas
For doctrinal works on Bodhisattvas, see BQ4293
4695 Descriptive works on various Bodhisattvas
Cultus
4700 General works
4705.A-Z By region or country, A-Z
4710.A-Z Individual Bodhisattvas, A-Z
4710.A35-A354 Ākāśagarbha (Table BQ11)
4710.A8-A84 Avalokiteśvara (Table BQ11)
Including the six types of Avalokiteśvara: Amoghapāśa, Ārya, Cintāmaṇicakra, Ekadaśamukha, Hayagrīva, and Sahasrabhūja
4710.K7-K74 Kṣitigarbha (Table BQ11)
4710.M3-M34 Maitreya (Table BQ11)
Cf. BQ4690.M3+, Maitreya as the future Buddha
4710.M4-M44 Mañjuśrī (Table BQ11)
4710.S3-S34 Samantabhadra (Table BQ11)
4710.T3-T34 Tārā (Table BQ11)
4710.V32-V324 Vajrapāṇi (Table BQ11)
4710.V34-V344 Vajrasattva (Table BQ11)
Eight kinds of mythological beings in Hinduism who protect Buddhism
Cf. BL1216+, Special deities in Hinduism (who have become protectors in Buddhism)
4718 General works
4720 General special
Cultus
4725 General works
4730.A-Z By region or country, A-Z
Devas
4735 General works
Cultus
4740 General works
4745.A-Z By region or country, A-Z
Individual Devas, A-Z
4750.D33-D334 Ḍākinī (Table BQ11)
4750.G35-G354 Gaṇeśa (Table BQ11)

Buddhist pantheon
Eight kinds of mythological beings in Hinduism who protect Buddhism
Devas
Individual Devas, A-Z -- Continued
4750.I6-I64 Indra (Table BQ11)
Cf. BL1225.I6+, Indra, Hindu deity
4750.M35-M354 Mahākāla (Table BQ11)
4750.S27-S274 Sarasvatī (Table BQ11)
Nāgas
4760 General works
4765 Cultus
Yakṣas
4770 General works
4775 Cultus
Gandharvas
4780 General works
4785 Cultus
Asuras
4790 General works
4795 Cultus
Garuḍas
4800 General works
4805 Cultus
Kiṃnaras
4810 General works
4815 Cultus
Mahoragas
4820 General works
4825 Cultus
Deities in other religions who protect Buddhism
4830 General works
4835.A-Z Individual deities, A-Z
Vidya-rājas
Class here works on the Tantric Buddhist guardians
4840 General works
4845 General special
Cultus
4850 General works
4855.A-Z By region or country, A-Z
Individual Vidya-rājas, A-Z
4860.A4-A44 Acala (Table BQ11)
4860.C35-C354 Cakrasamvara (Table BQ11)
4860.H47-H474 Hevajra (Table BQ11)
4860.K8-K84 Kuṇḍalī (Table BQ11)
4860.R3-R34 Rāgarāja (Table BQ11)
4860.T7-R74 Trailokyavijaya (Table BQ11)
4860.V3-V34 Vajrayakṣa (Table BQ11)
4860.Y3-Y34 Yamāntaka (Table BQ11)

	Buddhist pantheon -- Continued
	Arhats
	Including principally the saints in Hinayana Buddhism
	Cf. BQ900+, Buddhist disciples
	Cf. BQ4289, Doctrinal works
4865	General works
4870	General special
	Cultus
4875	General works
4880.A-Z	By region or country, A-Z
4890.A-Z	Others, A-Z
4890.A42-A424	A-phyi Chos-kyi-sgrol-ma (Table BQ12)
4890.D33-D334	Dam-tshig-rdo-rje (Table BQ12)
4890.D45-D454	Dgra-lha 'Ye-brdzu (Table BQ12)
4890.H37-H374	Hārītī (Table BQ12)
4890.K95-K954	Kun-dga'-gźon-nu (Table BQ12)
4890.K96-K964	Kurukullā (Table BQ12)
4890.M56-M564	Mgon-po Bse-khrab-can (Table BQ12)
4890.R37-R374	Rdo-rje-śugs-ldan-rtsal (Table BQ12)
4890.S76-S764	Srog-bdag-a-bse-chen-po-gdug-pa-sñiṅ-'byin (Table BQ12)
4890.V32-V324	Vajrabhairava (Table BQ12)
4890.V33-V334	Vajrakīla (Table BQ12)
4890.V336-V3364	Vajrakīlaya (Table BQ12)
4890.V339-V3394	Vajravārāhī (Table BQ12)
4890.V34-V344	Vajrayoginī (Table BQ12)
4890.V57-V574	Viśrāvaṇa (Table BQ12)
	Spirits, angels, demons, etc.
4900	General works
4905.A-Z	By region or country, A-Z
	Practice of Buddhism. Forms of worship
	For works limited to a particular sect, see BQ7001+
	Periodicals. Yearbooks. Societies
4911	Polyglot
4912	English
4913	Chinese
4914	French
4915	German
4916	Japanese
4918.A-Z	Other languages, A-Z
	Collected works
4920	Several authors
4925	Individual authors
4930	Encyclopedias. Dictionaries
	History
4935	General works
4940	Addresses, essays, lectures
	By period, see BQ286+
	General works
4945	Early works through 1800
4950	1801-
4953	General special

Practice of Buddhism. Forms of worship -- Continued
4955 Addresses, essays, lectures
4960.A-Z By region or country, A-Z
Ceremonies and rites. Ceremonial rules
For works limited to a particular sect, see BQ7001+
4965 Collections
4967 Dictionaries
General works
4970 Early works through 1800
4972 1801-1945
4975 1946-
4980 General special
4985 Ritualism (General)
4990.A-Z By region or country, A-Z
Apply table at BQ162.A-Z
4995 Service books for priests
4998 Books for laymen. "Buddhist Bible"
Special rites and ceremonies
Class here those works or rites and ceremonies which are applicable throughout Buddhism
5000 Triratna Service (100th day after birth)
5005 Confirmation. Jukai
5010 Initiation of novices
e.g. Shinbyu
5015 Marriage
5020 Funeral service. Wakes. Burial service. Cremation
5025 Memorial services for the dead
5030.A-Z Other, A-Z
5030.B63 Bodhi tree worship
5030.C6 Confession
Class here works principally for priests, monks, and nuns
Cf. BQ5720.U7, Uposatha
5030.C62 Consecration of Buddhist images
Including rites for consecration of new Buddha images, etc., for solemn enshrinement
5030.C64 Laying of cornerstones
5030.D4 Dedication
Including rites for blessing a new temple, a new house, a new family altar at home, for utensils which are no longer serviceable, and last respect rites for deceased pets, animals, fishes, etc.
5030.F47 Fetal propitiatory rites
5030.H6 Hōjōe
Class here works concerned with the ceremony for the release of captured birds, animals, or fish
5030.O43 Omizutori
5030.P73 Pretas, Offering to

Practice of Buddhism. Forms of worship -- Continued
Hymns. Chants. Recitations. Śabda-vidyā. Shōmyō. Goeika
For Buddhist music (General), see ML3197
For works limited to a particular sect, see BQ7001+
5035 Periodicals. Societies. Serials
Collections of hymns
5040 General
5042.A-Z By region or country, A-Z
5045 Dictionaries. Indexes. Concordances, etc.
History and criticism
5050 General works
5055 Addresses, essays, lectures
5060.A-Z By region or country, A-Z
Apply table at BQ1129.A-Z
5065 Individual texts. By author or title
Altar, liturgical objects, ornaments, memorials, etc.
Class here works limited to religious aspects
Cf. NK1676, Buddhist decoration and ornament
5070 General works
5075.A-Z Special objects, A-Z
5075.A6 Altars
Including both temple and home altars
5075.B4 Bells
5075.C3 Candles
5075.D7 Drums
5075.F6 Flowers
5075.G6 Gongs
5075.I6 Incense
5075.M4 Memorial tablets
Including Ihai, Sotōba, etc.
5075.P3 Pagodas
5075.P72 Prayer flags
5075.P73 Prayer wheels
5075.R7 Rosaries
5075.S4 Sepulchral monuments
5075.S8 Stūpas
For Gautama Buddha stūpas, see BQ925
5075.W6 Wooden fish (Mokugyo)
Vestments, altar cloths, etc.
5085 General works
5085.A-Z Special, A-Z
5085.H3 Habit (Kesa)
Liturgical functions
5090 General works
5095.A-Z Special functions, A-Z
Symbols and symbolism
Cf. N8193, Buddhist art (Visual art)
Cf. ND197, Buddhist paintings
Cf. NK1676, Buddhist decoration and ornament
Cf. NX676+, Buddhist arts (General)
5100 General works
5105 General special

Practice of Buddhism. Forms of worship
Symbols and symbolism -- Continued
5110 Addresses, essays, lectures
5115.A-Z By region or country, A-Z
5120 Liturgical symbolism
Including colors, lights, etc.
5125.A-Z Special symbols, A-Z
5125.B5 Bijas (Letters)
5125.D4 Dharmacakra (Wheel of the Buddha's teachings)
5125.F6 Flags and pennants
5125.H4 Hensō
Principally in Pure Land Buddhism
5125.M3 Mandala. Thang-ka
Principally in Tantric Buddhism
5125.M8 Mudrās (gestures of Buddhas or Bodhisattvas, etc.)
5125.P3 Padma (Lotus). Puṇḍarīka (White lotus)
5125.S8 Stūpas
Temple. Temple organization
5130 General works
5133 General works
Membership
For works limited to a particular sect, see BQ7001+
5133.3.A-Z By region or country, A-Z
Apply table at BQ1129.A-Z
Temple finance
For works limited to a particular sect, see BQ7001+
5136 General works. History
5136.3.A-Z By region or country, A-Z
Apply table at BQ1129.A-Z
Buddhist giving
Cf. BQ4420.G6, Buddhist virtues
5136.5 General works
5136.6 Special types of gifts (not A-Z)
5136.7 Fund raising
5137 Temple property
Buddhist ministry. Priesthood. Organization
Cf. BQ6140+, Monastic life
For works limited to a particular sect, see BQ7001+
5140 Periodicals. Societies. Serials
5145 Collections
5150 History
5155 General works
5160.A-Z By region or country, A-Z
5165 Sermons, addresses, essays
5170 Part-time ministry
5175 Ethics and etiquette
5180 Spiritual development. Religious life
5185 Professional development
5190 Ministerial work in cities
5195 Ministerial work in rural areas

Practice of Buddhism. Forms of worship
Buddhist ministry.
Priesthood. Organization -- Continued
5200 Popular works, anecdotes, etc.
5210 Handbooks, manuals, etc.
5213 Communication, correspondence, mass media, etc.
5215 Election, selection, succession, appointment, etc.
5220 Ordination
5225 Hierarchical offices
Heresy trials (General)
For works limited to a particular sect, see BQ7001+
5230 General works
5235 History
5240.A-Z By region or country, A-Z
Apply table at BQ1129.A-Z
Education and training for the ordained ministry
Including monasteries, Buddhist departments or schools in universities
For works limited to a particular sect, see BQ7001+
Periodicals, societies, etc.
5251 Polyglot
5252 English
5253 Chinese
5254 French
5255 German
5256 Japanese
5258.A-Z Other languages, A-Z
5260 General works
5265 Addresses, essays, lectures
5270 History of the study of Buddhism
5275.A-Z By region or country, A-Z
Under each country:
.x *General works*
.x2A-Z *Local, A-Z*
.x3A-Z *By institution, A-Z*
Training for lay workers
5280 General works. History
5285.A-Z By region or country, A-Z
Apply table at BQ162.A-Z
Kinds of ministries
5290 General works. History
5295 General special
5300.A-Z By region or country, A-Z
5305.A-Z Special ministeries, A-Z
5305.C4 Chaplains
5305.C6 Counselors
5305.P8 Public relations
Preaching
For works limited to a particular sect, see BQ7001+
5310 Periodicals. Societies. Serials

Practice of Buddhism. Forms of worship
Buddhist ministry. Priesthood. Organization
Preaching -- Continued
5315 Collected works
5320 History
5325.A-Z By region or country, A-Z
5330 General works. Treatises, etc.
5335 Addresses, essays, etc., on preaching
5336 Illustrations for sermons
Sermons
Classify sermons on a particular canonical text with the text; classify sermons on a particular subject with the subject
For sermons limited to a particular sect, see BQ7001+
General collections
5340 Several authors
5345 Individual authors
5350.A-Z Sermons on and/or for special occasions, A-Z
Including collections by one author or several authors and individual sermons
5350.M4 Memorial service sermons
Including funerals, wakes, etc.
5355.A-Z Other topics, A-Z
5355.B8 Buddhist name. Precepts-name
5355.M37 Marriage
Religious life
Cf. BJ2019.5.B8, Buddhist etiquette
For doctrinal works, see BQ4301+
For monasticism and monastic life, see BQ6001+
For works limited to a particular sect, see BQ7001+
For works limited to the minister's religious life, see BQ5180
5360 Periodicals
5365 Societies
5370 Dictionaries
5375 Collections
5380 History
General works
5385 Early works through 1800
5390 1801-1945
5395 1946-
5400 General special
5405 Popular works, stories, anecdotes, etc.
Including both collections and monographs
5410 Addresses, essays, lectures
Religious duties
5415 General works
5420 Religious leadership
5425 Duties of lay members
5430 Religion of the family
Cf. BQ200+, Religious education in the home
Religious life of special groups

Practice of Buddhism. Forms of worship
Religious life
Religious life of special groups -- Continued
5435 The aged
5436 Children
5440 Parents
Including works for mothers and fathers
5445 Men
Women
5450 General works
5455 Widows
5460 Young adults. Young married couples
Youth. Students
5465 General works
5470 Young men and boys
5475 Young women and girls
5480.A-Z Other groups, A-Z
5480.F37 Farmers
5480.S6 Soldiers
Precepts for laymen
Including the Five Precepts collectively
General works
5485 Early works through 1800
5490 1801-1945
5495 1946-
5500 General special
5505 Addresses, essays, lectures
5510.A-Z By region or country, A-Z
Apply table at BQ1129.A-Z
The Five Precepts
For works on the Five Precepts collectively, see BQ5485+
The Five Precepts individually
5521 First (Not to take life)
5522 Second (Not to take what is not given to one)
5523 Third (Not to commit adultery)
5524 Fourth (Not to tell lies)
5525 Fifth (Not to drink intoxicants)
5530.A-Z Other precepts, A-Z
Devotional literature. Meditations. Prayers
For works limited to a particular sect, see BQ7001+
5535 History and criticism
Collections by two or more authors
5538 Early works through 1800
1801-1945
5541 Polyglot
5542 English
5543 Chinese
5544 French
5545 German
5546 Japanese
5548.A-Z Other languages, A-Z

Practice of Buddhism. Forms of worship
Religious life
Devotional literature. Meditations. Prayers
Collections by two or more authors -- Continued
1946-
5551 Polyglot
5552 English
5553 Chinese
5554 French
5555 German
5556 Japanese
5558.A-Z Other languages, A-Z
Works by individual authors
5560 Early works through 1800
1801-1945
5561 Polyglot
5562 English
5563 Chinese
5564 French
5565 German
5566 Japanese
5568.A-Z Other languages, A-Z
1946-
5571 Polyglot
5572 English
5573 Chinese
5574 French
5575 German
5576 Japanese
5578.A-Z Other languages, A-Z
Selections for daily reading. Devotional calendars
5579 Several authors
5580 Individual authors
5585.A-Z Selections for special groups of readers, A-Z
5585.A5 Aged
5585.C4 Children
5585.F3 Families
5585.M3 Married people
5585.M4 Men
5585.P3 Parents
Including works for mothers and fathers
5585.P7 Prisoners
5585.S5 Sick
5585.S6 Soldiers. Armed forces. Veterans
5585.W6 Women
5585.Y5 Young adults. Young married couples
5585.Y6 Youth. Students
5585.Y7 Young men and boys
5585.Y8 Young women and girls
5590.A-Z Selections for special occasions and times, A-Z
5590.W3 Wartime
Special prayers and devotions

Practice of Buddhism. Forms of worship
Religious life
Devotional literature. Meditations. Prayers
Special prayers and devotions -- Continued
5592.A-Z Prayers and devotions to Buddhas, Bodhisattvas, etc., A-Z
5592.A44 Akṣobhya
5592.A45 Amitābha
5592.A8 Avalokiteśvara
5592.M3 Maitreya
5592.M35 Mañjuśrī
5592.T35 Tārā
5592.U75 Uṣṇīṣavijayā
5593.A-Z Prayers and devotions to Buddhist saints, A-Z
5593.P3 Padma Sambhava
5593.S55 Shōtoku Taishi
5594.A-Z Other, A-Z
5594.C65 Confession (Prayer)
5594.W4 Western Paradise (Pure Land). Rebirth in Western Paradise
Devotion. Meditation
For works limited to a particular sect, see BQ7001+
General works
5595 Early works through 1800
1801-1945
5601 Polyglot
5602 English
5603 Chinese
5604 French
5605 German
5606 Japanese
5608.A-Z Other languages, A-Z
1946-
5611 Polyglot
5612 English
5613 Chinese
5614 French
5615 German
5616 Japanese
5618.A-Z Other languages, A-Z
5620 General special
5625 Addresses, essays, lectures
5630.A-Z Special topics, A-Z
5630.A6 Ānāpānasmṛti. Breathing
5630.D4 Contemplation on death. Maraṇānusmṛti
5630.K6 Koan
5630.N4 Nembutsu
Cf. BQ4460, Buddhist doctrine
5630.P6 Postures
5630.P7 Psychoanalysis of meditation
5630.R6 Rosary
5630.S16 Samadhi

Practice of Buddhism. Forms of worship
Religious life
Devotion. Meditation
Special topics, A-Z -- Continued
5630.S2 Satipaṭṭhāna. Smṛty-upasthāna
5630.V5 Vipaśyanā
Prayer
5631 General works
5632 General special
5633.A-Z Special topics, A-Z
5633.T4 Temporal benefits, rewards, blessings, etc.
Spiritual life. Mysticism. Enlightenment.
Perfection
For doctrinal works, see BQ4301+
For works limited to a particular sect, see BQ7001+
5635 Collections
General works
5640 Early works through 1800
5650 1801-1945
5660 1946-
5670 General special
5675 Addresses, essays, lectures
5680.A-Z Other special religious practices or topics, A-Z
5680.C6 Copying of scriptures
5680.M85 Mummy cult
Festivals. Days and seasons
For works limited to a particular sect, see BQ7001+
5700 General works
5705 General special
5710 History
5715.A-Z By region or country, A-Z
Apply table at BQ162.A-Z
5720.A-Z Special, A-Z
Including international, national, and/or local celebrations
For works limited to a particular sect, see BQ7001+
5720.A8 Āsāḷha Pūjā. Dharmacakra Day
Class here those works concerned with the celebration (in July on the day of the full moon) of the Gautama Buddha's first sermon; observed principally in Sri Lanka
5720.B6 Birthday of Gautama Buddha. Hanamatsuri
5720.D5 Dhammasetkya
Observed in July; principally in Burma
5720.E6 Enlightenment Day of Gautama Buddha. Jodo-e
5720.E7 Equinox (Spring and Autumn). Higan-e
5720.K3 Kandy Esala Perahera
Class here those works concerned with the celebration of Gautama Buddha's Sacred Tooth Relic of the Dalada Maligawa Temple in Kandy (Sri Lanka)

Practice of Buddhism. Forms of worship
Festivals. Days and seasons
Special, A-Z -- Continued
5720.M2 Māgha Pūjā
Class here those works concerned with the celebration (in February on the day of the full moon) of the Gautama Buddha's discourse; observed principally in Sri Lanka
5720.M28 Mani Rimdu
5720.N6 Nirvana Day of Gautama Buddha. Nehan-e
5720.P7 Poson. Dhamma Vijaya
Class here those works concerned with the celebration (in June on the day of the full moon) of the sending out of missions to foreign lands by King Asoka; observed principally in Sri Lanka
5720.T4 Thadingyut. Festival of Lights
Observed in October at the end of the rainy season; principally in Burma
5720.T5 Thingyan. Water Festival
Observed in April before the rainy season; principally in Burma
5720.U6 Ullambana. Ollambana. O-bon (Memorial season)
5720.U7 Uposatha. Full moon night confession ceremony
Observed principally by monks and nuns in the Theravāda Buddhist countries
5720.U75 Chai. Ubonei. O-toki
Class here those works concerned with the abstention from food at certain periods for purification; observed principally by the laity
5720.W4 Wesak. Wisakha. Vesak. Vesākhā. Vaiśākha
Class here those works concerned with the combining of festivals venerating Gautama Buddha based on the Theravāda Buddhist traditions
Folklore
Cf. GR1+, Folklore
For works limited to a sect, see BQ7001+
5725 Collections
5730 History and criticism
5735.A-Z By region or country, A-Z
Apply table at BQ1029.A-Z
Mythological tales
Cf. BQ1460+, Jātakas
Cf. BQ1530+, Avadānas
Collections
5741 Polyglot
5742 English
5743 Chinese
5744 French
5745 German
5746 Japanese

Folklore
Mythological tales
Collections -- Continued
5748.A-Z Other languages, A-Z
5750 History and criticism
5755.A-Z By region or country, A-Z
Apply table at BQ1029.A-Z
Legends
Collections
5761 Polyglot
5762 English
5763 Chinese
5764 French
5765 German
5766 Japanese
5768.A-Z Other languages, A-Z
5770 History and criticism
5775.A-Z By region or country, A-Z
Apply table at BQ1029.A-Z
Parables
Cf. BQ1530+, Avadānas
5780 Collections
5785 History and criticism
5790.A-Z By region or country, A-Z
Apply table at BQ1029.A-Z
Proverbs
Collections
5791 Polyglot
5792 English
5793 Chinese
5794 French
5795 German
5796 Japanese
5798.A-Z Other languages, A-Z
5800 History and criticism
5805.A-Z By region or country, A-Z
Apply table at BQ1029.A-Z
5810 Miscellaneous stories (Collected)
5815 Individual legends, stories, etc.
Miracle literature
Collections
5821 Polyglot
5822 English
5823 Chinese
5824 French
5825 German
5826 Japanese
5828.A-Z Other languages, A-Z
5830 General works. History and criticism
5835.A-Z By region or country, A-Z
Apply table at BQ1029.A-Z
5840 Addresses, essays, lectures
5845.A-Z Special texts. By title or author, A-Z

Benevolent work. Social work. Welfare work, etc.
For works limited to a particular sect, see BQ7001+
Periodicals (General)
5851 Polyglot
5852 English
5853 Chinese
5854 French
5855 German
5856 Japanese
5858.A-Z Other languages, A-Z
5860 Societies. Associations (International)
5865 Congresses. Conferences (International)
5868 Directories. Yearbooks
5870 Museums. Exhibitions
5880 Collections
5882 Encyclopedias. Dictionaries
5884 Study and teaching
5886 History (General)
5888 Statistics. Theory and method
5890 Biography (Collective)
General works. Treatises
5892 Early works through 1800
5894 1801-
5896 Handbooks, manuals, etc.
5897 General special
5898 Addresses, essays, lectures
5899.A-Z By region or country, A-Z
Under each country:
.x *Periodicals. Societies. Collections*
.x2 *Congresses. Conferences*
.x3 *Directories. Yearbooks, etc.*
.x4 *History. General works. Statistics*
.x5 *Biography (Collective)*
.x6A-Z *By province or state, A-Z*
.x7A-Z *By city, etc., A-Z*
Missionary work
Cf. BV2618+, Christian missions to Buddhists
For works limited to a particular sect, see BQ7001+
Periodicals. Societies. Serials
5901 Polyglot
5902 English
5903 Chinese
5904 French
5905 German
5906 Japanese
5908.A-Z Other languages, A-Z
5910 Conferences, conventions, etc.
5912 Directories. Yearbooks
5914 Museums. Exhibitions
5916 Collections
5918 Encyclopedias. Dictionaries
5920 Study and teaching
5925 History (General)

Missionary work -- Continued
5930.A-Z Special methods and problems, A-Z
5935 Biography (Collective)
For works limited to a particular sect, see BQ7001+
General works. Treatises
5938 Early works through 1800
5940 1801-1945
5942 1946-
5945 General special
5950 Addresses, essays, lectures
5960.A-Z By region or country, A-Z
Apply table at BQ162.A-Z
Converts to Buddhism
Cf. BV2618.3+, Converts to Christianity from Buddhism
5970 Collective
5975.A-Z Individual, A-Z
5975.Z9 Anonymous
Monasticism and monastic life. Saṃgha (Order)
For works limited to a particular sect, see BQ7001+
Periodicals
6001 Polyglot
6002 English
6003 Chinese
6004 French
6005 German
6006 Japanese
6008.A-Z Other languages, A-Z
6010 Collections
6015 Encyclopedias. Dictionaries
History
General works
6020 Early works through 1800
6025 1801-1945
6030 1946-
By period
6040 Early to 1200
6045 1200-1850
6050 1850-
General works
6065 Early works to 1800
1801-1945
6071 Polyglot
6072 English
6073 Chinese
6074 French
6075 German
6076 Japanese
6078.A-Z Other languages, A-Z
1946-
6081 Polyglot
6082 English
6083 Chinese

Monasticism and monastic life. Saṃgha (Order)
General works
1946- -- Continued
6084 French
6085 German
6086 Japanese
6088.A-Z Other languages, A-Z
6100 General special
6105 Addresses, essays, lectures
6110 Origins
Monastic life. Vows. Discipline. Rules. Śīla
General works
6115 Early works through 1800
For collections or individual texts of Vinayapiṭaka (by piṭaka), see BQ1150+
For collections or individual texts of Vinayapiṭaka (by version), see BQ2250+
1801-
6121 Polyglot
6122 English
6123 Chinese
6124 French
6125 German
6126 Japanese
6128.A-Z Other languages, A-Z
6135 General special
Monks. Priests. Bhikṣu. Bhikkhu
6140 General works
6145 Novices. Śrāmaṇera
Nuns. Bhikṣuṇī. Bhikkhunī
6150 General works
6155 Novices. Śrāmaṇerikā
6160.A-Z By region or country, A-Z
Under each country:
.x History. General works
.x2A-Z Local, A-Z
Asceticism. Hermits. Wayfaring life
6200 History
6210 Biography (Collective)
6220 General works
6230 General special
6240.A-Z By region or country, A-Z
Apply table at BQ1129.A-Z
Monasteries. Temples. Shrines. Stūpas. Sites, etc.
For works limited to a particular sect, see BQ7001+
6300 Collected works
6305 Directories
For directories limited to a particular country, see BQ6330+
6310 History
6315 General works
6320 General special
6325 Addresses, essays, lectures

Monasteries. Temples.
Shrines. Stūpas. Sites, etc. -- Continued
By region or country
Asia
General works, see BQ6315
6330-6331 India (Table BQ13)
6332-6333 Sri Lanka (Table BQ13)
6334-6335 Burma (Table BQ13)
6336-6337 Thailand (Table BQ13)
6338-6339 Vietnam (Table BQ13)
6340-6341 Malaysia (Table BQ13)
Including Singapore
6342-6343 Indonesia (Table BQ13)
6344-6345 China (Table BQ13)
6346-6347 Mongolia (Table BQ13)
6348-6349 Tibet (Table BQ13)
6350-6351 Korea (Table BQ13)
6352-6353 Japan (Table BQ13)
6354.A-Z Other, A-Z
Under each:
.x *General*
.x2A-Z *Individual, A-Z*
Europe
6355 General works
6356-6357 Great Britain (Table BQ13)
6358-6359 Belgium (Table BQ13)
6360-6361 France (Table BQ13)
6362-6363 Germany (Table BQ13)
6364-6365 Netherlands (Table BQ13)
6366-6367 Sweden (Table BQ13)
6368-6369 Soviet Union (Table BQ13)
6370.A-Z Other, A-Z
Apply table at BQ6354.A-Z
6372-6373 Africa (Table BQ13)
America
6374 General works
6376-6377 United States (Table BQ13)
6378-6379 Canada (Table BQ13)
6380-6381 Brazil (Table BQ13)
6382.A-Z Other, A-Z
Apply table at BQ6354.A-Z
Oceanica
6383 General works
6384-6385 Australia (Table BQ13)
6386-6387 New Zealand (Table BQ13)
6388.A-Z Other, A-Z
Apply table at BQ6354.A-Z
Pilgrims and pilgrimages
6400 Collections
6410 General works
6420 General special
6430 Addresses, essays, lectures
6440 History

Pilgrims and pilgrimages -- Continued
6450.A-Z By region or country, A-Z
Under each country:
.x General works
.x2A-Z By province or state, A-Z
Sacred shrines of Gautama Buddha in India
6460 General works
6470 Lumbinī (Rummindei, Nepal)
Birthplace of Gautama Buddha
6480 Buddhagayā (Bodh-Gayā, Bihar)
Site of Gautama Buddha's Enlightenment
6490 Isipatana (Sārnāth, near Benares or Varanasi, Uttar Pradesh)
Site of Gautama Buddha's first sermon
6495 Kusinārā (Kusinagara, Uttar Pradesh)
Site of Gautama Buddha's death and cremation
Other individual places, see BQ6330+
Modifications, schools, etc.
For Original and Early Buddhism, see BQ4100+
Periodicals
7001 Polyglot
7002 English
7003 Chinese
7004 French
7005 German
7006 Japanese
7008.A-Z Other languages, A-Z
7010 Societies
7015 Congresses
Collections
7020 Several authors
7022 Individual authors
7025 Encyclopedias
7030 Dictionaries
7035 Directories
7040 Yearbooks
General works
7050 Early works through 1800
7055 1801-1945
7060 1946-
7070 History
7080 Miscellaneous works
Including works concerned with two or more sects, etc.
7085 General special
7090 Addresses, essays, lectures
By region or country, see BQ286+
Theravāda (Hinayana) Buddhism
7100 Periodicals
7110 Societies
7120 Congresses
Collections
7125 Several authors

Modifications, schools, etc.
Theravāda (Hinayana) Buddhism
Collections -- Continued
7130 Individual authors
7135 Dictionaries
7140 Encyclopedias
7145 Terminology
7150 Study and teaching
History
For particular regions or countries, see BQ320+
General works
7160 Early works through 1800
7165 1801-1945
7170 1946-
General works
7175 Early works through 1800
7180 1801-1945
7185 1946-
7190 General special
7200 Textbooks. Compends. Manuals
7205 Outlines, syllabi, etc.
7210 Addresses, essays, lectures
7212 Popular works
7215 Juvenile works
7220 Essence, genius, and nature
Doctrine
General works
7225 Early works through 1800
7227 1801-1945
7230 1946-
7235 General special
For Abhidharma (Abhidhamma), see BQ4195+
7240 History
7245 Introductions
Sthavira schools in India
General works
7250 Early works through 1800
7252 1801-
7255.A-Z Individual schools, A-Z
Under each:
.x *General works. Doctrines*
.x2 *Relations to other branches of Buddhism*
7255.M34 Mahāsāṅghika School
7255.S36 Sarvāstivāda (Vaibhāṣika) School
7255.S38 Sautrāntika School
Other schools or sects, see BQ8000+
Controversial works against Hinayana Buddhism
7260 Early works through 1800
7262 1801-
7265 Apologetic works
Relations to other religious and philosophical systems

Modifications, schools, etc.
Theravāda (Hinayana) Buddhism
Relations to other religious and philosophical systems -- Continued
7270 General works
Relations to Mahayana Buddhism, see BQ7432
7273 Relations to Hinduism
7276.A-Z Other, A-Z
7276.C5 Christianity
7280 Meditation. Mysticism. Perfection
7285 Religious life
Mahayana Buddhism
7300 Periodicals. Serials
7310 Societies
7320 Congresses
Collections
7325 Several authors
7330 Individual authors
7335 Dictionaries
7340 Encyclopedias
7345 Terminology
7350 Study and teaching
History
By region or country, see BQ286+
General works
7360 Early works through 1800
7362 1801-1945
7364 1946-
General works
7370 Early works through 1800
7372 1801-1945
7374 1946-
7380 General special
7382 Handbooks, manuals, etc.
7384 Outlines, syllabi, etc.
7386 Addresses, essays, lectures
7388 Popular works
7390 Juvenile works
7395 Essence, genius, and nature
Doctrine
General works
7400 Early works through 1800
7402 1801-1945
7405 1946-
7410 General special
7415 History
7420 Introductions
7422 Controversial works against Mahayana Buddhism
7424 Apologetic works
Relations to other religious and philosophical systems
7430 General works

Modifications, schools, etc.
Mahayana Buddhism
Relations to other religious and philosophical systems -- Continued
7432 Relations to Hinayana Buddhism
Including comparative studies
7434 Relations to Hinduism
7436.A-Z Other, A-Z
7436.C57 Christianity
7438 Meditation. Mysticism. Enlightenment
Religious life
7440 General works
7442 Bodhisattva vinaya. Mahayana discipline
Special schools
Including their philosophies
Mādhyamika School
7445 Periodicals
7447 Societies
7449 Congresses
Collections
7450 Several authors
7452 Individual authors
General works. History. Introductions
7454 Early works through 1800
7455 1801-1945
7457 1946-
7460 General special
7462 Addresses, essays, lectures
7464.A-Z By region or country, A-Z
7466 Controversial works against the Mādhyamika School
7468 Apologetic works
Relation to other religious and philosophical systems
7470 General works
7471 Relations to Yogācāra School
7472 Relations to other branches of Buddhism
7473 Relations to Hinduism
7474.A-Z Other, A-Z
7475 Meditation. Mysticism. Enlightenment. Perfection
Special branches of the Mādhyamika School
7476 General works
Including comparative studies
7477 Prāsaṅgika School
7478 Svātantrika School
7479 Madhyamaka-Yogācāra School
Biography
7479.7 Collective
7479.8.A-Z Founders and other important leaders, A-Z
Including local founders
Subarrange each person by Table BQ8
7479.8.N34-N349 Nāgārjuna, 2nd cent. (Table BQ8)

Modifications, schools, etc.
Mahayana Buddhism
Special schools -- Continued
Yogācāra (Vijñāna) School
7480 Periodicals
7482 Societies
7484 Congresses
Collections
7486 Several authors
7488 Individual authors
General works. History. Introductions
7490 Early works through 1800
7492 1801-1945
7494 1946-
7496 General special
7498 Addresses, essays, lectures
7500.A-Z By region or country, A-Z
7502 Controversial works against the Yogācāra School
7504 Apologetic works
Relations to other religious and philosophical systems
7506 General works
Relations to the Mādhyamika School, see BQ7471
7510 Relations to other branches of Buddhism
7512 Relations to Hinduism
7514.A-Z Other, A-Z
7516 Meditation. Mysticism. Enlightenment. Perfection
Special branches of the Yogācāra School
7518 General works
Including comparative studies
7520 Anākāra School
7522 Sākāra School
Biography
7528 Collective
7529.A-Z Founders and other important leaders, A-Z
Including local leaders
Subarrange each person by Table BQ8
7529.V36-V369 Vasubandhu (Table BQ8)
Other schools or sects, see BQ8000+
Tibetan Buddhism (Lamaism)
Including Dge-lugs-pa (Dga'-ldan, Shwa-ser, Yellow Cap)
7530 Periodicals. Societies
7540 Congresses
7545 Directories. Yearbooks
7547 Dictionaries. Encyclopedias
Collections. Collected works
For sacred books, see BQ1250+, etc.
7549 General
Special

Modifications, schools, etc.
Tibetan Buddhism (Lamaism)
Collections. Collected works
Special -- Continued
7550 Gsuṅ-'bum (Bka'-'bum)
Class individual parts of Gsuṅ-'bum with the person or the subject
7564.A-Z Other special, A-Z
Religious education
7565 General works
7566 Methods
7567 History
7568 Of the young
7569 In the home
History
Including Buddhist history of Tibet
7570 Collections. Collected works. Sources
General works
7572 Early works through 1750
For history written by Bu-ston, see BQ262
7574 1751-1949
7576 1950-
7578 Historiography
By period
Early to ca. 1000 A.D. (Introduction of Mādhyamika-Tantric Buddhism to Tibet)
7580 General works
7582 Debate to Lhasa, 792 A.D.
7584 1001-1350 (Red Cap golden era)
7586 1351-1719 (Foundation of Dalai lamas; Yellow Cap golden era)
7588 1720-1949
7590 1950-
By region or country
Tibet
General works, see BQ7572+
7592.A-Z Local, A-Z
Bhutan, see BQ400.B5+
Mongolia, see BQ580+
Sikkim, see BQ349.S57
7594.A-Z Other regions or countries, A-Z
Persecution
7596 General works. History
7598.A-Z By region or country, A-Z
Apply table at BQ162.A-Z
General works
Including Tibetan Buddhism in general
7600 Early works through 1750
7602 1751-1949
7604 1950-
7610 General special
7612 Addresses, essays, lectures
7614 Pictorial works

Modifications, schools, etc.
Tibetan Buddhism (Lamaism) -- Continued
7616 Popular works
7618 Juvenile works
Tibetan Buddhist literature
7620 General works
7622 History and criticism
7625 Essence, genius, nature
Doctrine
General works
7630 Early works through 1750
7632 1751-1949
7634 1950-
7640 General special
7642 History
7644 Introductions
7645.A-Z Special subjects, A-Z
7645.L35 Lam-rim
7646 Controversial works against Tibetan Buddhism
7648 Apologetic works
Relations to other religious and philosophical systems
7650 General works
7652 Relations to other branches of Buddhism
7654 Relations to Bonpo
7656.A-Z Other, A-Z
7656.H55 Hinduism
Special branches of Tibetan Buddhism
7660 General works
Individual branches
For founders and other important leaders, see BQ7950.A+
7662-7662.9 Rñiṅ-ma-pa (Nyingmapa) (Table BQ14)
7669-7669.9 Ni-guhi-ma-pa (Table BQ14)
7670-7670.9 Bka'-gdams-pa (Kadampa) (Table BQ14)
For Dge-lugs-pa (Gelugpa, Dga'-ldan, Shwa-ser, Yellow Cap), see BQ7530+
7672-7672.9 Sa-skya-pa (Sakyapa) (Table BQ14)
7673-7673.9 Ṅor-pa (Ngorpa) (Table BQ14)
7674-7674.9 Jo-naṅ-pa (Jonaṅ-pa) (Table BQ14)
7675-7675.9 Ṇa-len-dra-pa (Nalendrapa) (Table BQ14)
7676-7676.9 Źwa-lu-pa (Table BQ14)
7679-7679.9 Bka'-rgyud-pa (Kargyudpa) (Table BQ14)
7680-7680.9 Śaṅs-pa (Shangs-pa) (Table BQ14)
7681-7681.9 Dwags-po (Dakpo) (Table BQ14)
7682-7682.9 Kar-ma-pa (Karma) (Table BQ14)
7683-7683.9 'Brug-pa (Dukpa, Dookpa, Drukpa) (Table BQ14)
7684-7684.9 'Bri-guṅ-pa (Drigungpa) (Table BQ14)
7685-7685.9 Stag-luṅ-pa (Taklung) (Table BQ14)
7686-7686.9 'Ba'-rom-pa (Table BQ14)
7688.A-Z Other, A-Z
Subarrange each branch by Table BQ7
Forms of worship. Religious practice

Modifications, schools, etc.
Tibetan Buddhism (Lamaism)
Forms of worship. Religious practice -- Continued
7690 General works
Ceremonies and rites. Ceremonial rules
7695 General works
7697 Service books
7699.A-Z Special ceremonies and rites, A-Z
7699.B74 Basin offering (Buddhist rite)
For works limited to a sect, see the sect
7699.C65 Confession
7699.G87 Guru worship
Class here works limited to Tibetan Buddhism
For works limited to sects, see the sect
7699.H64 Homa (Rite)
Class here works limited to Tibetan Buddhism
For general works, see BQ8921.H6
7699.K34 Kālacakra (Tantric rite)
Class here works limited to Tibetan Buddhism
For general works, see BQ8921.K34
7699.M34 Mahāmudrā (Tantric rite)
Class here works limited to Tibetan Buddhism
For general works, see BQ8921.M35
Hymns. Chants. Recitations
7700 Collections
History and criticism
7705 General works
7710.A-Z Local, A-Z
7715.A-Z Individual texts. By author or title, A-Z
7720 Finance. Management
Ministry. Monkhood. Organization
7730 Collections
7735 History
General works
7740 Early works through 1750
7742 1751-1949
7744 1950-
7750 Handbooks, manuals, etc.
7752 Selection and succession of Dalai lama and Panchen lama
7754 Ordination of lamas
Education and training of lamas
7756 General works. History
7758.A-Z By region or country, A-Z
Under each country:
.x General works. History
.x2A-Z Local, A-Z
.x3A-Z Special institutions. By place, A-Z
Including monasteries
Sermons. Addresses. Lectures
Collections. Collected works
7760 General

Modifications, schools, etc.
Tibetan Buddhism (Lamaism)
Forms of worship. Religious practice
Sermons. Addresses. Lectures
General -- Continued
Dalai lamas
7762 General
7764.A-Z Individual, A-Z
Panchen lamas
7766 General
7768.A-Z Individual, A-Z
7770.A-Z Individual, A-Z
Religious life
7775 General works
7780 Discipline, duties, precepts, etc.
Devotional literature
7785 Collections
General works
7790 Early works through 1750
7795 1751-
Devotion. Meditation. Prayer. Mysticism. Enlightenment. Perfection
Including Tantric yoga
7800 Early works through 1750
7805 1751-
Devotions. Meditations. Prayers (Collected)
7810 Early works through 1750
7815 1751-
Festivals. Days and seasons
7820 General works
7825 Addresses, essays, lectures, etc.
7830.A-Z Special, A-Z
Folklore of Tibetan Buddhism
Cf. GR337, Folklore in Tibet
Collections
7850 Early works through 1750
7855 1751-
7860 History and criticism
7865.A-Z By region or country, A-Z
Under each country:
.x *Collections*
.x2 *History and criticism*
.x3A-Z *Local, A-Z*
7890 Monastic life. Discipline. Rules
Monasteries, temples, etc.
7900 General works
By region or country
See BQ6330+
Pilgrims and pilgrimages
7910 General works. History
7915.A-Z By region or country, A-Z
Apply table at BQ6450.A-Z
Biography

Modifications, schools, etc.
Tibetan Buddhism (Lamaism)
Biography -- Continued
7920 General collections
Dalai lamas
For collections of sermons, addresses, lectures, see BQ7762+
7930 Collective
7935.A-Z Individual, A-Z
Subarrange each person by Table BQ8
e.g.
7935.B77-B779 Bstan-'dzin-rgya-mtsho (Dalai Lama XIV) (Table BQ8)
7935.N34-N349 Ṅag-dbaṅ-blo-bzaṅ-rgya-mtsho (Dalai Lama V) (Table BQ8)
Panchen lamas
For collections of sermons, addresses, lectures, see BQ7766+
7940 Collective
7945.A-Z Individual, A-Z
Subarrange each person by Table BQ8
e.g.
7945.B75-B759 Bstan-pa'i-ñi-ma, Panchen Lama IV, 1781-1854 (Table BQ8)
7950.A-Z Other important leaders, A-Z
7950.A87-A879 Atīśa, 982-1054 (Table BQ8)
7950.M37-M379 Mar-pa Chos-kyi-blo-gros, 1012-1097 (Table BQ8)
7950.M55-M559 Mi-la-ras-pa, 1040-1123 (Table BQ8)
7950.N34-N349 Nāḍapāda (Nāropa) (Table BQ8)
7950.P32-P329 Padma Sambhava, ca. 717-ca. 762 (Table BQ8)
7950.S34-S349 Sa-skya Paṇḍi-ta Kun-dga'-rygal-mtshan, 1182-1251 (Table BQ8)
7950.S43-S439 Sgam-po-pa, 1079-1153 (Table BQ8)
7950.T75-T759 Tsoṅ-kha-pa Blo-bzaṅ-grags-pa, 1357-1419 (Table BQ8)
Other individuals, see BQ940+
Bonpo (Sect)
7960 Periodicals. Societies. Serials
7960.5 Congresses
7960.6 Directories
7961 Dictionaries. Encyclopedias
7962 General collections. Collected works
For collections of Bonpo literature, see BQ7965
7963 Religious education. Study and teaching
History
7964.2 General works
By region or country
Tibet, see BQ7964.2
7964.3.A-Z Other regions or countries, A-Z
Bonpo literature. Bonpo authors
For sacred books (Bonpo Kanjur), see BQ7968.2+
For individual works, see the subject

Modifications, schools, etc.
Bonpo (Sect)
Bonpo literature. Bonpo authors -- Continued
7965 Collections. Collected works
7966.2 General works. History and criticism
7966.5 General special
Sacred books. Sources
Collections
Original
7968.2 Comprehensive
Class here collections of Kanjur alone or of Kanjur and Tenjur combined
For collections of Tenjur alone, see BQ7976+
7968.5 Selections. Anthologies
Class here selections from two or more major groups of sacred books
Translations
7969.2.A-Z Comprehensive. By language, A-Z
7969.5.A-Z Selections. Anthologies. By language, A-Z
7970.2 General works. History and criticism
7970.5 General special
7970.7 Dictionaries
Including terminology, indexes, concordances, etc.
Special divisions and individual texts of Kanjur
7971.2-29 Mdo (Sūtras) and other canonical texts (Table BQ2a)
7971.5.A-Z Individual texts, A-Z
7971.5.B53-B539 Bla med go 'phan sgrub thabs kyi mdo (Table BQ3)
7971.5.B74-B749 Bskal pa bzan po'i mdo (Table BQ3)
7971.5.G84-G849 Gser 'od nor bu 'od 'bar gyi mdo (Table BQ3)
7971.5.G94-G949 Gzer mig (Table BQ3)
7971.5.G95-G959 Gzi brjid (Table BQ3)
7971.5.K45-K459 'Khor ba doṅ sprug ṅan soṅ skye sgo gcod pa'i mdo (Table BQ3)
7971.5.M45-M459 Mdo 'dus (Table BQ3)
7971.5.M46-M469 Mdo rnam 'brel par ti ka (Table BQ3)
7971.5.S26-S269 Saṅs rgyas mtshan mdo (Table BQ3)
7971.5.S59-S599 Skye sgo gcod pa'i mdo (Table BQ3)
7971.5.T48-T489 Theg pa'i rim pa mṅon du bśad pa'i mdo rgyud (Table BQ3)
7972.2-29 'Bum (Prajñāpāramitās) (Table BQ2a)
7972.5.A-Z Individual texts, A-Z
7972.5.B85-B859 'Bum Ñi ma dgu śar (Table BQ3)
7972.5.K53-K539 Khams brgyad stoṅ phrag brgya pa (Table BQ3)
7972.5.K54-K549 Khams 'briṅ (Table BQ3)
7972.5.K58-K589 Khams rtsa ṅes pa'i mdo (Table BQ3)
7973.2-29 Rgyud (Tantras) (Table BQ2a)
7973.5.A-Z Individual texts, A-Z
7973.5.G83-G839 Gsaṅ ba bsen thub (Table BQ3)

Modifications, schools, etc.
Bonpo (Sect)
Sacred books. Sources
Special divisions and individual texts of Kanjur
Rgyud (Tantras)
Individual texts, A-Z -- Continued
7973.5.M35-M359 Ma rgyud (Table BQ3)
7973.5.M37-M379 Ma rgyud saṅs rgyas rgyud gsum (Table BQ3)
7973.5.P45-P459 Pha rgyud rig pa khu byug (Table BQ3)
7973.5.S65-S659 Srid pa las kyi gtiṅ zlog (Table BQ3)
7974.2-29 Mdzod (Abhidharma) (Table BQ2a)
7974.5.A-Z Individual texts, A-Z
7974.5.M49-M499 Mdzod phug (Table BQ3)
7976-7976.9 Tenjur (Table BQ2)
For individual Tenjur texts which are commentaries of Kanjur texts, see the specific Kanjur text. For individual Tenjur texts and selections of subject oriented Tenjur texts, see the subject
7978 General works
Doctrines
7980.2 General works
7980.5 General special
Bonpo pantheon
7981.2 General works
7981.4.A-Z Individual deities, A-Z
7981.4.D322 Dbal-gsas
7981.4.L532 Lha-rgod-thog-pa
7981.4.M372 Ma-tri
7981.4.M422 Me-ri
7981.4.S572 Sitātapatrā
7981.4.S732 Stag-lha-me-'bar
7982.2 Religious life. Spiritual life
7982.3 Liturgy. Rituals
7982.4 Devotional literature. Prayers
7982.7 Organization. Government
7982.9 Benevolent work. Social work. Missionary work
7984.2 Monasticism and monastic life
Monasteries. Temples. Shrines. Sites
7984.5 General works
7984.7.A-Z By region or country, A-Z
Under each country:
.x *General works*
.x2A-Z *Local, A-Z, or individual, A-Z, if location is unnamed*
Biography
7986 Collective
Individual
7987.7 Gśen-rab, Mi-bo
For Gzer mig, Gzi brjid, and Mdo 'dus, see BQ7971.5.A+
7989.A-Z Other individuals, A-Z

	Modifications, schools, etc. -- Continued
	Special modifications, sects, etc.
8000-8049	Abhayagiri (Table BQ4)
8050-8059	Sāgaliya (Table BQ6)
8060-8069	Amarapura (Table BQ6)
(8080-8089)	Hommon Butsuryū see BQ8449.5.H66+
8100-8149	Hossō (Faxiang) (Table BQ4)
	Biography
8148	Collective
8149.A-Z	Founders and other important leaders, A-Z Including local founders
8149.H78-H789	Hsüan-tsang, ca. 596-664. Xuanzang, ca. 596-664 (Table BQ8)
	Xuanzang, ca. 596-664, see BQ8149.H78+
	Hua yan Buddhism, see BQ8200+
8150-8159	Jōjitsu (Chen Shih) (Table BQ6)
8200-8249	Kegon (Hua yan Buddhism) (Table BQ4)
	Biography
8248	Collective
8249.A-Z	Founders and other important leaders, A-Z Including local founders
8249.C45-C459	Chengguan, 738-839 (Table BQ8)
8249.F38-F389	Fazang, 643-712 (Table BQ8)
8249.G94-G949	Gyōnen, 1240-1321 (Table BQ8)
8249.M96-M969	Myōe, 1173?-1232 (Table BQ8)
8249.T78-T789	Tsung-mi, 780-841. Zongmi, 780-841 (Table BQ8)
8249.U37-U379	Ŭisang, 625-702 (Table BQ8)
	Zongmi, 780-841, see BQ8249.T78+
8250-8259	Kusha (Chü she) (Table BQ6)
8260-8269	Mahā-vihāra (Table BQ6)
8270-8279	Mahānikāya. Tamanikāya (Table BQ6)
8300-8349	Nichiren (Table BQ4)
8319.6.A-Z	Relations to other branches of Buddhism, A-Z
8319.6.S55	Shin (Sect)
	Biography
8348	Collective
8349.A-Z	Founders and other important leaders, A-Z Including local founders
8349.N56-N569	Nichiji, b. 1250 (Table BQ8)
8349.N57-N579	Nichiren, 1222-1282 (Table BQ8)
8350-8359	Bussho Gonenkai Kyōdan (Table BQ6)
8360-8369	Fuju-fuse (Table BQ6)
	Biography
8369.A2	Collective
8369.A3-Z	Founders and other important leaders, A-Z Including local founders
8369.N53-N539	Nichiō, 1565-1630 (Table BQ8)
8370-8379	Reiyūkai (Table BQ6)
	Biography
8379.A2	Collective

Modifications, schools, etc.
Special modifications, sects, etc.
Nichiren
Reiyūkai
Biography -- Continued
8379.A3-Z Founders and other important leaders, A-Z
Including local founders
8379.K82-K829 Kubo, Tsugunari, 1936- (Table BQ8)
8380-8389 Risshō Kōseikai (Table BQ6)
Biography
8389.A2 Collective
8389.A3-Z Founders and other important leaders, A-Z
Including local founders
8389.N54-N549 Niwano, Nichikō, 1938- (Table BQ8)
8389.N55-N559 Niwano, Nikkyō, 1906- (Table BQ8)
8400-8449 Sōka Gakkai (Nichiren Shōshū) (Table BQ4)
Biography
8448 Collective
8449.A-Z Founders and other important leaders, A-Z
Including local founders
8449.I38-I389 Ikeda, Daisaku (Table BQ8)
8449.M35-M359 Makiguchi, Tsunesaburō, 1871-1944 (Table BQ8)
8449.T64-T649 Toda, Jōsei, 1900-1958 (Table BQ8)
8449.5.A-Z Other Nichiren subsects, A-Z
8449.5.H63-H6392 Hokkeshū (Honmonryū) (Table BQ7)
8449.5.H66-H6692 Honmon Butsuryūshū (Table BQ7)
Biography
8449.5.H669 Collective
8449.5.H6692A-Z Founders and other important leaders, A-Z
Including local founders
8449.5.H6692N33-.H6692N3399 Nagamatsu, Seifū, 1817-1890 (Table BQ9)
8449.5.K45-K4592 Kenpon Hokke (Sect) (Table BQ7)
8450-8459 Nie pan (Table BQ6)
8500-8549 Pure Land Buddhism (Table BQ4)
Cf. BQ5125.H4, Hensō
For relations with Zen Buddhism, see BQ9269.6.P8
Biography
8548 Collective
8549.A-Z Founders and other important leaders, A-Z
Including local founders
Daochuo, 562-645, see BQ8549.T37+
8549.G46-G469 Genshin, Sōzu, 942-1017 (Table BQ8)
8549.K87-K879 Kūya, 903-972 (Table BQ8)
8549.S53-S539 Shandaodashi, 613-681 (Table BQ8)
8549.T36-T369 Tanluan, 476-542 (Table BQ8)
8549.T37-T379 Tao-ch'o, 562-645. Daochuo, 562-645 (Table BQ8)
Bailian jiao, see BQ8670+
8550-8559 Ji (Table BQ6)
Biography
8559.A2 Collective

Modifications, schools, etc.
  Special modifications, sects, etc.
    Pure Land Buddhism
      Ji
        Biography -- Continued
8559.A3-Z Founders and other important leaders, A-Z
            Including local founders
8559.I66-I669 Ippen, 1239-1289 (Table BQ8)
8559.S55-S559 Shinkyō, 1237-1319 (Table BQ8)
8600-8649 Jōdo (Table BQ4)
        Biography
8648 Collective
8649.A-Z Founders and other important leaders, A-Z
            Including local founders
8649.H66-H669 Hōnen, 1133-1212 (Table BQ8)
8649.J57-J579 Jishō, 1544-1620 (Table BQ8)
8650-8659 Seizan (Table BQ6)
8660-8669 Kōmyōkai (Table BQ6)
        Biography
8669.A2 Collective
8669.A3-Z Founders and other important leaders, A-Z
            Including local founders
8669.Y36-Y369 Yamazaki, Bennei, 1859-1920 (Table BQ8)
8670-8679 Pai lien chaio. Bailian jiao. White lotus (Table BQ6)
8700-8749 Shin (Table BQ4)
          Including Hompa Honganji and Ōtani-ha Honganji
          For relations with Nichiren sect, see BQ8319.6.S55
        Biography
8748 Collective
8749.A-Z Founders and other important leaders, A-Z
            Including local founders
8749.E85-E859 Eshin Ni, 1182?-1268? (Table BQ8)
8749.R46-R469 Rennyo, 1415-1499 (Table BQ8)
8749.S55-S559 Shinran, 1173-1263 (Table BQ8)
8750-8759 Kakushi Nembutsu (Table BQ6)
      White lotus, see BQ8670+
8760-8769 Yūzū Nembutsu (Table BQ6)
8770-8779 Rāmañña. Ramanya (Table BQ6)
8780-8789 Ritsu (Lü) (Table BQ6)
      Biography
8789.A2 Collective
8789.A3-Z Founders and other important leaders, A-Z
          Including local founders
8789.C47-C479 Chien-chen, 688-763. Jianzhen, 688-763 (Table BQ8)
        Jianzhen, 688-763, see BQ8789.C47+
8790-8799 San jie (Table BQ6)
8800-8809 Sanron (San lun) (Table BQ6)
      Biography
8809.A2 Collective

Modifications, schools, etc.
Special modifications, sects, etc.
Sanron (San lun)
Biography -- Continued
8809.A3-Z Founders and other important leaders, A-Z
Including local founders
8809.C55-C559 Chi-ts'ang, 549-623. Jicang, 549-623 (Table BQ8)
Jicang, 549-623, see BQ8809.C55+
8810-8819 She lun (Table BQ6)
8820-8829 Shugen (Table BQ6)
Including all branches
Biography
8829.A2 Collective
8829.A3-Z Founders and other important leaders, A-Z
Including local founders
8829.E55-E559 En no Ozunu, 634?-701? (Table BQ8)
8850-8859 Tachikawa School (Table BQ6)
8900-8949 Tantric Buddhism (Vajrayāna Buddhism) (Table BQ4)
Cf. BQ5125.M3, Mandala
8919.4.A-Z Relations to other religious and philosophical systems, A-Z
8919.4.T3 Tantrism
8921.A-Z Special rites and ceremonies, A-Z
8921.H6 Homa (Goma)
Cf. BQ7699.H64, Tibetan Buddhism
8921.K34 Kālacakra (Tantric rite)
Cf. BQ7699.K34, Tibetan Buddhism
8921.M35 Mahāmudrā (Tantric rite)
Cf. BQ7699.M34, Tibetan Buddhism
Lamaism, see BQ7530+
8950-8999 Shingon (Table BQ4)
Including Kogi Shingon shū
Biography
8998 Collective
8999.A-Z Founders and other important leaders, A-Z
Including local founders
8999.K33-K339 Kakuban, 1095-1144 (Table BQ8)
8999.K85-K859 Kūkai, 774-835 (Table BQ8)
8999.S55-S559 Shunjō, 1166-1227 (Table BQ8)
9000-9049 Buzan (Table BQ4)
Biography
9048 Collective
9049.A-Z Founders and other important leaders, A-Z
Including local founders
9049.S45-S459 Sen'yo, 1530-1604 (Table BQ8)
9050-9099 Chizan (Table BQ4)
9100-9149 Tendai (Tiantai) (Table BQ4)
Biography
9148 Collective
9149.A-Z Founders and other important leaders, A-Z
Including local founders
9149.C45-C45 Chih-i, 538-597. Zhiyi, 538-597 (Table BQ8)

Modifications, schools, etc.
Special modifications, sects, etc.
Tendai (T'ien-t'ai)
Biography
Founders and other important leaders, A-Z -- Continued

9149.E54-E549 Ennin, 794-864 (Table BQ8)
Genshin, Sōzu, 942-1017, see BQ8549.G46+
9149.S35-S359 Saichō, 767-822 (Table BQ8)
9149.S55-S559 Shinzei, Shōnin, 1443-1495 (Table BQ8)
9149.U38-U389 Ŭich'ŏn, 1055-1101 (Table BQ8)
Zhiyi, 538-597, see BQ9149.C45+

Taehan Pulgyo Ch'ŏnt'aejong
9149.5 Periodicals. Societies. Congresses. Directories. Collections
9149.51 Religious education
9149.52 History. General works
9149.53 Literature. Folklore, etc.
9149.54 Doctrine. Forms of worship
9149.55 Organization. Government
9149.56 Religious life. Devotional literature
9149.57 Benevolent work. Social work. Missionary work
9149.58 Monasticism. Temples
Biography
9149.59.A2 Collective
9149.59.A3-Z Founders and other important leaders, A-Z
Including local founders
Subarrange each person by Table BQ8
Other individuals
See BQ940-BQ999

9150-9199 Thammayut. Mahāyut (Table BQ4)
9200-9209 Ti lun (Table BQ6)
9210-9219 Wŏnhyo (Table BQ6)
Biography
9219.A2 Collective
9219.A3-Z Founders and other important leaders, A-Z
Including local founders
9219.W66-W669 Wŏnhyo, 617-686 (Table BQ8)
9220-9229 Wŏn Pulgyo (Table BQ6)
Biography
9229.A2 Collective
9229.A3-Z Founders and other important leaders, A-Z
Including local founders
9229.P36-P369 Pak, Chung-bin, 1891-1943 (Table BQ8)
9250-9299 Zen Buddhism (Table BQ4)
9269.6.A-Z Relations to other branches of Buddhism, A-Z
9269.6.H5 Hinayana Buddhism
9269.6.P8 Pure Land Buddhism
9288 Enlightenment. Satori
Biography
9298 Collective
9299.A-Z Founders and other important leaders, A-Z
Including local founders

Modifications, schools, etc.
Special modifications, sects, etc.
Zen Buddhism
Biography
Founders and other important leaders, A-Z -- Continued

9299.B62-B629	Bodhidharma, 6th cent. (Table BQ8)
	Congshen, 778-861, see BQ9299.T75+
9299.H83-H839	Huaihai, 720-814 (Table BQ8)
9299.H85-H859	Huineng, 638-713 (Table BQ8)
9299.S54-S549	Shenhui, 668?-760? (Table BQ8)
9299.T75-T759	Ts'ung-shen, 778-861. Congshen, 778-861 (Table BQ8)
9300-9309	Fuke (Table BQ6)
9310-9319	Ōbaku (Table BQ6)
	Biography
9319.A2	Collective
9319.A3-Z	Founders and other important leaders, A-Z. Including local founders
9319.I53-I539	Ingen, 1592-1673 (Table BQ8)
9350-9399	Rinzai (Table BQ4)
	Biography
9398	Collective
9399.A-Z	Founders and other important leaders, A-Z. Including local founders
	Bankei, 1622-1693, see BQ9399.E57+
9399.E52-E529	Eisai, 1141-1215 (Table BQ8)
9399.E57-E579	Eitaku, 1622-1693 (Table BQ8)
9399.E59-E599	Ekaku, 1686-1769 (Table BQ8)
	Hakuin, 1686-1769, see BQ9399.E59+
9399.I55-I559	I-hsüan, d. 867. Yixuan, d. 867 (Table BQ8)
9399.I56-I569	Ikkyū Oshō, 1394-1481 (Table BQ8)
9399.T33-T339	Takuan Sōhō, 1573-1645 (Table BQ8)
	Yixuan, d. 867, see BQ9399.I55+
9400-9449	Sōtō (Table BQ4)
	Biography
9448	Collective
9449.A-Z	Founders and other important leaders, A-Z. Including local founders
9449.D65-D659	Dōgen, 1200-1253 (Table BQ8)
9449.E37-E379	Ejō, 1198-1280 (Table BQ8)
	Keizan, 1268-1325, see BQ9449.S54+
9449.L52-L529	Liangjie, 807-869 (Table BQ8)
9449.R94-R949	Ryōkan, 1758-1831 (Table BQ8)
9449.S54-S549	Shōkin, 1268-1325 (Table BQ8)
9460-9469	Order of Buddhist Contemplatives (Table BQ6)
9510-9519	Taehan Pulgyo Chogyejong (Table BQ6)
	Biography
9519.A2	Collective
9519.A3-Z	Founders and other important leaders, A-Z. Including local founders
9519.C45-C459	Chinul, 1158-1210 (Table BQ8)

Modifications, schools, etc.
Special modifications, sects, etc.
Zen Buddhism
Taehan Pulgyo Chogyejong
Biography
Founders and other important leaders, A-Z -- Continued

9519.P68-P689 Pou Kuksa, 1301-1382 (Table BQ8)
9800.A-Z Other modifications, schools, sects, etc., A-Z
9800.A36-A3692 Agonshū (Table BQ7)
Biography
9800.A369 Collective
9800.A3692A-Z Founders and other important leaders, A-Z
Including local founders
9800.A3692K57-.A3692K5799 Kiriyama, Seiyū (Table BQ9)
9800.C48-C4892 Chen-fu (Sect). Zhen fo (Sect) (Table BQ7)
Biography
9800.C489 Collective
9800.C4892A-Z Founders and other important leaders, A-Z
Including local founders
9800.C4892L82-.C4892L8299 Lu, Shengyan, 1945- (Table BQ9)
9800.G43-G4392 Gedatsukai (Table BQ7)
9800.N35-N3592 Nakayama Shingo Shōshū (Table BQ7)
9800.N96-N9692 Nyoraikyō (Table BQ7)
Biography
9800.N969 Collective
9800.N9692A-Z Founders and other important leaders, A-Z
Including local founders
9800.N9692I77-.N9692I7799 Isson Nyorai Kino, 1756-1828 (Table BQ9)
9800.P45-P4592 Phât-giáo Hòa-Hảo (Table BQ7)
Biography
9800.P459 Collective
9800.P4592A-Z Founders and other important leaders, A-Z
Including local founders
9800.P4592H88-.P4592H8899 Huỳnh, Phú Sô, d. 1947 (Table BQ9)
9800.S25-S2592 Santi ‘Asōk (Organization) (Table BQ7)
Biography
9800.S259 Collective
9800.S2592A-Z Founders and other important leaders, A-Z
Including local founders
9800.S2592P45-.S2592P4599 Phōthirak, Phra, 1934- (Table BQ9)
9800.S46-S4692 Sesimjong (Table BQ7)
Biography
9800.S469 Collective
9800.S4692A-Z Founders and other important leaders, A-Z
Including local leaders
9800.S4692M82-.S4692M8299 Mubyŏn Taesa (Table BQ9)
9800.T53-T5392 Tiep Hien (Order of Interbeing) (Table BQ7)
Biography
9800.T539 Collective
9800.T5392A-Z Founders and other important leaders, A-Z
Including local founders
9800.T5392N45-.T5392N4599 Nhât Hạnh, Thích (Table BQ9)

Modifications, schools, etc.
Other modifications,
schools, sects, etc., A-Z -- Continued
Zhen fo (Sect), see BQ9800.C48+

	Comprehensive collections
.x	Original. By date
.x2.A-Z	Translations. By language, A-Z, and date
	Selections, anthologies, etc.
.x3	Original. By date
.x4.A-Z	Translations. By language, A-Z, and date
.x5.A-Z	Adaptations and paraphrases. By adaptor, A-Z
.x6	General works, commentaries, criticism, etc.
.x7	Special topics (not A-Z)
.x9	Dictionaries, terminology, indexes, concordances

BL2 TABLE FOR HINDU OR JAINA SACRED BOOKS (SUCCESSIVE DECIMAL NUMBERS) (2) BL2

	Complete texts
.x	Original. By date
.x2.A-Z	Translations. By language, A-Z, and date
.x2.A1	Polyglot
	Partial editions, selections, anthologies, etc.
	Original
.x3	General. By date
.x32.A-Z	Individual chapter, book, section, etc. By title, A-Z, and date
	Translations
.x4.A-Z	General. By language, A-Z, and date
.x4.A1	Polyglot
.x42.A-Z	Individual chapter, book, section, etc. By title, A-Z, language, A-Z, and date
.x5.A-Z	Adaptations and paraphrases. By adaptor, A-Z
.x6	General works, commentaries, criticism, etc.
.x7	Special topics (not A-Z)
.x9	Dictionaries, terminology, indexes, concordances

	Complete texts
.x	Original. By date
.x2A-Z	Translations. By language, A-Z, and date
.x2A1	Polyglot
	Partial editions, selections, anthologies, etc.
	Original
.x3	General. By date
.x32A-Z	Individual chapter, book, section, etc. By title, A-Z, and date
	Translations
.x4A-Z	General. By language, A-Z, and date
.x4A1	Polyglot
.x42A-Z	Individual chapter, book, section, etc. By title, A-Z, and date
.x5A-Z	Adaptations and paraphrases. By adaptor, A-Z, and date
.x6	General works, commentaries, criticism, etc.
.x7	Special topics (not A-Z)
.x9	Dictionaries, terminology, indexes, concordances

	Collected works
.xA2	Original texts. By date
.xA25	Partial editions. Selections. Quotations, etc. By date
.xA26-.xA269	Translations. By date
.xA27-.xA279	Separate works
	Biography, criticism, etc.
.xA28-.xA289	Periodicals. Societies. Congresses. Exhibitions
.xA29-.xA299	Dictionaries. Indexes. Concordances, etc.
.xA3-.xA39	Autobiography. Diaries, etc. By title
.xA4	Letters. By date
.xA6-.xZ	General works

.x	Periodicals. Societies. Directories. Congresses
.x2	Dictionaries. Encyclopedias
.x22	General collections. Collected works
	Including selections sacred to a particular sect
.x23	Religious education. Study and teaching
	History
.x3	General works
	By region or country
	India
	General works, see .x3
.x32.A-Z	Local, A-Z
.x35.A-Z	Other regions or countries, A-Z
	Under each country:
	.x *General works. History*
	.x2A-Z *Local, A-Z*
.x4	General works
.x42	General special
	Doctrines
.x45	General
.x47	General special. Special topics (not A-Z)
.x5.A-Z	Relations to other religious and philosophical systems and to other branches of Hinduism, A-Z
	Practice. Forms of worship. Religious life
.x52	General works
.x55	Liturgy. Rituals. Meditation. Devotion
.x6	Devotional literature. Prayers. Meditations. Hymns
.x7	Organization. Government. Ministry
.x73	Monasteries. Temples. Shrines. Sacred sites
	For local or individual temples, etc., see BL1243.76+
	Biography
.x9	Collective
.x92.A-Z	Founders and most important leaders, A-Z
	Subarrange each person by Table BL4
	Other individuals
	see BL1175

BL6 TABLE FOR ASIAN RELIGIONS, SECTS, ETC. (SUCCESSIVE CUTTER NUMBERS) BL6

.x	Periodicals. Societies. Directories. Congresses
.x2	Dictionaries. Encyclopedias
.x22	General collections. Collected works
	Including selections sacred to a particular sect
.x23	Religious education. Study and teaching
	History
.x3	General works
	By region or country
	General works of the country in which the religion or sect originated, see .x3
.x32A-Z	Local of the country in which the religion or sect originated, A-Z
.x35A-Z	Other regions or countries, A-Z
.x4	General works
.x42	General special
	Doctrines
.x45	General
.x47	General special. Special topics (not A-Z)
.x5A-Z	Relations to other religions, sects and philosophical systems, A-Z
	Practice. Forms of worship. Religious life
.x52	General works
.x55	Liturgy. Rituals. Meditation. Devotion
.x6	Devotional literature. Prayers. Meditations. Hymns
.x7	Organization. Government. Ministry
	Monasteries. Temples. Shrines. Sacred sites
.x73	General works
.x75A-Z	Local, A-Z, or individual, A-Z, if location is unnamed
	Biography
.x9	Collective
.x92A-Z	Founders and most important leaders, A-Z
.x93A-Z	Other individual, A-Z

BL7 TABLE FOR HINDU OR JAINA DEITIES (SUCCESSIVE CUTTER NUMBERS) BL7

.x	General works. India
.x2	Cult. Liturgy. Prayers
.x3A-Z	Local of India, A-Z
.x4A-Z	Other regions or countries, A-Z

	‘Abodah zarah (Avodah zarah)
.A15	Original texts (Hebrew or Aramaic). By date
.A15A-Z	Translations. By language, A-Z
	e.g.
.A15E5	English
.A15E65	English paraphrases
.A16	Selections. By date
.A17	Criticism. Commentaries, etc.
	Aboth (Avot)
.A2	Original texts (Hebrew or Aramaic). By date
.A2A-Z	Translations. By language, A-Z
.A22	Selections. By date
.A23	Criticism. Commentaries, etc.
	Ahilot, see .O3-.O5
	Arakhin
.A7	Original texts (Hebrew or Aramaic). By date
.A7A-Z	Translations. By language, A-Z
.A72	Selections. By date
.A73	Criticism. Commentaries, etc.
	Avodah zarah, see .A15-.A17
	Avot, see .A2-.A23
	Bavot
.B15	Original texts (Hebrew or Aramaic). By date
.B15A-Z	Translations. By language, A-Z
.B16	Selections. By date
.B17	Criticism. Commentaries, etc.
	Bava kamma
.B2	Original texts (Hebrew or Aramaic). By date
.B2A-Z	Translations. By language, A-Z
.B22	Selections. By date
.B23	Criticism. Commentaries, etc.
	Bava meẓia
.B3	Original texts (Hebrew or Aramaic). By date
.B3A-Z	Translations. By language, A-Z
.B32	Selections. By date
.B33	Criticism. Commentaries, etc.
	Bava batra
.B4	Original texts (Hebrew or Aramaic). By date
.B4A-Z	Translations. By language, A-Z
.B42	Selections. By date
.B43	Criticism. Commentaries, etc.
	Beḥirta, see .E3-.E5
	Bekhorot
.B5	Original texts (Hebrew or Aramaic). By date
.B5A-Z	Translations. By language, A-Z
.B52	Selections. By date
.B53	Criticism. Commentaries, etc.
	Berakhot
.B6	Original texts (Hebrew or Aramaic). By date
.B6A-Z	Translations. By language, A-Z
.B62	Selections. By date
.B63	Criticism. Commentaries, etc.
	Beẓah

	Beẓah -- Continued
.B7	Original texts (Hebrew or Aramaic). By date
.B7A-Z	Translations. By language, A-Z
.B72	Selections. By date
.B73	Criticism. Commentaries, etc.
	Bikkurim
.B8	Original texts (Hebrew or Aramaic). By date
.B8A-Z	Translations. By language, A-Z
.B82	Selections. By date
.B83	Criticism. Commentaries, etc.
	Demai
.D3	Original texts (Hebrew or Aramaic). By date
.D3A-Z	Translations. By language, A-Z
.D4	Selections. By date
.D5	Criticism. Commentaries, etc.
	Eduyyot. Beḥirta
.E3	Original texts (Hebrew or Aramaic). By date
.E3A-Z	Translations. By language, A-Z
.E4	Selections. By date
.E5	Criticism. Commentaries, etc.
	Eruvin
.E7	Original texts (Hebrew or Aramaic). By date
.E7A-Z	Translations. By language, A-Z
.E8	Selections. By date
.E9	Criticism. Commentaries, etc.
	Gittin
.G5	Original texts (Hebrew or Aramaic). By date
.G5A-Z	Translations. By language, A-Z
.G52	Selections. By date
.G53	Criticism. Commentaries, etc.
	Ḥagigah
.H3	Original texts (Hebrew or Aramaic). By date
.H3A-Z	Translations. By language, A-Z
.H32	Selections. By date
.H33	Criticism. Commentaries, etc.
	Ḥallah
.H4	Original texts (Hebrew or Aramaic). By date
.H4A-Z	Translations. By language, A-Z
.H42	Selections. By date
.H43	Criticism. Commentaries, etc.
	Horayot
.H5	Original texts (Hebrew or Aramaic). By date
.H5A-Z	Translations. By language, A-Z
.H6	Selections. By date
.H7	Criticism. Commentaries, etc.
	Ḥullin
.H8	Original texts (Hebrew or Aramaic). By date
.H8A-Z	Translations. By language, A-Z
.H82	Selections. By date
.H83	Criticism. Commentaries, etc.
	Kelim
.K2	Original texts (Hebrew or Aramaic). By date
.K2A-Z	Translations. By language, A-Z

	Kelim -- Continued
.K22	Selections. By date
.K23	Criticism. Commentaries, etc.
	Keritot
.K3	Original texts (Hebrew or Aramaic). By date
.K3A-Z	Translations. By language, A-Z
.K32	Selections. By date
.K33	Criticism. Commentaries, etc.
	Ketubbot
.K4	Original texts (Hebrew or Aramaic). By date
.K4A-Z	Translations. By language, A-Z
.K42	Selections. By date
.K43	Criticism. Commentaries, etc.
	Kiddushin
.K5	Original texts (Hebrew or Aramaic). By date
.K5A-Z	Translations. By language, A-Z
.K52	Selections. By date
.K53	Criticism. Commentaries, etc.
	Kilayim
.K6	Original texts (Hebrew or Aramaic). By date
.K6A-Z	Translations. By language, A-Z
.K62	Selections. By date
.K63	Criticism. Commentaries, etc.
	Kinnim
.K7	Original texts (Hebrew or Aramaic). By date
.K7A-Z	Translations. By language, A-Z
.K72	Selections. By date
.K73	Criticism. Commentaries, etc.
	Kodashim (Order)
.K8	Original texts (Hebrew or Aramaic). By date
.K8A-Z	Translations. By language, A-Z
.K82	Selections. By date
.K83	Criticism. Commentaries, etc.
	Ma'aser sheni
.M13	Original texts (Hebrew or Aramaic). By date
.M13A-Z	Translations. By language, A-Z
.M14	Selections. By date
.M15	Criticism. Commentaries, etc.
	Ma'aserot
.M17	Original texts (Hebrew or Aramaic). By date
.M17A-Z	Translations. By language, A-Z
.M18	Selections. By date
.M19	Criticism. Commentaries, etc.
	Makhshirin. Mashkim
.M2	Original texts (Hebrew or Aramaic). By date
.M2A-Z	Translations. By language, A-Z
.M22	Selections. By date
.M23	Criticism. Commentaries, etc.
	Makkot
.M3	Original texts (Hebrew or Aramaic). By date
.M3A-Z	Translations. By language, A-Z
.M32	Selections. By date
.M33	Criticism. Commentaries, etc.

	Mashkim, see .M2-.M23
	Mashkin, see .M8-.M83
	Megillah
.M4	Original texts (Hebrew or Aramaic). By date
.M4A-Z	Translations. By language, A-Z
.M42	Selections. By date
.M43	Criticism. Commentaries, etc.
	Me‘ilah
.M44	Original texts (Hebrew or Aramaic). By date
.M44A-Z	Translations. By language, A-Z
.M45	Selections. By date
.M46	Criticism. Commentaries, etc.
	Menaḥot
.M47	Original texts (Hebrew or Aramaic). By date
.M47A-Z	Translations. By language, A-Z
.M48	Selections. By date
.M49	Criticism. Commentaries, etc.
	Middot
.M5	Original texts (Hebrew or Aramaic). By date
.M5A-Z	Translations. By language, A-Z
.M52	Selections. By date
.M53	Criticism. Commentaries, etc.
	Mikva'ot
.M6	Original texts (Hebrew or Aramaic). By date
.M6A-Z	Translations. By language, A-Z
.M62	Selections. By date
.M63	Criticism. Commentaries, etc.
	Minor tractates
	See BM506.4
	Mo‘ed (Order)
.M7	Original texts (Hebrew or Aramaic). By date
.M7A-Z	Translations. By language, A-Z
.M72	Selections. By date
.M73	Criticism. Commentaries, etc.
	Mo‘ed katan. Mashkin
.M8	Original texts (Hebrew or Aramaic). By date
.M8A-Z	Translations. By language, A-Z
.M82	Selections. By date
.M83	Criticism. Commentaries, etc.
	Nashim (Order)
.N2	Original texts (Hebrew or Aramaic). By date
.N2A-Z	Translations. By language, A-Z
.N22	Selections. By date
.N23	Criticism. Commentaries, etc.
	Nazir
.N3	Original texts (Hebrew or Aramaic). By date
.N3A-Z	Translations. By language, A-Z
.N32	Selections. By date
.N33	Criticism. Commentaries, etc.
	Nedarim
.N4	Original texts (Hebrew or Aramaic). By date
.N4A-Z	Translations. By language, A-Z
.N42	Selections. By date

	Nedarim -- Continued
.N43	Criticism. Commentaries, etc.
	Nega'im
.N5	Original texts (Hebrew or Aramaic). By date
.N5A-Z	Translations. By language, A-Z
.N52	Selections. By date
.N53	Criticism. Commentaries, etc.
	Nezikin (Order)
.N6	Original texts (Hebrew or Aramaic). By date
.N6A-Z	Translations. By language, A-Z
.N62	Selections. By date
.N63	Criticism. Commentaries, etc.
	Niddah
.N7	Original texts (Hebrew or Aramaic). By date
.N7A-Z	Translations. By language, A-Z
.N72	Selections. By date
.N73	Criticism. Commentaries, etc.
	Oholot (Ahilot)
.O3	Original texts (Hebrew or Aramaic). By date
.O3A-Z	Translations. By language, A-Z
.O4	Selections. By date
.O5	Criticism. Commentaries, etc.
	Orlah
.O6	Original texts (Hebrew or Aramaic). By date
.O6A-Z	Translations. By language, A-Z
.O7	Selections. By date
.O8	Criticism. Commentaries, etc.
	Parah
.P2	Original texts (Hebrew or Aramaic). By date
.P2A-Z	Translations. By language, A-Z
.P3	Selections. By date
.P4	Criticism. Commentaries, etc.
	Pe'ah
.P5	Original texts (Hebrew or Aramaic). By date
.P5A-Z	Translations. By language, A-Z
.P6	Selections. By date
.P7	Criticism. Commentaries, etc.
	Pesaḥim
.P8	Original texts (Hebrew or Aramaic). By date
.P8A-Z	Translations. By language, A-Z
.P82	Selections. By date
.P83	Criticism. Commentaries, etc.
	Pirkei Avot, see .A2-.A23
	Rosh ha-Shanah
.R5	Original texts (Hebrew or Aramaic). By date
.R5A-Z	Translations. By language, A-Z
.R6	Selections. By date
.R7	Criticism. Commentaries, etc.
	Sanhedrin
.S2	Original texts (Hebrew or Aramaic). By date
.S2A-Z	Translations. By language, A-Z
.S22	Selections. By date
.S23	Criticism. Commentaries, etc.

	Shabbat
.S25	Original texts (Hebrew or Aramaic). By date
.S25A-Z	Translations. By language, A-Z
.S26	Selections. By date
.S27	Criticism. Commentaries, etc.
	Shebi'it (Shevi'it)
.S3	Original texts (Hebrew or Aramaic). By date
.S3A-Z	Translations. By language, A-Z
.S32	Selections. By date
.S33	Criticism. Commentaries, etc.
	Shebu'ot (Shevu'ot)
.S4	Original texts (Hebrew or Aramaic). By date
.S4A-Z	Translations. By language, A-Z
.S42	Selections. By date
.S43	Criticism. Commentaries, etc.
	Sheḥitat kodashim, see .Z5-.Z7
	Shekalim
.S5	Original texts (Hebrew or Aramaic). By date
.S5A-Z	Translations. By language, A-Z
.S52	Selections. By date
.S53	Criticism. Commentaries, etc.
	Shevi'it, see .S3-.S33
	Shevu'ot, see .S4-.S43
	Sotah
.S7	Original texts (Hebrew or Aramaic). By date
.S7A-Z	Translations. By language, A-Z
.S72	Selections. By date
.S73	Criticism. Commentaries, etc.
	Sukkah
.S9	Original texts (Hebrew or Aramaic). By date
.S9A-Z	Translations. By language, A-Z
.S92	Selections. By date
.S93	Criticism. Commentaries, etc.
	Ta'anit
.T2	Original texts (Hebrew or Aramaic). By date
.T2A-Z	Translations. By language, A-Z
.T22	Selections. By date
.T23	Criticism. Commentaries, etc.
	Tamid
.T3	Original texts (Hebrew or Aramaic). By date
.T3A-Z	Translations. By language, A-Z
.T32	Selections. By date
.T33	Criticism. Commentaries, etc.
	Tebul yom (Tevul yom)
.T4	Original texts (Hebrew or Aramaic). By date
.T4A-Z	Translations. By language, A-Z
.T42	Selections. By date
.T43	Criticism. Commentaries, etc.
	Temurah
.T5	Original texts (Hebrew or Aramaic). By date
.T5A-Z	Translations. By language, A-Z
.T52	Selections. By date
.T53	Criticism. Commentaries, etc.

	Terumot
.T6	Original texts (Hebrew or Aramaic). By date
.T6A-Z	Translations. By language, A-Z
.T62	Selections. By date
.T63	Criticism. Commentaries, etc.
	Tevul yom, see .T4-.T43
	Tohorot (Order)
.T7	Original texts (Hebrew or Aramaic). By date
.T7A-Z	Translations. By language, A-Z
.T72	Selections. By date
.T73	Criticism. Commentaries, etc.
	Tohorot
.T8	Original texts (Hebrew or Aramaic). By date
.T8A-Z	Translations. By language, A-Z
.T82	Selections. By date
.T83	Criticism. Commentaries, etc.
	Ukẓin
.U5	Original texts (Hebrew or Aramaic). By date
.U5A-Z	Translations. By language, A-Z
.U6	Selections. By date
.U7	Criticism. Commentaries, etc.
	Yadayim
.Y2	Original texts (Hebrew or Aramaic). By date
.Y2A-Z	Translations. By language, A-Z
.Y3	Selections. By date
.Y4	Criticism. Commentaries, etc.
	Yevamot
.Y5	Original texts (Hebrew or Aramaic). By date
.Y5A-Z	Translations. By language, A-Z
.Y6	Selections. By date
.Y7	Criticism. Commentaries, etc.
	Yoma
.Y8	Original texts (Hebrew or Aramaic). By date
.Y8A-Z	Translations. By language, A-Z
.Y82	Selections. By date
.Y83	Criticism. Commentaries, etc.
	Zavim
.Z2	Original texts (Hebrew or Aramaic). By date
.Z2A-Z	Translations. By language, A-Z
.Z3	Selections. By date
.Z4	Criticism. Commentaries, etc.
	Zebaḥim (Zevaḥim). Sheḥitat kodashim
.Z5	Original texts (Hebrew or Aramaic). By date
.Z5A-Z	Translations. By language, A-Z
.Z6	Selections. By date
.Z7	Criticism. Commentaries, etc.
	Zera'im (Order)
.Z8	Original texts (Hebrew or Aramaic). By date
.Z8A-Z	Translations. By language, A-Z
.Z82	Selections. By date
.Z83	Criticism. Commentaries, etc.
	Zevaḥim, see .Z5-.Z7

BM2 TABLE FOR LOCAL HISTORY OF JUDAISM (SUCCESSIVE CUTTER NUMBERS) BM2

.x	General works
.x2A-Z	Individual synagogues or congregations, A-Z

	Texts
.xA05	Facsimiles. By date
.xA1	Original language. By date
	Translations
.xA2	Hebrew. By date
.xA3	English. By date
.xA4	French. By date
.xA5	German. By date
.xA61-.xA619	Other languages. By language, alphabetically, and date
.xA7-.xZ	History and criticism

	Texts
.x	Original language (Aramaic or Hebrew). By date
.x12	English. Subarranged by translator
.x13	French. Subarranged by translator
.x14	German. Subarranged by translator
.x15	Hebrew (if translation). Subarranged by translator
.x16	Other languages, A-Z. Subarranged by date
.x19	Criticism

	Texts
.x	Original language (Aramaic or Hebrew). By date
.x2	English. Subarranged by translator
.x3	French. Subarranged by translator
.x4	German. Subarranged by translator
.x5	Hebrew (if translation). Subarranged by translator
.x6	Other languages, A-Z. Subarranged by date
.x9	Criticism

.xA3	By date (if author or editor is unknown)
.xA5-.xZ	By author or editor

	Texts
	Ashkenazi or unspecified rite
	Hebrew only
.xA3	By date (if editor is unknown)
.xA5-.xZ5	By editor, etc.
.xZ52-.xZ529	Manuscripts in facsimile. By name of manuscript or by name of artist or calligrapher
	Translations
.xZ54-.xZ549	Polyglot. By editor or translator
.xZ55-.xZ559	English. By editor or translator
.xZ56-.xZ569	French. By editor or translator
.xZ57-.xZ579	German. By editor or translator
.xZ58-.xZ589	Other languages
.xZ62-.xZ629	Other traditional rites. By rite as given in uniform title
	Non-traditional rites
.xZ64-.xZ649	Conservative. By editor or institution given in uniform title
.xZ65-.xZ659	Reconstructionist. By editor or institution given in uniform title
.xZ66-.xZ669	Reform. By editor or institution given in uniform title Including European liberal
.xZ67-.xZ679	Other. By editor or institution given in uniform title
.xZ68-.xZ689	Adaptations for children. By editor or institution given in uniform title or added entry
.xZ7-.xZ9	Criticism

BP1 TABLE FOR PARTS AND CHAPTERS OF THE KORAN (1 NUMBER) BP1

.A2	Original texts. By date
	Translations
.A3A-Z	English. By translator, A-Z
.A4A-Z	Other languages, A-Z
.A5-.Z	Criticism, etc.

.xA1-.xA29	General works
.xA3-.xZ	Local, A-Z, or individual, A-Z, if location is unnamed *Under each locality* *.x* *General* *.x2* *Individual*

.x1	General works
.x2A2	Collective biography
.x2A3	Works by the founder or central figure
.x2A5-.x2Z	Criticism and biography of the founder or central figure
	Including devotional literature, cultus, etc.
	For other individual biography, see BP80

.A1A-Z	Collected works. By editor, A-Z
.A2	Works by the Imam of a Shiite nature, apocryphal works, collections of his Hadith, etc. For orthodox Muslim works, see BP166+
.A3	Biography, criticism
.A5-.Z	Devotional literature, cultus, tomb, etc.

.x-.x19	Works by author
.x2A-Z	Works about author, A-Z

BQ1 TABLE FOR BUDDHIST SACRED BOOKS (10 NUMBERS) BQ1

0	Original texts (Pali, Sanskrit, Tibetan, Chinese, etc.)
	Subarrange by editor or date of imprint
1	Partial editions, selections, etc.
	Subarrange by editor or date of imprint
	For selections sacred to a particular sect, see Table BQ4 8, etc.
	Translations and adaptations (with or without original text)
	Subarrange by translator or adaptor
2.A1	Polyglot
2.A2-Z	Western languages, A-Z
3.A-Z	Oriental and other languages, A-Z
	Commentaries
5	Early works to 1800
7	1801-
	Including modern criticism, interpretation, etc.
8	Sermons
9	Dictionaries. Indexes. Concordances

0	Original texts (Pali, Sanskrit, Tibetan, Chinese, etc.)
	Subarrange by editor or date of imprint
0.1	Partial editions, selections, etc.
	Subarrange by editor or date of imprint
	For selections sacred to a particular sect, see Table BQ4 8, etc.
	Translations and adaptations (with or without original text)
	Subarrange by translator or adaptor
0.2.A1	Polyglot
0.2.A2-Z	Western languages, A-Z
0.3.A-Z	Oriental and other languages, A-Z
	Commentaries
0.5	Early works to 1800
0.7	1801-
	Including modern criticism, interpretation, etc.
0.8	Sermons
0.9	Dictionaries. Indexes. Concordances

.x	Original texts (Pali, Sanskrit, Tibetan, Chinese, etc.)
	Subarrange by editor or date of imprint
.x1	Partial editions, selections, etc.
	Subarrange by editor or date of imprint
	For selections sacred to a particular sect, see Table BQ4 8, etc.
	Translations and adaptations (with or without original text)
	Subarrange by translator or adaptor
.x2	Polyglot
.x22.A-Z	Western languages, A-Z
.x3.A-Z	Oriental and other languages, A-Z
	Commentaries
.x5	Early works to 1800
.x7	1801-
	Including modern criticism, interpretation, etc.
.x8	Sermons
.x9	Dictionaries. Indexes. Concordances

.x	Original texts (Pali, Sanskrit, Tibetan, Chinese, etc.)
	Subarrange by editor or date of imprint
.x1	Partial editions, selections, etc.
	Subarrange by editor or date of imprint
	For selections sacred to a particular sect, see Table BQ4 8, etc.
	Translations and adaptations (with or without original text)
	Subarrange by translator or adaptor
.x2	Polyglot
.x22A-Z	Western languages, A-Z
.x3A-Z	Oriental and other languages, A-Z
	Commentaries
.x5	Early works to 1800
.x7	1801-
	Including modern criticism, interpretation, etc.
.x8	Sermons
.x9	Dictionaries. Indexes. Concordances

0 Periodicals. Yearbooks
Societies, councils, associations, clubs, etc.
For societies, associations, etc. in local areas, see Table BQ4 2.A-2.Z
1 General works. History
1.2.A-Z International associations, A-Z
1.4 Young Buddhist associations
1.6 Young men's associations
1.8 Women's associations
2.A-Z By region or country, A-Z
Under each country:
.x General works. History
.x2A-Z Local, A-Z
.x3A-Z Individual, A-Z
Financial institutions. Trusts
3 General works
4.A-Z Individual, A-Z
Congresses. Conferences
5 General
5.5 Special. By date
6 Directories
7.A-Z Museums. Exhibitions. By city, A-Z
8 Collections. Collected works
Including selections sacred to a particular sect
9 Encyclopedias. Dictionaries
9.5 Terminology
Religious education
10 General works. History
11.A-Z By region or country, A-Z
Under each country:
.x General works. History
.x2A-Z Local, A-Z
11.2 Religious education of the young. Sunday schools, etc.
11.4 Religious education in the home
History
12 Collections. Collected works. Sources. Chronological tables
General works
12.2 Early works through 1800
12.3 1801-
12.4 Historiography
By period
12.5 Early to ca. 1200 A.D.
12.6 1200-1850
12.7 1850-1945
12.8 1945-
12.9.A-Z By region or country, A-Z
Under each country:
.x General works. History
.x2A-Z Local, A-Z
Persecutions
13 General works. History

Persecutions -- Continued
13.5.A-Z By region or country, A-Z
Under each country:
.x *General works. History*
.x2A-Z *Local, A-Z*
Literature
Including juvenile works
14 Collections
14.2 History and criticism
14.4.A-Z By region or country, A-Z
Under each country:
.x *Collections*
.x2 *History and criticism*
General works
15 Early works through 1800
15.2 1801-1945
15.4 1946-
15.6 Popular works. Pictorial works
15.7 Juvenile works
15.8 General special
e.g. Introduction to the sacred books of the sect, etc.
15.9 Essence, genius, and nature
16 Addresses, essays, lectures, etc.
17 Questions and answers. Maxims
Doctrine
General works
18 Early works through 1800
18.2 1801-1945
18.3 1946-
18.4 History
18.5 Introductions
18.6 General special
18.7 Addresses, essays, lectures, etc.
18.8 Creeds and catechism
18.9 Systemization of teachings based on the sect
19 Controversial works against the sect. Polemics
19.2 Apologetic works
19.4.A-Z Relations to other religious and philosophical systems, A-Z
19.4.C35 Catholic Church
19.4.C5 Christianity
19.4.C65 Confucianism
19.4.H37 Hasidism
19.4.S55 Shinto
19.4.T3 Taoism
19.6.A-Z Relations to other branches of Buddhism, A-Z
Prefer classification with smaller or less-known sect
20 Religious practice. Forms of worship
20.2 Ceremonies and rites. Ceremonial rules
Service books
20.4 For priests, etc.
20.6 For the laity

Religious practice.
Forms of worship
Ceremonies and rites.
Ceremonial rules -- Continued
21.A-Z Special ceremonies and rites, A-Z
21.A26 Abhiṣeka
21.F48 Fetal propitiatory rites
21.F8 Funeral service. Wakes. Burial service. Cremation
21.H6 Homa
21.M4 Memorial services for the dead
Hymns. Chants. Recitations.
Collections of hymns
22 General
22.5.A-Z By region or country, A-Z
Under each country:
.x General
.x2A-Z Local, A-Z
History and criticism
23 General works
23.5.A-Z By region or country, A-Z
Under each country:
.x General works
.x2A-Z Local, A-Z
24 Individual texts. By author or title
24.5 Liturgical objects. Vestments, etc.
25 Temple organization. Membership. Finance
Ministry. Organization. Government
26 General works
27 Handbooks. Manuals
28 Election, selection, succession, appointment, etc. Ordination
29 Hierarchical offices
30 Heresy trials. By date
31 Education and training of the ordained ministry
32.A-Z Special ministries, A-Z
Prefer classification in BQ5305 unless unique to the sect
Preaching
33 General works
33.5 Practical preaching
Sermons
Prefer classification with specific subject or canonical text
34 Several authors
35.A-Z Individual authors. By author and title, A-Z
Religious life
36 General works
36.2 Popular works, stories, etc.
Including exempla
36.4 Religious duties, etc. of the laity
Devotional literature
37 History and criticism

Religious practice.
Forms of worship
Religious life
Devotional literature -- Continued
Collections. Collected works
37.2 Early works through 1800
37.4 1801-
37.6 Selections for daily reading. Devotional calendars
38 Devotion. Meditation. Prayer. Spiritual life. Mysticism. Enlightenment
Devotions. Meditations. Prayers
39 Early works through 1800
39.5 1801-
Festivals. Days and seasons
40 General works. History
40.2.A-Z By region or country, A-Z
Under each country:
.x *General works*
.x2A-Z *Local, A-Z*
40.4.A-Z Special, A-Z
Prefer classification in BQ5720 unless unique to the sect
40.4.F6 Founder's Day
Folklore
41 Collections. General works
41.2 History and criticism
41.4.A-Z By region or country, A-Z
Under each country:
.x *Collections*
.x2 *History and criticism*
Benevolent work. Social work. Welfare work, etc.
42 Periodicals. Societies. Associations
42.2 Directories. Yearbooks
42.3 History
42.4 General works
42.6 Biography (Collective)
By region or country
See BQ5899
Missionary work
43 Museums. Exhibitions
43.2 History
43.4 General works. Treatises
43.6.A-Z By region or country, A-Z
Under each country:
.x *General works*
.x2A-Z *Local, A-Z*
Monasticism and monastic life
44 History
44.2 General works

Monasticism and
monastic life -- Continued
44.4A-Z By region or country, A-Z
Under each country:
.x *General works*
.x2A-Z *Local, A-Z*
Monastic life. Vows. Discipline. Rules
45 Early works through 1800
45.5 1801-
Monasteries. Temples. Shrines. Sites
46 History
46.5 General works
By region or country
See BQ6330-BQ6388
Biography
48 Collective
49.A-Z Founders and other important leaders, A-Z
Including local founders
Subarrange each person by Table BQ8
Other individuals
See BQ940-BQ999

0	Periodicals. Societies. Congresses. Directories. Collections
1	Religious education
2	History. General works
3	Literature. Folklore, etc.
4	Doctrine. Forms of worship
5	Organization. Government
6	Religious life. Devotional literature
7	Benevolent work. Social work. Missionary work
8	Monasticism. Temples
	Biography
9.A2	Collective
9.A3-Z	Founders and other important leaders, A-Z Including local founders Subarrange each person by Table BQ8
	Other individuals See BQ940-BQ999

.x	Periodicals. Societies. Congresses. Directories. Collections
.x1	Religious education
.x2	History. General works
.x3	Literature. Folklore, etc.
.x4	Doctrine. Forms of worship
.x5	Organization. Government
.x6	Religious life. Devotional literature
.x7	Benevolent work. Social work. Missionary work
.x8	Monasticism. Temples
	Biography
.x9	Collective
.x92A-Z	Founders and other important leaders, A-Z Including local founders Subarrange each person by Table BQ9
	Other individuals See BQ940-BQ999

.x	Collected works. By date
.x2	Partial editions. Selections. Quotations, etc. By date
.x3A-Z	Translations. By language, A-Z, and date
.x4A-Z	Individual works. By title, A-Z
.x5	Periodicals. Societies. Congresses. Exhibitions
.x6	Dictionaries. Indexes. Concordances
.x7	Biography and criticism Including autobiography, diaries, etc.
.x9	Sermons about the founder, etc.

.x	Collected works. By date
.x2	Partial editions. Selections. Quotations, etc. By date
.x3-.x39	Translations. By language, alphabetically, and date
.x4-.x49	Individual works. By title, alphabetically
.x5-.x59	Periodicals. Societies. Congresses. Exhibitions
.x6-.x69	Dictionaries. Indexes. Concordances
.x7-.x79	Biography and criticism Including autobiography, diaries, etc.
.x9-.x99	Sermons about the founder, etc.

.x	Periodicals. Collections, etc. Sources
.x2	General works. History
.x3	General special
.x4	Biography (Collective)
.x5A-Z	Local, A-Z

.x	General works
	Including nature, representation, own world, etc.
.x2	Historical development of concepts on the deity
	Cultus
.x3	General works
.x4A-Z	By region or country, A-Z

.x	General works
	Cultus
.x2	General works
.x3A-Z	By region or country, A-Z
.x4A-Z	Local, A-Z

BQ13 TABLE FOR BUDDHIST MONASTERIES, TEMPLES, ETC., IN SPECIFIC COUNTRIES (2 NUMBERS) BQ13

1.A2	Directories
1.A3-Z	General works
2.A-Z	Local, A-Z, or individual, A-Z, if location is unnamed
	Under each locality:
.x	*General works*
	Including directories
.x2A-Z	*Individual, A-Z*

0	Periodicals. Societies. Congresses. Directories. Collections
0.1	Religious education
0.2	History. General works
0.3	Literature. Folklore, etc.
0.4	Doctrine. Forms of worship
0.5	Organization. Government
0.6	Religious life. Devotional literature
0.7	Benevolent work. Social work. Missionary work
0.8	Monasticism. Temples
	Biography
0.9.A2	Collective
	Founders and other important leaders, A-Z see BQ7950
	Other individuals See BQ940-BQ999

INDEX

NUMERALS

48 Vows: BQ4455
613 commandments
  Halacha: BM520.8

A

A-phyi Chos-kyi-sgrol-ma: BQ4890.A42 +
A.C. Bhaktivedanta Swami, Prabhupāda: BL1285.892.A28
Aaron of Belz, 1880-1957: BM755.A115
Aatim (Hindu deity): BL1225.A37 +
Abadim: BM506.4.A15 +
Abba Arika
  Biography: BM755.A2
  Talmudist: BM502.3.A2
Abba Guryon (Midrash): BM517.A1 +
Abd-ru-shin, 1875-1941
  Biography: BP605.B54B4
  Works: BP605.B4 +
'Abdu'l-Bahá, 1844-1921
  Biography: BP393
  Works: BP363
Abhayagiri: BQ8000 +
Abhidhammapiṭaka: BQ1200 +
Abhidhānottaratantra: BQ2180.A24 +
Abhidharma (Abhidhamma): BQ4195 +
Abhidharmadīpa: BQ2660 +
Abhidharmahṛdayaśāstra (by Dharmaśreṣṭhi): BQ2730.A35 +
Abhidharmajñānaprasthānaśāstra (by Kātyāyanīputra): BQ2670 +
Abhidharmakośa. Kārikā and bhāṣya (by Vasubandhu): BQ2680 +
Abhidharmamahāvibhāṣaśāstra: BQ2690 +
Abhidharmāmṛtarasaśāstra: BQ2730.A36 +
Abhidharmanyāyānusārīśāstra: BQ2700 +
Abhidharmapiṭaka: BQ1160 +, BQ2490 +
  Chinese version: BQ1240 +
  Pali version: BQ1200 +
Abhidharmaprakaraṇabhāsya: BQ2730.A3697 +
Abhidharmaprakaraṇapāda (by Vasumitra): BQ2730.A37 +
Abhidharmasaṃgītiparyayapāda. Saṃgītiparyaya (by Mahākauṣṭhila): BQ2730.A39 +
Abhidharmasamuccaya. Mahāyānābhidharmasamuccaya (by Asaṅga): BQ3080.A25 +
Abhidharmāvatāraśāstra (by Skandhila): BQ2730.A44 +
Abhidharmavijñānakāyapāda: BQ2730.A46 +
Abhiniṣkramaṇasūtra: BQ1600.A23 +
Abhisamācārikā: BQ2429.8.A32 +
Abhisamayamañjarī (by Śubhākaragupta): BQ3340.A24 +
Abi-Ḥasira, Jacob ben Masoud, 1808-1880: BM755.A87
Abidji
  Religions: BL2480.A3
Abkir (Midrash): BM517.A2 +
Ablutions
  Islam: BP184.4
Abors
  Religion: BL2032.A2
Abraham (Biblical patriarch)
  Koran: BP133.7.A27
  Midrash: BM518.A2
Abrahamites (Bohemia): BP605.A2
Abravanel, Isaac, 1437-1508: BM755.A25
Abrogating and abrogated
  Hadith: BP136.78
Abrogator and abrogated verses
  Koran: BP130.3
Absolute mind (Buddhism): BQ4270

INDEX

Abū Bakr, Caliph, d. 634:
BP135.8.A28
Abū Dā'ūd Sulaymān ibn al-Ash'ath al-Sijistānī, 817 or 18-889
Hadith: BP135.A13+
Abubabaji: BP610.A32+
Abulafia, Abraham ben Samuel, 1240-ca. 1292:
BM755.A28
Abyssinian flight by followers of Muḥammad:
BP77.47
Academies for Talmudic study
Babylonia and Palestine: BM502
Acala: BQ4860.A4+
Ācāradaśa: BL1313.3.A83+
Ācārāṅga: BL1312.3.A93+
Ācāryakriyāsamuccaya (by Jagaddarpana):
BQ3340.A25+
Acoli
Religions: BL2480.A33
Acting
Hinduism: BL1239.5.A25
Actualism: BP605.A25
Adam (Biblical figure)
Koran: BP133.7.A3
Midrash: BM518.A4
Adapa
Assyro-Babylonian religions: BL1625.A35
Adar
Judaism: BM693.A32
Adbhutadharmaparyāya:
BQ2240.A24+
Addiction, Religious: BL53.5
Addicts, Recovering
Religious life: BL625.9.R43
Adhimukti: BQ4340+
Adhyardhaśatikā: BQ1890+
Adhyātmopaniṣad:
BL1124.7.A45+
Adi-Granth: BL2017.4+
Ādipurāṇa: BL1140.4.B74+
Aditi (Hindu deity): BL1225.A4+
Ādityas (Hindu deities):
BL1225.A443+
Administration
Synagogues: BM653
Admonition
Jewish way of life: BM723.5
Adolescence
Anthroposophy: BP596.A36
Adonis
Classical mythology: BL820.A25
Adult child abuse victims
Religious life: BL625.9.A37
Adult children of dysfunctional families
Religious life: BL625.9.A38
Advayasiddhi (by Lakṣmīṅkarā):
BQ3340.A34+
Advent, Second
Anthroposophy: BP596.S4
Advertising
Islam: BP185.72
Aeacus
Classical mythology: BL820.A3
Aeneas
Classical mythology: BL820.A34
Aesculapius
Classical mythology: BL820.A4
Aesthetics
Koran: BP134.A38
Aesthetics and religion:
BL65.A4
Aetherius Society: BP605.A33
African Americans
Islam
History: BP62.B56
Religious life: BL625.2
African Hebrew Israelite Nation of Jerusalem:
BP605.B63
African religions: BL2390+
Central Africa: BL2466
East Africa: BL2464
North Africa: BL2462
Southern Africa: BL2463
Sub-Saharan Africa: BL2462.5
West Africa: BL2465
Afro-Brazilian cults: BL2590.B7, BL2592.A+
Afro-Caribbean cults: BL2565+
Agadat Ester (Midrash):
BM517.A34+
Āgamas
Buddhism: BQ1280+
Hinduism: BL1141.4+
Jainism: BL1310+

INDEX

Agamemnon
Classical mythology: BL820.A46
Aged
Buddhism
Devotional literature: BQ5585.A5
Religious life: BQ5435
Hinduism
Religious life: BL1237.42
Judaism: BM540.A35
Prayer and service books: BM667.A35
Religious life: BL625.4
Aggada
Midrash: BM516+
Aggadat Bereshit (Midrash): BM517.A3+
Aggaññasutta: BQ1300.A35+
Aghorīs: BL1280.9+
Aging and religion: BL65.A46
Āgneyapurāṇa: BL1140.4.A46+
Agni (Hindu deity): BL1225.A45+
Agnicayana
Hinduism: BL1226.82.A33
Agnihotra
Hinduism: BL1226.82.A35
Agnipurāṇa: BL1140.4.A46+
Agniveśyagṛhyasūtra: BL1134.3+
Agnosticism: BL2747.2
Agonshū: BQ9800.A36+
Agriculture
Buddhism: BQ4570.A35
Comparative mythology: BL325.A35
Judaism: BM538.A4
Aharon ben Yiśakhar Dov, a.b.d. ḳ. Belza, 1880-1957: BM755.A115
Aharonim
Babylonian Talmud: BM501.9
Ahimsa
Jainism: BL1375.A35
Ahirbudhnyasaṃhitā: BL1141.8.A55+
Ahl-i Ḥadīth: BP195.A3+
Ahl-i Ḥaqq: BP195.A4+
Aḥmad, Ghulām, Hazrat Mirza, 1839?-1908: BP195.A5+
Ahmadiyya: BP195.A5+
Sufism: BP189.7.B3+
Ahoms
Religion: BL2032.A35
AIDS (Disease)
Buddhism: BQ4570.A37
Ainu
Religions: BL2370.A5
Aion
Classical mythology: BL820.A54
Aitareyabrāhmaṇa: BL1116.4+
Aitareyāraṇyaka: BL1122.4+
Aitareyopaniṣad: BL1124.7.A58+
Aïvanhov, Omraam Mikhaël: BP610.A35+
Aiyanār (Hindu deity): BL1225.A57+
Ājivikas: BL2020.A4+
Ājñāsaṃyakpramāṇa-nāma-ḍākinyupadeśa (by Tillopāda): BQ3340.A55+
Akans
Religions: BL2480.A4
Ākāśabhairavakalpa: BL1142.6.A35+
Ākāśagarbha: BQ4710.A35+
Akdamut millim: BM670.A42
Akhilananda
Hinduism: BL1272.2+
Akiba ben Joseph, ca. 50-ca. 132
Talmudist: BM502.3.A36
Akṣayamatinirdeśasūtra: BQ2240.A33+
Akṣobhya: BQ4690.A6+
Prayers and devotions to: BQ5592.A44
Akṣobhyatathāgatavyūha: BQ2240.A35+
Akṣyupaniṣad (Akṣikopaniṣad): BL1124.7.A65+
Akutobhaya mūlamadhyamakavṛtti (by Nāgārjuna): BQ2800+
Al yithalel (Midrash): BM517.A4+
Alagaddūpama Sutta: BQ1320.A42+
Alakhgīrs: BL1272.5+
Alakhiyas: BL1272.5+
Ālambanaparīkṣā (by Dignāga): BQ2930+
Ālavakasutta: BQ1419.5.A45+

Ālayavijñāna: BQ4445
Alcmene
Classical mythology: BL820.A56
Alcohol
Judaism: BM729.A34
Alcoholics
Religious life: BL625.9.A43
Alcoholics, Families of
Religious life: BL625.9.F35
Aleinu le-shabbe'aḥ: BM670.A44
Alekha: BL1272.7+
Aleph beth (Midrash):
BM517.A63+
Alexander, the Great
Koran: BP133.7.A42
Alfasi, Isaac ben Jacob,
1013-11-3. Halakhot:
BM520.82
'Alī al-Hādī ibn
Muḥammad, 827-868: BP193.2
'Alī al-Riḍā ibn
Mūsá, d. 818 or 19:
BP193.18
'Alī ibn Abī Ṭālib,
600 (ca.)-661: BP193.1
'Alī ibn Abī Ṭālib,
Caliph, 600 (ca.) - 661
Koran: BP133.7.A44
'Alī Muḥammad
Shīrāzī, called Bāb
1819-1850
Biography: BP391
Aliens
Judaism: BM720.N6
Allegory
Midrash: BM518.A45
'Almānīyah: BP190.5.S35
Alms
Islam: BP180
Alphabet
Hinduism: BL1215.L36
Sufism: BP189.65.A47
Altais
Religions: BL2370.A52
Altar cloths
Buddhism: BQ5080+
Altars: BL602
Buddhism: BQ5075.A6
Hinduism: BL1236.76.A48
Judaism: BM657.A5
Shinto: BL2224.35+
Amar Jyoti, Swami: BP605.T78
Amarapura: BQ8060+
Amaterasu Ōmikami: BL2226.2.A5
Amazons
Classical mythology: BL820.A6
Ambaṭṭha sutta: BQ1300.A45+
Amen
Judaism: BM670.A64
Ametsuchi no Kai: BP605.A4
Amidah: BM670.S5
Amitābha: BQ4690.A7+
Prayers and devotions to:
BQ5592.A45
Amitābha Buddha's Land:
BQ4535+
Amitārthasūtra: BQ2070+
Amitāyurdhyānasūtra: BQ2020+
Amitāyus: BQ4690.A7+
Amitiés spirituelles, Les:
BP610.S43+
Amon (Egyptian deity):
BL2450.A45
Amoraim: BM501.3
Amphibians
Comparative mythology:
BL325.A45
Amrit
Sikhism: BL2018.5.A47
Amṛta
Buddhism: BQ4570.I5
Hinduism: BL1215.I66
Amulets
Buddhism: BQ4570.A4
Hinduism: BL1236.76.A49
Islam: BP190.5.A5
Judaism: BM729.A4
Shinto: BL2227.8.A45
Amusements
Islam: BP190.5.A55
Amycus
Classical mythology: BL820.A63
Anada
Religions: BL2630.A68
Anahit (Goddess): BL2335.A52
Anākāra School: BQ7520
Abhidharmapiṭaka: BQ2920+
Ananda Cooperative Village:
BP605.S38A52
Ananda Marga: BL1272.8+
Ānandamūrti: BL1272.892.A5
Ānāpānasatisutta:
BQ1320.A48+
Ānāpānasmṛti: BQ5630.A6

Anat (Deity): BL1605.A5, BL1645.A53
Anātman: BQ4262
Anatomy, Human
  Talmudic literature: BM509.H84
Anattalakkhaṇasutta:
  BQ1339.5.A52+
Ancestor worship: BL467
  Buddhism: BQ4570.A5
  Hinduism: BL1239.5.A52
  India, Religions of: BL2015.A6
  Japan: BL2211.A5
  Judaism
    Ancient: BM178
  Korea: BL2236.A53
Andrews, Lynn V.: BP610.A54+
Androgyny
  Comparative mythology:
    BL325.B45
Andromeda
  Classical mythology: BL820.A64
Angas
  Buddhism: BQ1280+
  Jainism: BL1312.2+
Angas (African people)
  Religions: BL2480.A47
Angavijjā: BL1312.9.A56+
Angelic communion
  Theosophy: BP573.A5
Angels: BL477, BT965+
  Buddhism: BQ4900+
  Islam: BP166.89
  Judaism: BM645.A6
  Koran: BP134.A5
  Talmudic literature: BM509.A48
  Theosophy: BP573.A5
Aṅgulimāla Sutta: BQ1320.A53+
Anguttaranikāya: BQ1340+
Animal experimentation
  Nature worship: BL439.5
Animal slaughter
  Judaism: BM720.S6+
Animal worship: BL439+
  Japan: BL2211.A6
Animals
  Buddhism: BQ4570.A53
  Comparative mythology: BL325.A6
  Egyptian religion: BL2450.A54
  Greek religion and
    mythology: BL795.A54
  Hadith literature: BP135.8.A54
  India, Religions of: BL2015.A65
  Judaism: BM729.A5
  Koran: BP134.N3
Animals
  Nature worship: BL439+
  Talmudic literature: BM509.A5
  Theosophy: BP573.A55
Animals, Killing of
  Nature worship: BL439.5
Animism
  Buddhism: BQ4570.A54
  Egyptian religion: BL2450.A6
  Hinduism: BL1215.A56
  Islam: BP190.5.A6
Anitya: BQ4260
Anityātasutra: BQ2240.A54+
Anlo
  Religions: BL2480.A5
Annadākalpatantra:
  BL1142.6.A55+
Annapūrṇā (Hindu deity):
  BL1225.A64+
Ansaru Allah Community: BP212
Antagaḍadasāo: BL1312.3.A58+
Antakr̥tadaśa: BL1312.3.A58+
Antaryāptisamarthana (by
  Ratnākaraśanti): BQ3100+
Antenor
  Classical mythology: BL820.A65
Anteus
  Classical mythology: BL820.A67
Anthesteria
  Greek religion and
    mythology: BL795.A56
Anthropology and religion:
  BL256
Anthropology, Buddhist:
  BQ4570.M34
Anthropomorphism: BL215+
Anthroposophy: BP595+
Anti-cult movements: BP604+
Antichrist
  Islam: BP166.84
Antiquities
  Buddhism: BQ221+
  Hinduism: BL1109.2+
  Shinto: BL2227.8.A5
Anu (Deity): BL1625.A5
Anubis (Egyptian deity):
  BL2450.A62
Anūnatvāpūrṇatvanird
  eśaparivarta: BQ2240.A58+
Aṇuogadāra: BL1313.6.A58+

Anuttaropapātikadaśa:
BL1312.3.A59+
Anuttarovavāiyadasāo:
BL1312.3.A59+
Aṇuvrata: BL1380.A55
Anuvrati Sangh: BL1273.2+
Anuyogadvāra: BL1313.6.A58+
Apadāna: BQ1500+
Aparamitāyurjñānadhrd
aya: BQ2049.5.A63+
Aparimitāyur dhāranī.
Aparimitāyurjñananā
mamahāyānasūtra:
BQ1670.A63+
Āpastambagṛhyasūtra:
BL1133.8+
Āpastambakalpasūtra:
BL1126.3.A63+
Āpastambaśrautasūtra:
BL1128.6+
Āpastambaśulbasūtra:
BL1136.8.A63+
Apatani (Indic people)
Religion: BL2032.A63
Apedemak (Egyptian deity):
BL2450.A64
Aphrodite
Classical mythology: BL820.V5
Apocalyptic literature: BL501
Apocalypticism: BL501
Apohasiddhi (by
Ratnakīrti): BQ3110+
Apollo
Classical mythology: BL820.A7
Apologetics
Babylonian Talmud: BM503.3
Buddhism: BQ4050
Hinduism: BL1211.5
Islam: BP170
Judaism: BM648
Lamaism: BQ7648
Mādhyamika School: BQ7468
Mahayana Buddhism: BQ7424
Shiites: BP194.1
Theravāda Buddhism: BQ7265
Yogācāra School: BQ7504
Apostasy: BL639.5
Islam: BP168
Apostates, Treatment of
Judaism: BM720.H5
Apotheosis: BL465+
Appliances, Electrical
Judaism: BM729.E45
Appreciation of Hadith:
BP136.4+
Apsarases: BL1225.A65+
'Aqā'id: BP165.5
Aquarian Educational Group:
BP605.A617
Aquarian Foundation: BP605.A62
Arab contributions to
Islam: BP190.5.A67
Arab status in Islam:
BP190.5.A67
Arabian Peninsula
Islam: BP190.5.A66
Arabian religions: BL1680+
Arabs
Hadith literature: BP135.8.A7
Arabs in Islam: BP190.5.A67
Aramean religions: BL1610
Āraṇyakas: BL1122.2+
Arapesh
Religions: BL2630.A72
Arba'ah ṭurim
Halacha: BM520.86
Archaeology
Buddhism: BQ221+
Hinduism: BL1109.2+
Archaeology and religion:
BL65.A72, BL250
Arctic regions
Religions: BL2670+
Ares
Classical mythology: BL820.M2
Arete Truth Center: BP605.A67
Argonauts
Classical mythology: BL820.A8
Arhat: BQ4289
Arhats: BQ4865+
Ariadne
Classical mythology: BL820.A83
Arica Institute: BP605.A7
Arjun's Sukhamani: BL2017.44
Ark of the covenant
Judaism: BM657.A8
Ark of the law
Judaism: BM657.A85
Armed forces
Buddhism
Devotional literature:
BQ5585.S6

Armed Forces
  Judaism
    Prayer and service books: BM667.S6
Armenia, Religions of: BL2330+
Armenians
  Early religions: BL975.A75
Aromatic plants
  Greek religion and mythology: BL795.A7
Ārṣeyabrāhmaṇa: BL1121.3.A78+
Ārṣeyakalpasūtra: BL1126.3.A77+
Art
  Buddhism: BQ4570.A7
  Islam: BP190.5.A7
  Judaism: BM538.A7
Artemis (Greek deity)
  Classical mythology: BL820.D5
Arthaviniścayasūtra: BQ2240.A77+
Arts and Buddhism: BQ4570.A72
Aruṇopaniṣat: BL1124.7.A67+
Arvit: BM675.A78, BM675.S35
Arya-Samaj: BL1273.5+
Āryamūlasarvāstivādi śrāmaṇerakārikā: BQ2309.5.A7+
Aryan religions: BL660
Āryaśūra: BQ1460+
Asahara, Shōkō: BP605.O88
Āsāḷha Pūjā: BQ5720.A8
Asana
  Hinduism: BL1238.58.P67
Asbāb al-nuzūl: BP130.32
Ascension
  Muḥammad: BP166.57
  Religion: BL503.5
Asceticism
  Buddhism: BQ6200+
  Hinduism: BL1239.5.A82
  India, Religions of: BL2015.A8
  Islam: BP190.5.A75
  Jainism: BL1375.A75
  Religious life: BL625
  Sufism: BP189.52
Ascription
  Hadith literature: BP136.33, BP136.44
'Aśeret ha-dibrot (Midrash): BM517.A7+
Ash rite
  Hinduism: BL1226.82.V52
Ashantis
  Religions: BL2480.A8
Asharites: BP166.14.A84
Ash'arīyah: BP166.14.A84
Asherah
  Semitic religions: BL1605.A7
Ashkenazic rite: BM672.A8
Ashkenazim relations with Sephardim
  Medieval: BM182
Ashmorot: BM670.A69
Ashram life
  Hinduism: BL1238.72+
Ashrams
  Hinduism: BL1243.72+
Ashtoreth
  Semitic religions: BL1605.I8
'Āshūrā: BP186.3
  Sermons: BP183.63
Asian Buddhist Conference for Peace: BQ20.A74+
Asian religions: BL1000+
'Askarī, al-Ḥasan ibn Alī, d. 874: BP193.21
Asmat
  Religion: BL2123.A84
Aśoka
  Buddhism: BQ295
Aśokarājasūtra: BQ2240.A85+
Aśokāvadāna: BQ1540+
Āśramas
  Hinduism: BL1237.75
Assassins
  Islam: BP195.A8+
Association for Research and Enlightenment, Virginia Beach, Va.: BP605.A77
Assur (Assyrian deity): BL1625.A8
Assyro-Babylonian religion: BL1620+
Assyro-Babylonian religion and Judaism: BM536.A8
Aṣṭādaśasāhasrikā: BQ1900+
Astara: BP605.A8
Astarte
  Semitic religions: BL1605.I8
Aṣṭasāhasrikā: BQ1910+

Astral body
Theosophy: BP573.A7
Astrology
Anthroposophy: BP596.Z6
Talmudic literature: BM509.A7
Astronautics
Islam: BP190.5.A8
Judaism: BM538.A75
Astronautics and religion:
BL254
Astronomy
Koran: BP134.A8
Talmudic literature: BM509.A72
Astronomy and religion: BL253+
Asturians
Early religions: BL975.A8
Asura-gati: BQ4513
Asuras: BQ4790+
Āśvalāyanagṛhyapari
śiṣṭa: BL1131.6+
Āśvalāyanagṛhyasūtra:
BL1131.5+
Āśvalāyanaśrautapari
śiṣṭa: BL1126.8+
Āśvalāyanaśrautasūt
ra: BL1126.7+
Aśvamedha
Hinduism: BL1226.82.A8
Aśvins (Hindu deities):
BL1225.A7+
Atalanta
Classical mythology: BL820.A835
Aten (Egyptian deity):
BL2450.A83
Atharvaveda Brāhmaṇa:
BL1121.7+
Atharvaveda saṃhitās:
BL1114.6+
Atharvavedic Śrautasūtra:
BL1129.7+
Atheism: BL2747.3
Athena
Classical mythology: BL820.M6
Athene
Classical mythology: BL820.M6
Athletes
Religious life: BL625.9.A84
Atīśa, 982-1054: BQ7950.A87+
Atma Ram Pandurang:
BL1279.592.A84
Atman
Hinduism: BL1213.56
Jainism: BL1357.A85
Ātman-Brahman
Hinduism: BL1213.56
Ātmapūjopaniṣad:
BL1124.7.A75+
Atomic warfare and Judaism:
BM538.A8
Atomic warfare and
religion: BL65.A85
Atomism
Islam: BP166.25
Atonement
Hinduism: BL1214.32.A85,
BL1226.82.A85
Jainism: BL1375.A8
Judaism: BM645.A8
Atonement, Day of
Festivals and fasts: BM695.A8
Liturgical books: BM675.Y58
Atrisaṃhitā: BL1142.3.A87+
Aṭṭhakavagga: BQ1419.5.A86+
Attis
Classical mythology: BL820.A84
Atum (Egyptian deity):
BL2450.A89
Atuot
Religions: BL2480.A88
Aupapātika: BL1312.6.U83+
Aura
Theosophy: BP573.A8
Aurobindo Ashram: BL1273.8+
Australia
Religions: BL2610
Authority
Babylonian Talmud: BM503
Hadith: BP136.4+
Islam: BP165.7
Koran: BP130.7+
Religion: BL105
Avadānas: BQ1530+
Avadānaśataka: BQ1550+
Avadim: BM506.4.A15+
Avalokiteśvara: BQ4710.A8+
Prayers and devotions to:
BQ5592.A8
Avalokiteśvarasamantamu
khaparivarta: BQ2060+
Avarice
Islam: BP188.14.A92
Āvassaya: BL1313.9.A83+

Avaśyaka: BL1313.9.A83+
Avataṃsakasūtra. Buddhāvataṃsakamahā vaipulyasūtra: BQ1620+
Avatars
Hinduism: BL1213.36
Avayavinirākaraṇa (by Paṇḍita Aśoka): BQ3120+
Avesta: BL1515+
Aviḥatsira, Jacob, 1808-1880: BM755.A87
Avkir (Midrash): BM517.A2+
Avodah (Yom Kippur liturgy): BM670.A73
Avot de-Rabbi Nathan: BM506.4.A94+
Avyaktapaniṣad: BL1124.7.A88+
Awakening (Buddhism): BQ4315
Awqāf: BP170.25
Āyāradasāo: BL1313.3.A83+
Āyāraṅga: BL1312.3.A93+
Ayelet ha-shaḥar: BM675.R412
Ayyappan (Hindu deity): BL1225.A9+
Azāriqah: BP195.A84+
Azharot: BM670.A8
Azraqites: BP195.A84+

B

Ba
Egyptian religion: BL2450.B2
Ba da ren jue jing: BQ1529.5.P34+
Ba gua jiao: BL1943.P34
Ba ji ku nan tuo lo ni jing: BQ1670.P29+
'Ba'-rom-pa: BQ7686+
Baal
Canaanite religions: BL1671
Semitic religions: BL1605.B26
Baal Hammon
Semitic religions: BL1665.B3
Ba'al Shem Ṭov, ca. 1700-1760: BM755.I8
Bāb, 'Alī Muḥammad Shīrāzī, 1819-1850
Biography: BP391
Works: BP361
Babburukamme: BL1273.895+
Babism: BP340
Babylonian Talmud: BM499+
Special orders and tractates: BM506.A+
Babylonian Talmudic academies: BM502
Bacchus
Classical mythology: BL820.B2
Bachama
Religions: BL2480.B22
Badawiyah
Sufism: BP189.7.B3+
Bagalāmukhī (Hindu deity): BL1225.B3+
Baganda
Religions: BL2480.B225
Bahai Faith: BP300+
Bahá'u'lláh, 1817-1892
Biography: BP392
Works: BP362
Bahir: BM525.A3+
Bailian jiao: BQ8670+
Bajau
Religion: BL2135.B34
Bakoko
Religions: BL2480.B23
Bakossi
Religions: BL2480.B244
Balahāṛis: BL1273.9+
Balarāma (Hindu deity): BL1225.B345+
Balarāmīs: BL1273.9+
Balder
Germanic and Norse mythology: BL870.B3
Balisier plant and religion: BL65.B34
Balkar (Turkic people)
Early religions: BL975.B26
Baltic early religions: BL945
Baluba
Religions: BL2480.B25
Bambara
Religions: BL2480.B26
Bamileke
Religions: BL2480.B27
Bangladesh, Religions of: BL2040
Bangle
Sikhism: BL2018.5.B4
Bantus
Religions: BL2480.B3

Banum
Religions: BL2480.B32
Baoulé
Religions: BL2480.B33
Baptism
Judaism: BM703
Bar mitzvah: BM707+
Baraita
Talmudic literature: BM507+
Barakah
Islam: BP190.5.B3
Bareelly School: BP166.14.B37
Bargabhima (Hindu deity): BL1225.B35+
Basa
Religions: BL2480.B337
Basakata
Religions: BL2480.B34
Basava, fl. 1160: BL1281.292.B37
Basin offering (Buddhist rite)
Lamaism: BQ7699.B74
Basmalah: BP183.7.B3
Bat mitzvah: BM707+
Bāṭa Ṭhākurāṇī (Hindu deity): BL1225.B37+
Batak
Religion: BL2123.B38
Batetela
Religions: BL2480.B37
Bathing
Hinduism: BL1226.82.B38
Batinites: BP195.B3+
Batuque: BL2592.B3
Baucis and Philemon
Classical mythology: BL820.B28
Baudhāyanagṛhyasūtra: BL1133.6+
Baudhāyanapitṛmedhasū tra: BL1137.3.B38+
Baudhāyanaśrautasūtra: BL1128.2+
Baudhāyanaśulbasūtra: BL1136.8.B38+
Bauer, Michael, 1871-1929: BP597.B3
Bauls: BL1284.8+
Beads
Religion: BL619.B43
Beard
Islam: BP190.5.H3
Bears
Nature worship: BL443.B4
Beijing
Chinese religions: BL1812.P45
Bektashi
Sufism: BP189.7.B4+
Bells
Buddhism: BQ5075.B4
Hinduism: BL1236.76.B45
Belz
Hasidism: BM198.5
Bembas
Religions: BL2480.B4
Benedictions
Judaism
Liturgical books: BM675.B4
Oraḥ ḥayim law: BM523.3.B4
Benevolence (Gemilut ḥasadim)
Yoreh de'ah law: BM523.5.B4
Benevolent work
Buddhism: BQ5851+
Hinduism: BL1243.52+
Islam: BP170.2
Benito: BL2592.B45
Bennett, John Godolphin, 1897-1974: BP610.B46+
Berat gecesi: BP186.38
Sermons: BP183.638
Berawan
Religion: BL2083.B45
Bereaved children
Religious life: BL625.9.B47
Bereaved parents
Religious life: BL625.9.B48
Bereavement
Anthroposophy: BP596.B47
Islam: BP190.5.C57
Bereavement and religion: BL65.B47
Bereshit rabati (Midrash): BM517.B7+
Bereshit zuta (Midrash): BM517.B8+
Berit milah: BM705
Bernhardt, Oscar Ernst, 1875-1941
Biography: BP605.B54B4
Works: BP605.B4+

Besant, Annie Wood, 1847-1933
Biography: BP585.B3
Works: BP563
Besht
Biography: BM755.I8
Beth Hillel: BM501.25
Beth Shammai: BM501.25
Beti
Religions: BL2480.B47
Betsimisaraka
Religions: BL2480.B49
Bhadrakalpikasūtra: BQ2240.B49+
Bhadramāyākāravyākarana: BQ1800.B45+
Bhadrapāla: BQ1830+
Bhādū (Hindu deity): BL1225.B47+
Bhagavadgītā: BL1138.6+
Bhagavaī: BL1312.3.B53+
Bhāgavatapurāṇa: BL1140.4.B43+
Bhagavatas: BL1285.2+
Bhagavati (Hindu deity): BL1225.B48+
Bhagavatī (Jain literature): BL1312.3.B53+
Bhagwan Shree Rajneesh: BP605.R34+
Bhairava (Hindu deity): BL1225.B494+
Bhaiṣajyaguru: BQ4690.B5+
Bhaiṣajyaguruvaidūryaprabharājasūtra: BQ2240.B53+
Bhakti
Buddhism: BQ4340+
Hinduism: BL1214.32.B53
Sikhism: BL2018.5.B45
Bhakti yoga: BL1238.56.B53
Bhāradvājagṛhyasūtra: BL1133.7+
Bhāradvājapitṛmedhasutra: BL1137.3.B53+
Bhāradvājaśrautasūtra: BL1128.4+
Bhārasutta: BQ1339.5.B54+
Bhasma
Hinduism: BL1226.82.B48
Bhāvanākrama, Parts I-III (by Kamalaśīla): BQ3130+
Bhavānī (Hindu deity): BL1225.B5+
Bhāvanopaniṣad: BL1124.7.B53+
Bhaviṣyapurāạ: BL1140.4.B44+
Bhaviṣyottarapurāṇa: BL1140.4.B45+
Bhikkhu
Biography: BQ843
Monasticism: BQ6140+
Bhikkhunī
Biography: BQ855
Monasticism: BQ6150+
Bhikṣu
Biography: BQ843
Doctrines: BQ4550+
Monasticism: BQ6140+
Bhikṣunī
Biography: BQ855
Doctrines: BQ4550+
Monasticism: BQ6150+
Bhiksunivinaya: BQ2429.8.B48+
Bhils
Religion: BL2032.B48
Bhūtaḍāmaratantra: BL1142.6.B48+
Bhuvaneśvarī (Hindu deity): BL1225.B58+
Bible and the Koran: BP134.B4
Bible characters in the Koran: BP134.B5
Bible reading
Judaism: BM663
Biblical legends
Islam: BP137+
Bid'ah: BP165.7
Bie xing jing: BQ2180.B53+
Bīja: BQ4445
Bijas: BQ5125.B5
Bio-dynamics, Church of: BP605.C53
Biographers
Muḥammad, Prophet, d. 632: BP75.4+
Biography (as a concept)
Anthroposophy: BP596.B56
Biology and religion: BL255

Birds
  Comparative mythology:
    BL325.B43
  Nature worship: BL442
Birifor
  Religions: BL2480.B5
Birkat ha-ḥamah: BM675.B53
Birkat ha-ilanot: BM675.B48
Birkat kohanim: BM670.P74
Birkat She-heḥeyanu: BM670.B57
Birth
  Egyptian religion: BL2450.C65
Birth customs
  Religion: BL619.B57
Bisexuality
  Comparative mythology:
    BL325.B45
  Greek religion and
    mythology: BL795.B57
Bishnois
  Hinduism
    Religious life: BL1237.58.B57
Bka'-gdams-pa: BQ7670+
Bka'-rgyud-pa: BQ7679+
Bkaḥ-ḥgyur: BQ1260+
Bla med go 'phan sgrub
  thabs kyi mdo: BQ7971.5.B53+
Black Hebrew Israelite
  Nation: BP605.B63
Black Hebrews: BP605.B64
Black Muslims: BP221+
Blasphemy
  Islam: BP167.3
Blasphemy and religion:
    BL65.B54
Blavatsky, Helena
  Petrovna, 1831-1891
  Biography: BP585.B6
  Works: BP561.A1+
Blessing of the sun
  Judaism
    Liturgical books: BM675.B53
Blessings
  Buddhism: BQ5030.D4
Blood
  Comparative mythology: BL325.B5
  Japanese religions: BL2211.B56
  Theosophy: BP573.B5
Blood accusation cases
  Judaism: BM585.2
Blood as food or medicine
  Islam: BP184.9.B5
Bobo
  Religions: BL2480.B64
Bodhi: BQ4398+
Bodhi tree worship: BQ5030.B63
Bodhicaryāvatāra (by
  Śāntideva): BQ3140+
Bodhicitta: BQ4398.5
Bodhicittavivaraṇa (by
  Nāgārjuna, 9th cent.):
    BQ3340.B63+
Bodhidharma, 6th cent.:
    BQ9299.B62+
Bodhipakkhiyadhammas: BQ4399
Bodhisattva: BQ4293
Bodhisattva stages: BQ4330+
Bodhisattva vinaya
  Mahayana Buddhism: BQ7442
Bodhisattvabhūmi: BQ3060+
Bodhisattvamaṇyāvali (by
  Atīśa): BQ3300.B62+
Bodhisattvaprātimokṣa:
    BQ3060+
Bodhisattvas: BQ4695+
  Prayers and devotions to:
    BQ5592.A+
Body, Human
  Islam: BP190.5.B63
  Religious symbolism: BL604.B64
Boethusians
  Rabbinical literature:
    BM496.9.B63
Bona Dea
  Classical mythology: BL820.B64
Bonpo (Sect): BQ7960+
  Relations to Lamaism: BQ7654
Bonpo literature: BQ7965+
Book of life
  Judaism
    Liturgical books: BM675.M7
Book of Raziel: BM525.A36+
Book of temunah: BM525.A39+
Books and reading and
  religion: BL65.B66
Bōre Dēvaru (Hindu
  deity): BL1225.B65+
Boredom
  Religious life: BL625.92
Borvo
  Early Celtic religions:
    BL915.B67
Botany
  Talmudic literature: BM509.B6

Boys
Buddhism
Devotional literature: BQ5585.Y7
Religious life: BQ5470
Brahmā
Hinduism: BL1217+
Brahma-samaj: BL1274.5+
Brahmajālasutta: BQ1300.B73+
Brahmakumari: BL1274.2+
Brāhmaṇas: BL1116.2+
Brāhmanaśāsana rite: BL1226.82.B7
Brahmāṇḍapurāṇa: BL1140.4.B73+
Brahmanism and Buddhism: BQ4610.B7
Brahmans
Hinduism: BL1241.46
Brahmapurāṇa: BL1140.4.B74+
Brahmasaṃhitā: BL1141.8.B53+
Brahmāsutta: BQ1339.5.B72+
Brahmavaivartapurāṇa: BL1140.4.B75+
Brahmāvaivasvata: BL1140.4.B75+
Brahmosomaj: BL1274.5+
Branch Davidians: BP605.B72
Bratas
Hinduism: BL1237.78
Bratslav
Hasidism: BM198.52
Brazilian religions: BL2590.B7
Breaking the fast at the end of Ramadan: BP186.45
Breast feeding
Islam: BP190.5.B72
Breastplate of the High Priest
Judaism: BM657.B7
Breath
Theosophy: BP573.B7
Breathing (Buddhist religious practice): BQ5630.A6
Bṛhadāraṇyaka: BL1123.5+
Bṛhadāraṇyakopaniṣad: BL1124.7.B75+
Bṛhaddharmapurāṇa: BL1140.4.B76+
Bṛhannāradīyapurāṇa: BL1140.4.B77+
Bṛhannīlatantra: BL1142.6.B75+
Bṛhaspati (Hindu deity): BL1225.B7+
Bṛhat-kalpa: BL1313.3.K36+
'Bri-guṅ-pa: BQ7684+
Bribery
Islam: BP188.14.B75
Bridgewater treatises
Natural theology: BL175.B7+
Bṛihaspati (Hindu deity): BL1225.B7+
Brit bat
Judaism: BM706
Broadcasting, Religious
Islam: BP185.74+
Brodhisattvapiṭakasūtra: BQ1800.B63+
Brother XII, 1878-1934?: BP605.A62
Brotherhood
Islam: BP190.5.B74
Brotherhood (Brothers and Sisters of the Inner World): BP605.G44
Brotherhoods
Islam: BP189.68+
Brotherliness
Islam: BP190.5.B74
'Brug-pa: BQ7683+
Bskal pa bzan po'i mdo: BQ7971.5.B74+
Bstan-'dzin-rgya-mtsho (Dalai Lama XIV): BQ7935.B77+
Bstan-ḥgyur: BQ1270+
Bstan-pa'i-ñi-ma, Panchen Lama IV, 1781-1854: BQ7945.B75+
Bubba Free John, 1939- : BP610.B8+
Buddha: BQ4180
Buddhabhūmisūtra: BQ2240.B82+
Buddhacarita (by Aśvaghoṣa): BQ1606.B83+
Buddhagayā (Bodh-Gayā, Bihar): BQ6480
Buddhaghosa: BQ366
Buddhagotraśāstra (by Vasubandhu): BQ2940+
Buddhahood: BQ4450

Buddhapiṭakaduḥśīlan
igraha: BQ2240.B83+
Buddhas
Prayers and devotions to:
BQ5592.A+
Buddhatā: BQ4450
Buddhavaṃsa: BQ1510+
Buddhism: BQ1+
Biography: BQ840+
Controversial literature:
BQ4045
Deities: BQ4620+
Doctrines: BQ4061+
Folklore: BQ5725+
History: BQ251+
Ministry: BQ5140+
Missionary work: BQ5901+
Monasticism: BQ6001+
Pantheon: BQ4620+
Priesthood: BQ5140+
Relations to other
religions: BQ4600+
Islam: BP173.B9
Shinto: BL2222.23
Relations to special
subjects: BQ4570.A+
Religious life: BQ5360+
Ritual: BQ4965+
Sacred books: BQ1100+
Copying: BQ5680.C6
Sermons: BQ5340+
Worship: BQ4911+
Buddhist anthropology:
BQ4570.M34
Buddhist literature: BQ1001+
Buddhist name: BQ5355.B8
Buddhist precepts: BQ5485+
Buddhist saints
Prayers and devotions to:
BQ5593.A+
Bugis
Religion: BL2123.B83
Builsa
Religions: BL2480.B84
Bukhārī, Muḥammad ibn
Ismāʻīl, 810-870
Hadith: BP135.A12+
Bulgars (Turkic people)
Early religions: BL975.B84
Bulls
Nature worship: BL443.B8
'Bum (Prajñāpāramitās):
BQ7972.2+
'Bum Ñi ma dgu śar:
BQ7972.5.B85+
Burial service
Buddhism: BQ5020
Burial services for
freethinkers: BL2777.B8
Buriats
Religions: BL2370.B87
Burning bush
Midrash: BM518.B87
Business
Buddhism: BQ4570.B86
Businesspeople
Religious life: BL625.9.B87
Bussho Gonenkai Kyōdan:
BQ8350+
Buzan: BQ9000+
Byakkō Shinkōkai: BL2228.B92+

C

Cacus
Classical mythology: BL820.C127
Cadmus
Classical mythology: BL820.C13
Caduceus
Nature worship: BL457.C3
Caesarean section
Talmudic literature: BM509.C3
Cain (Biblical figure)
Midrash: BM518.C34
Cakradhara, 13th cent.:
BL1277.892.C35
Cakrasamvara: BQ4860.C35+
Cakrasamvāratantra:
BQ2180.C35+
Cakravartin: BQ4570.K5
Caliphate
Islam
Theology: BP166.9
Caliphs
Hadith literature: BP135.8.C35
Call to prayer
Islam: BP184.3
Calling
Religious life: BL629
Calls to prayer
Islam: BP183.4
Calydonian boar
Classical mythology: BL820.C15

Camephis (Egyptian deity):
BL2450.C3
Camilla
Classical mythology: BL820.C16
Campaigns, Military
Muḥammad, Prophet, d. 632:
BP77.7
Campanha do Quilo: BL2592.C34
Camps
Jewish religious education:
BM135
Cāmuṇḍā (Hindu deity):
BL1225.C24+
Cāmuṇḍī (Hindu deity):
BL1225.C24+
Canaanite religions: BL1670+
Caṇḍā (Hindu deity):
BL1225.C25+
Candakumārajātaka:
BQ1470.C34+
Caṇḍamahāroṣana:
BQ3340.C35+
Candapannatti: BL1312.6.C35+
Candāvejjhaya: BL1312.9.C35+
Caṇḍeśvara (Hindu
deity): BL1225.C247+
Caṇḍī (Hindu deity):
BL1225.C25+
Caṇḍikā (Hindu deity):
BL1225.C25+
Candles
Buddhism: BQ5075.C3
Judaism: BM657.C3
Candomblé: BL2592.C35
Candragarbha: BQ1820+
Candrajñānāgama:
BL1141.5.C35+
Candraprabhakumārasūtra:
BQ2240.C35+
Candraprajñapti: BL1312.6.C35+
Cantors
Judaism: BM658.2
Cao Daism (Vietnam) and
Buddhism: BQ4610.C3
Captured animals, Release
of
Buddhism: BQ5030.H6
Caregivers
Religious life: BL625.9.C35
Cariyāpiṭaka: BQ1520+
Caro, Joseph, 1488-1575
Biography: BM755.C28
Caro, Joseph, 1488-1575.
Shulḥan ʻarukh: BM520.88
Carthaginian religions: BL1660+
Cassandra
Classical mythology: BL820.C18
Caste
Buddhism: BQ4570.C3
Hinduism: BL1215.C3
Jainism: BL1375.C3
Castor and Pollux
Classical mythology: BL820.C2
Castration
Religion: BL619.C3
Catechisms
Buddhism: BQ196
Islam: BP45
Koran study: BP130.86
Shinto: BL2221.7
Catimbó: BL2592.C38
Cats
Nature worship: BL443.C3
Cattle
Hinduism: BL1215.C7
Catuḥśatakaśāstra (by
Āryadeva): BQ2760+
Catuḥstava (by
Nāgārjuna): BQ2910.C38+
Catuṣpariṣatsūtra:
BQ1300.C35+
Cauḍamma (Hindu deity):
BL1225.C38+
Causal body
Theosophy: BP573.C2
Causation (Buddhism): BQ4240+
Celestial bodies
Nature worship: BL438
Celibacy
Hinduism: BL1237.82.C46
Jainism: BL1375.C44
Celtiberi
Early religions: BL975.C4
Celtic early religions: BL900+
Censorship
Judaism: BM729.C4
Censorship and religion:
BL65.C45
Census
Rabbinical literature:
BM496.9.C45
Ceramics
Talmudic literature: BM509.C4

Cerebus
Classical mythology: BL820.C4
Ceremonial rules
Lamaism: BQ7695+
Ceremonies
Buddhism: BQ4965+
Chinese religions: BL1812.R57
Confucianism: BL1858+
Hinduism: BL1226.18+
India, Religions of: BL2015.R48
Islam: BP184+
Jainism: BL1377+
Japanese religions: BL2211.R5
Korean religions: BL2236.R58
Lamaism: BQ7695+
Religion: BL600+
Samaritans: BM980
Shiites: BP194.4
Shinto: BL2224.2+
Sufism: BP189.58+
Taoism: BL1940.4
Zoroastrianism: BL1590.L58
Ceres
Classical mythology: BL820.C5
Cerrahiye
Sufism: BP189.7.C47+
Chaga
Religions: BL2480.C43
Chai: BQ5720.U75
Chain of transmission
Hadith literature: BP136.33
Chaitanya (Sect): BL1285.3+
Chaitanya, 1486-1534:
BL1285.392.C53
Chakras
Hinduism: BL1215.C45
Theosophy: BP573.C5
Chaldean religions: BL1630
Chamba
Religions: BL2480.C45
Chan ch'a shan o yeh pao
ching: BQ2240.C39+
Chan yao jing: BQ3300.C47+
Chāndogyabrāhmaṇa:
BL1121.3.U63+
Chāndogyopaniṣad:
BL1124.7.C53+
Chang shou mieh tsui hu
chu t'ung tzu t'o lo ni
ching: BQ2240.C43+
Change
Anthroposophy: BP596.C37
Religious life: BL629.5.C53
Change and religion: BL65.C53
Chants
Buddhism: BQ5035+
Hinduism: BL1236.22+
Lamaism: BQ7700+
Chaplains, Buddhist: BQ5305.C4
Characters, Biblical, in
the Koran: BP134.B5
Charge of heresy
Islam: BP167.5
Charities
Buddhism: BQ4570.C45
Islam: BP170.25
Sikhism: BL2018.5.C4
Charity
Jainism: BL1375.C45
Charms
Shinto: BL2227.8.A45
Charon
Classical mythology: BL820.C55
Charybdis
Classical mythology: BL820.S39
Chedasūtras: BL1313.2+
Chemistry and religion:
BL265.C4
Chen-fu (Sect): BQ9800.C48+
Chen k'ung chiao: BL1943.C5
Chengguan, 738-839: BQ8249.C45+
Cherubim: BL478
Cheyasuttas: BL1313.2+
Chi-ts'ang, 549-623:
BQ8809.C55+
Chidvilasananda, Gurumayi:
BL1283.792.C45
Chien-chen, 688-763:
BQ8789.C47+
Chiga
Religions: BL2480.C48
Chih ch'an ping pi yao fa:
BQ1529.5.C55+
Chih-i, 538-597: BQ9149.C45+
Child and parent
Greek religion and
mythology: BL795.P37
Children
Buddhism: BQ4570.C47
Devotional literature:
BQ5585.C4
Religious life: BQ5436

Children
  Greek religion and
    mythology: BL795.C55
  Hinduism
    Religious life: BL1237.54
  Islam: BP173.3
    Devotional literature:
    BP188.3.C5
  Judaism
    Prayer and service books: BM666
    Religious duties: BM727
    Sermons: BM743
  Rationalism
    Religious training: BL2777.R4
  Religious life: BL625.5
Children and fathers
  Judaism
    Religious duties: BM725.5
Children and parents
  Even ha-'ezer law: BM523.7.P3
Children of God (Movement):
    BP605.C38
Children of the Koran: BP133.5+
Chimera
  Classical mythology: BL820.C57
Chinese religions: BL1790+
Chinnamastā (Hindu deity):
    BL1225.C54+
Chinul, 1158-1210: BQ9519.C45+
Chishtīyah
  Sufism: BP189.7.C49+
Chivalry
  Islam: BP188.16.C47
Chizan: BQ9050+
Chokossi
  Religions: BL2480.C49
Chokwe
  Religions: BL2480.C5
Cholas invasion, 1073
  Buddhism
    Sri Lanka: BQ367
Cholas rule
  Buddhism
    Sri Lanka: BQ367
Ch'ŏndogyo: BL2240.C5+
Ch'ŏnji Taean'gyo: BL2240.C6
Ch'ŏnjin'gyo: BL2240.C63
Chosen people
  Judaism: BM613+
Christ Foundation: BP605.C42
Christ International
  Community: BP605.I45
Christ Ministry Foundation:
    BP605.C43
Christengemeinschaft: BP605.C45
Christianity and Jews: BM535
Christianity in the Koran:
    BP134.C45
Christians
  Talmudic literature: BM509.C5
Christmas
  Anthroposophy: BP596.C4
Christmas trees
  Anthroposophy: BP596.C4
Christward Ministry: BP605.C5
Chronic pain patients
  Religious life: BL625.9.C47
Chu fen shuo jing: BQ2240.C45+
Ch'üan chen chiao: BL1943.C55
Chuang-tzu: BL1900.C45+
Church of Creative
  Bio-dynamics: BP605.C53
Church of God Unlimited:
    BP605.C534
Church of Religious
  Research: BP605.C54
Church of Religious
  Science: BP605.U53
Church of the Creator:
    BP605.C55
Church of the Path: BP605.C557
Church of the Truth: BP605.C56
Church Universal and
  Triumphant: BP605.S73
Chuvash
  Early religions: BL975.C46
Cīnācārasāratantra:
    BL1142.6.C56+
Circassians
  Religions: BL2370.C5
Circe
  Classical mythology: BL820.C6
Circle
  Religious symbolism: BL604.C5
Círculo Esotérico da
  Comunhão do Pensamento:
    BP605.C57
Circumcision
  Islam: BP184.8
  Judaism: BM705
  Midrash: BM518.C5
  Religion: BL619.C57

Cities and towns
Sacred places: BL582
Citragupta (Hindu deity):
BL1225.C57+
Citron
Judaism: BM657.C5
Citta: BQ4445
Cittaviśuddhiprakaraṇa
(by Āryadeva): BQ3340.C55+
Civil religion: BL98.5
Civil rights
Islam: BP173.44
Civil rights and religion:
BL65.C58
Civilization and Buddhism:
BQ4570.C8
Civilization and Islam:
BP190.5.C54
Civilization and Judaism: BM537
Civilization and religion: BL55
Clairvoyance
Buddhism: BQ4570.C58
Hinduism: BL1215.C53
Classical religion and
mythology: BL700+
Cleobis and Biton
Classical mythology: BL820.C62
Clothing
Islam: BP190.5.C6
Judaism: BM720.C6
Clouds
Comparative mythology:
BL325.C56
Cobras
Egyptian religion: BL2450.C62
Codependents
Religious life: BL625.9.C62
Codes
Halacha: BM520.82+
Cohanim
Judaism: BM720.C65
Coincidence
Religious life: BL625.93
College students
Islam
Devotional literature:
BP188.3.C64
Religious life: BL625.9.C64
Colonies
Greek religion and
mythology: BL795.C57
Colonization
Greek religion and
mythology: BL795.C57
Comic, The, and religion:
BL65.L3
Commandments
Halacha: BM520.7+
Commentators of Hadith:
BP135.62.A+
Communal religious
activities
Sufism: BP190
Communication
India, Religions of: BL2015.C65
Islam: BP184.27
Koran: BP134.C56
Communion, Angelic
Theosophy: BP573.A5
Community affairs,
Participation by rabbis:
BM652.7
Companions
Muḥammad
Hadith literature: BP136.46
Muḥammad, Prophet, d. 632:
BP75.5+, BP76.9
Comparative mythology: BL300+
Comparative religion,
Study of: BL41
Compassion (Buddhism): BQ4360
Compulsive gamblers
Religious life: BL625.9.C65
Computer network resources
Judaism: BM67
Religion: BL37
Computer science and
religion: BL255.5
Concentration
Theosophy: BP573.C7
Conception
Egyptian religion: BL2450.C65
Concordia
Classical mythology: BL820.C63
Concordia Augusta
Classical mythology: BL820.C63
Conduct of services,
meetings, etc.
Judaism
Work of the rabbi: BM652.6

Confession
  Buddhism: BQ5030.C6
    Prayer: BQ5594.C65
  Hinduism: BL1226.82.C66
  Judaism: BM723.7
    Liturgy: BM670.C64
  Lamaism: BQ7699.C65
  Religion: BL619.C6
Confirmation
  Buddhism: BQ5005
  Judaism: BM707+
Conflict management
  Islam: BP190.5.C56
Confucianism: BL1830+
Confucianism and Buddhism:
  BQ4610.C6
Confucianism and Islam:
  BP173.C65
Congregational Hebrew
  School: BM109.C6
Congregations
  Judaism: BM653+
Congshen, 778-861: BQ9299.T75+
Conscientious objectors
  and Judaism: BM538.P3
Consecration of images
  Buddhism: BQ5030.C62
Conservative Judaism: BM197.5
Consolation
  Islam: BP190.5.C57
  Judaism: BM729.C6
Constantinople, Council of
  (869-870)
  Anthroposophy: BP596.C68
Constellations
  Greek religion and
    mythology: BL795.C58
Contemplation
  Jainism: BL1378.85
Contemplation on death
  (Buddhism): BQ5630.D4
Contests
  Greek religion and
    mythology: BL795.C6
Conversion
  Judaism: BM645.C6
  Religion: BL639
Converts
  Buddhism: BQ5970+
  Islam: BP170.5
  Religion: BL639
Copper Scroll
  Dead Sea scrolls: BM488.C6
Coptic Church
  Relation to Islam: BP172.5.C6
Copying
  Tripiṭaka: BQ1136.C6
Corn
  Nature worship: BL457.C6
Cornerstone ceremonies
  Buddhism: BQ5030.C64
Cosmogony
  Assyro-Babylonian
    religions: BL1625.C6
  Buddhism: BQ4570.C6
  Egyptian religion: BL2450.C67
  Hinduism: BL1215.C6
  India, Religions of: BL2015.C67
  Islam: BP166.23
  Jainism: BL1375.C6
  Japan: BL2211.C67
  Koran: BP134.C6
Cosmology
  Buddhism: BQ4570.C6
  Hinduism: BL1215.C6
  India, Religions of: BL2015.C67
  Islam: BP166.23
  Jainism: BL1375.C6
  Koran: BP134.C6
Costume
  Islam: BP190.5.C6
Council of Constantinople
  (869-870)
  Anthroposophy: BP596.C68
Councils, Early
  Buddhism: BQ290+
Counseling
  Judaism
    Work of the rabbi: BM652.5
  Shinto: BL2224.55
Course in Miracles
  (Movement): BP605.C67+
Course in miracles (Text):
  BP605.C67
Covenant theology
  Judaism: BM612.5
Covenants
  Judaism: BM612.5
  Religion: BL617
Cows
  Egyptian religion: BL2450.C69
  Hinduism: BL1215.C7

Createdness
Koran: BP130.74
Creation
Comparative mythology: BL325.C7
Egyptian religion: BL2450.C74
Germanic and Norse mythology: BL870.C74
Islam: BP166.23
Koran: BP134.C6
Natural theology: BL224+
Talmudic literature: BM509.C67
Creative ability
Judaism: BM645.C73
Creative Bio-dynamics, Church of: BP605.C53
Creative Initiative Foundation: BP605.C74
Creator, Church of the: BP605.C55
Credibility
Koran: BP130.7+
Creeds
Religious doctrines (General): BL427
Shinto: BL2221.7
Cremation
Buddhism: BQ5020
Gautama Buddha: BQ938
Crime
Greek religion and mythology: BL795.C7
Islam: BP190.5.C75
Roman religion and mythology: BL815.C74
Crime and religion: BL65.C7
Criminals
Greek religion and mythology: BL795.C7
Roman religion and mythology: BL815.C74
Criminals and religion: BL65.C7
Criticism, Principles of
Koran: BP130.2+
Crocodile
Nature worship: BL440
Cross
Religious symbolism: BL604.C7
Crown of God
Rabbinical literature: BM496.9.C76
Cūlamālunkyasuttanta: BQ1320.C85+
Cūlavaṃśa: BQ2640.C85+
Cūlikasuttas: BL1313.5+
Cult tables
Greek religion and mythology: BL795.T32
Cults
Classical mythology: BL820.A+
Korea: BL2236.C6
Culture and Buddhism: BQ4570.C8
Culture and Hinduism: BL1215.C76
Culture and religion: BL65.C8
Cultus
Religion: BL550+
Sikhism: BL2018.3+
Cupid
Classical mythology: BL820.C65
Cups, Kiddush: BM657.K53
Curetes
Classical mythology: BL820.C7
Cybele
Classical mythology: BL820.C8
Cyclopes
Classical mythology: BL820.C83
Cyrene (nymph)
Classical mythology: BL820.C85

D

Da fang bian fo bao en jing: BQ2240.T313+
Da Free John, 1939- : BP610.B8+
Da sheng li qu liu bo lo mi jing: BQ2240.T32+
Da zang jing
Tripiṭaka: BQ1210+
Dacians
Early religions: BL975.D3
Dadu, 1544-1603: BL1285.592.D34
Dādūdayāla, 1544-1603: BL1285.592.D34
Dādūpanthīs: BL1285.5+
Daedalus
Classical mythology: BL820.D25
Daftar: BM960.3.D33+
Dagaaba
Religions: BL2480.D3
Daijōsai: BL2224.25.D34
Daikokuten: BL2211.D33

Daily prayers
  Judaism
    Liturgy: BM674.2+
Daivatabrāhmaṇa (Devatādhyāyabrāhmaṇa): BL1121.3.D35+
Dajjāl: BP166.84
Ḍākinī: BQ4750.D33+
Ḍākinījālasaṃvararahasya (by Anaṅgayogī): BQ3340.D34+
Dakpo: BQ7681+
Dakshiṇa Bhārata Jaina Sabhā: BL1380.D34
Dakṣiṇāmūrtyupaniṣad: BL1124.7.D35+
Dalai Lama V: BQ7935.N34+
Dalai Lama XIV: BQ7935.B77+
Dalai lama, Selection and succession of: BQ7752
Dalai lamas
  Biography: BQ7930+
Dalai lamas' sermons: BQ7762+
Dam-tshig-rdo-rje: BQ4890.D33+
Damamūkanidānasūtra: BQ2240.D33+
Dāmaratantra: BL1142.6.D35+
Dāna: BQ4420.G6
Danaids
  Classical mythology: BL820.D3
Dance
  Greek religion and mythology: BL795.D35
  Judaism: BM720.D2
  Religious life: BL625.94
  Religious ritual: BL605
  Sufism: BP189.65.D36
Dangaleat
  Religions: BL2480.D36
Dani
  Religion: BL2123.D35
Dao de jing: BL1900.L25+
Daochuo, 562-645: BQ8549.T37+
Dard
  Religion: BL2032.D37
Darkness
  Comparative mythology: BL325.L47
  Greek religion and mythology: BL795.L54
Darśanopaniṣad: BL1124.7.D37+
Darshan Singh, Sant: BP605.R85
Dāsa, Rāma Ratana: BL1279.892.D37
Daśabhūmīśvara: BQ1630+
Dasabodhisattuppattikathā: BQ2640.D37+
Daśacakrakṣitigarbha: BQ2240.D35+
Daśadigandhakāravidhvamsana: BQ2240.D36+
Dasam Granth: BL2017.455+
Dasara: BL1239.82.D37
Dasarathajātaka: BQ1470.D35+
Daśasāhasrikā: BQ2000.D37+
Daśavaikālika: BL1313.9.D38+
Dasaveāliya: BL1313.9.D38+
Daśnāmīs: BL1275.2+
Daswen Pādshāh kā Granth: BL2017.455+
Data processing
  Koran
    Criticism: BP130.38
Dāṭhāvaṃsa: BQ2570+
Dattapurāṇa: BL1140.4.D37+
Dattātreya (Deity): BL1225.D3+
Dattatreya (Sect): BL1275.5+
Dattātreyatantra: BL1142.6.D38+
Daughters
  Muḥammad, Prophet, d. 632: BP76.8
David, King of Israel
  Koran: BP133.7.D38
  Koranic legends: BP137.5.D3
Da'wah: BP170.85
Dawn
  Hinduism: BL1215.D3
Dawn Horse Communion: BP610.B8+
Dāwūd
  Koran: BP133.7.D38
Day of Atonement
  Liturgical books: BM675.Y58
Day of sacrifice
  Islam: BP186.6
    Sermons: BP183.66
Dayananda Sarvasti, Swami: BL1273.592.D38
Days of the week
  Comparative mythology: BL325.D33

Days, Sacred: BL590+
  Bahai Faith: BP385+
  Buddhism: BQ5700+
  Hinduism: BL1239.72+
  Islam: BP186+
  Lamaism: BQ7820+
  Shiites: BP194.5.A+
Dbal-gsas: BQ7981.4.D322
Dead
  Comparative mythology: BL325.D35
Dead Sea scrolls: BM487.A05+
Dead, Judgment of the: BL547
Dead, Worship of the: BL470
Death
  Buddhism: BQ4487
    Contemplation: BQ5630.D4
  Comparative mythology: BL325.D35
  Egyptian religion: BL2450.D43
  Gautama Buddha: BQ938
  Greek religion and mythology: BL795.D4
  Hinduism
    Doctrines: BL1214.72
    Religious observances: BL1237.82.D43
  Islam: BP166.815
  Japanese religions: BL2211.D35
  Judaism: BM635.4
  Koran: BP134.D35
  Muḥammad, Prophet, d. 632: BP77.75
  Religion: BL504
  Sikhism: BL2018.5.D4
  Theosophy: BP573.D4
Dedication
  Buddhism: BQ5030.D4
Dedication sermons
  Judaism: BM744.6
Dedication services
  Shinto: BL2224.25.D4
Dedication services for synagogues: BM675.S9
Deism: BL2747.4
Deities
  Assyro-Babylonian religions: BL1625.G6
  Bonpo: BQ7981.2+
  Buddhism: BQ4620+
Deities
  Chinese religions: BL1812.G63
  Egyptian religion: BL2450.G6
  Hinduism: BL1216+
  Jainism: BL1375.3+
  Shinto: BL2226+
Deity, Nature and attributes of: BL205+
Deliverance
  Hinduism: BL1213.58
Deluge
  Assyro-Babylonian religions: BL1625.D4
  Comparative mythology: BL325.D4
  Hinduism: BL1215.D45
Demeter
  Classical mythology: BL820.C5
Democracy
  Islam: BP190.5.D45
Demonology: BL480
  Buddhism: BQ4900+
  Greek religion and mythology: BL795.D5
  Hinduism: BL1215.D46
  Islam: BP166.89
  Japanese religions: BL2211.D4
  Koran: BP134.D4
Deoband School: BP166.14.D4
Depressed persons
  Religious life: BL625.9.D45
Ḍerā Saccā Saudā: BL2020.D47+
Derekh ereẓ: BM506.4.D4+
Dervishes: BP188.45+
Deserts
  Nature worship: BL446
Deśika: BL1288.592.V46
Desire
  Religious life: BL625.95
Destiny
  Natural theology: BL235
Determinism
  Islam: BP166.3+
  Judaism: BM645.F69
Deutschgläubige Gemeinschaft: BP605.D48
Dev-samaj: BL1275.8+
Deva-gati: BQ4508
Devadāsīs
  Hinduism
    Religious life: BL1237.58.D48

Devanārāyana (Hindu
deity): BL1225.D48+
Devandatthao: BL1312.9.D47+
Devarim zuta (Midrash):
BM517.D4+
Devas
Buddhism: BQ4735+
Developing countries
Religions: BL2680
Devībhāgavatapurāṇa:
BL1140.4.D47+
Devil
Buddhism: BQ4900+
Islam: BP166.89
Koran: BP134.D43
Devil worship: BL480
Devīpurāṇa: BL1140.4.D48+
Devotion
Buddhism: BQ5595+
Jainism: BL1378.6
Lamaism: BQ7800+
Sikhism: BL2018.4+
Devotional calendars,
Buddhist: BQ5579+
Devotional literature
Bonpo (Sect): BQ7982.4
Buddhism: BQ5535+
Hinduism: BL1144.52+
Islam: BP188.2+
Jainism: BL1378.7
Judaism: BM724
Lamaism: BQ7785+
Shiites: BP194.7
Shinto: BL2224.3
Sikhism: BL2018.38+
Sufism: BP189.62
Devotions
Bahai Faith: BP380
Lamaism: BQ7810+
Taoism: BL1942.8
Devyupaniṣad: BL1124.7.D48+
Dgah-ldan: BQ7530+
Dge-lugs-pa: BQ7530+
Dgra-lha 'Ye-brdzu: BQ4890.D45+
Dhamma Vijaya: BQ5720.P7
Dhammacakkapavattana Sutta:
BQ1339.5.D45+
Dhammanīti: BQ2640.D48+
Dhammapada: BQ1370+
Dhammapadaṭṭhakathā: BQ1375
Dhammasaṅgaṇi: BQ2500+
Dhammasetkya: BQ5720.D5
Dhāraṇīs: BQ1660+
Dharma
Buddhism: BQ4190
Hinduism: BL1213.52
Dharmacakra: BQ5125.D4
Dharmacakra Day: BQ5720.A8
Dharmadharmatāvibhaṅga
(by Maitreyanātha):
BQ3080.D53+
Dharmadhatu: BQ4210+
Dharmadhātu Origination:
BQ4250.D5
Dharmadhātustava (by
Nāgārjuna): BQ2910.D48+
Dharmagupta School
Vinayapiṭaka: BQ2400+
Dharmākara Bodhisattva,
Original Vow of: BQ4455
Dharmaranyapurāṇa:
BL1140.4.D53+
Dharmasamuccaya: BQ2240.D53+
Dharmasaṅgrahaḥ (by
Nāgārjuna): BQ2770+
Dharmaśarīrasūtra:
BQ2240.D54+
Dharmaskandha: BQ2730.D43+
Dharmatā: BQ4210+
Dharmaṭhākura: BL1276.2+
Dharmatrāta: BQ1380+
Dharmatrātadhyānasūtra:
BQ2240.D56+
Dhātukathā: BQ2520+
Dhimal
Religion: BL2034.5.D48
Dhū al-Qarnayn
Koran: BP133.7.A42
Dhvaja-stambha
Hinduism: BL1236.76.D45
Dialectal words
Koran: BP131.4
Dialectic
Talmudic literature: BM509.D5
Dialogue
Islam: BP190.5.D53
Diana
Classical mythology: BL820.D5
Dianetics: BP605.S2
Diaspora and Israel's
election
Judaism: BM613.5

Dietary laws
Islam: BP184.9.D5
Jainism: BL1375.D53
Judaism: BM710
Sikhism: BL2018.5.D5
Digambara: BL1380.D53
Dīghanikāya: BQ1290+
Dīkṣ
Hinduism: BL1226.82.D55
Diktynna
Classical mythology: BL820.D54
Dīn-i Ilāhī: BP195.D5+
Dinka
Religions: BL2480.D5
Dinkard: BL1520.D5A2+
Diola (African people)
Religions: BL2480.D53
Dionysus
Classical mythology: BL820.B2
Dioscuri, The
Classical mythology: BL820.C2
Dīpaṃkara: BQ4690.D5+
Dipavali: BL1239.82.D58
Dīpavaṃsa: BQ2580+
Direction of prayer
Islam: BP187.45
Directions
Bahai Faith: BP380
Dīrghāgama: BQ2240.D58+
Disciples
Gautama Buddha: BQ900+
Discipleship
Theosophy: BP573.D5
Discipline
Buddhist monasticism: BQ6115+
Hinduism: BL1237.32+
Lamaism: BQ7890
Lamaist religious life: BQ7780
Distribution of the Koran: BP131.18.A+
Diṭṭhivāya: BL1312.3.D58+
Divali: BL1239.82.D58
Divination
Religion: BL613
Divine Life Society: BL1276.3+
Divine Light Emissaries: BP605.E4
Divine Light Mission: BP605.D58
Divine-Love, International Society of: BP605.I55
Divine Revelation (Organization): BP605.D59
Divorce
Judaism: BM713.5
Divorced people
Religious life: BL625.9.D58
Divrei ha-yamim shel Moshe: BM517.D5+
Divyāvadāna: BQ1560+
Doctrine
Hinduism: BL1212.32+
Islam: BP166+
Jainism: BL1356+
Lamaism: BQ7630+
Mahayana Buddhism: BQ7400+
Shiites: BP194+
Shinto: BL2221+
Sufism: BP189.26+
Theravāda Buddhism: BQ7225+
Doctrine of Truth Foundation: BP605.S38D63
Doctrines (General), Religious: BL425+
Dōgen, 1200-1253: BQ9449.D65+
Dogma
Islam: BP165.5
Dogmas
Samaritans: BM945
Dogons
Religions: BL2480.D6
Dogs
Islam: BP190.5.D65
Dolphin
Greek religion and mythology: BL795.D6
Domestic life
Muḥammad, Prophet, d. 632: BP76.7
Domestic rites
Hinduism: BL1226.82.D66
Dookpa: BQ7683+
Dōrizas, Dionysēs: BP610.D65+
Dōsojin
Japanese religions: BL2211.D68
Dove
Religious symbolism: BL604.D6
Dragons
Greek religion and mythology: BL795.D7
Drāhyāyaṇagṛhyasūtra: BL1136.2+
Drāhyāyaṇaśrautasūt ra: BL1129.4+
Dravidian religion: BL2020.D7+

Dream interpretation
Rabbinical literature: BM496.9.D73
Dreams
Islam: BP190.5.D73
Jainism: BL1375.D73
Japanese religions: BL2211.D73
Dreams and religion: BL65.D67
Dress
Islam: BP190.5.C6
Judaism: BM720.C6
Dri ma med pa'i bśags rgyud: BQ2180.D74+
Drigunpa: BQ7684+
Drinking vessels
Religious symbolism: BL604.D7
Drinks and drinking
Germanic and Norse mythology: BL870.D7
Dṛṣṭivāda: BL1312.3.D58+
Drugs and religion: BL65.D7
Druids: BL910
Drukpa: BQ7683+
Drumakinnarājaparipṛcchāsūtra: BQ2240.D78+
Drums
Buddhism: BQ5075.D7
Druzes
Semitic religions: BL1695
Dualism
Hinduism: BL1215.D8
Natural theology: BL218
Duḥkha (Dukkha): BQ4235
Dukpa: BQ7683+
Dunhuang manuscripts: BQ244.T8+
Durgā (Hindu deity): BL1225.D8+
Durgā-pūjā: BL1239.82.D87
Duties, Religious
Buddhism: BQ5415+
Hinduism: BL1237.75+
Islam: BP176+
Judaism: BM725+
Lamaism: BQ7780
Duty
Hinduism: BL1214.32.D88
Dvādaśanikāyaśāstra (by Nāgārjuna): BQ2780+
Dwags-po: BQ7681+
Dwellings
Sacred places: BL588
Dyaks
Religion: BL2123.D9
Dybbuk
Judaism: BM729.D92

E

Eagle
Comparative mythology: BL325.E3
Earth
Nature worship: BL438.2
Earth, Theory of the
Natural theology: BL224+
Earthquakes
Nature worship: BL457.E3
East African religions: BL2464
Ebisu
Japanese religions: BL2211.E24
Echerian Church: BP605.E27
Eckankar: BP605.E3
Eclipses
Comparative mythology: BL325.E35
Ecology
Bahai Faith: BP388.E36
Buddhism: BQ4570.E23
Hinduism: BL1215.N34
Islam: BP190.5.N38
Ecology, Human, and Judaism: BM538.H85
Economics
Anthroposophy: BP596.E25
Buddhism: BQ4570.E25
Greek religion and mythology: BL795.E25
Hadith literature: BP135.8.E28
Hinduism: BL1215.E27
Islam: BP173.75
Koran: BP134.E25
Sikhism: BL2018.5.E36
Talmudic literature: BM509.E27
Ecstasy
Hinduism: BL1215.E3
Religious life: BL626
Edens
Comparative mythology: BL325.E4
Education
Hadith literature: BP135.8.E3
Koran: BP134.E38
Shiites: BP194.9.E3
Talmudic literature: BM509.E3

Education and training
Hindu ministry and
leadership: BL1241.64
Education of lamas: BQ7756+
Education, Religious: BL42+
Bonpo (Sect): BQ7963
Buddhism: BQ141+
Hinduism: BL1108.2+
Islam
Young people: BP44+
Lamaism: BQ7565+
Educational activities' management
Synagogues: BM653.7
Educational methodology
Islam: BP44
Eggs
Comparative mythology:
BL325.E45
Egoism
Hinduism: BL1214.32.E35
Egypt
Koran: BP134.E5
Egyptian religion, Ancient:
BL2428+
Egyptian religions: BL2420+
Egyptian religions and
Judaism: BM536.E3
Egyptian religions, Modern:
BL2460
Eḥad mi yode'a: BM670.E32
Eightfold Path: BQ4320
Eileithyia
Classical mythology: BL820.E5
Eisai, 1141-1215: BQ9399.E52+
Eitaku, 1622-1693: BQ9399.E57+
Ejō, 1198-1280: BQ9449.E37+
Ekādaśī: BL1239.82.E36
Ekaku, 1686-1769: BQ9399.E59+
Ekāmrapurāṇa: BL1140.4.E42+
Ekaviṃśatistotra: BQ2000.E53+
Eleazar ben Azariah
Talmudist: BM502.3.E38
Election
Judaism: BM613+
Electrical apparatus and
appliances
Judaism: BM729.E45
Electricity
Comparative mythology:
BL325.E47
Electricity and religion:
BL265.E6
Eleh ezkerah (Midrash):
BM517.E5+
Eleusinian mysteries
Greek religion and
mythology: BL795.E5
Eliezer ben Hyrcanus
Talmudist: BM502.3.E4
Elijah ben Solomon, gaon
of Vilna, 1720-1797:
BM755.E6
Elijah, the prophet
Rabbinical literature:
BM496.9.E4
Elul: BM693.E48
Elysium
Classical religion and
mythology: BL735
Greek religion and
mythology: BL795.E6
Emblems
Religion: BL603+
Emigration and immigration
Koran: BP134.E55
Emissaries of Divine Light:
BP605.E4
Emotions
Confucianism: BL1883.E56
Emotions and religion: BL65.E46
Emperor worship
Japan: BL2211.E46
Emptiness (Buddhism): BQ4275
En no Ozunu, 634?-701?:
BQ8829.E55+
End of the world
Buddhism: BQ4480
Religion: BL503
Endogamy
Hinduism: BL1215.E5
Endowments
Islam: BP170.25
Enemies of Muḥammad
Koran: BP133.6.E5
Enki (Sumerian deity):
BL1616.E54
Enlightenment
Buddhism: BQ4398+, BQ5635+
Gautama Buddha: BQ935
Lamaism: BQ7800+
Mādhyamika School: BQ7475

Enlightenment
Mahayana Buddhism: BQ7438
Yogācāra School: BQ7516
Zen Buddhism: BQ9288
Ennin, 794-864: BQ9149.E54+
Ennōkyō: BL2228.E55+
Entertainments, exercises
Judaism: BM125+
Entity Mission: BP605.E57
Envy
Islam: BP188.14.E58
Epaphus
Classical mythology: BL820.E7
Ephod
Judaism: BM657.E7
Epistemology, Buddhist: BQ4440
Epithets
Hadith literature: BP135.8.E64
Equality
Hinduism: BL1215.E68
Islam: BP173.45
Religion: BL65.E68
Equinox
Buddhism: BQ5720.E7
EREVNA (Organization):
BP605.E73
Erichthonius
Classical mythology: BL820.E8
Erinyes
Classical mythology: BL820.F8
Eros
Classical mythology: BL820.C65
Escape to Mt. Thaur
Muḥammad, Prophet, d. 632:
BP77.65
Eschatology: BL500+
Buddhism: BQ4475+
Egyptian religion: BL2450.E8
Greek religion and
mythology: BL795.E7
Hinduism: BL1214.56+
Islam: BP166.8+
Judaism: BM635+
Koran: BP134.E7
Talmudic literature: BM509.E8
Eser galuyyot (Midrash):
BM517.E6+
Esfah (Midrash): BM517.E7+
Eshin Ni, 1182?-1268?:
BQ8749.E85+
Espiritualistas
Trinitarios Marianos:
BL2532.E86
Essenes: BM175.E8
Eternity
Egyptian religion: BL2450.T55
Etheric double
Theosophy: BP573.E7
Ethical culture movement:
BP605.E84
Ethics
Koran: BP134.E8
Ethiopian religions: BL1710
Ethnic relations and
religion: BL65.E75
Ethnic religions: BL380
Ethnicity and religion:
BL65.E75
Ethnology and religion: BL256
Etrog
Judaism: BM657.C5
Etruscan religion and
mythology: BL740+
Europa
Greek religion and
mythology: BL795.E8
European Congress
(Buddhist association):
BQ20.E8+
European religions: BL689+
Eurythmy
Anthroposophy: BP596.R5
Evel (Talmud): BM506.4.S4+
Even ha-'ezer
Halacha: BM520.86.A56+,
BM520.88.A56+
Even ha-'ezer law
Halacha: BM523.6+
Evil
Comparative mythology:
BL325.G58
Koran: BP134.G65
Evil eye
Rabbinical literature:
BM496.9.E9
Evil spirits
Religious doctrine: BL480
Evocation
Roman religion and
mythology: BL815.E8

Evolution
Bahai Faith: BP388.E94
Islam: BP190.5.E86
Judaism: BM538.E8
Natural theology: BL263
Theosophy: BP573.E8
Ewe (African people)
Religions: BL2480.E96
Excommunication
Judaism: BM720.E9
Exegetics
Tripiṭaka: BQ1115.5
Exercises, entertainments
Judaism: BM125+
Exodus, The
Judaism: BM645.E9
Exogamy
Hinduism: BL1215.E5
Experience, Religious: BL53+, BR110+
Buddhism: BQ4570.P76
Experimentation, Animal
Nature worship: BL439.5
Extrasensory perception
Theosophy: BP573.E9
Eye
Comparative mythology: BL325.E93
Religion: BL619.E9

F

Fa ju pi yu jing: BQ1389.5.F32+
Fa mie jin jing: BQ2240.F32+
Fafnir
Germanic and Norse mythology: BL870.F28
Failure
Religious life: BL629.5.F33
Fairies
Comparative mythology: BL325.F4
Faith
Buddhism: BQ4340+
Confirmation: BQ5005
Hadith literature: BP135.8.F35
Hinduism: BL1214.32.S72
Islam: BP166.78+
Judaism: BM729.F3
Koran: BP134.F23
Religious life: BL626.3
Faith and reason
Sikhism: BL2018.5.F34
Faith and works
Islam: BP166.78+
Faith cure
Buddhism: BQ4570.F3
Sufism: BP189.65.F35
Faithists: BP605.F34
Fakirs
India, Religions of: BL2015.F2
Falasha
Liturgical books: BM672.F3
Fall of man
Comparative mythology: BL325.F3
Falsehood
Islam: BP188.14.F3
Families
Assyro-Babylonian religions
Religious life: BL1625.F35
Buddhism
Devotional literature: BQ5585.F3
Religious life: BQ5430
Islam
Devotional literature: BP188.3.F3
Religious life: BP188.18.F35
Religious life: BL625.6
Families of alcoholics
Religious life: BL625.9.F35
Family
Confucianism: BL1883.F35
Gautama Buddha: BQ933
Jainism: BL1375.F35
Koran: BP134.F25
Muḥammad, Prophet, d. 632: BP76.8
Family of Love: BP605.C38
Family relations
Koran: BP134.F25
Family violence, Victims of
Religious life: BL625.9.V52
Fan wang jing: BQ2460+
Fanaticism
Religion: BL53.5
Fang (African people)
Religions: BL2480.F3
Fans
Japanese religions: BL2211.F34
Fantasy and religion: BL65.I43

Farewell pilgrimage
  Muḥammad, Prophet, d. 632:
    BP77.68
Farmers
  Buddhism
    Religious life: BQ5480.F37
Farming, Organic
  Anthroposophy: BP596.O73
Fast-breaking at the end
  of Ramadan: BP186.45
  Sermons: BP183.645
Fast-day prayers
  Judaism
    Liturgical books: BM675.F3
Fasting
  Hadith literature: BP135.8.F37
  Hinduism: BL1237.76
  Islam: BP179, BP184.5
  Judaism: BM720.F3
  Koran: BP134.F3
Fasts
  Anthroposophy: BP596.F37
  Bahai Faith: BP385+
  Egyptian religion: BL2450.F28
  Hinduism: BL1239.72+
  India, Religions of: BL2015.F3
  Islam: BP186+
  Jainism: BL1355.5+
  Japanese religions: BL2211.F37
  Judaism: BM690+
  Samaritans: BM970
  Shiites: BP194.5.A+
Fate and fatalism
  Egyptian religion: BL2450.F3
  Germanic and Norse
    mythology: BL870.F3
  Greek religion and
    mythology: BL795.F37
  Hinduism: BL1215.F34
  Islam: BP166.3+
  Jainism: BL1375.F37
  Natural theology: BL235
Fatherhood
  Attributes of deity: BL215.3
Fathers
  Buddhism
    Devotional literature:
    BQ5585.P3
    Religious life: BQ5440
  Comparative mythology:
    BL325.F35
Fathers and children
  Judaism
    Religious duties: BM725.5
Fazang, 643-712: BQ8249.F38+
Fear
  Islam: BP190.5.F42
  Judaism: BM645.F4
Fear and religion: BL65.F4
Fear of the dead
  Religious doctrine: BL470
Feast of Esther: BM695.P8
Feast of Lights
  Judaism: BM695.H3
Feasts
  Anthroposophy: BP596.F37
  Bahai Faith: BP385+
  Egyptian religion: BL2450.F28
  Hinduism: BL1239.72+
  India, Religions of: BL2015.F3
  Islam: BP186+
  Jainism: BL1355.5+
  Japanese religions: BL2211.F37
  Shiites: BP194.5.A+
Fellowship
  Judaism: BM720.F4
Fellowship of Isis: BP605.F44
Female deities
  Comparative mythology: BL325.F4
Femininity
  Attributes of deity: BL215.5
Feminism
  Theosophy: BP573.F46
Festival day sermons
  Judaism: BM745+
Festival of Lights
  (Buddhism): BQ5720.T4
Festival prayers
  Judaism: BM674.4+
Festivals
  Anthroposophy: BP596.F37
  Bahai Faith: BP385+
  Buddhism: BQ5700+
  Hinduism: BL1239.72+
  Islam: BP186+
  Judaism: BM690+
  Lamaism: BQ7820+
  Samaritans: BM970
  Shiites: BP194.5.A+
Fetal propitiatory rites
  Buddhism: BQ5030.F47
Fetishism
  Japanese religions: BL2211.F47

Field cults: BL583
Finance
  Hinduism
    Temple organization, etc.: BL1241.62
  Lamaist religious practice: BQ7720
Financial institutions
  Buddhism: BQ96+
Financial management
  Synagogues: BM653.3
Findhorn Community: BP605.F5
Finno-Ugrians
  Early religions: BL975.F8
Fire
  Comparative mythology: BL325.F5
  Greek religion and mythology: BL795.F55
  India, Religions of: BL2015.F55
  Judaism: BM729.F57
  Nature worship: BL453
Fire rite
  Hinduism: BL1226.82.F5
Fire walking
  Religion: BL619.F57
First of Muḥarram
  Islam: BP186.2
Firstborn, Redemption of
  Judaism: BM720.R4
Fish
  Egyptian religion: BL2450.F5
Five duties of a Moslem: BP176+
Five Precepts (Buddhism): BQ5521+
Five Wisdoms (Tantric Buddhism): BQ4394
Flags and pennants
  Buddhism: BQ5125.F6
Fleeing
  Comparative mythology: BL325.F6
Flight to Medina
  Muḥammad, Prophet, d. 632: BP77.5
Flowers
  Buddhism: BQ4570.F56, BQ5075.F6
  Egyptian religion: BL2450.F55
  Umbanda: BL2592.U514P55
Fo yi jiao jing: BQ1680+
Folklore
  Buddhism: BQ5725+
  Tibetan Buddhism: BQ7850+
Followers
  Hadith literature: BP136.47
Fon
  Religions: BL2480.F65
Food
  Buddhism: BQ4570.F6
  Hinduism: BL1215.F66
  Jainism: BL1375.F65
  Koran: BP134.F58
Food and religion: BL65.F65
Food offering
  Hinduism: BL1236.76.F66
Foot
  Greek religion and mythology: BL795.F6
Foot worship rite
  Hinduism: BL1226.82.F6
Footprints
  Gautama Buddha: BQ922
Forgery
  Hadith literature: BP136.74
Forgiveness
  Anthroposophy: BP596.F67
Forgiveness and religion: BL65.F67
Forgiveness of sin
  Hadith literature: BP135.8.F67
  Islam: BP166.793
  Koran: BP134.F6
Former lives
  Gautama Buddha: BQ930
Forms of worship
  Jainism: BL1376+
  Judaism: BM656+
  Lamaism: BQ7690+
  Shinto: BL2224+
Formularies of worship, texts, etc.
  Islam: BP183+
  Shiites: BP194.3
  Sufism: BP189.55
Fortuna
  Classical mythology: BL820.F7
Forty-eight Vows: BQ4455
Foundation for Inner Peace: BP605.C67+
Foundation sacrifices: BL571
Four Noble Truths: BQ4230+
Four pairs of stages (Hinayana Buddhism): BQ4324
Four species (Sukkot): BM657.F68

Four stages
  Hinduism: BL1237.75
Fourth Way (Gurdjieff movement): BP605.G8+
Fraternidade Eclética Espiritualista Universal: BL2592.F73
Fravashis
  Zoroastrianism: BL1590.F73
Free thought: BL2747.5
Free will
  Judaism: BM645.F69
Freedom
  Buddhism: BQ4570.F7
  Islam: BP190.5.F7
  Judaism: BM645.F7
Freedom and religion: BL65.L52
Freedom of religion and Islam: BP173.65
Freedom of speech
  Islam: BP173.66
  Judaism: BM645.F73
Freethinkers, Burial services for: BL2777.B8
French Sanhedrin under Napoleon
  Judaism: BM655.5
Freyr
  Germanic and Norse mythology: BL870.F5
Friday evening service
  Judaism
    Liturgical books: BM675.S35
Fridays
  Islam: BP186.15
Friends
  Gautama Buddha: BQ900+
  Muḥammad, Prophet, d. 632: BP76.9
Friends International: BP605.I5
Friendship
  Buddhism: BQ4570.F74
  Islam: BP190.5.F73
Frigg
  Germanic and Norse mythology: BL870.F6
Fringes
  Judaism: BM657.F7
Fu mu en zhong jing: BQ1690+
Fujidō: BL2228.F85+
Fuju-fuse: BQ8360+
Fuke: BQ9300+
Full moon night confession ceremony (Buddhism): BQ5720.U7
Functionaries, Religious
  Islam: BP185+
  Shiites: BP194.9.G68
Fund raising
  Buddhist temple finance: BQ5136.7
Fundamentalism
  Islam: BP166.14.F85
  Natural theology: BL238
Funeral rites
  Buddhism: BQ5020
  Egyptian religion: BL2450.F8
  Germanic and Norse mythology: BL870.F7
  Hinduism: BL1226.82.F86
  Islam: BP184.9.F8
  Japanese religions: BL2211.F86
  Judaism: BM712
  Shinto: BL2224.25.F8
Funeral sermons
  Buddhism: BQ5350.M4
  Judaism: BM744.3
Funeral services
  Religion: BL619.F85
Furies
  Classical mythology: BL820.F8
Fusōkyō: BL2222.F88+
Future life
  Anthroposophy: BP596.F85
  Assyro-Babylonian religions: BL1625.F8
  Buddhism: BQ4530+
  Chinese religions: BL1812.F87
  Classical religion and mythology: BL735
  Egyptian religion: BL2450.F83
  Germanic and Norse mythology: BL870.F8
  Greek religion and mythology: BL795.F8
  Hinduism: BL1214.58
  Islam: BP166.8+
  Japanese religions: BL2211.F87
  Judaism: BM635+
  Koran: BP134.F8
  Religion: BL535+
  Roman religion and

Future life
  mythology: BL815.F8
 Sumerian religions: BL1616.F87
 Theosophy: BP573.F8
Future punishment
 Egyptian religion: BL2450.F84

G

Gā
 Religions: BL2480.G3
Gabai
 Judaism: BM659.G3
Gabbra
 Religions: BL2480.G32
Gacchācāra: BL1312.9.G35+
Gagá: BL2532.G33
Gallas
 Religions: BL2480.G34
Gamaliel II, fl. 80-110
 Talmudist: BM502.3.G35
Gamblers, Compulsive
 Religious life: BL625.9.C65
Gambling
 Islam: BP188.14.G35
Gaṇapatyātharvásirṣo
 paniṣad: BL1124.7.G36+
Gaṇḍavyūha: BQ1640+
Gandhara manuscripts:
  BQ244.G35+
Gandharvas
 Buddhism: BQ4780+
 Hinduism: BL1225.G29+
Gandharvatantra: BL1142.6.G35+
Gaṇḍīstotragāthā:
  BQ3300.G35+
Gaṇeśa (Hindu deity):
  BL1225.G34+
 Buddhism: BQ4750.G35+
Gaṇeśapurāṇa: BL1140.4.G36+
Gaṅgā (Hindu deity):
  BL1225.G35+
Gaṇividyā: BL1312.9.G37+
Garbhakośa: BQ4220
Garbhopaniṣad: BL1124.7.G37+
Gardening
 Religious life: BL629.5.G37
Gardens
 Greek religion and
  mythology: BL795.L3
 Religious life: BL629.5.G37
Garībadāsīs: BL1276.4+
Garuḍapurāṇa: BL1140.4.G38+
Garuḍas: BQ4800+
Gaskin, Stephen: BP610.G37+
Gāthāsaṅgraha (by
 Vasubandhu): BQ3080.G37+
Gatis (Buddhism): BQ4500+
Gaurī (Hindu deity):
  BL1225.G37+
Gautama Buddha: BQ860+
 Birthday celebration: BQ5720.B6
 Enlightenment Day
  celebration: BQ5720.E6
 Nirvana Day celebration:
  BQ5720.N6
 Poems, etc., on his life:
  BQ1603+
 Shrines in India: BQ6460+
Gautamīyatantra: BL1142.6.G36+
Gāyatrī (Deity): BL1225.G38+
Gāyatrī (Mantra):
  BL1236.52.G38
Gāyatrītantra: BL1142.6.G37+
Gays
 Judaism: BM729.H65
 Religious life: BL625.9.G39
Gbaya
 Religions: BL2480.G36
Gedatsukai: BQ9800.G43+
Gehenna
 Rabbinical literature:
  BM496.9.H4
Geiger, Abraham, 1810-1874:
  BM755.G4
Gemilut ḥasadim
 Yoreh de'ah law: BM523.5.B4
Gems
 Egyptian religion: BL2450.G42
 Theosophy: BP573.G4
Generosity
 Islam: BP188.16.G45
Genshin, Sōzu, 942-1017:
  BQ8549.G46+
Gentiles
 Judaism: BM720.N6
Gentle Wind Retreat: BP605.G44
Geography
 Koran: BP131.2
 Talmudic literature: BM509.G4
Geography and religion: BL65.G4
Geology and religion: BL259
Geonim: BM501.5
Gerim: BM506.4.G4+

Germanic mythology: BL830+
Geryon
  Classical mythology: BL820.G47
Gesture
  Buddhism: BQ5125.M8
Getae (Zalmoxis cult)
  Early religions: BL975.G5
Ghadīr
  Shiites: BP194.5.G45
Ghanavyūhasūtra: BQ2240.G52+
Ghāsī Vimaladattajātaka:
    BQ1470.G53+
Ghazzālī, 1058-1111
  Biography: BP80.G3
Ghose, Aurobindo:
    BL1273.892.G56
Giants
  Classical mythology: BL820.G5
  Comparative mythology: BL325.G5
  Germanic and Norse
    mythology: BL870.G53
Gift of tongues
  Religion: BL54
Gilgit manuscripts: BQ244.G5+
Girimānanda Sutta:
    BQ1349.5.G57+
Girls
  Buddhism
    Devotional literature:
    BQ5585.Y8
    Religious life: BQ5475
  Greek religion and
    mythology: BL795.G57
  Islam
    Religious life: BP188.18.G57
  Judaism
    Prayer and service books:
    BM667.G5
Giryama
  Religions: BL2480.G57
Giving
  Buddhism: BQ4420.G6
    Temple support: BQ5136.5+
  Hinduism: BL1239.5.G58
  Jainism: BL1375.G58
Glossolalia
  Religion: BL54
Gnosticism and Judaism:
    BM536.G54
Gobhilagṛhyasūtra: BL1134.9+
God
  Gautama Buddha: BQ918.G6
  Greek religion and
    mythology: BL795.G6
  Hinduism: BL1213.32+
  Islam: BP166.2
  Judaism: BM610
    Providence and government:
    BM645.P7
  Koran: BP134.G6
  Religious doctrine: BL473
  Sikhism: BL2018.22
  Theosophy: BP573.G6
God and man, Mediation
  between
  Islam: BP166.76
Goddesses
  Comparative mythology: BL325.F4
  Egyptian religion: BL2450.G58
  Greek religion and
    mythology: BL795.G63
  India, Religions of: BL2015.G6
  Korea: BL2236.G62
  Religious doctrine: BL473.5
Gods
  Assyro-Babylonian
    religions: BL1625.G6
  Buddhism: BQ4620+
  Chinese religions: BL1812.G63
  Egyptian religion: BL2450.G6
  Hinduism: BL1216+
  India, Religions of: BL2015.G63
  Japanese religions: BL2211.G6
  Korea: BL2236.G63
  Religious doctrine: BL473
  Semitic religions: BL1605.G63
  Talmudic literature: BM509.G63
  Umbanda: BL2592.U514G6
God's suffering
  Rabbinical literature:
    BM496.9.S93
Golden age
  Comparative mythology:
    BL325.G55
Goldsmith, Joel: BP610.G64+
Golem
  Rabbinical literature
    Myths and legends: BM531
Goma (Rite): BQ8921.H6
Gonds
  Religion: BL2032.G6

Gongs
Buddhism: BQ5075.G6
Good
Comparative mythology: BL325.G58
Good and evil
Koran: BP134.G65
Good spirits
Religious doctrine: BL477
Gopālatāpanīyopaniṣad: BL1124.7.G66+
Gopathabrāhmaṇa: BL1121.7+
Gorakhnāth: BL1278.892.G67
Gorakhnāthīs: BL1278.8+
Goraksa: BL1278.892.G67
Gorgons
Classical mythology: BL820.G7
Comparative mythology: BL325.G6
Gosānī (Hindu deity): BL1225.G67+
Gotra: BQ4285+
Government
Hinduism: BL1241.32+
Islam: BP185+
Shiites: BP194.9.G68
Sikhism: BL2018.5.P64
Zoroastrianism: BL1590.S73
Government and politics
Japanese religions: BL2211.S73
Government of God
Judaism: BM645.P7
Roman religion and mythology: BL815.P74
Goyim
Judaism: BM720.N6
Grace at meals
Judaism
Liturgical books: BM675.G7
Graces, The
Classical mythology: BL820.G8
Grail
Anthroposophy: BP596.G7
Grail movement: BP605.B4+
Grasses
Hinduism: BL1236.76.G7
Gratitude
Islam: BP188.16.G7
Religion: BL65.G73
Great mother of the gods
Classical mythology: BL820.C8
Great White Brotherhood: BP605.G68
Greater Community Way of Knowledge: BP605.S58
Greek religion and mythology: BL780+
Greek religions and Judaism: BM536.G7
Gṛhyasūtras: BL1131.2+
Griffins
Comparative mythology: BL325.G7
Griscom, Chris, 1942- : BP605.L53
Grottoes
Sacred places: BL584
Groves
Sacred places: BL583
Gsaṅ ba bsen thub: BQ7973.5.G83+
Gśen-rab, Mi-bo: BQ7987.7
Gser 'od nor bu 'od 'bar gyi mdo: BQ7971.5.G84+
Guan wu liang shou jing: BQ2020+
Guarantors
Hadith literature: BP136.48+
Guardian-of-the-Faithful
Hasidism: BM198.53
Guga Chauhan (Hindu deity): BL1225.G78+
Guhyagarbhatantra (Guhyamūlatantra): BQ2180.G93+
Guhyamūlatantra: BQ2180.G93+
Guhyasamājatantra: BQ2150+
Guṇa: BQ4363
Gunavatī Mahāmāya: BQ3340.G85+
Guo qu xian zai yin guo jing: BQ1600.K85+
Guptasādhanatantra: BL1142.6.G87+
Gur
Hasidism: BM198.56.G87
Gurdjieff Foundation: BP605.G8+
Gurdjieff movement: BP605.G8+
Gurdjieff, Georges Ivanovitch, 1872-1949
Biography: BP605.G94G87
Works: BP605.G8A+
Guru worship
Hinduism: BL1214.32.G87
Lamaism: BQ7699.G87

Gurupañcāśikā (by
Aśvaghoṣa): BQ3340.G87+
Gurus
India, Religions of: BL2015.G85
Jainism: BL1375.G87
Sikhism: BL2018.5.G85
Guruship
Hinduism: BL1241.48
Gurutantra: BL1142.6.G88+
Guruvayurappan (Hindu
deity): BL1225.G8+
Gusains: BL1276.5+
Gyōnen, 1240-1321: BQ8249.G94+
Gzer mig: BQ7971.5.G94+
Gzi brjid: BQ7971.5.G95+

H

Habad
Hasidism: BM198.54
Habit (Religious garb)
Buddhism: BQ5085.H3
Hachiman: BL2226.2.H3
Ḥad gadya: BM670.H28
Haddāwā: BP189.7.H3+
Hades
Classical religion and
mythology: BL735
Hadith literature: BP135+
Shiites: BP193.25+
Hadith scholars and
commentators: BP135.62.A+
Hadith stories: BP136.9
Hadith studies: BP135.6+
Hadith, Abrogated: BP136.78
Hadjerai
Religions: BL2480.H28
Hadranim
Babylonian Talmud: BM502.7
Haftaroth: BM670.H3
Haggadah: BM674.6+
Karaites: BM185.4.H35+
Hagiography
Sufism: BP189.43
Hair
Hinduism: BL1239.5.H35
Islam: BP190.5.H3
Sikhism: BL2018.5.H3
Haircutting
Hinduism: BL1239.5.H35
Islam: BP190.5.H3
Sikhism: BL2018.5.H3
Hajj: BP187.3
Hājj 'Umar ibn Sa'īd
al-Fūtī, 1794?-1864:
BP80.H23
Ḥajjat al-wadā'
Muḥammad, Prophet, d. 632:
BP77.68
Halacha
Midrash: BM515
Rabbinical literature: BM520+
Halakhot
Halacha: BM520.82
Ḥalitsah: BM720.H3
Hallah
Yoreh de'ah law: BM523.5.H3
Hallel: BM670.H35
Hallucinogenic drugs and
religion: BL65.D7
Halvetiyye: BP189.7.K44+
Ḥamadsha: BP189.7.H34+
Haman
Midrash: BM518.H35
Hamitic religions: BL2410
Hamzah Fansuri, 16th/17th
cent.: BP80.H279
Hanafites: BP166.14.H2
Hanamatsuri: BQ5720.B6
Hanbalites: BP166.14.H3
Hand
Comparative mythology:
BL325.H23
Hand washing
Judaism: BM704
Handicapped and Judaism:
BM540.H35
Handicraft
Judaism: BM729.H35
Ḥanina, Segan ha-Kohanim,
lst. cent.
Talmudist: BM502.3.H35
Hanŏlgyo: BL2240.H36+
Hansadutta, Swami,
1941- : BP610.H35+
Hanukkah: BM695.H3
Hanukkah lamp: BM657.H3
Hanukkah prayers: BM675.H33
Hanukkah sermons: BM747.H3
Hanumān (Hindu deity):
BL1225.H3+
Haoma
Zoroastrianism: BL1590.H36

Happiness
Islam: BP190.5.H34
Judaism: BM729.J4
Happiness and religion: BL65.H36
Harai: BL2224.25.H3
Haridasas: BL1285.7+
Hariharanātha (Hindu deity): BL1225.H343+
Hārītī: BQ4890.H37+
Harranian religions: BL1635
Harṣavardhana, King of Thānesar and Kanauj, fl. 606-647
Buddhism: BQ308
Ḥasan ibn ʻAlī, d. ca. 669: BP193.12
Ḥaserot vi-yeterot (Midrash): BM517.T2+
Ḥashwīya: BP195.H3+
Hasideans: BM175.H36
Hasidic rite: BM672.A82
Hasidic tales and legends: BM532
Hasidim: BM198+
Hasidism: BM198+
Haskalah: BM194
Hastapūjāvidhi (by Śāśvatavajra): BQ3340.H38+
Hastavālanāmprakaraṇa vṛtti (by Āryadeva): BQ2910.H38+
Hatarat nedarim: BM675.H35
Haṭha yoga
Hinduism: BL1238.56.H38
Hathor (Egyptian deity): BL2450.H3
Hausas
Religions: BL2480.H3
Hawaiians
Religions: BL2630.H38
Hawthorn
Nature worship: BL457.H3
Hayagrīva (Hindu deity): BL1225.H347+
Hayaśiras (Hindu deity): BL1225.H347+
Hayavadana (Hindu deity): BL1225.H35+
Head
Comparative mythology: BL325.H25
Headgear
Religion: BL619.H4
Headless gods
Comparative mythology: BL325.H3
Healing gods
Comparative mythology: BL325.H4
Japan: BL2211.H32
Healing, Spiritual
Buddhism: BQ4570.F3
Sufism: BP189.65.F35
Healing, Spiritual, and religion: BL65.M4
Health
Islam: BP166.72
Judaism: BM538.H43, BM729.J4
Shiites: BP194.9.H34
Theosophy: BP573.H4
Health and religion: BL65.M4
Heat
India, Religions of: BL2015.F55
Heathen
Judaism: BM720.N6
Heaven
Bahai Faith: BP388.H43
Buddhism: BQ4508
Confucianism: BL1883.H43
Egyptian religion: BL2450.H35
Hinduism: BL1214.76
Judaism: BM645.H43
Heaven's Gate: BP605.H36
"Hebrew" as a name
Judaism: BM729.N3
Hebrew book of Enoch
Cabala
Zohar supplements: BM525.A6H4+
Hebrew religions: BL1650
Hecate
Classical mythology: BL820.H43
Heder: BM109.H4
Heikhalot rabbati
Cabala: BM525.A364+
Heikhalot zutrati
Cabala: BM525.A365+
Heimdallr
Germanic and Norse mythology: BL870.H4
Heimholungswerk Jesu Christi: BP605.H4

Hekhalot
  Cabala
    Zohar supplements: BM525.A6H4+
Helen of Troy
  Classical mythology: BL820.H45
Helios
  Classical mythology: BL820.S62
Hell
  Buddhism: BQ4525
  Chinese religions: BL1812.H44
  Hinduism: BL1214.78
  Islam: BP166.88
  Jainism: BL1375.H45
  Rabbinical literature:
    BM496.9.H4
Hellenistic movements
  Judaism: BM176
Hemavatasutta: BQ1419.5.H45+
Hensō: BQ5125.H4
Hephaestus
  Classical mythology: BL820.V8
Hera
  Classical mythology: BL820.J6
Heracles
  Classical mythology: BL820.H5
Hercules
  Classical mythology: BL820.H5
Ḥerem: BM720.E9
Hereros
  Religions: BL2480.H4
Heresies
  Islam: BP167.5
  Judaism: BM646
Heresy
  Islam: BP167.5
  Judaism: BM646
Heresy trials
  Buddhism: BQ5230+
Heretics
  Islam: BP167.5
  Judaism: BM646
Heretics, Treatment of
  Judaism: BM720.H5
Hermaphroditism
  Comparative mythology:
    BL325.B45
  Talmudic literature: BM509.H4
Hermeneutics
  Babylonian Talmud: BM503.7
  Koran: BP130.2+
  Tripiṭaka: BQ1115.5
Hermes
  Classical mythology: BL820.M5
Hermitage life
  Hinduism: BL1239.5.H47
Hermits
  Buddhism: BQ6200+
  Japanese religions: BL2211.H4
Heroes
  Comparative mythology:
    BL325.H46
  Roman religion and
    mythology: BL815.H47
Heroines
  Greek religion and
    mythology: BL795.H47
Hetubindu (by
  Dharmakīrti): BQ3150+
Hetucakranirnaya (by
  Dignāga): BQ3300.H47+
Hetutattvopadeśa (by
  Jitāri): BQ3160+
Hevajra: BQ4860.H47+
Hevajratantra: BQ2160+
Hides and skins
  Talmudic literature: BM509.H54
Hidushim
  Babylonian Talmud: BM504.2
Hierarchies
  Theosophy: BP573.H5
Higan-e: BQ5720.E7
High Holiday prayers: BM675.H5
High Holiday sermons: BM746
High Holidays
  Judaism: BM693.H5
High Holy Day prayers: BM675.H5
High Holy Day sermons: BM746
High Holy Days
  Judaism: BM693.H5
High Priest's Breastplate
  Judaism: BM657.B7
Hijrah
  Muḥammad, Prophet, d. 632:
    BP77.5
Ḥikmati-i nuvīn: BP605.H5
Hillel, lst cent.
  B.C./lst. cent.
  Talmudist: BM502.3.H55
Hinayana Abhidharma: BQ289
Hinayana Buddhism: BQ7100+
  Abhidharmapiṭaka: BQ2650+
  Relations
    Mahayana Buddhism: BQ7432
    Zen Buddhism: BQ9269.6.H5

Hindu authors: BL1144.52+
Hindu interpretations of
Muḥammad: BP76.45
Hindu literature: BL1144.52+
Hinduism: BL1100+
Relations to other
religions
Buddhism: BQ4610.H6
Islam: BP173.H5
Jainism: BL1358.2
Judaism: BM536.H5
Lamaism: BQ7656.H55
Mādhyamika School of
Buddhism: BQ7473
Mahayana Buddhism: BQ7434
Theravāda Buddhism: BQ7273
Yogācāra School of
Buddhism: BQ7512
Relations with Muḥammad,
Prophet, d. 632: BP76.45
Hinomoto: BL2222.H56+
Hippolyta
Classical mythology: BL820.H55
Hippopotamus
Egyptian religion: BL2450.H5
Hiraniyakeśipitr̥medhas
ūtra: BL1137.3.H57+
Hiraṇyakeśinśrautasū
tra: BL1128.7+
Hiraṇyakeśyagr̥hyasūt
ra: BL1133.9+
Historians of Islam
Biography: BP49.5.A+
Historiography
Buddhism: BQ280
Classical religion and
mythology: BL717
Islam: BP49+
Koran: BP134.H5
Muḥammad, Prophet, d. 632:
BP75.3
Religion: BL41
Sufism
Biography: BP189.43
History and anthroposophy:
BP596.H57
History and Buddhism: BQ4570.H5
History and Hinduism:
BL1215.H57
History and Islam: BP190.5.H5
History and religion: BL65.H5
History and the Koran:
BP134.H57
History of events
Koran: BP130.5
Hita Harivaṃśa Gosvāmī:
BL1287.292.H58
Hittites
Religions: BL2370.H5
Hmong (Asian people)
Religion: BL2150.H57
Hohm Community: BP605.H58
Hōjōe: BQ5030.H6
Hokkeshū (Honmonryū):
BQ8449.5.H63+
Hol ha-Moed: BM693.H64
Holde
Germanic and Norse
mythology: BL870.H65
Holī
Hinduism: BL1239.82.H65
Holidays
Bahai Faith: BP385+
Shiites: BP194.5.A+
Holiness
Judaism: BM645.H58
Holocaust
Jewish theology: BM645.H6
Holocaust Remembrance Day
prayers: BM675.H55
Holy Order of Mans: BP605.H6
Holy Spirit
Judaism: BM612.7
Holy War
Islam: BP182
Holyearth Foundation: BP605.H64
Holymen
Hinduism: BL1241.44+
Homa (Rite): BQ8921.H6
Lamaism: BQ7699.H64
Home
Sacred places: BL588
Homiletics
Islam: BP184.25
Judaism: BM730+
Homosexuality
Buddhism: BQ4570.H65
Greek religion and
mythology: BL795.H6
Islam: BP188.14.H65
Judaism: BM729.H65
Homosexuality and religion:
BL65.H64

Hompa Honganji: BQ8700+
Hōnen, 1133-1212: BQ8649.H66+
Honmiti: BL2222.H66+
Honmon Butsuryūshū:
BQ8449.5.H66+
Honmonryū: BQ8449.5.H63+
Hope
Judaism: BM645.H64
Horatii
Classical mythology: BL820.H7
Horned god: BL460
Horns
Religious symbolism: BL604.H6
Horowitz, Jacob Isaac,
1745-1815: BM755.H73
Horowitz, Naphtali Zebi,
1760-1827: BM755.H76
Horses
Nature worship: BL443.H6
Horus (Egyptian deity):
BL2450.H6
Hoshana Rabba prayers: BM675.H6
Hoshanot: BM670.H67
Ḥoshen
Judaism: BM657.B7
Ḥoshen mishpaṭ
Halacha: BM520.86.A58+,
BM520.88.A58+
Hospitality
Islam: BP188.16.H67
Judaism: BM720.H6
Hossō (Faxiang): BQ8100+
Host desecration
accusation
Judaism: BM585.4
Hours of prayer
Islam: BP184.3
House blessings
Religion: BL619.H68
Hsi Wang Mu (Deity)
Taoism: BL1942.85.H75
Hsiao tzu ching: BQ2240.H76+
Hsien t'ien tao: BL1943.H74
Hsien yü yin yüan ching:
BQ1600.H74+
Hsüan-tsang, ca. 596-664:
BQ8149.H78+
Hua
Religions: BL2630.H82
Hua yan Buddhism: BQ8200+
Huaihai, 720-814: BQ9299.H83+
Hubbard, L. Ron (La
Fayette Ron), 1911- :
BP605.S2
Huineng, 638-713: BQ9299.H85+
Human anatomy
Talmudic literature: BM509.H84
Human beings, Worship of:
BL465+
Human body
Religious symbolism: BL604.B64
Theosophy: BP573.H8
Human ecology
Buddhism: BQ4570.E23
Judaism: BM538.H85
Human-etisk forbund
(Norway): BP605.H85
Human rights
Buddhism: BQ4570.H78
Hinduism: BL1215.H84
Judaism: BM645.H85
Koran: BP134.H85
Human rights and religion:
BL65.H78
Human sacrifice
Greek religion and
mythology: BL795.H83
Roman religion and
mythology: BL815.S3
Humanism: BL2747.6
Rabbinical literature:
BM496.9.H85
Relation to religions
Buddhism: BQ4570.H8
Hinduism: BL1215.H86
Judaism: BM538.H87
Humanistic Judaism: BM197.8
Humanities and religion:
BL65.H8
Humor
Buddhism: BQ4570.H85
Islam: BP190.5.H8
Humor and religion: BL65.L3
Hunger
Islam: BP190.5.H85
Hunting
Greek religion and
mythology: BL795.H85
Hurufis: BP195.H8+
Ḥusayn ibn 'Alī, d. 680:
BP193.13
Husparam nask: BL1515.5.H8A2+

Húynh, Phú S'o, d. 1947:
BQ9800.P4592H88+
Hyacinthus
Classical mythology: BL820.H9
Hydra
Classical mythology: BL820.H93
Hygieia
Classical mythology: BL820.S25
Hygiene
Shiites: BP194.9.H34
Hygiene and religion: BL65.M4
Hymns
Buddhism: BQ5035+
Free thought: BL2777.R5
Hinduism: BL1236.22+
Islam: BP183.5
Jainism: BL1377.3
Judaism: BM678+
Lamaism: BQ7700+
Sikhism: BL2018.32
Worship: BL560
Hypnotism and religion: BL65.H9
Hypocrisy
Islam: BP188.14.H94

I

I AM Movement: BP605.I18
I AM Religious Activity:
BP605.I18
I-hsüan, Shih, d. 867:
BQ9399.I55+
I kuan tao: BL1943.I35
Ibadites: BP195.I3+
Iberians
Early religions: BL975.I2
Iblīs
Koran: BP134.D43
Ibn Mājah, Muḥammad ibn
Yazīd, d. 887
Hadith: BP135.A17+
Ibrāhīm (Biblical
patriarch)
Koran: BP133.7.A27
Icarus
Classical mythology: BL820.I33
Icchantika: BQ4297
'Īd al-Aḍḥā: BP186.6
Sermons: BP183.66
'Īd al-Fiṭr: BP186.45
Sermons: BP183.645
'Id al-Ghadīr
Shiites: BP194.5.G45
Ideals, Social
Judaism: BM729.S6
Idolatry
India, Religions of: BL2015.I4
Religious doctrine: BL485
Yoreh de'ah law: BM523.5.I3
Idra de-mashkena
Cabala
Zohar supplements: BM525.A6I22+
Idra rabba
Cabala
Zohar supplements: BM525.A6I3+
Idra zuta
Cabala
Zohar supplements: BM525.A6I5+
Iemanjá: BL2592.I35
Ifa: BL2532.I33
Igbo
Religions: BL2480.I2
I'jāz
Koran: BP130.73
Ijun Mitto: BL2228.I35+
Ikeda, Daisaku: BQ8449.I38+
Ikhlāṣ: BP166.783
Ikkyū Oshō, 1394-1481:
BQ9399.I56+
Ill, Terminally
Religious life: BL625.9.S53
Illiteracy
Muḥammad, Prophet, d. 632:
BP75.6
Illness, Last
Gautama Buddha: BQ938
Illyrians
Early religions: BL975.I57
'Ilm al-Ḥadīth: BP135.6+
Image of God
Rabbinical literature:
BM496.9.I5
Image worship
Religious doctrine: BL485
Images
Islam: BP190.5.A7
Imagination and religion:
BL65.I43
Imamate
Islamic theology: BP166.94

Imams
  Islam: BP185.4
  Shiites
    Biography: BP193+
Imiut
  Egyptian religion: BL2450.I44
Immortalism
  Greek religion and
    mythology: BL795.I49
Immortality: BL530
  Buddhism: BQ4570.I5
  Egyptian religion: BL2450.I5
  Germanic and Norse
    mythology: BL870.I6
  Greek religion and
    mythology: BL795.I5
  Hinduism: BL1215.I66
  India, Religions of: BL2015.I6
  Judaism: BM645.I5
  Roman religion and
    mythology: BL815.I4
  Theosophy: BP573.I5
Impermanence (Buddhism): BQ4260
Impugning transmission of
  a tradition
  Hadith literature: BP136.6
Inanna (Sumerian deity):
  BL1616.I5
Inari cult: BL2211.I5
Incantations
  Japanese religions: BL2211.I53
Incarnation
  Religion: BL510
Incas
  Religions: BL2590.P4
Incense
  Buddhism: BQ5075.I6
  Judaism: BM720.I6
  Rabbinical literature:
    BM496.9.I53
Incest
  Comparative mythology:
    BL325.I48
Incubation
  Comparative mythology: BL325.I5
India, Religions of: BL2000+
Indo-European religions: BL660
Indonesia, Religions of:
  BL2110+
Indra (Hindu deity): BL1225.I6+
  Buddhism: BQ4750.I6+
Indriyabhāvanāsutta:
  BQ1320.I53+
Infernal regions
  Religion: BL545
Information services
  Judaism: BM66
Information technology
  Buddhism: BQ4570.I55
Information technology and
  religion: BL265.I54
Ingassana (African people)
  Religions: BL2480.I53
Ingen, 1592-1673: BQ9319.I53+
Ingersoll, Robert Green
  Works on religious
    subjects: BL2720+
Inimitability
  Koran: BP130.73
Initiation rites
  Hinduism: BL1226.82.I54
Initiations
  Religion: BL615
Inner World Brothers and
  Sisters: BP605.G44
Ino
  Classical mythology: BL820.M3
Insadi-sūtra: BQ2240.I55+
Inscriptions
  Buddhism: BQ246+
  Hinduism: BL1109.2+
Insects
  Comparative mythology:
    BL325.I57
Inspiration
  Koran: BP130.7+
Inspiration of Hadith: BP136.4+
Installation sermons of
  rabbis: BM744.7
Installation sermons of
  synagogue officials: BM744.8
Institute for Research in
  Human Happiness: BP605.K55
Institute for the
  Development of the
  Harmonious Human Being:
    BP605.I44
Institutions, Religious
  Organization: BL632+
Insufficiency of natural
  theology: BL190
Integrism
  Islam: BP166.14.F85

Intellect
Koran: BP134.R33
Intellectuals and religion: BL237
Intention
Hadith literature: BP135.8.I65
Islam: BP166.783
Intercession
Islam: BP166.825
Interest
Yoreh de'ah law: BM523.5.I5
Interfaith movements, Participation by rabbis: BM652.7
Intermediate state
Buddhism: BQ4490
Islam: BP166.82
International affairs and religion: BL65.I55
International Buddhist Conference (International Brotherhood Association): BQ20.I58+
International Community of Christ: BP605.I45
International date line
Oraḥ ḥayim law: BM523.3.I5
International Friends: BP605.I5
International Rajneesh Foundation: BP605.R34+
International Society for Krishna Consciousness: BL1285.8+
International Society of Divine-Love: BP605.I55
Internet
Judaism: BM538.I58
Computer network resources: BM67
Religion
Computer network resources: BL37
Interpersonal relations
Anthroposophy: BP596.I57
Hadith literature: BP135.8.I67
Islam: BP190.5.I57
Religious life: BL626.33
Interpolating transmission of a tradition
Hadith literature: BP136.6
Interpolation
Hadith literature: BP136.72
Interpretation of dreams
Rabbinical literature: BM496.9.D73
Invitation
Islam: BP170.85
Invocations
Islam: BP183.3
Iphigenia
Classical mythology: BL820.I65
Ippen, 1239-1289: BQ8559.I66+
Iqbal, Muhammad, Sir, 1877-1938
Biography: BP80.I6
Iran
Hadith literature: BP135.8.I7
Koran: BP134.I72
Talmudic literature: BM509.I6
Iran, Religions of: BL2270+
Iranians
Koran: BP134.I72
Iraq, Religions of: BL2350.I7
Irmandade da Santa Cruz: BL2592.I75
Isaac
Midrash: BM518.I8
Isaā'īl
Koran: BP133.7.I85
'Īsāwīyah
Sufism: BP189.7.I7+
Ise Shintō: BL2221.9.I8
Išhara (Semitic goddess): BL1605.I77
Ishmael (Biblical figure)
Koran: BP133.7.I85
Ishmael ben Elisha, 2nd cent.: BM502.3.I8
Ishrāqīyah
Sufism: BP189.7.I74+
Ishtar
Semitic religions: BL1605.I8
Isipatana (Sārnāth, India)
Buddhism: BQ6490
Isis (Egyptian deity): BL2450.I7
Isis Fellowship: BP605.F44
Islam: BP1+
Apologetics: BP170
Biography: BP70+
Controversial literature: BP169
Doctrine: BP166+

Islam
Relations to other religions: BP171+
Buddhism: BP173.B9
Christianity: BP172+
Confucianism: BP173.C65
Coptic Church: BP172.5.C6
Religious life: BP188+
Islamic legends: BP137+
Islamic literature: BP85.42+
Islamic sociology: BP173.25+
Ismā'īl ibn Ja'far: BP195.I8+
Ismailites: BP195.I8+
Isnād
Hadith literature: BP136.33
Īśopaniṣad: BL1124.7.I76+
Isrā'
Muḥammad: BP166.57
"Israel" as a name
Judaism: BM729.N3
Israel ben Eliezer: BM755.I8
Israel in relation to the Messianic era
Judaism: BM625.5
Israel Independence Day prayers: BM675.I87
Israel Meir, ha-Kohen, 1838-1933: BM755.K25
Israel's mission
Judaism: BM613+
Isson Nyorai Kino, 1756-1828: BQ9800.N9692I77+
Istadeva
Hinduism: BL1213.32+
Itivuttaka: BQ1400+
Ittōen: BP605.I8
Itys
Classical mythology: BL820.I8
Iyov (Midrash): BM517.I7+
Izumo Taisha: BL2222.I99+

J

Jacob (Biblical patriarch)
Koran: BP133.7.J33
Jacob ben Asher, ca. 1269-ca. 1340. Arba'ah ṭurim
Halacha: BM520.86
Jacob Isaac, ha-Ḥozeh, mi-Lublin, 1745-1815: BM755.H73
Ja'far al-Ṣādiq, 702?-765 or 6
Imams: BP193.16
Jagannātha (Hindu deity): BL1225.J3+
Jahmīyah: BP195.J3+
Jaiminīyabrāhmaṇa: BL1121.3.J35+
Jaiminīyagṛhyasūtra: BL1136.3+
Jaiminīyārṣeyabrāhmaṇa: BL1121.3.J36+
Jaiminīyasaṃhitā: BL1114.3+
Jaiminīyaśrautasūtra: BL1129.6+
Jaiminīyopaniṣadbrāhmaṇa: BL1121.3.J37+, BL1123.8+
Jain literature: BL1315+
Jainism: BL1300+
Relations to other religions
Buddhism: BQ4610.J3
Hinduism: BL1358.2
Jambuddīvapannattī: BL1312.6.J35+
Jambūdvīpaprajñapti: BL1312.6.J35+
Jambūdvīpasaṅgrahaṇī: BL1314.2.J35+
Janus
Classical mythology: BL820.J2
Japan, Religions of: BL2195+
Jātakamāla: BQ1460+
Jatakarma
Hinduism: BL1215.J3
Jātakas: BQ1460+
Jātinirākṛti (by Jitāri): BQ3170+
Jayākhyasaṃhitā: BL1141.8.J38+
Jen wang po je ching: BQ1930+
Jerusalem
Hadith literature: BP135.8.J47
Islam: BP190.5.P3
Judaism: BM729.P3
Midrash: BM518.J4
Jerusalem Day sermons
Judaism: BM747.J47

Jerusalem night journey
Muḥammad: BP166.57
Jesus Christ
Anthroposophy: BP596.J4
Koran: BP134.J37
Jesus Christ, Attitude toward
Judaism: BM620
"Jew" as a name
Judaism: BM729.N3
Jewish science
Judaism: BM729.J4
Jewish tradition: BM529
Jewish way of life: BM723+
Jews
Hadith literature: BP135.8.J48
Koran: BP134.J4
Talmudic literature: BM509.J48
Jews, Relations with
Muḥammad, Prophet, d. 632: BP76.4
Ji: BQ8550+
Jianzhen, 688-763: BQ8789.C47+
Jicang, 549-623: BQ8809.C55+
Jihad
Hadith literature: BP135.8.J54
Islam: BP182
Koran: BP134.J45
Jikkōkyō: BL2222.J55+
Jin gang san mei jing: BQ2240.V35+
Jinacarita (by Vanaratna Medhaṃkara): BQ1606.J53+
Jing tu san bu jing: BQ2010+
Jing zang: BQ1220+
Jinn
Islam: BP166.89
Koran: BP134.J52
Jishō, 1544-1620: BQ8649.J57+
Jīva
Hinduism: BL1213.56
Jīvābhigama: BL1312.6.J58+
Jīvājīvābhigamasūtra: BL1312.6.J62+
Jñāna: BQ4380+
Jñānārṇavatantra: BL1142.6.J53+
Jñānasaṅkalinītantra: BL1142.6.J54+
Jñānasiddhi (by Indrabhūti): BQ3340.J65+
Jñānodayatantra: BQ2180.J54+
Jñānolkanāmadhāraṇī sarvagatipariśdhanī: BQ1670.J52+
Jñātādharmakathāṅga: BL1312.3.N39+
Jo-naṅ-pa: BQ7674+
Jōdo: BQ8600+
Jodo-e: BQ5720.E6
Jōdo sambukyō: BQ2010+
John the Baptist
Koran: BP133.7.J65
John, Bubba Free, 1939- : BP610.B8+
John, Da Free, 1939- : BP610.B8+
Jōjitsu (Chen Shih): BQ8150+
Jonaṅ-pa: BQ7674+
Jones, Jim, 1931-1978: BP605.P46
Jordan
Rabbinical literature: BM496.9.J67
Jose the Galilean
Talmudist: BM502.3.J67
Joseph (Son of Jacob)
Koran: BP133.7.J67
Joshua ben Ḥananiah, lst cent.
Talmudist: BM502.3.J68
Journals, Spiritual
Religious life: BL628.5
Journey to Jerusalem at night
Muḥammad: BP166.57
Joy
Judaism: BM645.J67
Religious life: BL626.35
Judah Löw ben Bezaleel, ca. 1525-1609: BM755.J8
Judah, ha-Levi, 12th cent.: BM550.J79
Judaism: BM1+
Biography: BM750+
Doctrine: BM600+
History: BM150+
Koran: BP134.J4
Liturgy and ritual: BM660+
Relations to other religions: BM534+
Buddhism: BQ4610.J8
Christianity: BM535

Judaism
Relations to other religions
Islam: BP173.J8
Samaritans: BM915
Zoroastrianism: BL1566.J8
Relations to special subjects: BM533.32+
Judgment
Islam: BP166.85
Judgment and religion: BL65.J83
Judgment of God
Religious doctrine: BL475.6
Judgment of the dead: BL547
Jukai: BQ5005
Jum'ah: BP186.15
Juno
Classical mythology: BL820.J6
Jupiter
Classical mythology: BL820.J8
Jupiter Dolichenus
Classical mythology: BL820.J83
Justice
Bahai Faith: BP388.J87
Islam
Religious life: BP188.16.J88
Sociology: BP173.43
Judaism: BM645.J8
Justice and religion: BL65.J87
Juz' al-Ḥamd: BP128.15
Juz' Alif-lām-rā': BP128.46
Juz' 'Amma: BP129.42
Juz' Fa-mā kān: BP128.66
Juz' Fa-man aẓlam: BP128.84
Juz' Ḥā'-mīm: BP128.93
Juz' Ilayh: BP128.87
Juz' Innamā al-sabīl: BP128.36
Juz' Iqtarab: BP128.55
Juz' Kull al-ṭa'ām: BP128.22
Juz' La-tajidanna: BP128.27
Juz' Lā yuḥibb: BP128.25
Juz' Qad aflaḥ: BP128.58
Juz' Qad sami': BP129.18
Juz' Qāla a-lam aqul: BP128.52
Juz' Qāla al-mala': BP128.32
Juz' Qāla fa-mā khaṭbukum: BP129
Juz' Sa-yaqūl: BP128.18
Juz' Subḥān: BP128.48
Juz' Tabārak: BP129.29
Juz' Tilka al-rusul: BP128.19
Juz' Wa-al-muḥṣanāt: BP128.24
Juz' Wa-i 'lamū: BP128.34
Juz' Wa-lā tujādilū: BP128.69
Juz' Wa-law annanā: BP128.29
Juz' Wa-mā anzalnā: BP128.79
Juz' Wa-mā min dābbah: BP128.39
Juz' Wa-mā ubarri': BP128.42
Juz' Wa-man yaqnut: BP128.75
Juz' Wa-qāla alladhīna: BP128.63
Jyotibā (Hindu deity): BL1225.J96+

K

Ka (Egyptian religion): BL2450.K3
Ka'bah: BP187.4
Kabīrpanthīs: BL2020.K3+
Kabre
Religions: BL2480.K32
Kacchapajātaka: BQ1470.K33+
Kadampa: BQ7670+
Kaddish: BM670.K3
Kafirs
Religions: BL1750.7.K34
Kagura: BL2224.25.K3
Kahan, Israel Meir, 1838-1933: BM755.K25
Kaivalyopaniṣad: BL1124.7.K35+
Kakṣapuṭa (by Nāgārjuna, Siddha): BQ3340.K33+
Kakuban, 1095-1144: BQ8999.K33+
Kakushi Nembutsu: BQ8750+
Kālacakra (Tantric rite): BQ8921.K34
Lamaism: BQ7699.K34
Kālacakramūlatantra: BQ2170+
Kālacakratantra: BQ2170+
Kālacakrāvatāra (by Abhayākaragupta): BQ3340.K35+
Kālakārāma Sutta: BQ1349.5.K35+
Kalām: BP166+

Kalash
  Religion: BL2036.5.K34
Kalenjin
  Religions: BL2480.K35
Kālī (Hindu deity):
  BL1225.K3+
Kālikāpurāṇa: BL1140.4.K34+
Kālītantra: BL1142.6.K34+
Kalki (Hindu deity):
  BL1225.K35+
Kalkipurāṇa: BL1140.4.K35+
Kallah: BM506.4.K3+
Kallah rabbati: BM506.4.K35+
Kalmyks
  Early religions: BL975.K34
Kalpasūtras: BL1126.2+
Kalpāvatasmikā: BL1312.6.K36+
Kalpikā: BL1312.6.N57+
Kāma (Hindu deity):
  BL1225.K36+
Kāma (Hindu doctrine):
  BL1214.36
Kāmadhenutantra: BL1142.6.K35+
Kamagami
  Japanese religions: BL2211.K35
Kāmākhyātantra:
  BL1142.6.K3592+
Kāmikāgama: BL1141.5.K35+
Kanaphātās: BL1278.8+
Kandhs
  Religion: BL2032.K3
Kandy Esala Perahera: BQ5720.K3
Kaniṣka, Kushan emperor,
  ca. 144-170
  Buddhism: BQ302+
Kanjur
  Bonpo: BQ7968.2
  Tripiṭaka
    Tibetan version: BQ1260+
Kaṅkālamālinītantra:
  BL1142.6.K36+
Kaṇṇaki (Hindu deity):
  BL1225.K37+
Kānphaṭas: BL1278.8+
Kāṇvasaṃhitā: BL1113.7+
Kāpālikas: BL1280.8+
Kapilapurāṇa: BL1140.4.K36+
Kapisthalakathasaṃhitā:
  BL1112.8+
Kappa
  Jainism: BL1313.3.K36+
Kappāvadamsiāo: BL1312.6.K36+
Kar-ma-pa: BQ7682+
Karaites: BM185+
  Treatment: BM720.K3
Karam: BP188.16.G45
Kāraṇāgama: BL1141.5.K37+
Kāraṇḍavyūhasūtra:
  BQ2240.K34+
Karbis
  Religion: BL2032.K34
Kargyudpa: BQ7679+
Karma
  Buddhism: BQ4435
  India, Religions of: BL2015.K3
  Jainism: BL1357.K37
  Lamaism: BQ7682+
  Theosophy: BP573.K3
Karma yoga
  Hinduism: BL1238.56.K37
Karmaśataka: BQ1570+
Karmasiddhiprakaraṇa (by
  Vasubandhu): BQ2950+
Karmathians
  Islam: BP195.K3+
Karmavācanā: BQ2260+
Karmavibhaṅga: BQ2240.K36+
Karo-Batak
  Religion: BL2123.K35
Karo, Joseph ben Ephraim,
  1488-1575
  Biography: BM755.C28
Karo, Joseph ben Ephraim,
  1488-1575. Shulḥan
  'arukh
  Halacha: BM520.88
Karramites: BP195.K35+
Karrāmīyah: BP195.K35+
Karthābhajā: BL1276.8+
Kārttikeya (Hindu deity):
  BL1225.K38+
Karumāri (Hindu deity):
  BL1225.K39+
Karunā: BQ4360
Karuṇāpuṇḍarīka: BQ1700+
Kashmir Saivism: BL1281.15+
Kāśyapaparivarta: BQ1760+
Kathabrāhmaṇa
  (Kāṭhakabrāhmaṇa):
  BL1118.3+
Kāṭhakagṛhyasūtra
  (Laugākṣigṛhyasūst
  ra): BL1133.2+
Kāṭhakasaṃhitā: BL1112.7+

Kāṭhakaśrautasūtra:
BL1127.5+
Kaṭhāraṇyaka: BL1123.3+
Kathāvatthu: BQ2540+
Kaṭhopaniṣad: BL1124.7.K38+
Kātīyagṛhyasūtra: BL1134.5+
Kātyāyanaśrautasūtra:
BL1127.6+
Kaulas: BL1277.2+
Kauṣītakagṛhyasūtra:
BL1131.8+
Kauṣītakibrāhmaṇa:
BL1116.6+
Kauṣītakibrāhmaṇopan
iṣad: BL1124.7.K39+
Kauthumasaṃhitā: BL1114.4+
Kavvanot (Cabala): BM670.K39
Kaysāniyah: BP195.K38+
Keepers of the Flame
(Fraternity): BP605.S73
Kegon (Hua yan Buddhism):
BQ8200+
Kenopaniṣad: BL1124.7.K46+
Kenpon Hokke (Sect):
BQ8449.5.K45+
Kesa: BQ5085.H3
Kha mchu nag po źi bar
byed pa źes bya ba
theg pa chen po'i mdo:
BQ2240.K42+
Khaḍir
Koranic legends: BP137.5.K5
Khādiragṛhyasūtra: BL1136.2+
Khaggavisāṇasutta:
BQ1419.5.K48+
Khalq al-Qur'ān: BP130.74
Khalsa: BL2018.7.K44
Khalwatīyan: BP189.7.K44+
Khamlāṃba (Hindu deity):
BL1225.K48+
Khams brgyad stoṅ phrag
brgya pa: BQ7972.5.K53+
Khams 'briṅ: BQ7972.5.K54+
Khams rtsa ṅes pa'i mdo:
BQ7972.5.K58+
Khānaqāh-i Ni'mat
Allāhī: BP189.7.K46+
Khandhaka: BQ2360+
Khaṇḍobā (Hindu deity):
BL1225.K5+
Khanty
Religions: BL2370.K53
Kharia
Religion: BL2032.K43
Kharijites: BP195.K4+
Khasis
Religion: BL2032.K45
Khatmīyah
Sufism: BP189.7.K5+
Khiḍr
Koranic legends: BP137.5.K5
Khōḍiyāra Mātā (Hindu
deity): BL1225.K56+
Khoikhoi
Religions: BL2480.K45
Khojahs: BP195.N58+
'Khor ba doṅ sprug ṅan
soṅ skye sgo gcod pa'i
mdo: BQ7971.5.K45+
Khordah Avesta: BL1515.5.K5A2+
Khuddakanikāya: BQ1350+
Khuddakapāṭha: BQ1360+
Kiddush: BM670.K52
Kiddush cups: BM657.K53
Kikuyu
Religions: BL2480.K54
Kīlayadvādaśatantrama
hāyānasūtra: BQ2180.K54+
Killing of animals
Nature worship: BL439.5
Kiṃnaras: BQ4810+
Kindness
Islam: BP188.16.K56
King (Buddhist concept):
BQ4570.K5
King, George, 1919- :
BP605.A33
Kinga
Religions: BL2480.K56
Kings and rulers
Comparative mythology: BL325.K5
Hinduism: BL1215.K56
India, Religions of: BL2015.K5
Islam
Devotional literature:
BP188.3.K55
Judaism: BM645.P64
Midrash: BM518.K5
Rabbinical literature:
BM496.9.K5
Kinot: BM675.K5
Kiraṇāgama: BL1141.5.K57+
Kiranti
Religion: BL2034.5.K55

Kirghiz
Religions: BL2370.K57
Kiriyama, Seiyū:
BQ9800.A3692K57+
Kirpal Ruhani Satsang:
BP605.R85
Kissing
Judaism: BM720.K5
Kleśa: BQ4425+
Knayakāparamēśvari
(Hindu deity): BL1225.K377+
Knowledge
Hadith literature: BP135.8.E3
Koran: BP134.K6
Koan: BQ5630.K6
Kōfuku no Kagaku
(Organization): BP605.K55
Kogi Shingon shū: BQ8950+
Kogo shūi: BL2217.5.K6+
Kohelet (Midrash): BM517.K5+
Kojiki: BL2217.2+, BL2217.3
Kol nidre: BM675.Y58
Kol nidrei: BM670.K6
Kōmyōkai: BQ8660+
Konen (Midrash): BM517.K8+
Konkōkyō: BL2222.K66+
Kono
Religions: BL2480.K6
Koran: BP100+
Relation to Hadith
literature: BP136.38
Works against: BP169
Koran stories: BP130.58
Koran studies: BP130.77+
Koranic legends: BP137+
Korea, Religions of: BL2230+
Koreshanity: BP605.K6
Kōshin cult: BL2211.K6
Kosumomeito: BP605.K63
Kpelle
Religions: BL2480.K72
Kposo
Religions: BL2480.K74
Krama: BL1277.5+
Krishna
Hinduism: BL1220+
Krishnamurti, J. (Jiddu),
1895- : BP585.K7
Kriya yoga
Hinduism: BL1238.56.K74
Kriyāsaṅgraha (by
Kuladatta): BQ3340.K75+
Kriyoḍḍīśantantra:
BL1142.6.K74+
Kriyoḍḍīśatantra:
BL1142.6.K75+
Kṛṣṇa
Hinduism: BL1220+
Kṛṣṇyāmalatantra:
BL1142.6.K76+
Kṣaṇabhangasiddhi (by
Ratnakīrti): BQ3300.K73+
Kṣitigarbha: BQ4710.K7+
Kṣitigarbhapraṇidhāna
sūtra: BQ1710+
Ku-i Buddhism: BQ630.K8
Kubjikāmatatantra:
BL1142.6.K78+
Kubjikātantra: BL1142.6.K82+
Kubjikopaniṣad: BL1124.7.K82+
Kubo, Tsugunari, 1936- :
BQ8379.K82+
Kufr: BP166.785
Kujiki: BL2217.5.K8+
Kujō shakujōkyo: BQ2240.K93+
Kūkai, 774-835: BQ8999.K85+
Kulacūḍāmaṇitantra:
BL1142.6.K83+
Kulaprakāśatantra:
BL1142.6.K84+
Kulārṇavatantra:
BL1142.6.K85+
Kumbha Melā: BL1239.82.K85
Kumina: BL2532.K85
Kun-dga'-gźon-nu: BQ4890.K95+
Kuṇḍalī: BQ4860.K8+
Kuṇḍalinī yoga
Hinduism: BL1238.56.K86
Kuntīdevīdhāraṇī:
BQ1670.K85+
Kuo ch'ü hsien tsai yin
kuo ching: BQ1600.K85+
Kurds
Religions: BL2370.K8
Kuria
Religions: BL2480.K85
Kūrmapurāṇa: BL1140.4.K87+
Kurozumikyō: BL2222.K88+
Kurukullā: BQ4890.K96+
Kusha (Chū she): BQ8250+
Kushi, Michio: BP610.K8+
Kusinārā (Kusinagara,
Uttar Pradesh)
Buddhism: BQ6495

Kutim: BM506.4.K8+
Kūya, 903-972: BQ8549.K87+
Kwaio
 Religions: BL2630.K85
Kyōzō
 Tripiṭaka: BQ1126+
Kyōzuka
 Tripiṭaka: BQ1128
Kyōzutsu
 Tripiṭaka: BQ1128
Kyūseishukyō: BL2228.K98+

L

Laban
 Midrash: BM518.L32
Labor
 Buddhism: BQ4570.E25
 Koran: BP134.L34
 Talmudic literature: BM509.L2
Labyrinths
 Comparative mythology: BL325.L3
Ladon
 Classical mythology: BL820.L25
Lag b'Omer: BM695.L3
Laghukālacakratantra (by Mañjuśrīyaśa): BQ3340.L33+
Laghuprāmāṇyaparīkṣ ā (by Dharmottara): BQ3300.L34+
Lajjā Gaurī (Hindu deity): BL1225.L28+
Lakshmi (Hindu deity): BL1225.L3+
Lakṣmaṇa (Hindu deity): BL1225.L345+
Lakṣmītantra: BL1141.8.L35+
Lāladāsa: BL1277.692.L34
Lāladāsī: BL1277.6+
Lalitāgama: BL1141.5.L35+
Lalitavistara: BQ1580+
Lamaism: BQ7530+
Lamas
 Education and training: BQ7756+
 Ordination: BQ7754
Lamia
 Classical mythology: BL820.L28
Lamps
 Hanukkah: BM657.H3
Landscapes
 Greek religion and mythology: BL795.L3
Language
 Buddhism: BQ4570.L3
 Hinduism: BL1215.L36
 Jainism: BL1375.L35
 Judaism: BM538.L34
 Muḥammad, Prophet, d. 632: BP75.84
Language and religion: BL65.L2
Laṅkāvatārasūtra: BQ1720+
Laos, Religions of: BL2067
Laozi
 Biography: BL1930
 Dao de jing: BL1900.L25+
Lares
 Classical mythology: BL820.L3
Latvians
 Early religions: BL945
Lāṭyāyanaśrautasūtra: BL1129.3+
Laugākṣigṛhyasūtra: BL1133.2+
Laughter and religion: BL65.L3
Laurel
 Roman religion and mythology: BL815.L3
Law
 Buddhism: BQ4570.L37
 India, Religions of: BL2015.L38
Law and religion: BL65.L33
Lay Buddhism: BQ4565
Laya yoga
 Hinduism: BL1238.56.L38
Laylat al-Barā'ah: BP186.38
 Sermons: BP183.638
Laylat al-Mi'rāj: BP186.36
 Sermons: BP183.636
Laylat al-Qadr: BP186.43
 Sermons: BP183.643
Leadership
 Comparative mythology: BL325.L4
 Hinduism: BL1241.44+
 Islam: BP190.5.L4
 Religious life: BL626.38
Leadership and religion: BL65.L42
Legends
 Buddhism: BQ5761+
 Islam: BP137+
 Rabbinical literature: BM530+

Legião da Boa Vontade:
BL2592.L4
Lekharāja, Dada:
BL1274.292.L44
Lesbians
Judaism: BM729.H65
Letters (Alphabet)
Buddhism: BQ5125.B5
Jainism: BL1375.L35
Sufism: BP189.65.A47
Leucothea
Classical mythology: BL820.M3
Levinsohn, Isaac Baer,
1788-1860: BM755.L45
Lha-rgod-thog-pa: BQ7981.4.L532
Li shi a Pi tan lun:
BQ2730.L52+
Liangjie, 807-869: BQ9449.L52+
Liberalism (Religion): BL99
Liberty and religion: BL65.L52
Liberty, Religious: BL640
Life
Koran: BP134.L54
Life after death
Islam: BP166.8+
Judaism: BM635+
Koran: BP134.F8
Life and death
Japanese religions: BL2211.D35
Life of poverty
Hinduism: BL1214.32.P68
Life sciences and religion:
BL261
Life, Meaning of
Buddhism: BQ4570.L5
Hinduism: BL1215.L54
Light
Comparative mythology:
BL325.L47
Greek religion and
mythology: BL795.L54
Islam: BP190.5.L47
Judaism: BM645.L54
Light and religion: BL265.L5
Light Institute: BP605.L53
Lights and candles
Judaism: BM657.C3
Liḳuṭe Tsevi: BM675.R42
Lilith
Comparative mythology: BL325.L5
Semitic religions: BL1605.L55
Limbus
Religion: BL2034.5.L55
Lindisfarne Association:
BP605.L56
Liṅgapurāṇa: BL1140.4.L56+
Lingayats: BL1281.2+
Lions
Comparative mythology:
BL325.L56
Egyptian religion: BL2450.L5
Lipkin, Israel, 1810-1883:
BM755.L54
Lisu
Religion: BL2078.L57
Literary discoveries
Buddhism: BQ240+
Lithuanians
Early religions: BL945
Litolatria: BL2592.L56
Liturgical objects
Buddhism: BQ5070+
Islam: BP184.95+
Shinto: BL2224.35+
Liturgical symbolism
Buddhism: BQ5120
Liturgy
Hinduism: BL1226.18+
Judaism: BM660+
Karaites: BM185.3+
Samaritans: BM960+
Zoroastrianism: BL1590.L58
Llamas
Nature worship: BL443.L6
Loki
Germanic and Norse
mythology: BL870.L6
Lorber, Jakob, 1800-1864:
BP610.L67+
Lotus
Buddhism: BQ5125.P3
Lotus and religion: BL65.L67
Love
Anthroposophy: BP596.L67
Buddhism: BQ4359, BQ4570.L6
Germanic and Norse
mythology: BL870.L64
Islam: BP188.16.L68
Koran: BP134.L67
Religious life: BL626.4
Sufism: BP189.65.L68
Lü: BQ8780+

Lü zang
Tripiṭaka: BQ1230+
Lu, Shengyan, 1945- :
BQ9800.C4892L82+
Lubavitch
Hasidism: BM198.54
Lucumí: BL2532.S3
Lugbara
Religions: BL2480.L76
Lulab
Judaism: BM657.L8
Lulav
Judaism: BM657.L8
Lumbinī (Rummindei, Nepal)
Buddhism: BQ6470
Lun zang
Tripiṭaka: BQ1240+
Luo
Religions: BL2480.L8
Lupercalia
Roman religion and mythology: BL815.L8
Luqmān
Koran: BP133.7.L84
Luria, Isaac ben Solomon
Cabala: BM525.L83+
Lushai
Religion: BL2032.L87
Lustration
Religion: BL619.L8
Luzzatto, Samuel David, 1800-1865: BM755.L8
Lynn, James Jesse: BP605.S43L9

M

Ma rgyud: BQ7973.5.M35+
Ma rgyud saṅs rgyas rgyud gsum: BQ7973.5.M37+
Ma-tri: BQ7981.4.M372
Maʻamadot: BM675.R44
Maʻaśeh ʻaśarah haruge malkhut (Midrash): BM517.E5+
Maʻaśeh merkavah
Cabala: BM525.A367+
Maʻaśeh Torah (Midrash): BM517.M2+
Maat (Egyptian deity): BL2450.M33
Macumba: BL2592.M23
Madhva, 13th cent.: BL1286.292.M34
Mādhvas: BL1286.2+
Madhyamā pratipad: BQ4280
Madhyamaka-Yogācāra School of Buddhism: BQ7479
Madhyamakahṛdayakārikā (by Bhāvaviveka): BQ2910.M34+
Madhyamakakārikā (by Nāgārjuna): BQ2790+
Madhyamakālaṅkāra (by Śātarakṣita): BQ3180+
Madhyamakaratnapradīpa (by Bhāvaviveka): BQ2910.M35+
Mādhyamakaśāstra (by Piṅgala): BQ2810+
Madhyamakāvatāra (by Candrakīrti): BQ2910.M36+
Mādhyamika School of Buddhism: BQ7445+
Abhidharmapiṭaka: BQ2750+
Madhyāntānugamaśāstra (by Asaṅga): BQ2820+
Madhyāntavibhāgasūtra (by Maitreyanātha): BQ2960+
Magen David
Judaism: BM657.5.M3
Māgha Pūjā: BQ5720.M2
Magic
Buddhism: BQ4570.M3
Islam: BP190.5.M25
Magic and religion: BL65.M2
Magid
Judaism: BM659.M3
Magnanimity
Islam: BP188.16.M3
Mah-Meri
Religion: BL2083.M34
Mah tovu: BM670.M33
Mahā Ummagga Jātaka: BQ1470.M35+
Mahā-vihāra: BQ8260+
Mahābalasūtra: BQ2240.M27+
Mahābhāgavatapurāṇa: BL1140.4.M32+
Mahābhārata: BL1138.2+
Mahābodhivaṃsa (by Upatissa): BQ2590+
Mahācattārisakasutta: BQ1320.M34+

Mahājanakajātaka:
BQ1470.M3594+
Mahajjātakamālā: BQ1600.M34+
Mahākāla: BQ4750.M35+
Mahākālatantra: BQ2180.M32+
Mahākapijātaka: BQ1470.M362+
Mahākāruṇikacittadhā
raṇi: BQ1670.M35+
Mahāmāyūrīvidyārāj
ñī: BQ1730+
Mahāmokṣasūtra: BQ2240.M33+
Mahāmokṣatantra:
BL1142.6.M34+
Mahāmudrā (Tantric rite):
BQ8921.M35
Lamaism: BQ7699.M34
Mahānārāyaṇopaniṣad:
BL1124.7.M34+
Mahānidānasutta: BQ1300.M33+
Mahānikāya: BQ8270+
Mahānirvāṇatantra:
BL1142.6.M35+
Mahānubhāva: BL1277.8+
Mahāpadānasutta: BQ1300.M34+
Mahāparinibbānasutta:
BQ1300.M35+
Mahāparinirvāṇasūtra:
BQ1740+
Mahāpradoṣa
Hinduism: BL1226.82.M27
Mahāprajñāpāramitās
ūtra: BQ1940+
Mahāpratyākhyāna:
BL1312.9.M34+
Mahāratnakūṭasūtra: BQ1750+
Mahars
Religion: BL2032.M34
Mahāsaṃnipātasūtra: BQ1810+
Mahāsāṅghika School of
Buddhism: BQ7255.M34
Vinayapiṭaka: BQ2420+
Mahāsannipātaratnaketu
dhāraṇī: BQ1670.M36+
Mahāsatipaṭṭhānasutta:
BQ1300.M36+
Mahāsudassanasutta:
BQ1300.M37+
Mahāsutasomajātaka:
BQ1470.M365+
Mahātaṇhāsaṅkhayasut
ta: BQ1300.M38+
Mahāvaipulyapūrnabuddh
asūtraprasannārthsū
tra: BQ2230+
Mahāvairocanasūtra: BQ1870+
Mahāvaṃsa (by
Mahānāma): BQ2600+
Mahāvastu: BQ1590+
Mahāvidyātantra:
BL1142.6.M3594+
Mahāvīra: BL1370+
Mahāvrata
India, Religions of: BL2015.M27
Mahāyāna Bodhisattva
Vinaya: BQ2450+
Mahayana Buddhism: BQ7300+
Abhidharmapiṭaka: BQ2740+
Development: BQ300
Sūtrapiṭaka: BQ1610+
Mahayana discipline: BQ7442
Mahāyānamadhyamakaśā
stravyākhyā (by
Sthiramati): BQ2830+
Mahāyānasaṅgraha (by
Asaṅga): BQ2980+
Mahāyānaśraddhotpāda
śāstra (by
Aśvaghoṣa): BQ2990+
Mahāyānasūtrālaṅkā
ra (by Asaṅga): BQ3000+
Mahāyānaviṃśaka (by
Nāgārjuna): BQ2910.M42+
Mahāyānottaratantrāś
astra: BQ3010+
Mahāyut: BQ9150+
Mahdī, Muḥammad ibn
al-Ḥasan, b. 869: BP193.22
Mahdism: BP166.93
Mahdiyah
Sufism: BP189.7.M26+
Mahima Dharma: BL2020.M3+
Mahīśāsaka School
Vinayapiṭaka: BQ2430+
Mahiṣāsura (Hindu deity):
BL1225.M25+
Mahoragas: BQ4820+
Maḥzor: BM674.4+
Maimonides, Moses, 1135-
1204
Biography: BM755.M6
Halacha: BM520.84
Principles of Judaism: BM545+

Mainōkyō
 Tripiṭaka: BQ1128
Maitrāyaṇīsaṃhitā:
 BL1113.3+
Maitrāyaṇīyagṛhyasū
 tra: BL1133.3+
Maitrayāṇiyopaniṣad:
 BL1124.7.M35+
Maitreya: BQ4690.M3+, BQ4710.M3+
 Prayers and devotions to:
 BQ5592.M3
Maitreyapraṇidhāna (by
 Sthiramati): BQ3080.M34+
Maitreyavyākaraṇa:
 BQ2240.M343+
Maitrī (Mettā): BQ4360
Majjhimanikāya: BQ1310+
Majjhimapaṇṇāsa:
 BQ1319.5.M34+
Makhādevajātaka: BQ1470.M367+
Makiguchi, Tsunesaburō,
 1871-1944: BQ8449.M35+
Maktab Tarighe Oveyssi
 Shamaghsoudi: BP189.7.M28+
Malamāsa: BL1239.82.M34
Malāmatīyah
 Sufism: BP189.7.M3+
Malaysia, Religions of: BL2080+
Malê: BL2592.M3
Maleya Mādēśvara (Hindu
 deity): BL1225.M27+
Malicious accusation
 Koran: BP134.M24
Malikites: BP166.14.M3
Mālinīvijayottaratantra:
 BL1142.6.M36+
Malkhuyyot: BM670.M34
Mallapurāṇa: BL1140.4.M35+
Mambila
 Religions: BL2480.M22
Man
 Buddhism: BQ4570.M34
 Hinduism: BL1213.54
 Islam: BP166.7+
 Judaism: BM627
 Koran: BP134.M3
 Sikhism: BL2018.5.M35
 Theosophy: BP573.M3
Man and God, Mediation
 between
 Islam: BP166.76
Man Núóng: BQ4690.M36+
Manala
 Religions: BL2480.M25
Manasā (Hindu deity):
 BL1225.M3+
Mānava Sevā Saṅgha:
 BL1277.9+
Mānavagṛhyasūtra: BL1133.3+
Maṇavāḷa Māmuṇi,
 1370-1444: BL1288.292.M35
Mānavaśrautasūtra: BL1127.7+
Mandala
 Buddhism: BQ5125.M3
 India, Religions of: BL2015.M3
 Religious symbolism: BL604.M36
Maṇḍalabrāhmaṇopani.
 sad: BL1124.7.M36+
Mandari
 Religions: BL2480.M28
Māṇḍūkyopaniṣad:
 BL1124.7.M37+
Maṅgalasutta: BQ1369.5.M35+
Mani Rimdu: BQ5720.M28
Maṇibhadra (Jaina deity):
 BL1375.7.M35
Maṇicūḍajātaka: BQ1470.M38+
Mañjuśrī: BQ4710.M4+
 Prayers and devotions to:
 BQ5592.M35
Mañjuśrīmūlakalpa:
 BQ2180.M34+
Mañjuśrīnāmasaṅgīti:
 BQ2240.M35+
Mannus
 Germanic and Norse
 mythology: BL870.M3
Mansi
 Religions: BL2370.M34
Mantrabrāhmaṇa: BL1121.3.U63+
Mantras
 Hinduism: BL1236.22+
 Jainism: BL1377.3
Mantrasaṃhitā: BL1142.3.M36+
Manual of discipline
 Dead Sea scrolls: BM488.M3
Manus (Hindu mythology):
 BL1225.M35+
Manuscript preservation
 Tripiṭaka: BQ1126+
Manuscripts
 Samaritan Pentateuch: BM922
Manuscripts, Arabic
 Koran: BP100.3

Manuṣya-gati: BQ4510
Maori
  Religions: BL2615
Mar-pa Chos-kyi-blo-gros, 1012-1097: BQ7950.M37+
Maraṇānusmṛti: BQ5630.D4
Maranos, Treatment of
  Judaism: BM720.M3
Marduk (Deity): BL1625.M37
María Lionza: BL2592.M35
Marīcisaṃhitā: BL1142.3.M37+
Māriyammaṉ (Hindu deity): BL1225.M3715+
Mārkaṇḍeyapurāṇa: BL1140.4.M37+
Marriage
  Bahai Faith: BP388.M37
  Buddhism: BQ4570.M36
    Priesthood: BQ5355.M37
  Judaism: BM713
  Religious doctrine: BL462
Marriage rites
  Buddhism: BQ5015
  Hinduism: BL1226.82.M3
Marriage service
  Religious ceremonies: BL619.M37
Marriage, Sacred
  Greek religion and mythology: BL795.S22
Married people
  Buddhism
    Devotional literature: BQ5585.M3
  Islam
    Devotional literature: BP188.3.M3
Mars
  Classical mythology: BL820.M2
Marsyas
  Classical mythology: BL820.M26
Martyrdom
  Islam: BP190.5.M3
  Judaism: BM645.M34
  Religious life: BL626.5
Martyrs
  Islam: BP72
Marut (Hindu deity): BL1225.M38+
Maruyamakyō: BL2228.M37+
Marxism and anthroposophy: BP596.M37
Mary, Blessed Virgin, Saint
  Jewish attitude toward: BM621
  Koran: BP133.7.M37
Maryam
  Koran: BP133.7.M37
Masaharu Taniguchi: BL2228.S45+
Masculinity
  Attributes of deity: BL215.3
Mashona
  Religions: BL2480.M3
Masks
  Japanese religions: BL2211.M37
Masoretic Pentateuch and Samaritan Pentateuch compared: BM927
Mass media
  Islam: BP185.7+
  Religion: BL638+
Mataṅgaparameśvarāgama: BL1141.5.M38+
Mathematics
  Islam: BP190.5.M34
  Talmudic literature: BM509.M3
Mathematics and religion: BL265.M3
Mati: BQ4380+
Matn
  Hadith literature: BP136.36
Matriarchy
  Comparative mythology: BL325.M3
Mātṛkābhedatantra: BL1142.6.M37+
Matsyapurāṇa: BL1140.4.M38+
Matsyendra: BL1278.592.M38
Matter
  Buddhist interpretations: BQ4570.M37
Matuta
  Classical mythology: BL820.M3
Mawlid al-Nabī: BP186.34
  Sermons: BP183.634
Mawri
  Religions: BL2480.M32
Maxims
  Buddhism: BQ135
Māya
  Hinduism: BL1214.38
Mayan religions: BL2560.M3
Māyātantra: BL1142.6.M38+
Mazda
  Zoroastrianism: BL1580

Mazdaznan: BP605.M37
Mazdeism: BL1500+
Mbala
  Religions: BL2480.M33
Mbundu
  Religions: BL2480.M35
Mdo (Sutras)
  Bonpo (Sect): BQ7971.2+
Mdo 'dus: BQ7971.5.M45+
Mdo rnam 'brel par ti ka:
    BQ7971.5.M46+
Mdzod (Abhidharma)
  Bonpo (Sect): BQ7974.2+
Mdzod phug: BQ7974.5.M49+
Me-ri: BQ7981.4.M422
Meadows
  Greek religion and
    mythology: BL795.L3
Meals, Sacred
  Greek religion and
    mythology: BL795.S23
  Roman religion and
    mythology: BL815.S15
Mealtime prayers
  Judaism
    Liturgical books: BM675.G7
Measures and weights
  Talmudic literature: BM509.W4
Mecca
  Islam: BP187.2+
  Muḥammad, Prophet, d. 632:
    BP77.4+, BP77.7
  Pilgrimage to: BP181, BP187.3
Medea
  Classical mythology: BL820.M37
Mediation
  Judaism: BM645.M37
Mediation between God and
  man
  Islam: BP166.76
Medicine
  Buddhism: BQ4570.M4
  Hadith literature: BP135.8.M43
  Islam: BP166.72
  Judaism: BM538.H43
  Religion: BL65.M4
Medina (Saudi Arabia)
  Hadith literature: BP135.8.M45
  Muḥammad, Prophet, d. 632:
    BP77.5, BP77.6+
Meditation
  Buddhism: BQ5595+
    Psychoanalysis: BQ5630.P7
  Hinayana Buddhism: BQ7280
  Hinduism: BL1238.32+
  India, Religions of: BL2015.M4
  Jainism: BL1378.6
  Japanese religions: BL2211.M43
  Lamaism: BQ7800+
  Mādhyamika School: BQ7475
  Mahayana Buddhism: BQ7438
  Religious life: BL627
  Shinto: BL2224.73
  Sikhism: BL2018.4+
  Theravāda Buddhism: BQ7280
  Yogācāra School: BQ7516
Meditations
  Buddhism: BQ5535+
  Jewish way of life: BM724
  Lamaism: BQ7810+
  Religious life: BL624.2+
  Shinto: BL2224.3
  Taoism: BL1942.8
Medusa
  Classical mythology: BL820.M38
Meera, Mother, 1960- :
    BP610.M42+
Meher Baba, 1894-1969:
    BP610.M43+
Mehitsah
  Synagogues: BM653.2
Meir, 2nd cent.
  Talmudist: BM502.3.M44
Meitheis
  Religion: BL2032.M4
Mekhilta of Rabbi Ishmael:
    BM517.M4+
Mekhilta of Rabbi Simeon
  ben Yoḥai: BM517.M45+
Melampus
  Classical mythology: BL820.M39
Melchizedek Synthesis
  Light Academy: BP605.M44
Melodic reading
  Koran: BP131.6
Membership
  Hinduism: BL1241.58
Memmon
  Classical mythology: BL820.M4
Memorial sermons
  Judaism: BM744.3

Memorial service sermons,
Buddhist: BQ5350.M4
Memorial services
Buddhism: BQ5025
Confucianism: BL1859.M45
Judaism
Liturgical books: BM675.M4
Memorial tablets
Buddhism: BQ5075.M4
Memorials
Islam: BP184.95+
Religion: BL619.M45
Memory
Assyro-Babylonian religions: BL1625.M45
Theosophy: BP573.M4
Men
Buddhism
Devotional literature: BQ5585.M4
Religious life: BQ5445
Hinduism
Religious life: BL1237.44
Judaism
Prayer and service books: BM667.M45
Religious duties: BM725
Religious life: BL625.65
Men believers
Buddhism
Biography: BQ846
Men of the Koran: BP133.5+
Menander, Indo-Greek king, fl. 150 B.C.
Buddhism: BQ298
Mende
Religions: BL2480.M4
Menorah: BM657.M35
Mens (Roman deity)
Classical mythology: BL820.M45
Men's clubs management
Synagogues: BM653.5
Mensuration
Comparative mythology: BL325.M35
Mental healing
Theosophy: BP573.H4
Mental health and religion: BL65.M45
Mental illness
Greek religion and mythology: BL795.M4
Mercury (Roman deity)
Classical mythology: BL820.M5
Mercy
Koran: BP134.M47
Merit
Buddhism: BQ4363
Islam: BP166.33
Judaism: BM645.M4
Mert-seger (Egyptian deity): BL2450.M4
Meru
Religions: BL2480.M43
Merutantra: BL1142.6.M47+
Messiah
India, Religions of: BL2015.M47
Judaism: BM615+
Rabbinical literature: BM496.9.M47
Talmudic literature: BM509.M4
Messiahs
Religious doctrine: BL475
Messianic era
Judaism: BM625+
Messianism
India, Religions of: BL2015.M47
Metals
Nature worship: BL457.M4
Metamorphosis
Comparative mythology: BL325.M4
Greek religion and mythology: BL795.M47
Religion: BL515+
Metaphor
Buddhism: BQ4570.M45
Hinduism: BL1215.M48
Koran: BP131.3
Methodology
Classical religion and mythology: BL717
Religion: BL41
Mettāsutta: BQ1349.5.M43+
Metteyya: BQ4690.M3+
Mevleviyeh
Sufism: BP189.7.M4+
Meyvaḻi (Sect): BL1295.M47+
Mezuzah (Liturgical object): BM657.M4
Mezuzah (Talmudic literature): BM506.4.M48+
Mgon-po Bse-khrab-can: BQ4890.M56+

Mi-la-ras-pa, 1040-1123:
BQ7950.M55+
Mice
Comparative mythology: BL325.M5
Mid-Sha'bān, Night of:
BP186.38
Sermons: BP183.638
Midas
Classical mythology: BL820.M55
Middle aged persons
Religious life: BL625.3
Middle East
Anthroposophy: BP596.M52
Middle Way (Buddhism): BQ4280
Midrash: BM510+
Midrash ha-gadol: BM517.M5+
Midrash ha-ne'lam
Cabala
Zohar supplements: BM525.A6M5+
Midrash rabbah: BM517.M6+
Midrash zuta: BM517.Z8+
Mikoshi
Shinto: BL2227.8.M54
Mikveh
Judaism: BM703
Milandapañhā: BQ2610+
Military campaigns
Muḥammad, Prophet, d. 632:
BP77.7
Millennialism: BL503.2
Mills
Comparative mythology:
BL325.M53
Millstones
Comparative mythology:
BL325.M53
Min (Egyptian deity):
BL2450.M55
Mīnākṣī (Hindu deity):
BL1225.M48+
Minas
Religion: BL2032.M5
Minbar
Islam: BP184.95+
Mind
Koran: BP134.R33
Minerva
Classical mythology: BL820.M6
Ministerial work
Buddhism: BQ5140+
Ministry
Buddhism: BQ5140+
Hinduism: BL1241.32+
Lamaism: BQ7730+
Shinto: BL2224.4+
Minor Tractates (Talmudic
literature): BM506.2+
Minotaur
Classical mythology: BL820.M63
Miogarosormr
Germanic and Norse
mythology: BL870.M5
Miracle literature
Buddhism: BQ5821+
Miracles
Buddhism: BQ4570.M5
Hinduism: BL1215.M57
Islam: BP166.65
Muḥammad, Prophet, d. 632:
BP75.8
Religious doctrine: BL487
Mi'rāj
Muḥammad: BP166.57
Mīrghanīyah
Sufism: BP189.7.M5+
Misconstruction
Hadith literature: BP136.76
Mishle (Midrash): BM517.M77+
Mishnah: BM497+
Special orders and
tractates: BM506.A+
Mishneh Torah: BM520.84
Misogi: BL2224.25.M57
Misogikyō: BL2222.M57+
Mission of Islam: BP170.85
Mission of Israel
Judaism: BM613+
Mission of Muḥammad: BP166.55
Missionary activities
Religion: BL637
Missionary work
Buddhism: BQ5901+
Early history: BQ296
Hinduism: BL1243.32+
Islam: BP170.3
Mitake: BL2222.M58+
Mithraism: BL1585
Mithras (God): BL1585
Mitnaggedic rite: BM672.A8
Mitnaggedim
Hasidism: BM198.8
Mitra (Hindu deity): BL1225.M5+

Mixed pews
  Synagogues: BM653.2
Miyaza: BL2224.63
Mnemonic devices
  Talmudic literature: BM509.M6
Moabite religion: BL1675
Moba
  Religions: BL2480.M63
Mode of fasting
  Islam: BP184.5
Moderation
  Buddhism: BQ4420.M6
  Greek religion and mythology: BL795.M6
  Islam: BP188.16.M59
Modesty
  Islam: BP188.16.M6
Mokṣa
  Hinduism: BL1213.58
  India, Religions of: BL2015.M64
Mokugyo: BQ5075.W6
Moloch
  Semitic religions: BL1605.M6
Monasteries
  Buddhism: BQ6300+
  Hinduism: BL1243.72+
  Islam: BP187.62+
  Jainism: BL1378+
  Lamaism: BQ7900+
Monastic life
  Buddhism: BQ6001+, BQ6115+
  Hinduism: BL1238.72+
  Lamaism: BQ7890
Monasticism
  Bonpo (Sect): BQ7984.2
  Buddhism: BQ6001+
  Hinduism: BL1238.72+
  India, Religions of: BL2015.M66
  Islam: BP189.68+
  Jainism: BL1378+
  Organization: BL631
Mongols
  Religions: BL2370.M7
Monkhood
  Lamaism: BQ7730+
Monks
  Buddhism: BQ6140+
    Biography: BQ843
Monotheism: BL221
  Assyro-Babylonian religions: BL1625.M6
  Roman religion and mythology: BL815.M6
Monotheistic religions: BL360
Monro, Kiyo Sasaki, 1941- : BP610.M65+
Monsters
  Greek religion and mythology: BL795.M65
Moon
  Comparative mythology: BL325.M56
  Nature worship: BL438
  Roman religion and mythology: BL815.M64
Moorish Science Temple of America: BP232
Moral theology
  Judaism: BM728
Mordvinians
  Early religions: BL975.M6
Morning prayer
  Hinduism: BL1236.52.M67
Moses (Biblical leader)
  Koran: BP133.7.M67
  Midrash: BM518.M6
Moses ben Maimon, 1135-1204
  Biography: BM755.M6
  Principles of Judaism: BM545+
Moses ben Naḥman, ca. 1195-ca. 1270: BM755.M62
Mosque officials: BP185+
Mosques: BP187.62+
Mossi
  Religions: BL2480.M67
Motazilites: BP195.M6+
Mother goddesses
  Classical mythology: BL820.M65
  Comparative mythology: BL325.M6
  India, Religions of: BL2015.M68
  Japan: BL2211.M57
Motherhood
  Attributes of deity: BL215.5
  Islam: BP190.5.M67
  Judaism: BM726
Mothers
  Buddhism
    Devotional literature: BQ5585.P3
    Religious life: BQ5440
  Religious life: BL625.68
Mountain gods
  Japan: BL2211.M59

Mountains
Chinese religions: BL1812.M68
Comparative mythology: BL325.M63
Japanese religions: BL2211.M6
Korean religions: BL2236.M68
Nature worship: BL447
Mourners' prayers
Judaism: BM675.M7
Mourning customs
Islam: BP184.9.M68
Judaism: BM712
Movement of Spiritual Inner Awareness: BP605.M68
Mr.t (Egyptian deity): BL2450.M4
Mṛgendratantra: BL1142.6.M75+
Mt. Thaur, Escape to
Muḥammad, Prophet, d. 632: BP77.65
Mubyŏn Taesa: BQ9800.S4692M82+
Mudgalapurāṇa: BL1140.4.M84+
Mudrās
Buddhism: BQ5125.M8
Hinduism: BL1226.82.M93, BL1236.76.M84
Muezzin: BP185.3
Muḥammad al-Bāqir ibn 'Alī Zayn al-'Ābidīn, d. 731 or 2: BP193.15
Muḥammad al-Jawād ibn 'Alī al-Riḍā, 810 or 11-835 or 6: BP193.19
Muḥammad ibn 'Abd al-Wahhāb, 1703 or 4-1792: BP195.W2+
Muḥammad, Prophet, d. 632: BP75+
Hadith literature: BP135.8.M85
Islamic theology: BP166.5+
Koran: BP133.7.M84
Muḥammad's enemies
Koran: BP133.6.E5
Muḥammad's mission: BP166.55
Muḥarram, First of
Islam: BP186.2
Muḥarram, Tenth of
Islam: BP186.3
Sermons: BP183.63
Shiites: BP194.5.T4
Muktananda, Swami: BL1283.792.M84
Mukti
Hinduism: BL1213.58
Mūlamadhyamakavṛtti (by Buddhapālita): BQ2840+
Mūlapaṇṇāsa: BQ1319.5.M84+
Mūlasūtras: BL1313.8+
Mūlasuttas: BL1313.8+
Mulian jing: BQ2240.M84+
Mummy cult (Buddhism): BQ5680.M85
Munāiqūn
Koran: BP134.M86
Muṇḍakopaniṣad: BL1124.7.M86+
Muṇḍamālātantra: BL1142.6.M86+
Mundas
Religion: BL2032.M84
Murīdīyah: BP195.M66+
Murids: BP195.M66+
Murjites: BP195.M7+
Murngin
Religions: BL2630.M87
Murugan (Hindu deity): BL1225.M8+
Mūsá (Biblical leader)
Koran: BP133.7.M67
Mūsá al-Kāẓim ibn Ja'far, 745?-799: BP193.17
Muses
Classical mythology: BL820.M8
Music
Buddhism: BQ4570.M97
Hinduism: BL1215.M87
Islam: BP190.5.M8
Religious ritual: BL605
Sufism: BP189.65.M87
Music in Jewish worship: BM658+
Muslim ibn al-Ḥajjāj al-Qushayrī, ca. 821-875
Hadith: BP135.A14+
Muslims in non-Muslim countries: BP52.5
Muspilli
Germanic and Norse mythology: BL870.M8
Myōe, 1173?-1232: BQ8249.M96+
Myōgō: BQ4460

Mysteries
Egyptian religion: BL2450.M9
Greek religion and mythology: BL795.M9
Religion: BL610
Mysticism
Buddhism: BQ5635+
Chinese religions: BL1812.M94
Hinayana Buddhism: BQ7280
Hinduism: BL1215.M9
India, Religions of: BL2015.M9
Islam: BP188.45+
Jainism: BL1378.8+
Judaism: BM723+
Lamaism: BQ7800+
Mādhyamika School: BQ7475
Mahayana Buddhism: BQ7438
Rabbinical literature: BM496.9.M87
Religious life: BL625
Roman religion and mythology: BL815.M8
Sikhism: BL2018.43
Theravāda Buddhism: BQ7280
Yogācāra School: BQ7516
Zoroastrianism: BL1590.M9
Myth
Religion: BL300+
Myth and ritual school
Religion: BL304.2
Mythical characters
Hinduism: BL1216+
Jainism: BL1375.3+
Mythological tales
Buddhism: BQ5741+
Mythology: BL1+
Mythology, Comparative: BL300+
Mythology, Shinto: BL2226+
Myths and legends
Rabbinical literature: BM530+

N

Na-len-dra-pa: BQ7675+
Nabataean religion: BL1677
Nabu (Deity): BL1625.N32
Nāḍapāda: BQ7950.N34+
Nag-dban-blo-bzan-rgya-m tsho (Dalai Lama V): BQ7935.N34+
Nāgakumāra (Jaina diety): BL1375.7.N34
Nagamatsu, Seifū, 1817-1890: BQ8449.5.H6692N33+
Nāgārjuna, 2nd cent.: BQ7479.8.N34+
Nāgas: BQ4760+
Nage
Religion: BL2123.N32
Nagesh sect: BL1278.2+
Naḥman ben Simḥah, of Bratzlav, 1722-1811: BM755.N25
Naḥmanides, ca. 1195-ca. 1270: BM755.M62
Nakayama Shingo Shōshū: BQ9800.N35+
Nakṣatramātṛkānāmad hāraṇī: BQ1670.N35+
Nalendrapa: BQ7675+
Namdharis: BL2018.7.N34
Name (Jew, Israel, Hebrew)
Judaism: BM729.N3
Names
Hinduism: BL1215.N3
Semitic religions: BL1605.N3
Talmudic literature: BM509.N3
Nan-hua ching: BL1900.C45+
Nānak's Japujī: BL2017.422
Nānak's Sidha gosati: BL2017.424
Nanda
Buddhism: BQ905.N2
Nandadevi (Hindu deity): BL1225.N34+
Nandīsūtra: BL1313.6.N34+
Nandisutta: BL1313.6.N34+
Nanhua jing: BL1900.C45+
Naqshabandīyah
Sufism: BP189.7.N35+
Nāradapañcarātra: BL1141.8.N37+
Nāradapurāṇa: BL1140.4.N37+
Nāradīyapurāṇa: BL1140.4.N37+
Nāradīyasaṃhitā: BL1141.8.N38+
Naraka-gati: BQ4525
Narasiṃha (Hindu deity): BL1225.N35+
Narasiṃhapurāṇa: BL1140.4.N39+
Nārāyaṇa (Hindu deity): BL1225.N36+

Nārāyaṇopaniṣad: BL1124.7.N37+
Narmadā (Hindu deity): BL1225.N37+
Naropa Institute: BP605.N3
Nasā'ī, Aḥmad ibn Shu'ayb, 830 or 31-915
Hadith: BP135.A16+
Nasi
Judaism: BM655.45
Nāsikh wa-al-mansūkh: BP130.3
Naṭarāja (Hindu deity): BL1225.N378+
Nāthas: BL1278.5+
National religions: BL385
Nationalism
India, Religions of: BL2015.N26
Islam: BP173.55
Nationalism and religion: BL65.N3
Nativistic movements
India, Religions of: BL2015.N3
Nats (Burmese religion): BL2052.N37
Natural history
Buddhism: BQ4570.N3
Koran: BP134.N3
Talmudic literature: BM509.N4
Tripiṭaka: BQ1136.N38
Natural history and religion: BL262+
Natural theology: BL175+
Nature
Buddhism: BQ4570.N3
Hinduism: BL1215.N34
Islam: BP190.5.N38
Koran: BP134.N3
Sikhism: BL2018.5.N37
Nature and religion: BL65.N35
Nature worship: BL435+
Japan: BL2211.N37
Navagraha (Hindu deity): BL1225.N38+
Navalapanthīs: BL1278.895+
Navel
Comparative mythology: BL325.N35
Egyptian religion: BL2450.N3
Greek religion and mythology: BL795.N3
Semitic religions: BL1605.N35
Navigation
Comparative mythology: BL325.N37
Nawrúz
Bahai Faith: BP387.N38
Nāyādhammakahāo: BL1312.3.N39+
Naẓar: BP188.16.M6
Nazarite
Judaism: BM720.N3
Ndebele
Religions: BL2480.N33
Ndembu
Religions: BL2480.N35
Near-death experiences
Anthroposophy: BP596.N43
Near East
Anthroposophy: BP596.M52
Nehan-e: BQ5720.N6
Neith Egyptian deity): BL2450.N45
Nembutsu
Doctrine: BQ4460
Practice: BQ5630.N4
Nemean lion
Classical mythology: BL820.N47
Nemesis
Classical mythology: BL820.N48
Neo-American Church: BP605.N44
Neo-paganism: BP605.N46
Nepal, Religions of: BL2033+
Neptune
Classical mythology: BL820.N5
Nergal (Deity): BL1625.N37
Nerthus
Germanic and Norse mythology: BL870.N4
Netratantra: BL1142.6.N47+
Netti: BQ1369.5.N48+
Nettipakaraṇa: BQ2640.N45+
Neurosis, Religious: BL53.5
New Age movement: BP605.N48
New Jerusalem Scroll
Dead Sea Scrolls: BM488.N48
New moon
Jewish festival: BM695.N4
New moon prayers
Judaism: BM675.N45
New Universal Union: BP605.H5

New Year
Assyro-Babylonian religions: BL1625.N4
Judaism: BM695.N5
New Year prayers
Judaism: BM675.R67
New Year's Day
Islam: BP186.2
New Zealand
Religions: BL2615
Newbrough, John Ballou, 1828-1891: BP605.F34
Newhouse, Flower Arlene Sechler, 1909- : BP605.C5
Nfaropa: BQ7950.N34+
Ngaju
Religion: BL2123.N43
Ngbaba-Ma'bo
Religions: BL2480.N45
Ngorpa: BQ7673+
Nhât Hạnh, Thích: BQ9800.T5392N45+
Ni-guhi-ma-pa: BQ7669+
Nichiji, b. 1250: BQ8349.N56+
Nichiō, 1565-1630: BQ8369.N53+
Nichiren: BQ8300+
Relations
Shin (Sect): BQ8319.6.S55
Nichiren Shōshū: BQ8400+
Nichiren, 1222-1282: BQ8349.N57+
Nidānakathā: BQ1470.N53+
Niddesa: BQ1480+
Nie pan: BQ8450+
Night
Comparative mythology: BL325.N5
Night journey to Jerusalem
Muḥammad: BP166.57
Night of mid-Sha'bān: BP186.38
Sermons: BP183.638
Nigrodhamigajātaka: BQ1470.N55+
Nihon shoki: BL2217.2+, BL2217.4
Nika
Religions: BL2480.N458
Nikāyas: BQ1280+
Nīlamatapurāṇa: BL1140.4.N55+
Nīlatantra: BL1142.6.N55+
Nile River
Islam: BP190.5.N54
Nīmānandins: BL1286.5+
Ni'mat Allāhī Order: BP189.7.K46+
Nimbārka: BL1286.592.N55
Nimbarka (Sect): BL1286.5+
Nine grades of life (Buddhism): BQ4465
Ninth of Av
Judaism: BM695.T57
Ninth of Av prayers
Judaism: BM675.K5
Nirankaris: BL2018.7.N57
Nirayāvaliyāo: BL1312.6.N57+
Nirmalas: BL2018.7.N59
Nirodhasamāpatti: BQ4327
Niruttaratantra: BL1142.6.N5595+
Nirvana
Buddhism: BQ4263
Theosophy: BP573.N5
Nirvāṇatantra: BL1142.6.N56+
Nishida, Tenkō, 1872-1968: BP605.I8
Nisīha: BL1313.3.N58+
Niśītha: BL1313.3.N58+
Niṣpannayogāvali (by Abhayākaragupta): BQ3340.N57+
Nītiśāstrajantupoṣaṇabindu (by Nāgārjuna): BQ2910.N56+
Nityāṣoḍaśikārṇava: BL1142.6.N57+
Niwano, Nichikō, 1938- : BQ8389.N54+
Niwano, Nikkyō, 1906- : BQ8389.N55+
Nīyah
Islam: BP166.783
Nizārīs: BP195.N58+
No-mind (Zen Buddhism): BQ4375
Noachide movement: BP605.N63
Noah (Biblical figure)
Koran: BP133.7.N63
Noahide Laws
Halacha: BM520.73
Noahides: BP605.N63
Nocturnal ceremonies
Religion: BL619.N7
Non-Attachment (Buddhism): BQ4275
Non-Jews
Judaism: BM720.N6

Non-self (Buddhism): BQ4262
Nonviolence
  Buddhism: BQ4570.V5
  Hinduism: BL1214.32.V56
  India, Religions of: BL2015.N64
  Islam: BP190.5.V56
  Judaism: BM538.P3
  Religion: BL65.V55
  Sikhism: BL2018.5.N65
Ṅor-pa: BQ7673+
Norito: BL2224.3
Norse mythology: BL830+
North African religions: BL2462
Northern Sect (Hinduism): BL1288.5+
Nosairians: BP195.N7+
Novellae
  Babylonian Talmud: BM504.2
Novices
  Buddhism
    Biography: BQ843
    Initiation: BQ5010
  Buddhist nuns: BQ6155
  Buddhist priests: BQ6145
Nuclear energy and religion: BL65.N83
Nuer
  Religions: BL2480.N7
Nūḥ (Biblical figure)
  Koran: BP133.7.N63
Numbers and religion: BL65.N85
Numeric value of letters
  Sufism: BP189.65.A47
Nuns
  Buddhism
    Biography: BQ855
  Buddhist monasticism: BQ6150+
Nupe
  Religions: BL2480.N8
Nurculuk: BP251+
Nyāyabindu (by Dharmakīrti): BQ3190+
Nyāyamukha (by Dignāga): BQ3300.N93+
Nyāyānusāra (by Saṅghabhadra): BQ2730.N83+
Nyāyapraveśa (by Śaṅkarasvāmin): BQ3200+
Nyingmapa: BQ7662+
Nymphs
  Classical mythology: BL820.N95
  Comparative mythology: BL325.F4
Nyoraikyō: BQ9800.N96+
Nzima
  Religions: BL2480.N9

O

O-bon (Memorial season)
  Buddhism: BQ5720.U6
Oahspe: BP605.F34
Oaths
  Assyro-Babylonian religions: BL1625.O2
  Judaism: BM720.O3
  Koran: BP134.O27
Ōbaku: BQ9310+
Obeah: BL2532.O23
Occasional prayers
  Judaism: BM675.O25
Occasional sermons
  Judaism: BM744+
Occidental religions: BL689+
Occultism
  Buddhism: BQ4570.O3
Ocean
  Semitic religions: BL1605.W3
Oceania
  Religions: BL2600+
Odin
  Germanic and Norse mythology: BL870.O3
Odysseus
  Classical mythology: BL820.O3
Oedipus
  Classical mythology: BL820.O43
  Comparative mythology: BL325.O4
Offering, Basin (Buddhist rite)
  Lamaism: BQ7699.B74
Offerings
  Worship: BL570+
Officials of the mosque: BP185+
Oghaniryukti: BL1313.9.O53+
Ohanijjutti: BL1313.9.O53+
Ōkuninushi no kami: BL2226.2.O48
Ollambana: BQ5720.U6
Om
  Hinduism: BL1236.52.O46
Omens
  Islam: BP188.14.O4
Omizutori: BQ5030.O43
Ōmoto: BL2222.O65+

Ōnie no Matsuri: BL2224.25.D34
Opposites
Comparative mythology: BL325.P7
Ops
Classical mythology: BL820.O6
Oracles
Religion: BL613
Oraḥ ḥayim
Halacha: BM520.86.A52+, BM520.88.A52+
Oraḥ ḥayim law
Halacha: BM523.2+
Oral tradition
Babylonian Talmud: BM503
Oraons
Religion: BL2032.O73
Order
Comparative mythology: BL325.O74
Order of Buddhist Contemplatives: BQ9460+
Order of Interbeing (Buddhist sect): BQ9800.T53+
Order of the Lily and the Eagle: BP605.O65
Ordination
Buddhism: BQ5220
Judaism: BM652
Sermons: BM744.7
Lamaism: BQ7754
Ordo Arcanorum Gradalis: BP605.O7
Ordo Novi Templi: BP605.O73
Ordre du temple solaire: BP605.O77
Ordure (Use)
Religion: BL619.O6
Organic farming
Anthroposophy: BP596.O73
Organization
Lamaism: BQ7730+
Synagogues: BM653
Organization of Hadith: BP136.3+
Organization, Religious: BL630+
Oriental religions: BL1000+
Orientation
Religion: BL619.O7
Original vow of Dharmākara Bodhisattva: BQ4455
Origins of religion: BL430
Ormazd
Zoroastrianism: BL1580
Ornaments
Islam: BP184.95+
Orphans
Islam: BP173.33
Orpheus
Classical mythology: BL820.O7
Greek religion and mythology: BL795.O7
Osiris (Egyptian deity): BL2450.O7
Ōtani-ha Honganji: BQ8700+
Other Power (Buddhism): BQ4453+
Otiyyot de-Rabbi Akiva (Midrash): BM517.O8+
Oumu Shinrikyō: BP605.O88
Ouziel, Ben-Zion Meir Ḥai, 1880-1953: BM755.U72
Ovambo
Religions: BL2480.O77
Oveyssi School
Sufism: BP189.7.M28+
Owegbe Society: BL2480.O8

P

Pa chi k'u nan t'o lo ni ching: BQ1670.P29+
Pa kua chiao: BL1943.P34
Pa ta jen chüeh ching: BQ1529.5.P34+
Paccaināyaki (Hindu deity): BL1225.P23+
Pacific Ocean islands
Religions: BL2600+
Padma: BQ5125.P3
Padma Sambhava: BQ7950.P32+
Prayers and devotions to: BQ5593.P3
Padmanābha (Hindu deity): BL1225.P24+
Padmapurāṇa: BL1140.4.P34+
Pādmasaṃhitā: BL1141.8.P34+
Padmāvatī (Jaina deity): BL1375.7.P33
Paganism: BL432
Paganism, Attitudes toward
Muḥammad, Prophet, d. 632: BP76.3

Pagodas
Buddhism: BQ5075.P3
Sacred places: BL586
Paguyuban Sumarah: BL2122.P3
Pai lien chaio: BQ8670+
Pain
Religious life: BL627.5
Paine, Thomas
Works on religious subjects: BL2735+
Paiṇṇas: BL1312.8+
Paippalāda: BL1114.7+
Pak, Chung-bin, 1891-1943: BQ9229.P36+
Pakistan, Religions of: BL2035+
Palatu: BL1279.2+
Palaṭū Sāhiba: BL1279.292.P35
Palestine
Islam: BP190.5.P3
Judaism: BM729.P3
Midrash: BM518.P25
Talmudic literature: BM509.P3
Palestine, Religions of: BL2340+
Palestinian religions, Ancient: BL1640+
Palestinian Talmud: BM498+
Special orders and tractates: BM506.A+
Palestinian Talmudic academies: BM502
Palms
Egyptian religion: BL2450.P3
Pan
Classical mythology: BL820.P2
Panbabylonism
Assyro-Babylonian religions: BL1625.P3
Pañcarakṣā: BQ1670.P35+
Pāñcarātra: BL1141.7+
Pāñcarātra (Sect): BL1286.8+
Pañcaviṃśatisāhasrikā: BQ1950+
Panchen Lama IV, 1781-1854: BQ7945.B75+
Panchen lamas
Biography: BQ7940+
Selection and succession: BQ7752
Panchen lamas' sermons: BQ7766+
Pandora
Classical mythology: BL820.P23
Panegyrics
Muḥammad, Prophet, d. 632: BP76.2
Pangestu (Organization): BL2122.P34
Paṇhāvāgaraṇa: BL1312.3.P35+
Panim aḥerim le-Esther (Midrash): BM517.P1+
Paññāsajātaka: BQ1470.P35+
Paṇṇāvanā: BL1312.6.P35+
Pantheism: BL220
Hinduism: BL1213.38
India, Religions of: BL2015.P3
Pantheon, Hindu: BL1216+
Pantheon, Jaina: BL1375.3+
Panthoibi (Hindu deity): BL1225.P25+
Papa
Talmudist: BM502.3.P36
Paper
Religious use: BL619.P3
Papuans
Religions: BL2630.P3
Parables
Buddhism: BQ5780+
Gautama Buddha: BQ915
Hinduism: BL1215.P3
Midrash: BM518.P3
Tripiṭaka: BQ1136.P35
Paradise
Buddhism: BQ4535+
Islam: BP166.87
Religion: BL540
Paramānandatantra: BL1142.6.P37+
Paramārtha-satya: BQ4255
Paramasaṃhitā: BL1141.8.P37+
Pārameśvarasaṃhitā: BL1141.8.P38+
Paramitas: BQ4336
Pāramitāsmāsa (by Āryaśūra): BQ3300.P37+
Parapsychology
Buddhism: BQ4570.P75
Jainism: BL1375.P37
Judaism: BM538.P2
Religion: BL65.P3
Pāraskaragṛhyasūtra: BL1134.5+

Paraśurāma (Hindu deity):
BL1225.P27+
Pārāyanasutta: BQ1419.5.P36+
Parchment
Judaism: BM729.P35
Parent and child
Even ha-'ezer law: BM523.7.P3
Greek religion and
mythology: BL795.P37
Parents
Buddhism
Devotional literature:
BQ5585.P3
Religious life: BQ5440
Hadith literature: BP135.8.P37
Hinduism
Religious life: BL1237.48
Religious life: BL625.8
Pari-nirvana
Gautama Buddha: BQ938
Parināma: BQ4365
Paritta: BQ1529.5.P35+
Parivāra: BQ2390+
Parnasabaridhāraṇī:
BQ1670.P37+
Parseeism: BL1500+
Part-time ministry
Buddhism: BQ5170
Participation in community
affairs, interfaith
movements, etc.
Rabbis: BM652.7
Parvati (Hindu deity):
BL1225.P3+
Paryuṣaṇā
Jainism: BL1355.6.P37
Paseban Jati
(Organization): BL2122.P36
Passover: BM695.P3+
Liturgy: BM675.P3
Passover sermons: BM747.P3
Pastoral theology
Shinto: BL2224.55
Pāśupatas: BL1281.5+
Pataḥ Eliyahu: BM670.P47
Patidars
Religion: BL2032.P38
Patience
Islam: BP188.16.P37
Patients
Religious life: BL625.9.S53
Pāṭikavagga: BQ1295.5.P35+
Pātimokkha: BQ2320+
Paṭisaṁbhidāmagga: BQ1490+
Paṭṭhāna: BQ2560+
Pattini (Hindu deity):
BL1225.P344+
Pauṣkarasaṃhitā:
BL1141.8.P42+
Peace
Buddhism: BQ4570.P4
Hinduism: BL1215.P4
Islam: BP190.5.P34
Judaism: BM538.P3
Religion: BL65.P4
Theosophy: BP573.P3
Peace of mind
Religious life: BL627.55
Pegasus
Classical mythology: BL820.P4
Peking
Chinese religions: BL1812.P45
Peli'ah (Midrash): BM517.P2+
Penance
Jainism: BL1375.P4
Penates
Classical mythology: BL820.P43
Penelope
Classical mythology: BL820.P45
Pentateuch, Samaritan: BM920+
Pentecost
Judaism: BM695.S5
Liturgy: BM675.P5
Peoples Temple: BP605.P46
Percival, Harold W.: BP605.W67
Peregrinos: BL2592.P45
Pereḳ shirah: BM675.P6
Perfection
Buddhism: BQ4301+, BQ5635+
Hinayana Buddhism: BQ7280
Lamaism: BQ7800+
Mādhyamika School: BQ7475
Theravāda Buddhism: BQ7280
Yogācāra School: BQ7516
Performing arts
Islam: BP190.5.P4
Periodicity
Theosophy: BP573.P4
Persecution
Buddhism: BQ800+
Lamism: BQ7596+
Muḥammad, Prophet, d. 632:
BP77.47
Religion: BL65.P47

Persephone
Classical mythology: BL820.P7
Perseus
Classical mythology: BL820.P5
Personal religion
Judaism: BM723+
Personality
Religious life: BL627.57
Pesikta (Midrash): BM517.P3+
Pesikta de-Rav Kahana (Midrash): BM517.P34+
Pesikta rabbati (Midrash): BM517.P4+
Petavatthu: BQ1430+
Peṭirat Aharon (Midrash): BM517.P5+
Pha rgyud rig pa khu byug: BQ7973.5.P45+
Phaethon
Classical mythology: BL820.P53
Phallicism: BL460
Japanese religions: BL2211.P48
Pharisees
Judaism
Ancient: BM175.P4
Phât-giáo Hòa-Hảo: BQ9800.P45+
Philemon and Baucis
Classical mythology: BL820.B28
Philippines, Religions of: BL2130+
Philistine religion: BL1675
Philo
Judaism: BM177
Philosophical theology
Shinto: BL2220.7
Philosophies, Contemporary, Attitude toward
Gautama Buddha: BQ910
Philosophy
Koran: BP134.P5
Philosophy and Buddhism: BQ4040
Philosophy and religion: BL51
Philosophy of religion: BL51
Philosophy of science
Theosophy: BP573.S35
Phoenician religions: BL1660+
Phoenician religions and Judaism: BM536.P5
Phoenix
Comparative mythology: BL325.P45
Phōthirak, Phra, 1934- : BQ9800.S2592P45+
Photography
Islam: BP190.5.A7
Phylacteries
Judaism: BM657.P5
Physicians
Islam
Religious life: BP188.18.P45
Physics and religion: BL265.P4
Physiology
Anthroposophy: BP596.P47
Pilgrim Festival prayers: BM675.P59
Pilgrim Festival sermons (Three Festivals): BM746.5
Pilgrim Festivals (Judaism): BM693.P5
Pilgrimage, Farewell
Muḥammad, Prophet, d. 632: BP77.68
Pilgrimages: BL619.P5
Buddhism: BQ6400+
Greek religion and mythology: BL795.P48
Hinduism: BL1239.32+
Islam: BP184.7
Jainism: BL1378.52+
Japanese religions: BL2211.P5
Korean religions: BL2236.P54
Lamaism: BQ7910+
Pilgrimages to Mecca: BP181, BP187.3
Pilgrims: BL619.P5
Buddhism: BQ6400+
Greek religion and mythology: BL795.P48
Hinduism: BL1239.32+
Jainism: BL1378.52+
Japanese religions: BL2211.P5
Korean religions: BL2236.P54
Lamaism: BQ7910+
Pillars of Islam: BP176+
Pilpul
Babylonian Talmud: BM503.8
Pirḳe shirah: BM675.P6
Pirkei de-Rabbi Eliezer (Midrash): BM517.P7+
Pitr̥medhasūtras: BL1137.2+

Piyutim
Biography of authors: BM678.4+
Liturgy: BM670.P5
PL Kyōdan: BL2228.P23+
Plants
Comparative mythology: BL325.P6
Hinduism: BL1215.P54
Koran: BP134.P55
Nature worship: BL444
Talmudic literature: BM509.B6
Tripiṭaka: BQ1136.P56
Umbanda: BL2592.U514P55
Play
Hinduism: BL1215.P56
Play and religion: BL65.P6
Pluralism, Religious
India: BL2015.R44
Poetry and Islam: BP190.5.P56
Polarity
Comparative mythology: BL325.P7
Political science
Koran: BP134.P6
Theosophy: BP573.P7
Political science and religion: BL65.P7
Politics
Greek religion and mythology: BL795.P57
Hinduism: BL1215.P65
Islam: BP173.7
Jainism: BL1375.P64
Japanese religions: BL2211.S73
Judaism: BM645.P64
Rabbinical literature: BM496.9.P64
Shiites: BP194.185
Sikhism: BL2018.5.P64
Zoroastrianism: BL1590.S73
Politics and religion: BL65.P7
India: BL2015.P57
Polity
Islam: BP185+
Shiites: BP194.9.G68
Pollution
Islam: BP190.5.P57
Polytheism: BL217
Islam: BP166.22
Polytheistic religions: BL355
Poseidon
Classical mythology: BL820.N5
Posḳim
Halacha: BM520.82+
Poson: BQ5720.P7
Postmodernism and religion: BL65.P73
Posture
Buddhism: BQ5630.P6
Hinduism: BL1238.58.P67
Poṭṭhapādasutta: BQ1300.P68+
Pou Kuksa, 1301-1382: BQ9519.P68+
Poverty
India, Religions of: BL2015.P6
Islam: BP190.5.P6
Poverty and religion: BL65.P75
Poverty, Life of
Hinduism: BL1214.32.P68
Power
Islam: BP190.5.P63
Power (Society): BP605.P68
Practice of Hinduism: BL1225.2+
Practice of Islam: BP174+
Pradyumna (Hindu deity): BL1225.P72+
Praises
Islam: BP183.3
Prajāpati (Hindu deity): BL1225.P73+
Prajñā: BQ4380+
Prajñādaṇḍa (by Nāgārjuna): BQ2910.P69+
Prajñāpanā: BL1312.6.P35+
Prajñāpāramitāhṛday asūtra: BQ1960+
Prajñāpāramitāratnag uṇasamcayagatha: BQ1920+
Prajñāpāramitās: BQ1880+
Prajñāpradīpamūlamad hyamakavṛtti (by Bhāvaviveka): BQ2850+
Prajñāśataka (by Nāgārjuna): BQ2910.P72+
Prajñopāyaviniścayasi ddhi (by Anaṅgavajra): BQ3340.P74+
Prakīrṇas: BL1312.8+
Pramānāntarbhāva: BQ3210+
Pramāṇasamuccaya (by Dignāga): BQ3220+
Pramāṇavārttika (by Dharmakīrti): BQ3230+
Pramāṇaviniścaya (by Dharmakīrti): BQ3300.P73+

Prāṇāyāma
Hinduism: BL1238.58.P73
Praṇidhāna: BQ4355
Prānnāthīs: BL2020.P7+
Prapañcasāratantra: BL1142.6.P73+
Prasāda: BQ4340+
Prāsaṅgika School of Buddhism: BQ7477
Prasannapadā (by Candrakīrti): BQ2860+
Praśnavyākaraṇa: BL1312.3.P35+
Praśnopaniṣad: BL1124.7.P73+
Prāthanā Samāj: BL1279.5+
Prātimokṣa: BQ2270+
Pratipattisāraśataka (by Āryadeva): BQ3340.P75+
Pratītyasamutpāda: BQ4240+
Pratītyasamutpādahṛda yakārikā (by Nāgārjuna): BQ2910.P73+
Pratītyasamutpādāvad ana: BQ1600.P72+
Pratītyasamutpādavyāk hyā (by Vasubandhu): BQ3080.P73+
Pratyekabuddha: BQ4290
Pratyutpannabuddhasammuk hāvasthitasamādhisū tra: BQ2240.P73+
Pratyutpannasūtra: BQ1830+
Prayer: BL560
Bahai Faith: BP388.P73
Buddhism: BQ5631+
Greek religion and mythology: BL795.P6
Hadith literature: BP135.8.P66
Hinduism: BL1237.77
Islam: BP178, BP184.3
Jainism: BL1378.6
Judaism: BM669
Koran: BP134.P7
Lamaism: BQ7800+
Roman religion and mythology: BL815.P68
Shiites: BP194.9.P7
Shinto: BL2224.73
Sikhism: BL2018.4+
Prayer books
Judaism: BM665+
Prayer flags
Buddhism: BQ5075.P72
Prayer wheels
Buddhism: BQ5075.P73
Prayer, Call to
Islam: BP184.3
Prayer, Calls to
Islam: BP183.4
Prayer, Direction of
Islam: BP187.45
Prayer, Hours of
Islam: BP184.3
Prayer, Morning
Hinduism: BL1236.52.M67
Prayers: BL560
Agnostics, atheists, etc.: BL2777.P7
Buddhism: BQ5535+
Hinduism: BL1236.22+
Islam: BP183.3
Jainism: BL1378.7
Lamaism: BQ7810+
Shiites: BP194.9.P7
Shinto: BL2224.3
Taoism: BL1942.8
Zoroastrianism: BL1590.P7
Pre-Columbian American religions: BL2510
Pre-Islamic Arabian religions: BL1685
Pre-Islamic prophets
Koran: BP134.P745
Pre-Talmudic Jewish literature: BM480+
Preachers
Judaism: BM659.M3
Preaching
Buddhism: BQ5310+
Hinduism: BL1241.72+
Islam: BP184.25
Judaism: BM730+
Precepts-name (Buddhism): BQ5355.B8
Precepts, Buddhist: BQ5485+
Lamism: BQ7780
Predestination
Hadith literature: BP135.8.P7
Islam: BP166.3+
Preludes, Religious
Islam: BP183.3
Premananda, Swami: BP605.S82+
Premaprakāśis: BL1279.7+

Preservation of manuscripts, books, etc.
  Tripiṭaka: BQ1126+
Preta-gati: BQ4520
Pretas, Offering to: BQ5030.P73
Pride
  Islamic religious life
    Sins: BP188.14.P74
Priestesses
  Greek religion and mythology: BL795.P7
  Shinto: BL2224.5+
Priesthood
  Buddhism: BQ5140+
  Hinduism: BL1241.32+
  Samaritans: BM950
Priestly blessing
  Judaism
    Liturgy: BM670.P74
Priests: BL635
  Buddhism
    Biography: BQ843
  Buddhist monasticism: BQ6140+
  Egyptian religion: BL2450.P69
  Greek religion and mythology: BL795.P7
  Judaism: BM651+
  Roman religion and mythology: BL815.P7
  Shinto: BL2224.5+
Princes
  Islam
    Devotional literature: BP188.3.K55
Printing
  Judaism: BM729.P65
Prison
  Japanese religions: BL2211.P7
Prisoners
  Buddhism
    Devotional literature: BQ5585.P7
  Islam
    Devotional literature: BP188.3.P7
Procrustes
  Classical mythology: BL820.P65
Profession of faith
  Islam: BP177
Professional development
  Rabbis: BM652.4
Prohibited work
  Oraḥ ḥayim law: BM523.3.P7
Prometheus
  Classical mythology: BL820.P68
Promises
  Islam: BP188.16.P74, BP190.5.P74
Prophecies
  Buddhism: BQ4570.P7
  Gautama Buddha: BQ929.P7
  Hinduism: BL1215.P77
  Koran: BP134.P74
Prophecy
  Islam: BP166.38+
  Judaism: BM645.P67
  Religion: BL633
Prophet, Elizabeth Clare: BP605.S73
Prophet, Mark: BP605.S73
Prophets
  Assyro-Babylonian religions: BL1625.P7
  Buddhism: BQ4570.P7
  Islam: BP166.38+
  Koran: BP134.P745
  Rabbinical literature: BM496.9.P75
  Religion: BL633
  Semitic religions: BL1605.P7
Prophets prior to Muḥammad
  Islam: BP166.4
Proposed religions: BL390
Proselytes
  Judaism: BM729.P7
Proselyting
  Judaism: BM729.P7
Proserpina
  Classical mythology: BL820.P7
Proserpine
  Classical mythology: BL820.P7
Protection of animals
  Judaism: BM729.A5
Proverbs
  Buddhism: BQ5791+
  Hadith literature: BP135.8.P75
  Koran: BP131.85
Proverbs (Midrash): BM517.M77+
Providence
  Natural theology: BL230+

Providence of God
Judaism: BM645.P7
Roman religion and mythology: BL815.P74
Prussians (Baltic tribe)
Early religions: BL945
Pseudo-Messiahs
Judaism
Biography: BM752
Pseudo-Sabian religions: BL1635
Psyche
Classical mythology: BL820.P8
Psychiatry for the rabbi: BM652.5
Psychical research
Buddhism: BQ4570.P75
Shinto: BL2227.8.P7
Psychoanalysis and Judaism: BM538.P68
Psychology
Buddhism: BQ4570.P76
Hinduism: BL1215.P8
Judaism: BM538.P68
Koran: BP134.P747
Sikhism: BL2018.5.P75
Sufism: BP189.65.P78
Talmudic literature: BM509.P8
Psychology for the rabbi: BM652.5
Psychology of Islam: BP175
Psychology of religion: BL53+
Psychology, Applied
Judaism: BM729.J4
Psychotherapy
Islam: BP190.5.P79
Ptah (Egyptian deity): BL2450.P7
Pu sa ying lo ben ye jing: BQ2470+
Public relations
Buddhism: BQ5305.P8
Islam: BP185.72
Public worship
Islam: BP184.2
Publication and distribution of Rabbinical literature: BM496.8
Publication of the Koran: BP131.18.A+
Publicity
Islam: BP185.72
Puerto Rican Spiritualism: BL2532.P83
Puggalapaññatti: BQ2530+
Pūjā
Hinduism: BL1226.82.P85
Puṇḍarīka: BQ5125.P3
Punishment
Koran: BP134.P8
Punishment, Future
Egyptian religion: BL2450.F84
Pupphacūliāo: BL1312.6.P85+
Pupphiāo: BL1312.6.P87+
Purāṇas: BL1140.2+
Pure Land (Buddhism): BQ4535+
Pure Land Buddhism: BQ8500+
Relations
Zen Buddhism: BQ9269.6.P8
Pure Land sūtras: BQ2010+
Pure life Society: BP605.P8
Purification
Judaism: BM702+
Purification rites
Hinduism: BL1226.82.P87
Purifications
Islam: BP184.4
Purim: BM695.P8
Purim prayers: BM675.P8
Purim sermons: BM747.P8
Puritan movements
Natural theology: BL237.5
Purity
Zoroastrianism: BL1590.P85
Purity, Ritual
Hadith literature: BP135.8.P87
Samaritans: BM982
Pūrṇapramukhāvadānaśataka: BQ2240.P87+
Puruṣa
Hinduism: BL1213.54
Pūṣan (Hindu deity): BL1225.P8+
Puṣikā: BL1312.6.P87+
Puṣpacūlikā: BL1312.6.P85+
Pyrros
Classical mythology: BL820.P9
Pyrrus
Classical mythology: BL820.P9

Q

Qādirīyah
 Sufism: BP189.7.Q3+
Qādiyānī: BP195.A5+
Qiblah: BP187.45
Qirā'āt: BP131.5
Quality of transmission
 Hadith literature: BP136.5
Quan zhen jiao: BL1943.C55
Quaternities
 Religious doctrine: BL474.5
Quatrains
 Islam: BP183.3
Queens
 Egyptian religion: BL2450.Q44
Questions and answers
 Judaism: BM51
Quimbanda: BL2592.Q54
Qumran community: BM175.Q6

R

Ra (Egyptian deity): BL2450.R2
Ra'aya mehemana
 Cabala
  Zohar supplements: BM525.A6R2+
Rab, 3rd cent.
 Biography: BM755.A2
 Talmudist: BM502.3.A2
Rabaris
 Religion: BL2032.R32
Rabbah bar Bar Ḥana, 3rd cent.
 Talmudist: BM502.3.R3
Rabbinical literature: BM495+
Rabbinical manuals: BM676
Rabbis: BM651+
 Installation and ordination
  Sermons: BM744.7
Rabinowitz, Elijah David, 1845-1905: BM755.R15
Race
 Buddhism: BQ4570.R3
 Hinduism: BL1215.R34
 Islam: BP190.5.R3
 Judaism: BM645.R3
Race and religion: BL65.R3
Race problems
 Islam: BP190.5.R3
Rādhā (Hindu deity): BL1225.R24+
Radhasoami Satsang: BP605.R33+
Rādhātantra: BL1142.6.R33+
Rādhāvallabha: BL1287.2+
Radio broadcasting
 Islam: BP185.76
Rāgarāja: BQ4860.R3+
Rāgs, The (Adi-Granth): BL2017.427+
Rain
 Judaism: BM720.R3
 Rabbinical literature: BM496.9.R33
Rain gods
 Japan: BL2211.R33
Rain-wishing prayer
 Hinduism: BL1236.52.R35
Rainbow
 Comparative mythology: BL325.R2
Rainmaking rite
 Japan: BL2211.R34
Rāja yoga: BL1238.56.R35
Rājapraśnīya: BL1312.6.R38+
Rajneesh Foundation (International): BP605.R34+
Rajneesh, Bhagwan Shree, 1931- : BP605.R34
Rajputs
 Religion: BL2032.R34
Rām Sanehīs
 Hinduism: BL1279.8+, BL1287.3+
Rāma (Hindu deity): BL1225.R3+
Rāmacandra (Hindu deity): BL1225.R3+
Rāmacaraṇa, Swami: BL1287.392.R36
Ramadan: BP186.4
 Hadith literature: BP135.8.R3
 Sermons: BP183.64
Ramakrishna Mission: BL1280.2+
Ramakrishna, 1836-1886: BL1280.292.R36
Ramala Centre: BP605.R35
Ramalinga, 1823-1874: BL1282.592.R36
Rāmananda: BL1287.592.R56
Rāmānandins: BL1287.5+
Rāmānandīs: BL1287.5+
Rāmañña: BQ8770+
Rāmānuja: BL1288.292.R36
Rāmānuja sect: BL1288.2+

Ramanya: BQ8770+
Rāmatāpinīyopaniṣad:
BL1124.7.R36+
Rāmavats: BL1287.5+
Rāmāyaṇa: BL1139.2+
Rammohun Roy, Raja:
BL1274.592.R36
Ramthat School for
Enlightenment: BP605.R37
Raṇachoḍarāya (Hindu
deity): BL1225.R344+
Raṅganātha (Hindu deity):
BL1225.R345+
Rashi, 1040-1105
Babylonian Talmud: BM501.8
Biography: BM755.S6
Raśmivimalaviśuddhapra
bhānāmadhāraṇī:
BQ1670.R37+
Rastafarians: BL2532.R37
Rāṣṭrapālaparipṛcch
ā: BQ1770+
Rathvi
Religion: BL2032.R38
Rationalism: BL2700+, BL2747.7
Ratnadhvaja: BQ1840+
Ratnagotravibhāga: BQ3020+
Ratnajāliparipṛcchān
āmamahāyānasūtra:
BQ2240.R38+
Ratnārāśisūtra: BQ1780+
Ratnasambhava: BQ4690.R3+
Ratnāvalī (by
Nāgārjuna): BQ2870+
Rauravāgama: BL1141.5.R37+
Rauravatantra: BL1142.6.R38+
Rav, 3rd cent.
Biography: BM755.A2
Talmudist: BM502.3.A2
Rāyapaseṇiya: BL1312.6.R38+
Rays, Seven
Theosophy: BP573.S47
Raziel, Book of
Cabala: BM525.A36+
Rdo-rje-śugs-ldan-rtsal:
BQ4890.R37+
Reading of the Bible
Judaism: BM663
Readings
Judaism
Liturgy: BM675.R4
Koran: BP131.5
Reason
Islam: BP190.5.R4
Koran: BP134.R33
Sikhism: BL2018.5.F34
Rebirth
Buddhism: BQ4485+
Hinduism: BL1214.74
Rebirth in Western
Paradise (Pure Land
Buddhism): BQ4540
Recital of the Names of
God
Sufism: BP189.58+
Recitation
Koran: BP131.6
Recitations
Hinduism: BL1236.22+
Lamaism: BQ7700+
Reconciliation
Religious doctrine: BL476.5
Reconstructionist Judaism:
BM197.7
Recovering addicts
Religious life: BL625.9.R43
Recreation in the
synagogue: BM135
Redemption
Judaism: BM645.R4
Religious doctrine: BL476
Redemption of the
firstborn
Judaism: BM720.R4
Reform movements
Judaism: BM197
Regeneration
Religion: BL619.R42
Regifugium
Roman religion and
mythology: BL815.R4
Reincarnation: BL515+
Anthroposophy: BP596.R44
Buddhism: BQ4485+
Germanic and Norse
mythology: BL870.R4
India, Religions of: BL2015.R4
Theosophy: BP573.R5
Reiyūkai: BQ8370+
Relativity (Buddhism): BQ4240+
Relics
Gautama Buddha: BQ924
Islam: BP186.97
Muḥammad, Prophet, d. 632:
BP75.9
Religion: BL619.R44

Religion: BL1+
Psychology: BL53+
Relation to other subjects: BL65.A+
Religion and anthroposophy: BP596.R45
Religion and civilization: BL55
Religion and sociology: BL60
Religions: BL1+
Religions and anthroposophy: BP596.R45
Religions of the world: BL74+
Religions, Contemporary, Attitude toward
Gautama Buddha: BQ910
Religious activities, Communal
Sufism: BP190
Religious addiction: BL53.5
Religious broadcasting
Islam: BP185.74+
Religious communities
Organization: BL632+
Religious customs
Islam: BP184+
Religious dancing
Judaism: BM720.D2
Religious duties
Jewish way of life: BM725+
Religious education: BL42+
Bonpo (Sect): BQ7963
Buddhism: BQ141+
Hinduism: BL1108.2+
Lamaism: BQ7565+
Shiites: BP194.9.E3
Religious education in the home
Buddhism: BQ200+
Lamaism: BQ7569
Religious education of the young
Buddhism: BQ171+
Islam: BP44+
Judaism: BM100+
Lamaism: BQ7568
Religious experience: BL53+, BR110+
Buddhism: BQ4570.P76
Islam: BP175
Religious functionaries
Islam: BP185+
Shiites: BP194.9.G68
Religious instinct (Buddhism): BQ4285+
Religious leadership
Buddhism: BQ5420
Religious liberty and Islam: BP173.65
Religious life: BL624+
Bonpo (Sect): BQ7982.2
Buddhism: BQ4301+, BQ5360+
Confucianism: BL1857
Hadith literature: BP135.8.R4
Hinayana Buddhism: BQ7285
Hinduism: BL1214.22+, BL1225.2+, BL1237.32+
Islam: BP188+
Koran: BP134.R35
Lamaism: BQ7775+
Mahayana Buddhism: BQ7440+
Shiites: BP194.7
Shinto: BL2224.7+
Sikhism: BL2018.37+
Sufism: BP189.6+
Theravāda Buddhism: BQ7285
Religious neurosis: BL53.5
Religious orders
India, Religions of: BL2015.M66
Organization: BL631
Religious organization: BL630+
Religious pluralism
India: BL2015.R44
Religious preludes
Islam: BP183.3
Religious Research, Church of: BP605.C54
Religious Science International: BP605.U53
Religious stories
Islam: BP45
Religious tolerance
India, Religions of: BL2015.R46
Sikhism: BL2018.5.R44
Religious training of children
Agnostics, atheists, etc.: BL2777.R4
Reliquaries
Religion: BL619.R44
Ren wang bo re jing: BQ1930+
Renenet (Egyptian deity): BL2450.R25
Rennyo, 1415-1499: BQ8749.R46+

Rēṇukāmbe (Hindu deity): BL1225.R45+
Renunciation
  Buddhism: BQ4555
  Gautama Buddha: BQ934
Repentance
  Islam: BP166.79
  Judaism: BM645.R45
  Religious doctrine: BL476.7
Reporters
  Hadith literature: BP136.48+
Rešep (Canaanite deity): BL1672.R47
Reshpu (Egyptian deity): BL2450.R3
Respect to parents and teachers
  Yoreh de'ah law: BM523.5.R4
Responsa
  Halacha: BM522+
Restoration proposals
  Judaism
    The temple: BM655.6
Resurrection
  Egyptian religion: BL2450.R4
  Islam: BP166.83
  Judaism: BM645.R47
  Koran: BP134.R4
  Religion: BL505
Retelling of the Hadith: BP136.9
Retreats
  Religious life: BL628
Rēvaṇasiddha, ca. 1075-ca. 1205: BL1281.292.R48
Revanta (Hindu deity): BL1225.R47+
Revealed religions: BL365
Revelation
  Hinduism: BL1215.R4
  Islam: BP166.6+
  Judaism: BM645.R5
  Religious doctrine: BL475.5
Revelation on Sinai
  Judaism: BM612
Revelations
  Muḥammad, Prophet, d. 632: BP77.43
Revolutions and religion: BL65.R48
Reward
  Buddhism: BQ4358
  Japanese religions: BL2211.R44
  Judaism: BM645.R55
Ṛgveda Āraṇyaka: BL1122.3+
Ṛgveda Brāhmaṇas: BL1116.3+
Ṛgveda saṃhitā: BL1112.5+
Ṛgvedic Gṛhyasūtras: BL1131.3+
Ṛgvedic Śrautasūtras: BL1126.6+
Rgyud (Tantras): BQ7973.2+
Rhea Cybele
  Classical mythology: BL820.C8
Rhythm
  Anthroposophy: BP596.R5
Ribhus (Hindu mythology): BL1225.R5+
Rice gods
  Japan: BL2211.R47
Rider-gods
  Zoroastrianism: BL1590.R5
Riḍván
  Bahai Faith: BP387.R53
Rifā'īyah
  Sufism: BP189.7.R5+
Rinzai: BQ9350+
Risen Christ Foundation: BP605.R56
Rishis
  Hinduism: BL1111.72.R57, BL1241.52
Rishonim: BM501.6
Risshō Kōseikai: BQ8380+
Rites
  Buddhism: BQ4965+
  Chinese religions: BL1812.R57
  Hinduism: BL1226.18+
  India, Religions of: BL2015.R48
  Islam: BP184+
  Jainism: BL1310.8.R57
  Japanese religions: BL2211.R5
  Judaism: BM700+
  Korean religions: BL2236.R58
  Lamaism: BQ7695+
  Religion: BL600+
  Samaritans: BM980
  Shiites: BP194.4
  Sufism: BP189.58+
  Zoroastrianism: BL1590.L58
Ritsu (Lü): BQ8780+
Rittelmeyer, Friedrich, 1872-1938: BP605.C45

Ritual
  Confucianism: BL1858+
  Freethinkers: BL2777.R5
  Greek religion and
    mythology: BL788
  Jainism: BL1377+
  Judaism: BM660+
  Karaites: BM185.3+
  Roman religion and
    mythology: BL808
  Samaritans: BM960+
  Semitic religions: BL1605.R5
  Shinto: BL2224.2+
  Sikhism: BL2018.3+
  Taoism: BL1940.4
Ritual baths
  Judaism: BM703
Ritual purity
  Hadith literature: BP135.8.P87
  Judaism: BM702+
  Samaritans: BM982
Rivers
  Greek religion and
    mythology: BL795.R58
  Hinduism: BL1215.R5
  India, Religions of: BL2015.R5
  Sacred places: BL583
Rñiṅ-ma-pa: BQ7662+
Rohiṇījātaka: BQ1470.R63+
Roma
  Classical mythology: BL820.R65
Roman religion and
  mythology: BL798+
Rome
  Comparative mythology: BL325.R6
  Rabbinical literature:
    BM496.9.R66
Romulus & Remus
  Classical mythology: BL820.R67
Ropshitser, Naphtali
  Ẓevi, 1760-1827: BM755.H76
Rosaries
  Buddhism: BQ5075.R7, BQ5630.R6
  Islam: BP184.96.R66
Rosenzweig, Franz, 1886-
  1929: BM755.R6
Rosh ha-Shanah: BM695.N5
Rosh ha-Shanah prayers:
  BM675.R67
Rosh ha-Shanah sermons:
  BM747.R6
Rosh Hodesh: BM695.N4
Ṛshipañcamī
  Hinduism: BL1226.82.R75
Rudra (Hindu deity): BL1225.R8+
Rudrayāmalatantra:
  BL1142.6.R84+
Ruhani Satsang: BP605.R85
Rule of the congregation
  Dead Sea scrolls: BM488.R85
Rulers
  Comparative mythology: BL325.K5
  Hinduism: BL1215.K56
  India, Religions of: BL2015.K5
  Islam
    Devotional literature:
    BP188.3.K55
  Judaism: BM645.P64
  Midrash: BM518.K5
  Rabbinical literature:
    BM496.9.K5
Rules
  Buddhist monasticism: BQ6115+
  Lamaism: BQ7890
Rules, Ceremonial
  Lamaism: BQ7695+
Ryōkan, 1758-1831: BQ9449.R94+

S

Sa-skya-pa: BQ7672+
Sa-skya Paṇḍi-ta
  Kun-dga'-rygal-mtshan,
  1182-1251: BQ7950.S34+
Saadiah ben Joseph, 882-
  942
  Biography: BM755.S2
  Principles of Judaism:
    BM550.S25
Sabbath
  Judaism: BM685
  Midrash: BM518.S24
Sabbath prayers
  Judaism: BM675.S3
Sabbath schools
  Judaism: BM100+
Sabbathaians: BM199.S3
Sabbatical year
  Judaism: BM720.S2
Sabian Assembly: BP605.S113
Saboraim: BM501.4
Ṣabr: BP188.16.P37
Sacraments: BL619.S3
  Hinduism: BL1226.82.S24

Sacred books: BL70+
Egyptian religion: BL2430
Hinduism: BL1111+
Islam: BP100+
Jainism: BL1310+
Shinto: BL2217+
Taoism: BL1900.A1+
Sacred marriage
Greek religion and mythology: BL795.S22
Sacred meals
Greek religion and mythology: BL795.S23
Roman religion and mythology: BL815.S15
Sacred places
Islam: BP187+
Shiites: BP194.6.A2+
Worship: BL580+
Sacred shrines
Gautama Buddha: BQ6460+
Sacred sites
Hinduism: BL1243.72+
Sacred thread ceremony
Hinduism: BL1226.82.S2
Sacred times, seasons, days: BL590+
Sacrifice
Egyptian religion: BL2450.S23
Germanic and Norse mythology: BL870.S2
Greek religion and mythology: BL795.S25
Worship: BL570+
Sacrifice, Human
Roman religion and mythology: BL815.S3
Sacrifices
Hinduism: BL1236.76.S23
Islam: BP184.6
Judaism: BM715
Sacrifices, Foundation
Worship: BL571
Saddhammapakāsinī: BQ1495
Saddharmapuṇḍarīkasū tra: BQ2050+
Saddharmasmṛtyupasthān asūtra: BQ2240.S33+
Saddharmavipralopa: BQ4480
Sādhanā
Hinduism: BL1238.58.S24
Sādhanamālā: BQ3340.S34+
Sadhs: BL1280.3+
Sadhus
Hinduism: BL1241.53
Saducees: BM175.S2
Ṣaḍviṃśabrāhmaṇa: BL1121.3.S34+
Sāgaliya: BQ8050+
Sagara (Hindu mythology): BL1225.S16+
Sahā: BQ4510
Ṣaḥābah
Hadith literature: BP136.46
Muḥammad, Prophet, d. 632: BP75.5+
Sahajānanda, Swami: BL1289.292.S25
Sahajasiddhi (by Dombī-heruka): BQ3340.S35+
Sahajiyā: BL1287.8+
Sāhebadhanīs: BL2020.S25+
Saichō, 767-822: BQ9149.S35+
Sailors
Semitic religions: BL1665.S24
Saint Germain Foundation: BP605.I18
Saint worship
Sufism: BP189.585
Sainthood
Hinduism: BL1241.44+
Sufism: BP189.33
Saints
Hinayana Buddhism: BQ4865+
India, Religions of: BL2015.S3
Religious doctrine: BL488
Sufism
Biography: BP189.4+
Śaiva Āgamas: BL1141.2+
Saiva Siddhānta: BL1281.8+
Saiva Siddhanta Church: BL1281.9+
Saivism: BL1280.5+
Saka
Religions: BL2370.S25
Sakalamata (Sect): BL1295.S23+
Sakalava (Malagasy people)
Religions: BL2480.S23
Sākāra School of Buddhism: BQ7522
Abhidharmapiṭaka: BQ2920+
Śakti (Hindu concept): BL1214.34

Śakti (Hindu deity):
 BL1225.S18+
Śaktisaṅgamatantra:
 BL1142.6.S35+
Saktism: BL1282.2+
Śaktiviśiṣṭādvaitav
 edānta: BL1283.2+
Sakyamuni Buddha: BQ4690.S3+
Sakyapa: BQ7672+
Salafīyah
 Islam: BP195.S18+
Salanter, Israel, 1810-
 1883: BM755.L54
Saḷāytanavagga: BQ1339.3.S4+
Sālimīyah: BP195.S2+
Śālistambasūtra: BQ2240.S35+
Sallekhanā
 Jainism: BL1375.S26
Salus
 Classical mythology: BL820.S25
Salutations
 Hinduism: BL1239.5.S24
Salvation
 Buddhism: BQ4453+
 Hadith literature: BP135.8.S24
 Hinduism: BL1213.72
 Islam: BP166.77+
 Jainism: BL1375.S3
 Religious doctrine: BL476
 Sikhism: BL2018.5.S3
Sam'
 Sufism: BP189.65.M87
Samadhi
 Buddhism: BQ5630.S16
 Hinduism: BL1238.58.S26
 Jainism: BL1378.85
Samādhirājasūtra: BQ2080+
Sāmaññaphalasutta:
 BQ1300.S25+
Samantabhadra: BQ4710.S3+
Samantabhadracaryāpraṇ
 idhānarāja: BQ1640+
Sāmānyadūṣaṇādikpr
 asāritā (by Paṇḍita
 Aśoka): BQ3300.S22+
Samarasa Suddha Sanmarga
 Sathia Sangam: BL1282.5+
Samaritan Pentateuch: BM920+
Samaritan Targum: BM930+
Samaritans: BM900+
 Semitic religions: BL1640+
Samartha Sampradaya: BL1282.8+
Samavāyāṅga: BL1312.3.S35+
Sāmaveda Āraṇyakas:
 BL1123.7+
Sāmaveda Brāhmaṇas:
 BL1121.2+
Sāmavedic Gṛhyasūtras:
 BL1134.8+
Sāmavedic Śrautasūtras:
 BL1129.2+
Sāmavidhānabrāhmaạ:
 BL1121.3.S35+
Samayabhedoparacanacakra
 (by Vasumitra): BQ2710+
Sambandhaparīkṣā (by
 Dharmakīrti): BQ3300.S24+
Sāmbapurāṇa: BL1140.4.S23+
Saṃdhinirmocanasūtra: BQ2090+
Saṃgha: BQ4545+
Saṃgha (Order): BQ6001+
Saṃhitās: BL1112.4+
Saṃhitopanisadbrāhmaṇa:
 BL1121.3.S36+
Sām̐īndātās: BL1295.S25+
Sammohanatantra: BL1142.6.S36+
Samoyeds
 Religions: BL2370.S3
Sampasādaniyasutta:
 BQ1300.S27+
Sampatkumāra (Hindu
 deity): BL1225.S19+
Saṃsāra: BQ4485+
Samsara
 Hinduism: BL1214.74
Saṃskāras
 Hinduism: BL1226.82.S24
Samson
 Comparative mythology: BL325.S3
Saṃstāraka: BL1312.9.S25+
Samuel (Midrash): BM517.S4+
Samuel ben Naḥman,
 3rd/4th cent.
 Talmudist: BM502.3.S34
Samuel of Nehardea, ca.
 177-257
 Talmudist: BM502.3.S37
Samvarodayatantra: BQ2180.S24+
Saṃvṛti-satya: BQ4255
Saṃyuttanikāya: BQ1330+
San
 Religions: BL2480.S24
San jie (Buddhist sect):
 BQ8790+

San lun: BQ8800+
San shi yin guo jing:
BQ2240.S36+
Sanaka: BL1286.5+
Sanatkumārasaṃhitā:
BL1141.8.S36+
Sañcayagāthā: BQ2000.S24+
Sanctuaries
Greek religion and
mythology: BL795.S47
Sandhyā
Hinduism: BL1226.82.S25
Śāṇḍilya: BL1286.892.S36
Sangha Sabhā (Council) of
the United Kingdom: BQ54+
Saṅghāṭasūtra:
BQ2240.S3695+
Sangreal Sodality: BP605.S116
Sanhedrin
Judaism
The temple: BM655.4
Sanhedrin (Tractate): BM506.S2+
Sanhedrin under Napoleon
Judaism
The temple: BM655.5
Śani (Hindu deity):
BL1225.S22+
Śāṅkhāyanabrāhmaṇa:
BL1116.7+
Śāṅkhāyanagṛhyasūt
ra: BL1131.7+
Śāṅkhāyanāraṇyaka:
BL1122.5+
Śāṅkhāyanaśrautasū
tra: BL1127.2+
Śāṅkhyāyanatantra:
BL1142.6.S37+
Sannyasins
Hinduism: BL1241.54
Sanron (San lun): BQ8800+
Śaṅs-pa: BQ7680+
Saṅs rgyas mtshan mdo:
BQ7971.5.S26+
Sant Bani Ashram: BP605.R85
Sant Mat: BP605.R335
Sant Nirankari Mandal:
BP605.S12
Santals
Religion: BL2032.S24
Santānāntarasiddhi (by
Dharmakīrti): BQ3300.S26+
Santeria: BL2532.S3
Santi 'Asōk
(Organization): BQ9800.S25+
Santo Daime: BL2592.S25
Santoshī Mātā (Hindu
deity): BL1225.S23+
Sanūsīyah
Sufism: BP189.7.S4+
Saptaśatikā: BQ2000.S36+
Saptatathāgatapūrvapra
ṇidhānaviśeṣavista
ranāmamahāyānasūtra:
BQ2240.S37+
Sara (African people)
Religions: BL2480.S25
Sarada Devi, 1853-1920:
BL1280.292.S27
Śāradātilakatantra:
BL1142.6.S38+
Śaraṇāgati
Hinduism: BL1214.32.S25
Sarasvatī (Hindu deity):
BL1225.S25+
Buddhism: BQ4750.S27+
Sarasvatītantra: BL1142.6.S39+
Śārdūlakarṇāvadāna:
BQ2240.S3793+
Sarutahiko no Kami:
BL2226.2.S27
Sarvabuddhaviṣayāvatā
rajñānālokālaṅkā
rasūtra: BQ2240.S3795+
Sarvadharmamahāśāntib
odhicittakulayarāja:
BQ2180.S25+
Sarvadurgatipariśodhana
tantra: BQ2180.S26+
Sarvānanda: BQ1470.S26+
Sarvapuṇyasamuccayasamā
adhisūtra: BQ2240.S38+
Sarvāstivāda School of
Buddhism: BQ7255.S36
Sarvāstivāda School
Vinaya: BQ2250+
Sarvatathāgatādhiṣṭh
ānahṛdayaguhyadhātu
karaṇḍmudrādhāraṇ
ī: BQ1670.S27+
Sarvatathāgatatattvasa·
ngraha: BQ2180.S28+
Sasajātaka: BQ1470.S27+
Sat-sanga Society: BP605.S36
Śatapathabrāhmaṇa: BL1118.5+

Śatapathāraṇyaka
(Bṛhadāraṇyaka):
BL1123.5+
Śatasāhasrikā: BQ1970+
Śataśāstra (by
Āryadeva): BQ2880+
Satipaṭṭhāna: BQ5630.S2
Satipaṭṭhānasutta:
BQ1320.S25+
Satmar: BM198.55
Satori (Zen Buddhism): BQ9288
Śaṭpraśnopaniṣad:
BL1124.7.S27+
Ṣaṭsāhasrasaṃhitā:
BL1142.6.S43+
Saturn
Classical mythology: BL820.S29
Comparative mythology:
BL325.S37
Sātvatasaṃhitā:
BL1141.8.S38+
Satyā-nārāyan (Hindu
deity): BL1225.S28+
Satyanand Agnihotri:
BL1275.892.S27
Satyasiddhiśāstra (by
Harivarman): BQ2720+
Satyaśodhaka Samāja:
BL1283.2924+
Satyrs
Classical mythology: BL820.S3
Saubhāgyalakṣmītantra:
BL1142.6.S45+
Saul, King of Israel
Rabbinical literature:
BM496.9.S38
Śaunaka: BL1114.8+
Saundarananda (by
Aśvaghoṣa): BQ905.N2A7
Saurapurāṇa: BL1140.4.S27+
Sautrāntika School of
Buddhism: BQ7255.S38
Saviors
Religious doctrine: BL475
Savitar (Hindu deity):
BL1225.S8+
Sāvitrī (Hindu deity):
BL1225.S3+
Sawan Kirpal Ruhani
Mission: BP605.R85
Scapegoat
Rabbinical literature:
BM496.9.S43
Scarabée (Association):
BP605.S18
Schapiro, Joshua Isaac ben
Jehiel, 1801-1873:
BM755.S256
Scholars
Hadith studies: BP135.62.A+
Islam
Biography: BP49.5.A+
School prayers
Judaism: BM667.S4
Schools
Islam: BP48.A+
Judaism: BM90+
Theosophy: BP528
Schools of theology
Islam: BP166.14.A+
Schreiber, Moses, 1762-
1839: BM755.S33
Science
Buddhism: BQ4570.S3
Hinduism: BL1215.S36
Islam: BP190.5.S3
Jainism: BL1375.S35
Judaism: BM538.S3
Koran: BP134.S3
Sikhism: BL2018.5.S35
Talmudic literature: BM509.S34
Theosophy: BP573.S35
Urantia Book: BP605.U76S3
Science and religion: BL239+
Scientology: BP605.S2
Scribes
Judaism: BM659.S3
Scriptures
Bahai Faith: BP360+
Scrolls of Torah: BM657.T6
Scylla
Classical mythology: BL820.S39
Scythians
Early religions: BL975.S38
Seafaring life
Semitic religions: BL1665.S24
Seal of Three Laws: BQ4260+
Seasonal festivals
Anthroposophy: BP596.F37
Seasons
Hinduism: BL1239.72+
Lamaism: BQ7820+

Seasons, Sacred: BL590+
Second Advent
  Anthroposophy: BP596.S4
Secrecy and religion: BL65.S37
Secrets and religion: BL65.S37
Sects
  Buddhism: BQ7001+
  Hinduism: BL1271.2+
  Islam: BP191+
  Jainism: BL1379+
  Judaism
    Ancient: BM175.A+
    Modern: BM196+
  Samaritans: BM913.A+
  Shinto: BL2222.A+
Secularism: BL2747.8
  Islam: BP190.5.S35
Seder berakhot le-kohl ha-shanah: BM185.4.S43+
Seder Haḳafot: BM670.S4
Seder Tashlikh: BM670.S42
Sédir, Paul, 1871-1926: BP610.S43+
Sedulur Sejati (Organization): BL2122.S43
Sefer ha-razim
  Cabala: BM525.A37+
Sefer ha-temunah
  Cabala: BM525.A39+
Sefer Yeẓirah
  Cabala: BM525.A4+
Sefirah period
  Judaism: BM695.S4
Seged: BM695.S43
Seichō no Ie: BL2228.S45+
Seizan: BQ8650+
Sekai Kyūseikyō: BL2228.S55+
Sekai Shintō: BL2222.S45+
Sekhmet (Egyptian deity): BL2450.S34
Sekoddeśa: BQ2180.S44+
Self
  Hinduism: BL1213.56
  Jainism: BL1375.S4
Self and religion: BL65.S38
Self-esteem
  Religious life: BL629.5.S44
Self-preparation
  Theosophy: BP573.S4
Self-realization
  Jainism: BL1375.S43
Self-Realization Fellowship: BP605.S36
Self-realization movement: BP605.S35+
Self-Revelation Church of Absolute Monism: BP605.S85W3
Self-worship
  Hinduism: BL1226.82.S3
Seliḥot: BM675.S4
Semaḥot: BM506.4.S4+
Semitic religions: BL1600+
Sen, Keshub Chunder: BL1274.592.S35
Senā, b. 1330: BL1287.692.S45
Senāpanthīs: BL1287.6+
Senufo
  Religions: BL2480.S44
Senussites
  Sufism: BP189.7.S4+
Sen'yo, 1530-1604: BQ9049.S45+
Separation of sexes in seating
  Synagogues: BM653.2
Sephardic rite
  Liturgy: BM672.S4
Sephardim
  Medieval: BM182
Sepulchral monuments
  Buddhism: BQ5075.S4
  Japanese religions: BL2211.S33
Serapis (Egyptian deity): BL2450.S37
Serekh shirot olat ha-Shabbat
  Dead Sea scrolls: BM488.S47
Serer
  Religions: BL2480.S45
Sermons
  Bar mitzvah: BM707.3
  Buddhism: BQ5340+
    Life of Gautama Buddha: BQ912
  Hinduism: BL1241.76+
  Islam: BP183.6
  Jainism: BL1377.5
  Judaism: BM735+
  Lamaism: BQ7760+
Serpent worship: BL441
  Hinduism: BL1239.5.S37
  India, Religions of: BL2015.S4
Serpents
  Japanese religions: BL2211.S34
  Religious symbolism: BL604.S4

Service books
  Judaism: BM665+
  Lamaism: BQ7697
Śeṣasaṃhitā: BL1141.8.S47+
Sesimjong: BQ9800.S46+
Set (Egyptian deity): BL2450.S4
Seth (Egyptian deity):
    BL2450.S4
Sevāpanthas: BL2018.7.S48
Seven gods of fortune
  Japan: BL2211.S36
Seven rays
  Theosophy: BP573.S47
Sex
  Buddhism: BQ4570.S48
  Comparative mythology:
    BL325.S42
  Hinduism: BL1215.S48
  Islam: BP190.5.S4
  Judaism: BM720.S4
  Rabbinical literature:
    BM496.9.S48
Sex and religion: BL65.S4
Sex crimes and religion:
    BL65.S42
Sex role
  Hinduism: BL1215.S49
Sex worship: BL460
Sexton
  Judaism: BM659.S5
Sgam-po-pa, 1079-1153:
    BQ7950.S43+
Sha'are Tsiyon: BM675.R46
Shaatnez
  Yoreh de'ah law: BM523.5.S5
Shabak
  Islam: BP195.S5+
Shabat ḥol-mo'ed Sukot
  Samaritans: BM960.3.S52+
Shabbat ha-gadol: BM685.5
Shabbethai Tzevi, 1626-
  1676: BM755.S45
Shādhilīyah
  Sufism: BP189.7.S5+
Shadows
  Egyptian religion: BL2450.S55
Shafā'ah: BP166.76
Shafiites: BP166.14.S4
Shaḥarit: BM675.S44
Shaḥarit (Sabbath): BM675.S45
Shai (Egyptian deity):
    BL2450.S56
Shamanism
  Asian religions: BL2370.S5
  Buddhism: BQ4570.S5
  Chinese religions: BL1812.S45
  Indonesia: BL2122.S52
  Japanese religions: BL2211.S38
  Korea: BL2236.S5
  Nepal: BL2033.5.S52
Shambulinga (Hindu deity):
    BL1225.S48+
Shamesh
  Judaism: BM659.S5
Shamlaji (Hindu deity):
    BL1225.S5+
Shan e yin guo jing: BQ2100+
Shandaodashi, 613-681:
    BQ8549.S53+
Shango: BL2532.S5
Shangs-pa: BQ7680+
Shans
  Religions: BL2370.S53
Shapira, Joshua Isaac ben
  Jehiel, 1801-1873:
    BM755.S256
Share International
  Foundation: BP605.S49
Shaving
  Yoreh de'ah law: BM523.5.S53
Shavuot: BM695.S5
  Liturgy: BM675.P5
Shavuot sermons: BM747.S53
Shaykh al-Islām: BP185.5.S53
Shaykhī: BP195.S55+
Shayṭān
  Koran: BP134.D43
She lun: BQ8810+
Shehitah
  Judaism: BM720.S6+
Shema
  Judaism
    Liturgy: BM670.S45
Shemini 'atseret
  Samaritans: BM960.3.S53+
Shemini Atzeret: BM695.S53
Shemiṭah: BM720.S2
Shemoneh 'esreh: BM670.S5
Shemu'el (Midrash): BM517.S4+
Shenhui, 668?-760?: BQ9299.S54+
Sherman, Ingrid, 1919- :
    BP610.S5+
Sherpas
  Religion: BL2034.5.S53

Shīʻah and politics: BP194.185
Shiites: BP192+
Shikōkai: BP605.S53
Shiloh, the Lightbringer,
 1937- : BP610.S54+
Shin (Sect): BQ8700+
 Relations to Nichiren sect:
 BQ8319.6.S55
Shinbyu: BQ5010
Shingon: BQ8950+
Shinkyō, 1237-1319:
 BQ8559.S55+
Shinran, 1173-1263: BQ8749.S55+
Shinri: BL2222.S54+
Shinri Jikkōkai: BL2228.S56+
Shinri no Kai: BP605.S55
Shinshu: BL2222.S55+
Shinto: BL2216+
Shinto-Honkyoku: BL2222.S56+
Shinto religion and
 Judaism: BM536.S5
Shintō Taiseikyō: BL2222.S57+
Shinzei, Shōnin, 1443-
 1495: BQ9149.S55+
Ships
 Religion: BL619.S45
 Talmudic literature: BM509.S55
Shir ha-shirim (Midrash):
 BM517.S45+
Shir ha-yiḥud: BM670.S55
Shirakawa Shintō: BL2221.9.S5
Shirk
 Islam: BP166.22
Shirkûtu
 Assyro-Babylonian
 religions: BL1625.S38
Shiʻur komah
 Cabala: BM525.A42+
Shiva (Hindu deity): BL1218+
Shizensha: BL2222.S58+
Shneor Zalman ben Baruch,
 1747-1813: BM755.S525
Shneur Zalman, of Lyady,
 1745-1813: BM755.S525
Shochet
 Judaism: BM720.S6+
Shofar
 Judaism: BM657.S5
Shoghi, Effendi
 Bahai Faith
 Scriptures: BP364
Shōkin, 1268-1325: BQ9449.S54+
Shophar
 Judaism: BM657.S5
Shōtoku Taishi
 Prayers and devotions to:
 BQ5593.S55
Shree Rajneesh Ashram,
 Pune, India: BP605.R34+
Shri Ram Chandra Mission:
 BL1283.3+
Shrine management
 Shinto: BL2224.6+
Shrines
 Bahai Faith: BP420+
 Buddhism: BQ6300+
 Shrines of Gautama Buddha
 in India: BQ6460+
 Confucianism: BL1880+
 Greek religion and
 mythology: BL795.S47
 Hinduism: BL1243.72+
 India, Religions of: BL2015.T4
 Islam: BP187+
 Jainism: BL1378.4+
 Japanese religions: BL2211.S4
 Korea: BL2236.S54
 Shiites: BP194.6.A2+
 Shinto: BL2225+
 Sikhism: BL2018.35+
 Taoism: BL1941+
Shu (Egyptian deity): BL2450.S6
Shugen: BQ8820+
Shulḥan ʻarukh
 Halacha: BM520.88
Shunjō, 1166-1227: BQ8999.S55+
Shūsei: BL2222.S59+
Shuʻūbīyah: BP190.5.S5
Shūyōdan: BL2228.S57+
Shūyōdan Hōseikai:
 BL2228.S5796+
Shwa-ser: BQ7530+
Si shi er zhang jing: BQ2110+
Siberia, Religions of: BL2300
Sick
 Buddhism
 Devotional literature:
 BQ5585.S5
 Islam
 Devotional literature:
 BP188.3.S5
 Religious life: BP188.18.S53
 Judaism
 Prayer and service books:
 BM667.S55
 Visitation: BM729.V5

Sickness
  Islam: BP166.72
Siddhām: BQ4570.L3
Siddhānta literature
  Jainism: BL1310+
Siddhas
  Buddhism: BQ4570.S55
  Hinduism: BL1241.56
Siddur: BM674.2+
Sidur
  Karaites: BM185.4.S53+
Sifatites: BP195.S6+
Sifra (Midrash): BM517.S6+
Sifra di-tseni'uta
  Cabala
    Zohar supplements: BM525.A6S5+
Sifrei (Midrash): BM517.S7+
Sifrei zuta (Midrash): BM517.S85+
Sikh Gurus (Ten Gurus): BL2017.83+
Sikh religion: BL2017+
Sikhism: BL2017+
  Relation to Islam: BP173.S5
Śikṣāsamuccaya (by Śāntideva): BQ3240+
Śīla
  Buddhist monasticism: BQ6115+
Sīlakkhandha: BQ1295.5.S65+
Śīlaparikathā (by Vasubandhu): BQ3080.S55+
Śīlasamyuktasūtra: BQ2240.S54+
Silence
  Religious life: BL628.2
  Worship: BL619.S5
Silica
  Anthroposophy: BP596.S54
Silvanus
  Classical mythology: BL820.S47
Simeon bar Yoḥai, 2nd cent.
  Talmudist: BM502.3.S5
Simḥat Torah: BM695.S6
Simḥat Torah prayers: BM675.S5
Sin
  Assyro-Babylonian religions: BL1625.S5
  Islam: BP166.75
  Judaism: BM630
  Religious doctrine: BL475.7
Sin (Deity)
  Assyro-Babylonian religions: BL1625.S49
Sin, Forgiveness of
  Hadith literature: BP135.8.F67
  Islam: BP166.793
  Koran: BP134.F6
Sinai revelation
  Judaism: BM612
Sincerity
  Islam: BP166.783
Siṅgalovadāsutta: BQ1300.S56+
Singapore, Religions of: BL2085
Singh, Darshan, Maharaj: BP605.R85
Singh, Kirpal: BP605.R85
Singh, Thakar: BP605.R85
Singing
  Sufism: BP189.65.M87
Sinhalese
  Religion: BL2032.S55
Sins
  Islamic religious life: BP188.13+
Sins, Confession of
  Judaism
    Liturgy: BM670.C64
Sirens
  Classical mythology: BL820.S5
Śirgula (Hindu deity): BL1225.S55+
Sisterhoods' management
  Synagogues: BM653.5
Sisters
  Comparative mythology: BL325.S47
Sisters of the Inner World: BP605.G44
Sisyphus
  Classical mythology: BL820.S53
Sītā (Hindu deity): BL1225.S57+
Śītalā (Hindu deity): BL1225.S59+
Sitātapatrā: BQ7981.4.S572
Śiva (Hindu deity): BL1218+
Śiva Nārāyaṇīs: BL1283.5+
Sivananda Swami: BL1276.392.S59
Śivapurāṇa: BL1140.4.S48+
Six gatis (Buddhism): BQ4506+

Six Great Origination
(Tantric Buddhism):
BQ4250.S6
Six hundred and thirteen
commandments
Halacha: BM520.8
Six paramitas: BQ4336
Six worlds (Buddhism): BQ4506+
Skadi
Germanic and Norse
mythology: BL870.S5
Skanda: BQ2300+
Skandapurāṇa: BL1140.4.S53+
Skins and hides
Talmudic literature: BM509.H54
Sky
Egyptian religion: BL2450.S65
Sky gods
Comparative mythology: BL325.S5
Skye sgo gcod pa'i mdo:
BQ7971.5.S59+
Slander
Islam: BP188.14.S55
Slaughter of animals
Judaism: BM720.S6+
Slavic early religions: BL930+
Small groups
Religious life: BL628.4
Smṛty-upasthāna: BQ5630.S2
Snāna
Hinduism: BL1226.82.B38
Sobo
Religions: BL2480.S63
Social classes
Buddhism: BQ4570.C3
Social conflict and
religion: BL65.S62
Social ideals
Judaism: BM729.S6
Social justice
Islam: BP173.43
Social life in the
synagogue: BM135
Social movements and
religion: BL65.S64
Social security
Islam: BP190.5.S57
Social service
Judaism: BM729.S7
Social teachings
Koran: BP134.S6
Social work
Buddhism: BQ5851+
Hinduism: BL1243.52+
Islam: BP170.2
Society and religion
India: BL2015.S6
Society for the Greater
Community Way of
Knowledge: BP605.S58
Society, the state, and
Judaism: BM538.S7
Sociology
Buddhism: BQ4570.S6
Hinduism: BL1215.S64
Islam: BP173.25+
Theosophy: BP573.S6
Sociology and religion: BL60
Sod ha-egoz
Cabala: BM525.A426+
Sofer
Judaism: BM659.S3
Sofer, Moses, 1762-1839:
BM755.S33
Soferim: BM501.17
Soferim (Tractate): BM506.4.S6+
Sōgōgaku Gakuin: BP605.S6
Sōka Gakkai (Nichiren
Shōshū): BQ8400+
Sokar (Egyptian deity):
BL2450.S72
Sol
Classical mythology: BL820.S62
Solar Quest (Organization):
BP605.S65
Soldiers
Buddhism
Devotional literature:
BQ5585.S6
Religious life: BQ5480.S6
Hinduism
Religious life: BL1237.58.S65
Islam
Devotional literature:
BP188.3.S6
Judaism
Prayer and service books:
BM667.S6
Religious duties: BM727.5
Solitude
Islam: BP190.5.S6

Solomon ben Isaac, called
  Rashi, 1040-1105
  Biography: BM755.S6
Solomon, King of Israel
  Koran: BP133.7.S64
Solstice, Winter
  Sacred days: BL595.W55
Soma
  Hinduism
    Liturgical object:
    BL1236.76.S66
Soma (Hindu deity): BL1225.S63+
Soma sacrifices
  Hinduism: BL1226.82.V3
Sonanandajātaka: BQ1470.S65+
Sonārāya (Hindu deity):
    BL1225.S65+
Songhai
  Religions: BL2480.S65
Songs
  Islam: BP183.5
Songs of the Sabbath
  sacrifice
  Dead Sea scrolls: BM488.S47
Sopdu (Egyptian deity):
    BL2450.S75
Sotho
  Religions: BL2480.S67
Sōtō: BQ9400+
Soul
  Anthroposophy: BP596.S63
  Greek religion and
    mythology: BL795.S62
  Hinduism: BL1213.56
  Islam: BP166.73
  Jainism: BL1375.S65
  Judaism: BM645.S6
  Koran: BP134.S67
Soul and religion: BL290
Sound
  Hinduism: BL1215.S67
South American religions:
    BL2580+
Southern African religions:
    BL2463
Southern Sect (Hinduism):
    BL1288.8+
Space and time
  Buddhism: BQ4570.T5
Special days and seasons
  Islam: BP186+
Speech, Freedom of, and
  Islam: BP173.66
Sphere
  Greek religion and
    mythology: BL795.S63
Sphinxes
  Classical mythology: BL820.S66
Spice boxes
  Judaism: BM657.S64
Spirals
  Comparative mythology: BL325.S7
Spirit
  Koran: BP134.S7
Spirit possession
  Religious doctrine: BL482
Spirit world
  Buddhism: BQ4900+
  Islam: BP166.89
Spirits
  Anthroposophy: BP596.S65
  Buddhism: BQ4900+
Spirits, Evil
  Religious doctrine: BL480
Spirits, Good
  Religious doctrine: BL477
Spiritual exercises
  Hinduism: BL1238.32+
Spiritual Frontiers
  Fellowship: BP605.S66
Spiritual healing
  Buddhism: BQ4570.F3
  Sufism: BP189.65.F35
Spiritual healing and
  religion: BL65.M4
Spiritual Inner Awareness
  Movement: BP605.M68
Spiritual journals
  Religious life: BL628.5
Spiritual life
  Anthroposophy: BP596.S66
  Bonpo (Sect): BQ7982.2
  Buddhism: BQ5635+
  Hinduism: BL1237.32+
  Judaism: BM723+
  Shinto: BL2224.73
Spiritualism
  Buddhism: BQ4570.O3
Spring
  Semitic religions: BL1605.S65
Springs
  Greek religion and
    mythology: BL795.S65

Śraddhā
Buddhism: BQ4340+
Hinduism: BL1214.32.S72
Śrāddhā rite
Hinduism: BL1226.82.S73
Śrāmaṇera
Buddhist priests: BQ6145
Śrāmaṇerikā
Buddhist nuns: BQ6155
Sraosha (God)
Zoroastrianism: BL1588
Śrautasūtras: BL1126.4+
Śrāvaka: BQ4287+
Śrāvakabhūmi: BQ3070.S7+
Śrāvaṇi
Hinduism: BL1226.82.S75
Sri Lanka, Religions of: BL2045+
Śrī Vēṅkaṭēśvara (Hindu deity): BL1225.S7+
Srid pa las kyi gtiṅ zlog: BQ7973.5.S65+
Śrīghanācārasaṅgraha: BQ2429.8.S75+
Śrījñānaguṇabhadranāmastuti (by Vajravarman): BQ3300.S74+
Śrīmālādevīsiṃhanādasūtra (Śrīmālāsūtra): BQ1790+
Śrīmālāsūtra: BQ1790+
Śrīnārāyanīs: BL1283.5+
Śrīpraśnasaṃhitā: BL1141.8.S75+
Śrīśrībrahmasaṃhitā: BL1141.8.S76+
Śrīvaisnavas: BL1288.2+
Śrīvidyā (Hindu deity): BL1225.S76+
Srog-bdag-a-bse-chen-po-gdug-pa-sñiṅ-'byin (Buddhist deity): BQ4890.S76+
Stag-lha-me-'bar: BQ7981.4.S732
Stag-luṅ-pa: BQ7685+
Stars
Greek religion and mythology: BL795.C58
Nature worship: BL438
State and religion: BL65.S8
Buddhism: BQ4570.S7
Hinduism: BL1215.S83
India, Religions of: BL2015.S72
Islam: BP173.6
Japanese religions: BL2211.S73
Shinto: BL2223.S8
Zoroastrianism: BL1590.S73
State/society and Judaism: BM538.S7
Steiner, Rudolf, 1861-1925
Anthroposophy: BP595.S894+
Stewardship
Buddhism: BQ4420.G6
Sthānāṅga: BL1312.3.T53+
Sthavira schools of Buddhism: BQ7250+
Stone
Japanese religions: BL2211.S76
Korean religions: BL2236.S76
Stone, Hal: BP610.S75+
Stones (Sacred)
Nature worship: BL457.S7
Stories for Sabbath schools
Judaism: BM107
Storms
Nature worship: BL457.S75
Storytelling
Hinduism: BL1215.S85
Religious life: BL628.7
Students
Buddhism
Devotional literature: BQ5585.Y6
Religious life: BQ5465+
Hinduism
Religious life: BL1237.52
Judaism
Religious duties: BM727
Stūpa worship
Gautama Buddha: BQ925
Stūpas: BQ5075.S8, BQ6300+
Gautama Buddha: BQ925
Symbolism: BQ5125.S8
Su yao jing: BQ2240.S85+
Sub-Saharan African religions: BL2462.5
Subhāṣitaratnakaraṇḍakakathā (by Āryaśūra): BQ3340.S93+

Subsidiary organization
management
Synagogues: BM653.5
Subud: BP605.S7
Relation to Islam: BP173.S92
Success and religion: BL65.S84
Succession of Dalai lama:
BQ7752
Succession of Panchen lama:
BQ7752
Sudhābhojanajātaka:
BQ1470.S93+
Suffering
Buddhism: BQ4235, BQ4263
India, Religions of: BL2015.S86
Judaism: BM645.S9
Sikhism: BL2018.5.S84
Suffering and religion:
BL65.S85
Suffering of God
Rabbinical literature:
BM496.9.S93
Sufi orders: BP189.68+
Sufism: BP188.45+
Relations to Shiites: BP194.17
Sugawara Michizane as
Tenjin: BL2226.2.S84
Suicide
Jainism: BL1375.S95
Suika Shintō: BL2221.9.S9
Suk (African people)
Religions: BL2480.S78
Sukhāvatī: BQ4535+
Sukhāvatīvyūha (Larger):
BQ2030+
Sukhāvatīvyūha
(Smaller): BQ2040+
Sukkot: BM695.S8
Liturgy: BM675.T2
Sukkot sermons: BM747.S84
Sukkoth: BM695.S8
Suku
Religions: BL2480.S8
Sūkyō Mahikari: BL2228.S58+
Sulaymān
Koran: BP133.7.S64
Śulbasūtras: BL1136.7+
Sumāgadhāvadāna: BQ1600.S94+
Sumaṅgalavilāsinī (by
Buddhaghosa): BQ1295
Sumerian religion: BL1615+
Summer
Judaism: BM729.S85
Summit Lighthouse (Group):
BP605.S73
Summons
Islam: BP170.85
Sun
Comparative mythology: BL325.S8
India, Religions of: BL2015.S9
Theosophy: BP573.S95
Sun worship: BL438
Germanic and Norse
mythology: BL870.S8
Greek religion and
mythology: BL795.S85
India: BL2015.S9
Japanese religions: BL2211.S84
Roman religion and
mythology: BL815.S8
Sunburst Communities: BP605.S74
Sunday
Sacred days: BL595.S9
Sunday schools
Buddhism: BQ171+
Sunna: BP135+
Sunnite theology: BP166+
Sunnites
Relations to Shiites: BP194.16
Sunyata: BQ4275
Śūnyatāsaptatikārikā
(by Nāgārjuna):
BQ2910.S94+
Supererogation
Rabbinical literature:
BM496.9.S95
Superman
Religious doctrine: BL465+
Supernatural
Koran: BP134.S94
Supernatural and religion:
BL100
Superstition
Buddhism: BQ4570.S9
Hinduism: BL1215.S87
Judaism: BM538.S8
Superstitions and religion:
BL490
Supriyasārthavāhajāta
ka: BQ1470.S94+
Śūraṅgamasamādhisūt
ra: BQ2120+
Sūraṅgamasūtra: BQ2120+

Sūrapannatti: BL1312.6.S87+
Sūrat 'Abas: BP129.45
Sūrat al-'Ādiyāt: BP129.67
Sūrat al-Aḥqaf: BP128.94
Sūrat al-Aḥzāb: BP128.74
Sūrat al-A'lá: BP129.53
Sūrat al-'Alaq: BP129.63
Sūrat al-An'ām: BP128.28
Sūrat al-Anbiyā': BP128.56
Sūrat al-Anfāl: BP128.33
Sūrat al-'Ankabūt: BP128.68
Sūrat al-A'rāf: BP128.3
Sūrat al-'Aṣr: BP129.7
Sūrat al-Balad: BP129.56
Sūrat al-Baqarah: BP128.17
Sūrat al-Bayyinah: BP129.65
Sūrat al-Burūj: BP129.5
Sūrat al-Dahr: BP129.4
Sūrat al-Dhāriyāt: BP128.99
Sūrat al-Ḍuḥá: BP129.59
Sūrat al-Dukhān: BP128.9
Sūrat al-Fajr: BP129.55
Sūrat al-Falaq: BP129.82
Sūrat al-Fatḥ: BP128.96
Sūrat al-Fātiḥah: BP128.16
Sūrat al-Fīl: BP129.73
Sūrat al-Furqān: BP128.62
Sūrat al-Ghāshiyah: BP129.54
Sūrat al-Ḥadīd: BP129.17
Sūrat al-Ḥajj: BP128.57
Sūrat al-Ḥāqqah: BP129.33
Sūrat al-Ḥashr: BP129.2
Sūrat al-Ḥijr: BP128.45
Sūrat al-Ḥujurāt: BP128.97
Sūrat al-Humazah: BP129.72
Sūrat al-Ikhlāṣ: BP129.8
Sūrat Āl 'Imrān: BP128.2
Sūrat al-Infiṭār: BP129.47
Sūrat al-Insān: BP129.4
Sūrat al-Inshiqāq: BP129.49
Sūrat al-Isrā': BP128.49
Sūrat al-Jāthiyah: BP128.92
Sūrat al-Jinn: BP129.36
Sūrat al-Jumu'ah: BP129.24
Sūrat al-Kāfirūn: BP129.77
Sūrat al-Kahf: BP128.5
Sūrat al-Kawthar: BP129.76
Sūrat al-Layl: BP129.58
Sūrat al-Ma'ārij: BP129.34
Sūrat al-Mā'idah: BP128.26
Sūrat al-Masad: BP129.79
Sūrat al-Mā'ūn: BP129.75
Sūrat al-Muddaththir: BP129.38
Sūrat al-Mujādalah: BP129.19
Sūrat al-Mulk: BP129.3
Sūrat al-Mu'minūn: BP128.59
Sūrat al-Mumtaḥinah: BP129.22
Sūrat al-Munāfiqūn: BP129.25
Sūrat al-Mursalāt: BP129.41
Sūrat al-Muṭaffifīn: BP129.48
Sūrat al-Muzammil: BP129.37
Sūrat al-Naba': BP129.43
Sūrat al-Naḥl: BP128.47
Sūrat al-Najm: BP129.13
Sūrat al-Naml: BP128.65
Sūrat al-Nās: BP129.83
Sūrat al-Naṣr: BP129.78
Sūrat al-Nāzi'āt: BP129.44
Sūrat al-Nisā': BP128.23
Sūrat al-Nūr: BP128.6
Sūrat al-Qadr: BP129.64
Sūrat al-Qalam: BP129.32
Sūrat al-Qamar: BP129.14
Sūrat al-Qāri'ah: BP129.68
Sūrat al-Qaṣaṣ: BP128.67
Sūrat al-Qiyāmah: BP129.39
Sūrat al-Ra'd: BP128.43
Sūrat al-Raḥmān: BP129.15
Sūrat al-Rūm: BP128.7
Sūrat al-Ṣaff: BP129.23
Sūrat al-Ṣāffāt: BP128.8
Sūrat al-Sajdah: BP128.73
Sūrat al-Shams: BP129.57
Sūrat al-Sharḥ: BP129.6
Sūrat al-Shu'arā': BP128.64
Sūrat al-Shūrá: BP128.88
Sūrat al-Taghābun: BP129.26
Sūrat al-Taḥrīm: BP129.28
Sūrat al-Takāthur: BP129.69
Sūrat al-Takwīr: BP129.46
Sūrat al-Ṭalāq: BP129.27
Sūrat al-Ṭāriq: BP129.52
Sūrat al-Tawbah: BP128.35
Sūrat al-Tīn: BP129.62
Sūrat al-Ṭūr: BP129.12
Sūrat al-Wāqi'ah: BP129.16
Sūrat al-Zalzalah: BP129.66
Sūrat al-Zukhruf: BP128.89
Sūrat al-Zumar: BP128.83
Sūrat Fāṭir: BP128.77
Sūrat Fuṣṣilat: BP128.86
Sūrat Ghāfir: BP128.85
Sūrat Hūd: BP128.38

Sūrat Ibrāhīm: BP128.44
Sūrat Luqmān: BP128.72
Sūrat Maryam: BP128.53
Sūrat Muḥammad: BP128.95
Sūrat Nūḥ: BP129.35
Sūrat Qāf: BP128.98
Sūrat Quraysh: BP129.74
Sūrat Saba': BP128.76
Sūrat Ṣād: BP128.82
Sūrat Ṭā-hā: BP128.54
Sūrat Yā-sīn: BP128.78
Sūrat Yūnus: BP128.37
Sūrat Yūsuf: BP128.4
Sūriyapannatti: BL1312.6.S87+
Sūrya (Hindu deity): BL1225.S8+
Sūryagarbha: BQ1850+
Susanoo no Mikoto: BL2226.2.S94
Sūtradṛtāṅga: BL1312.3.S88+
Sūtrālamkāra (by Maitreyanātha): BQ3080.S97+
Sūtrapiṭaka: BQ1140+, BQ1280+
Chinese version: BQ1220+
Pali version: BQ1190+
Sūtrasamuccaya (by Śāntideva): BQ3250+
Suttanipāta: BQ1410+
Suttapiṭaka: BQ1190+
Suttas, Early Buddhist: BQ1280+
Suttavibhaṅga: BQ2330+
Suvarṇaprabhāsasūtra: BQ2130+
Suvarṇavarṇāvadāna: BQ1600.S96+
Suvikrāntavikrāmiparipṛcchā: BQ1980+
Sūyagaḍa: BL1312.3.S88+
Svacchandatantra: BL1142.6.S94+
Svāmīnārāyaṇa: BL1289.2+
Svantovit (Slavic deity): BL935.S92
Svarodaya: BQ2180.S94+
Svarog (Slavic deity): BL935.S94
Svātantrika School of Buddhism: BQ7478
Śvetāmbara: BL1380.S8
Śvetāśvataropaniṣad: BL1124.7.S84+
Swami-Narayanis: BL1289.2+
Swami Order of America: BP605.S8+
Swastika
Religious symbolism: BL604.S8
Sword
Religious symbolism: BL604.S85
Sword of Moses
Cabala: BM525.A43+
SYDA Foundation: BL1283.7+
Symbolism
Buddhism: BQ5100+
Chinese religions: BL1812.S95
Gautama Buddha: BQ927
Germanic and Norse mythology: BL870.S87
Hinduism: BL1215.S9
Islam: BP182.5+
Judaism: BM657.2+
Koran: BP132.5
Zoroastrianism: BL1590.S95
Symbols, Religious: BL603+
Synagogue dedication services: BM675.S9
Synagogue officials, Sermons for the installation of: BM744.8
Synagogue seating: BM653.2
Synagogues: BM653+
Syria
Hadith literature: BP135.8.S95
Syria, Religions of: BL2340+
Syrian religions, Ancient: BL1640+

T

Ta fang pien fo pao en ching: BQ2240.T313+
Ta sheng li ch'ü liu po lo mi ching: BQ2240.T32+
Ta'ame ḥaserot vi-yeterot (Midrash): BM517.T2+
Tabernacle
Judaism: BM654
Tabernacle service
Judaism: BM675.T2
Tābi'īn
Hadith: BP136.47
Tables
Greek religion and mythology: BL795.T32
Tachikawa School: BQ8850+
Tadshe (Midrash): BM517.T3+

Taehan Pulgyo Chogyejong:
BQ9510 +
Taehan Pulgyo
Ch'ŏnt'aejong: BQ9149.5 +
Taejonggyo: BL2240.T33 +
Taesun Chillihoe: BL2240.T34 +
Tagbana
Religions: BL2480.T25
Taḥanun: BM670.T35
Taita
Religions: BL2480.T27
Taittirīyabrāhmaṇa:
BL1118.4 +
Taittirīyāraṇyaka: BL1123.4 +
Taittirīyasaṃhitā: BL1113.4 +
Taittirīyopaniṣad:
BL1124.7.T35 +
Taiwa Kyōdan: BL2222.T35 +
Tajiks
Religions: BL2370.T19
Tajwīd
Koran: BP131.6
Takamagahara
Japanese religions: BL2211.T3
Taklung: BQ7685 +
Takuan Sōhō, 1573-1645:
BQ9399.T33 +
Talāntāntarakaśāstra
(by Bhāvaviveka):
BQ2910.T35 +
Talavakārāraṇyaka: BL1123.8 +
Tales, Mythological
Buddhism: BQ5741 +
Talismans
Buddhism: BQ4570.A4
Islam: BP190.5.A5
Judaism: BM729.A4
Shinto: BL2227.8.A45
Tallensi
Religions: BL2480.T3
Talmud Torah: BM109.T3
Talmud, Babylonian: BM499 +
Talmud, Palestinian: BM498 +
Talmudic academies
Babylonia and Palestine: BM502
Talmudic Aggada: BM516 +
Talmudic literature: BM497 +
Talmudists
Collective: BM501.15 +
Individual
Biography: BM755.A +
Criticism: BM502.3.A +
Tamang (Nepalese people)
Religions: BL2370.T23
Tamanikāya: BQ8270 +
Tamils
Religion: BL2370.T25
India: BL2032.T3
Tammuz (Deity): BL1625.T3
Tanaquil legend
Roman religion and
mythology: BL815.T3
Tandulavaicārika:
BL1312.9.T35 +
Tandulaveyāliya: BL1312.9.T35 +
Tāṇḍyabrāhmaṇa:
BL1121.3.T35 +
Tan'gun: BL2236.T35
Tanḥuma (Midrash): BM517.T35 +
Tanit
Semitic religions: BL1665.T3
Tanjur
Tripiṭaka
Tibetan version: BQ1270 +
Tanluan, 476-542: BQ8549.T36 +
Tanna de-vei Eliyahu
(Midrash): BM517.T4 +
Tannaim: BM501.2
Tantalus
Classical mythology: BL820.T37
Tantrarājatantra:
BL1142.6.T35 +
Tantras: BQ2140 +
Tantric Buddhism: BQ8900 +
Tantric Buddhist texts: BQ3320 +
Tantric texts: BL1141.2 +
Tantric yoga: BQ7800 +
Tantrism: BL1283.8 +
Relations to Tantric
Buddhism: BQ8919.4.T3
Tao-ch'o, 562-645: BQ8549.T37 +
Tao te ching: BL1900.L25 +
Taoism: BL1899 +
Relation to Buddhism: BQ4610.T3
Tapas
Hinduism: BL1238.58.T36
Tapuḥe zahev
Cabala
Zohar supplements: BM525.A6M5 +
Taqlīd: BP165.7
Tārā
Buddhism: BQ4710.T3 +
Prayers and devotions:
BQ5592.T35

Tārā (Hindu deity):
BL1225.T3+
Tārābhaṭṭārikānām
āṣṭaśataka: BQ2240.T37+
Tārākā
(Hindu deity): BL1225.T3+
Tārātantra
Tantric texts: BL1142.6.T37+
Tripiṭaka: BQ2180.T35+
Tarfon
Talmudist: BM502.3.T37
Targum, Samaritan: BM930+
Tarkabhāṣā (by
Mokṣākaragupta): BQ3260+
Tarkarahasyam: BQ3300.T37+
Tarkasōpāna (by
Vidyākaraśānti): BQ3270+
Tashlikh: BM670.S42
Tasmiyah: BP183.7.B3
Tatars
Religions: BL2370.T3
Tatenen (Egyptian deity):
BL2450.T37
Tathāgata: BQ4180
Tathāgatagarbha: BQ4450
Tathāgatagarbhasūtra: BQ2190+
Tathāgatoṣṇīsaṣitā
tapatrāparājitamahā
pratyaṅgiratparmasidd
hanāmadhāranī:
BQ1670.T35+
Tathatā: BQ4210+
Tattvārthadhigamasūtra:
BL1314.2.T38+
Tattvasaṅgraha (by
Śāntarakṣita): BQ3280+
Taurobolium
Roman religion and
mythology: BL815.T35
Tawāzun: BP188.16.M59
Tawbah: BP166.79
Teacher training for
sabbath schools
Judaism: BM108
Teachings
Gautama Buddha: BQ915, BQ937
Teachings of the Koran: BP132+
Technology
Buddhism: BQ4570.T42
Technology and religion:
BL265.T4
Teed, Cyrus Reed, 1838-
1908: BP605.K6
Teenage girls
Religious life: BL625.9.T44
Tefilat ha-derekh: BM675.T38
Tefillin: BM657.P5
Tehillim (Midrash): BM517.T5+
Tehinnot: BM675.T4
Teisei: BL2222.T34+
Tejāji (Hindu deity):
BL1225.T45+
Tekhelet (Dye): BM657.T44
Telecommunication
Islam: BP185.7+
Television broadcasting
Islam: BP185.77
Temple
Judaism: BM655+
Temple finance
Buddhism: BQ5136+
Temple membership
Buddhism: BQ5133+
Temple organization
Buddhism: BQ5140+
Hinduism: BL1241.32+
Temple property
Buddhism: BQ5137
Temple scroll
Dead Sea scrolls: BM488.T44
Temple seas
Egyptian religion: BL2450.T42
Temples
Assyro-Babylonian
religions: BL1625.T42
Bahai Faith: BP420+
Buddhism: BQ5130+, BQ6300+
Egyptian religion: BL2450.T43
Germanic and Norse
mythology: BL870.T4
Greek religion and
mythology: BL795.S47
Hinduism: BL1243.72+
India, Religions of: BL2015.T4
Jainism: BL1378.4+
Lamaism: BQ7900+
Sacred places: BL586
Sikhism: BL2018.35+
Sumerian religions: BL1616.T45
Taoism: BL1941+
Temurah (Midrash): BM517.T6+
Ten commandments
Halacha: BM520.75

Ten stages (Mahayana
Buddhism): BQ4330+
Ten worlds (Buddhism): BQ4500+
Tendai (Tiantai): BQ9100+
Tengalais: BL1288.8+
Tengenkyō: BL2228.T42+
Tenjur
Bonpo: BQ7968.2, BQ7976+
Tenkalais: BL1288.8+
Tennō: BL2222.T45+
Tenrikyō: BL2222.T46+
Tenshō Kōtai Jingūkyō:
BL2228.T45+
Tenth of Muḥarram
Islam: BP186.3
Sermons: BP183.63
Shiites: BP194.5.T4
Tēr
Hinduism: BL1215.T4
Terehpanth: BL1380.T4
Terminally ill
Religious life: BL625.9.S53
Terminus
Roman religion and
mythology: BL815.T45
Terrorism and religion:
BL65.T47
Terumah: BM720.T4
Testing transmission of
traditions
Hadith literature: BP136.6
Tetum
Religion: BL2123.T47
Teutates
Early Celtic religions:
BL915.T4
Thadingyut: BQ5720.T4
Thailand, Religions of: BL2075+
Thammayut: BQ9150+
Ṭhāṇāṅga: BL1312.3.T53+
Thang-ka: BQ5125.M3
Thanksgiving Psalms
Dead Sea scrolls: BM488.T5
Thanksgiving scroll
Dead Sea scrolls: BM488.T5
Thedick, Eleanore Mary,
1883-1973: BP605.C43
Theg pa'i rim pa mṅon du
bśad pa'i mdo rgyud:
BQ7971.5.T48+
Theism: BL200
Themis
Classical mythology: BL820.T47
Theodicy: BL216
Theological movements
Islam: BP166.14.A+
Theology
Babylonian Talmud: BM504.3
Hinduism: BL1212.32+
Islam: BP166+
Koran: BP132+
Shiites: BP194+
Shinto: BL2221+
Sikhism: BL2018.2+
Urantia Book: BP605.U75
Theology, Moral
Judaism: BM728
Theology, Pastoral
Shinto: BL2224.55
Theology, Philosophical
Shinto: BL2220.7
Theology, Schools of
Islam: BP166.14.A+
Theomachy
Semitic religions: BL1605.T45
Theory of knowledge
Buddhism: BQ4440
Koran: BP134.K6
Theosophical Society,
Covina, California:
BP510.T52
Theosophy: BP500+
Relation to Buddhism:
BQ4610.T46
Relation to Islam: BP173.T45
Theragāthā: BQ1440+
Therapeutae
Judaism: BM175.T5
Theravāda Buddhism: BQ7100+
Abhidharmapiṭaka: BQ2490+
Vinayapiṭaka: BQ2310+
Therīgāthā: BQ1450+
Theseus
Classical mythology: BL820.T5
Thesmophoria
Greek religion and
mythology: BL795.T54
Thingyan: BQ5720.T5
Thirteen (The number)
Comparative mythology:
BL325.T45
Thirteen articles of faith
Judaism: BM607

Thor
Germanic and Norse mythology: BL870.T5
Thoth (Egyptian deity): BL2450.T5
Thought
Theosophy: BP573.T5
Thracians
Early religions: BL975.T5
Three Festivals
Judaism: BM693.P5
Three Jewels (Buddhism): BQ4000+, BQ4131+
Three Svabhāva theory (Buddhism): BQ4443
Three Weeks (Jewish mourning period): BM695.T4
Threefold Buddhakāya: BQ4180
Threefold Refuges: BQ4350
Thūpavaṃsa (by Vācissara): BQ2640.T45+
Ti lun: BQ9200+
Tianfei (Deity): BL1942.85.T53
Tiantai: BQ9100+
Tiber River
Classical mythology: BL820.T6
Tiberinus
Classical mythology: BL820.T6
Tibetan Buddhism: BQ7530+
Tibetan Buddhist literature: BQ7620+
Tibetan religions: BL1945.T5
Tiep Hien (Order of Interbeing): BQ9800.T53+
Tijānīyah
Sufism: BP189.7.T5+
Tikkun: BM675.R48
Tikkun ḥazot: BM675.T5
Tikkun leil Hoshana Rabba: BM675.H6
Tikkunei Zohar
Cabala
Zohar supplements: BM525.A6T5+
Tiḳun: BM675.R48
Tiḳun shovavim: BM675.T52
Tiḳune ha-Zohar: BM525.A6T5+
Tilakas
Hinduism: BL1236.76.T54
Time
Buddhism: BQ4205.T5, BQ4570.T5
Comparative mythology: BL325.T55
Egyptian religion: BL2450.T55
Time
Islam: BP190.5.T54
Judaism: BM729.T55
Time and religion: BL65.T55
Times, Sacred: BL590+
Timiti
Hinduism: BL1226.82.T5
Tingley, Katherine Augusta Westcott, 1847-1929: BP585.T5
Tipiṭaka: BQ1170+
Tirmidhī, Muḥammad ibn ʻĪsá, d. 892
Hadith: BP135.A15+
Tiryañ-gati: BQ4515
Tish'ah be-Av: BM695.T57
Liturgy: BM675.K5
Tishri: BM693.T6
Titans
Classical mythology: BL820.T63
Tithes
Judaism: BM720.T4
Titus, emperor of Rome
Midrash: BM518.T5
Talmudic literature: BM509.T5
Tivi
Religions: BL2480.T5
Toba-Batak
Religion: BL2123.T62
Toda, Jōsei, 1900-1958: BQ8449.T64+
Toḍalatantra: BL1142.6.T64+
Tolai
Religions: BL2630.T64
Tolerance
Buddhism: BQ4570.T6
Tolerance, Religious
Islam: BP171.5
Sikhism: BL2018.5.R44
Tongues, Gift of
Religion: BL54
Torah cases: BM657.T59
Torah scrolls: BM657.T6
Toraja
Religion: BL2123.T67
Torat Kohanim (Midrash): BM517.S6+
Tosafists
Babylonian Talmud: BM501.8
Tosefta: BM508+
Tractate Sanhedrin: BM506.S2+

Tractates
Mishnah: BM506.A+
Tosefta: BM508.5.A+
Tractates, Minor (Talmudic literature): BM506.2+
Tradition
Babylonian Talmud: BM503
Traditions
Islam: BP135+
Shiites: BP193.25+
Trailokyavijaya: BQ4860.T7+
Training of lamas: BQ7756+
Translating the Koran: BP131.13
Translation history
Tripiṭaka: BQ1120+
Transmigration
Buddhism: BQ4485+
Hinduism: BL1214.74
Judaism: BM635.7
Religion: BL515+
Transmission of tradition, Testing of
Hadith literature: BP136.6
Transmission quality
Hadith literature: BP136.5
Transmission, Chain of
Hadith literature: BP136.33
Transmitters
Hadith literature: BP136.48+
Shiites: BP193.28
Transmitters, Women
Hadith literature: BP136.485
Travel
Islam: BP184.9.T73, BP190.5.T73
Judaism: BM720.T7
Religious life: BL628.8
Treatment of animals
Judaism: BM729.A5
Tree planting
Hinduism: BL1239.5.T74
Tree worship: BL444
Greek religion and mythology: BL795.T8
Hinduism: BL1239.5.T75
India: BL2015.T7
Trees
Comparative mythology: BL325.P6
Hinduism: BL1215.T75
India, Religions of: BL2015.T7
Umbanda: BL2592.U514P55
Trees, Christmas
Anthroposophy: BP596.C4
Trials
Greek religion and mythology: BL795.T85
Triangle
Religious symbolism: BL604.T7
Trikālaparīksā (by Dignāga): BQ3300.T75+
Triṃśikāvijñaptimāt ratāsiddhi (by Vasubandhu): BQ3030+
Trimurti
Hinduism: BL1213.34
Trinities
Religious doctrine: BL474
Tripiṭaka: BQ1100+
Biography: BQ1132+
Tripurā Bhairavī (Hindu deity): BL1225.T68+
Tripurārṇavatantra: BL1142.6.T75+
Tripurasundarī (Hindu deity): BL1225.T73+
Tripurātāpinyupaniṣad: BL1124.7.T74+
Triratnānusmṛtisūtra: BQ2240.T74+
Trisaṃvaraprabhāmālā (by Vibhūticandra): BQ3300.T77+
Trisvabhāvanirdeśa (by Vasubandhu): BQ3080.T75+
Truce with the Meccans
Muḥammad, Prophet, d. 632: BP77.7
True Life Foundation: BP605.T69
Trust in God
Judaism: BM729.T7
Trusts
Buddhism: BQ96+
Truth
Buddhism: BQ4255
Hinduism: BL1213.74
Truth Consciousness: BP605.T78
Truth, Church of: BP605.C56
Truthfulness
Islam: BP188.16.T78
Tsa pao tsang ching: BQ1600.T73+
Tsitsit: BM506.4.Z5+
Tsoṅ-kha-pa Blo-bzaṅ-grags-pa, 1357-1419: BQ7950.T75+

Tsung-mi, 780-841: BQ8249.T78+
Ts'ung-shen, 778-861:
BQ9299.T75+
Tswana
Religions: BL2480.T76
Tu bi-Shevat: BM695.T9
Tu bi-Shevat prayers: BM675.T82
Tulasī (Hindu deity):
BL1225.T83+
Tun-huang manuscripts:
BQ244.T8+
Tunguses
Religions: BL2370.T8
Turkana
Religions: BL2480.T87
Turkic peoples
Hadith literature: BP135.8.T87
Turks (General)
Religions: BL2370.T84
Tushu (Hindu deity):
BL1225.T86+
Tutelaries
Japanese religions: BL2211.T8
Twelve-linked Chain of
Dependent Origination:
BQ4250.T9
Twelve-step programs
Judaism: BM538.T85
Meditations: BL624.5
Twilight
Oraḥ ḥayim law: BM523.3.T9
Twins
Comparative mythology: BL325.T8
Two realms (Tantric
Buddhism): BQ4220
Tyāgarāja (Hindu deity):
BL1225.T93+
Tyche
Classical mythology: BL820.F7
Typology (Psychology)
Religious life: BL627.57

U

U-netanneh tokef: BM670.U25
Udāna: BQ1390+
Udānavarga: BQ1380+
Udāsī (Sect): BL2018.7.U33
Uḍḍīśatantra: BL1142.6.U44+
Udmurts
Early religions: BL975.U34
Uduk
Religions: BL2480.U38
Uetsufumi: BL2217.5.U3+
UFO cults and religion:
BL65.U54
Ŭich'ŏn, 1055-1101:
BQ9149.U38+
Ŭisang, 625-702: BQ8249.U37+
Ulama
Islam: BP185+
Ull
Germanic and Norse
mythology: BL870.U4
Ulla I
Talmudist: BM502.3.U44
Ullambana: BQ5720.U6
'Ulūm al-Qu'ān: BP130.77+
Ulysses
Classical mythology: BL820.O3
Umbanda: BL2592.U4+
Ummaggajātaka: BQ1470.U45+
Unarius Academy of Science:
BP605.U52
Unarius Educational
Foundation: BP605.U52
Unbelief
Islam: BP166.785
Underdeveloped areas and
religion: BL65.U5
Underground places
Sacred places: BL584
Unidentified flying
objects and religion:
BL65.U54
United Church of Religious
Science: BP605.U53
Unity and plurality: BL270
Unity of God
Islam: BP166.2
Unity of Islam: BP170.82
Universal and Triumphant,
Church: BP605.S73
Universal Great
Brotherhood: BP605.U536
Universal religions: BL390
Universal Union, New: BP605.H5
Universality of Islam: BP170.8
Upālipariprcchāsūtra:
BQ2480.U57+
Upālisutta: BQ1320.U63+
Upanayana
Hinduism: BL1226.82.S2

Upāṅgas: BL1312.5+
Upaniṣadbrāhmaṇa:
BL1121.3.U63+
Upaniṣads: BL1124.5+
Uparipaṇṇāsa: BQ1319.5.U62+
Upāsaka
Biography: BQ846
Doctrine: BQ4560+
Upāsakadaśā: BL1312.3.U83+
Upāsakaśīlasūtra:
BQ2480.U62+
Upāsikā
Biography: BQ858
Doctrine: BQ4560+
Upāya: BQ4370
Uposatha: BQ5720.U7
Uragasutta: BQ1419.5.U72+
Ural-Altaic religions: BL685
Urantia Book: BP605.U74+
Urantia Brotherhood: BP605.U7+
Urim and Thummim
Judaism: BM657.U7
Uṣas (Hindu deity):
BL1225.U82+
Usiel, Ben-Zion Meir Hai,
1880-1953: BM755.U72
Uṣṇīṣavijayā: BQ4690.U75+
Prayers and devotions to:
BQ5592.U75
Uspenskiĭ, P. D., 1878-
1947: BP605.G94U75
Usūlīyah: BP166.14.F85
'Uthmān ibn 'Affān,
Caliph, d. 656
Hadith literature: BP135.8.U85
Uttarādhyayana: BL1313.9.U77+
Uttarajjhayaṇa: BL1313.9.U77+
Uttaraṣaṭkatantra:
BL1142.6.U77+
Uvangas: BL1312.5+
Uvāsagadasāo: BL1312.3.U83+
Uvavāiya: BL1312.6.U83+

V

V symbol
Religious symbolism: BL604.V2
Va-yekhullu (Midrash):
BM517.V2+
Va-yissa'u (Midrash): BM517.V4+
Va-yosha' (Midrash): BM517.V5+
Vadagalais: BL1288.5+
Vadakalais: BL1288.5+
Vādanyāya (by
Dharmakīrti): BQ3290+
Vādhūlagṛhyasūtra:
BL1134.2+
Vādhūlaśrautasūtra:
BL1128.3+
Vahagn: BL2335.V34
Vaidalyasūtra (by
Nāgārjuna): BQ2910.V34+
Vaikhānasa: BL1142.2+
Vaikhānasagṛhyasūtra:
BL1134.4+
Vaikhanasas: BL1289.4+
Vaikhānasaśrautasūtra:
BL1128.8+
Vaipulyasūtra: BQ2240.V33+
Vairocana: BQ4690.V3+
Vaiśākha: BQ5720.W4
Vaishnavism: BL1284.5+
Relation to Islam: BP173.H58
Vaiṣṇava saṃhitās:
BL1141.2+
Vaitānaśrautasūtra:
BL1129.7+
Vājapeya: BL1226.82.V3
Vājasaneyisaṃhitā: BL1113.6+
Vajrabhairava: BQ4890.V32+
Vajrabhairavatantra:
BQ2180.V34+
Vajracchedikā: BQ1990+
Vajrakīla: BQ4890.V33+
Vajrakīlaya: BQ4890.V336+
Vajrakosá: BQ4220
Vajrapāṇi: BQ4710.V32+
Vajrasamādhisūtra:
BQ2240.V35+
Vajrasattva: BQ4710.V34+
Vajraśekharasūtra:
BQ2180.S28+
Vajraśekharavimānasarv
ayogayogisūtra:
BQ2180.V3496+

Vajraśekharayogānuttar asamyaksambodhicittop-adaśāstra: BQ3340.V33+
Vajrasūcī (by Aśvaghoṣa): BQ2890+
Vajrāvalī: BQ3340.V35+
Vajravārāhi: BQ4890.V339+
Vajravidāraṇānāmadh-aranī: BQ2180.V35+
Vajrayāna Buddhism: BQ8900+
Vajrayoginī: BQ4890.V34+
Vajraysakṣa: BQ4860.V3+
Valetudo
  Classical mythology: BL820.V34
Valkyrites
  Germanic and Norse mythology: BL870.V3
Vallabha sect: BL1289.5+
Vallabhācārya, 1479-1531?: BL1289.592.V35
Vallabhācāryas (Sect): BL1289.5+
Vallabheśopaniṣad: BL1124.7.V35+
Vaḻḻi (Hindu deity): BL1225.V24+
Values
  Islam: BP190.5.V3
Vāmakeśvaratantra: BL1142.6.V33+
Vāmanapurāṇa: BL1140.4.V35+
Vammīkasutta: BQ1320.V35+
Vaṃśabrāhmaṇa: BL1121.3.V36+
Vaṇhidsāo: BL1312.6.V35+
Vārāhagṛhyasūtra: BL1133.4+
Varāhapurāṇa: BL1140.4.V37+
Vārāhaśrautasūtra: BL1127.8+
Varṇārhavarṇastotra (by Mātṛceṭa): BQ3300.V37+
Varuṇa (Hindu deity): BL1225.V3+
Vasava, fl. 1160: BL1281.292.B37
Vāstu-pūjā: BL1226.82.V36
Vasubandhu: BQ7529.V36+
Vasugupta: BL1281.1592.V38
Vāsukipurāṇa: BL1140.4.V3793+
Vātulāgama: BL1141.5.V38+
Vavahāra: BL1313.3.V38+
Vāyavīyapurāṇa: BL1140.4.S48+
Vāyu (Hindu deity): BL1225.V38+
Vāyupurāṇa: BL1140.4.V38+
Ve-hizhir (Midrash): BM517.V6+
Vedic texts: BL1112.2+
Vegetarianism
  Buddhism: BQ4570.V43
  Hinduism: BL1214.32.V45
  Jainism: BL1375.V44
  Judaism: BM538.V43
Vegetarianism and religion: BL65.V44
Velikoe beloe bratstvo: BP605.V44
Vendidād: BL1515.5.V4A2+
Veneration
  Islam: BP186.97
Veneti (Italic people)
  Early religions: BL975.V46
Veṅkaṭanātha: BL1288.592.V46
Venus
  Classical mythology: BL820.V5
Ver sacrum
  Roman religion and mythology: BL815.V3
Verahaccānisutta: BQ1339.5.V45+
Veritat Foundation: BP605.V47
Vesak: BQ5720.W4
Vesākhā: BQ5720.W4
Vessantarājātaka: BQ1470.V48+
Vesta
  Classical mythology: BL820.V55
Vestals
  Roman religion and mythology: BL815.V4
Vestments, Religious
  Buddhism: BQ5080+
  Shinto: BL2224.38.V47
Veterans
  Buddhism
    Devotional literature: BQ5585.S6
Vibhaṅga: BQ2510+
Vibhūti: BL1226.82.V52
Vices
  Buddhism: BQ4401+, BQ4425+
  Islam: BP188.13+
Victims of family violence
  Religious life: BL625.9.V52

Victory
Classical mythology: BL820.V6
Vidui
Judaism
Liturgy: BM670.C64
Vidya-rājas: BQ4840+
Vietnam, Religions of: BL2055+
Vigrahavyāvarttanī (by Nāgārjuna): BQ2900+
Vijñāna: BQ4445
Vijñānabhairava: BL1142.6.V55+
Vijñaptimātratā: BQ4445
Vilemurk
Early Celtic religions: BL915.V54
Vimalakīrtinirdeśa: BQ2210+
Vimalāvatīavadāna: BQ1600.V56+
Vimānavatthu: BQ1420+
Vimokṣa: BQ4263
Viṃśatikāvijñaptimā tratāsiddhi (by Vasubandhu): BQ3040+
Vimuttimagga (by Upatissa): BQ2620+
Vīṇāśikhatantra: BL1142.6.V56+
Vinayakārikā: BQ2429.8.V52+
Vinayapiṭaka: BQ1150+, BQ2250+
Chinese version: BQ1230+
Pali version: BQ1180+
Violence
Buddhism: BQ4570.V5
Hinduism: BL1214.32.V56
Islam: BP190.5.V56
Judaism: BM538.P3
Violence and religion: BL65.V55
Vipāka: BL1312.3.V58+
Vipaśyanā: BQ5630.V5
Vīrabhadra (Hindu deity): BL1225.V48+
Vīrāgama: BL1141.5.V57+
Vīraśaivas: BL1281.2+
Vīrastava: BL1312.9.V57+
Virgin birth
Comparative mythology: BL325.V5
Virginity
Comparative mythology: BL325.V55
Greek religion and mythology: BL795.V57
Virtues
Anthroposophy: BP596.V5
Buddhism: BQ4401+, BQ4415+
Islam: BP188.15+
Viśeṣacintabrahmaparip ṛcchāsūtra: BQ2240.V55+
Viśeṣastava (by Mtho-btsun-grub-rje): BQ3300.V57+
Vishnu (Hindu deity): BL1219+
Visions
India, Religions of: BL2015.V5
Visiting the sick
Judaism: BM729.V5
Viṣṇudharmottarapurā. na: BL1140.4.V56+
Viṣṇupurāṇa: BL1140.4.V57+
Viṣṇusaṃhitā: BL1141.8.V54+
Viśrāvaṇa: BQ4890.V57+
Visuddhimagga (by Buddhaghosa): BQ2630+
Viśvakarman (Hindu deity): BL1225.V49+
Viṣvaksenasaṃhitā: BL1141.8.V57+
Viśvāmitra (Hindu deity): BL1225.V495+
Viṭhobā (Hindu deity): BL1225.V5+
Vivāgasuya: BL1312.3.V58+
Vivekananda, 1863-1902: BL1280.292.V58
Vivisection
Nature worship: BL439.5
Vocation
Religious life: BL629
Voodooism: BL2490
Voorthuyzen, Louwrens: BP610.V6+
Voting
Islam: BP190.5.V63
Votive offerings
Buddhism: BQ4570.V6
Etruscan religion and mythology: BL760.V6
Greek religion and mythology: BL795.V6
Japanese religions: BL2211.V6
Vows
Buddhist monasticism: BQ6115+
Buddhist religious life: BQ4355
Worship: BL570+

Voyages and travels
Comparative mythology: BL325.V68
Vratas
Hinduism: BL1237.78
Vratyas: BL2020.V7+
Vṛhannāradīyapurāṇa: BL1140.4.V75+
Vṛṣṇidaśā: BL1312.6.V35+
Vulcan
Classical mythology: BL820.V8
Vyavahāra: BL1313.3.V38+

W

Wahhabis: BP195.W2+
Wahhābīyah: BP195.W2+
Walls
Religious symbolism: BL604.W3
Wampar
Religions: BL2630.W35
Waqf: BP170.25
War
Buddhism: BQ4570.W3
Greek religion and mythology: BL795.W28
Islam: BP190.5.W35
Judaism: BM538.P3
War and religion: BL65.W2
War of the Sons of Light against the Sons of Darkness
Dead Sea scrolls: BM488.W3
War, Holy
Islam: BP182
Wartime
Devotional literature for Buddhist: BQ5590.W3
Washington (D.C.).
Self-Revelation Church of Absolute Monism: BP605.S85W3
Water
Anthroposophy: BP596.W38
Greek religion and mythology: BL795.W3
Hinduism: BL1215.W38
Islam: BP190.5.W37
Judaism: BM729.W38
Koran: BP134.W37
Nature worship: BL450
Religion: BL619.W3
Water
Semitic religions: BL1605.W3
Water Festival (Buddhism): BQ5720.T5
Wayfaring life
Buddhism: BQ6200+
Hinduism: BL1239.5.W38
Wealth
Buddhism: BQ4570.W4
Islam: BP190.5.W4
Wealth and religion: BL65.W42
Wedding sermons
Judaism: BM744.5
Weights and measures
Talmudic literature: BM509.W4
Welfare work
Buddhism: BQ5851+
Hinduism: BL1243.52+
Islam: BP170.2
Wenchang (Deity): BL1942.85.W45
Wesak: BQ5720.W4
West African religions: BL2465
West Indies
Religions: BL2520+
Western Paradise (Buddhism): BQ4535+
Prayers and devotions: BQ5594.W4
Wetlands
Japanese religions: BL2211.W48
Wheel
Religious symbolism: BL604.W4
Wheel of the Buddha's teachings: BQ5125.D4
Wheels
Comparative mythology: BL325.W45
White Brotherhood: BP605.W48
White Eagle Lodge: BP605.W49
White lotus (Sect): BQ8670+
White Yajurveda saṃhitā: BL1113.6+
Whole and parts
Theosophy: BP573.W56
Widows
Buddhism
Religious life: BQ5455
Winds
Greek religion and mythology: BL795.W56

Wine
  Egyptian religion: BL2450.W55
  Nature worship: BL457.W5
Wine and wine making
  Yoreh de'ah law: BM523.5.W5
Winter solstice
  Sacred days: BL595.W55
Winti: BL2592.W56
Wisakha: BQ5720.W4
Wisdom
  Buddhism: BQ4380+
  Comparative mythology:
    BL325.W56
Wisdom and religion: BL65.W57
Wise, Isaac Mayer, 1819-
  1900: BM755.W5
Wit and religion: BL65.L3
Wittek, Gabriele, 1933- :
    BP605.H4
Wives and daughters
  Muḥammad, Prophet, d. 632:
    BP76.8
Women
  Buddhism
    Biography: BQ850+
    Devotional literature:
    BQ5585.W6
    Doctrines: BQ4570.W6
    Religious life: BQ5450+
  Comparative religion: BL458
  Greek religion and
    mythology: BL795.W65
  Hadith literature: BP135.8.W6
  Hinduism
    Religious life: BL1237.46
  India, Religions of: BL2015.W6
  Islam
    Biography: BP73
    Devotional literature:
    BP188.3.W6
    Islamic sociology: BP173.4
    Religious life: BP188.18.W65
  Jainism: BL1375.W65
  Japanese religions: BL2211.W65
  Judaism: BM729.W6
    Biography: BM753
    Prayer and service books:
    BM667.W6
    Religious duties: BM726
  Koran: BP134.W6
    Biography: BP133.6.W6
  Religious life: BL625.7
Women
  Roman religion and
    mythology: BL815.W6
  Sikhism: BL2018.5.W65
  Talmudic literature: BM509.W7
  Tripiṭaka: BQ1133.W6
Women believers
  Buddhism
    Biography: BQ858
Women heroes
  Comparative mythology:
    BL325.W65
Women transmitters
  Hadith literature: BP136.485
Wŏn Pulgyo: BQ9220+
Wong Tai Sin (Taoist
  deity): BL1942.85.W65
Wŏnhyo (Sect): BQ9210+
Wŏnhyo, 617-686: BQ9219.W66+
Wood cults: BL583
Wooden fish
  Buddhism: BQ5075.W6
Word Foundation: BP605.W67
Work and Islam: BP173.77
Work and religion: BL65.W67
Work ethic
  Koran: BP134.L34
Work, Prohibited
  Oraḥ ḥayim law: BM523.3.P7
Work, The (Gurdjieff
  movement): BP605.G8+
Working class
  Talmudic literature: BM509.L2
Works and faith
  Islam: BP166.78+
Works, Good
  Islam: BP170.2
World and Buddhism: BQ4570.W64
World Buddhist Sangha
  Council: BQ20.W5+
World Buddhist Union: BQ20.W6+
World Fellowship of
  Buddhists: BQ20.W7+
World of Animals
  (Buddhism): BQ4515
World of Asuras (Buddhism):
    BQ4513
World of devas (Buddhism):
    BQ4508
World of hungry spirits
  (Buddhism): BQ4520
World of men (Buddhism): BQ4510

World politics and Islam:
BP173.5
World religions: BL390
Worlds (Buddhism): BQ4500+
Worship: BL550+
Buddhism: BQ4911+
Judaism: BM656+
Lamaism: BQ7690+
Shinto: BL2224+
Sikhism: BL2018.3+
Worship of saints
Sufism: BP189.585
Worship, Guru
Lamaism: BQ7699.G87
Worship, Public
Islam: BP184.2
Wounding transmission of a tradition
Hadith literature: BP136.6
Wreaths
Greek religion and mythology: BL795.W74
Religious symbolism: BL604.W7
Wu liang yi jing: BQ2070+

X

Xangô: BL2592.X36
Xhosa
Religions: BL2480.X55
Xi Wang Mu (Deity):
BL1942.85.X58
Xian tian dao: BL1943.H74
Xian yu yin yuan jing:
BQ1600.H74+
Xiao zi jing: BQ2240.H76+
Xuanzang, ca. 596-664:
BQ8149.H78+

Y

Y symbol
Religious symbolism: BL604.Y2
Yahweh Ben Yahweh: BP610.Y34+
Yaḥyá
Koran: BP133.7.J65
Yajña
Hinduism: BL1226.82.Y35
Yajurveda Āraṇyaka: BL1123.2+
Yajurveda Brāhmaṇas:
BL1118.2+
Yajurveda saṃhitās: BL1112.6+
Yajurvedic Gṛhasūtras:
BL1131.9+
Yajurvedic Śrautasūtras:
BL1127.4+
Yaka
Religions: BL2480.Y32
Yakṣas (Deities)
Buddhism: BQ4770+
Hinduism: BL1225.Y27+
Jainism: BL1375.7.Y34
Yakṣī (Hindu deity):
BL1225.Y28+
Yakuts
Religions: BL2370.Y34
Yalkut ha-Makhiri
(Midrash): BM517.Y2+
Yalkut Shimoni (Midrash):
BM517.Y3+
Yama (Hindu deity): BL1225.Y3+
Yamaka: BQ2550+
Yamakage: BL2222.Y35+
Yamāntaka: BQ4860.Y3+
Yamazaki, Bennei, 1859-1920: BQ8669.Y36+
Yamma, King of Hell: BQ4525
Yantra
Hinduism: BL1236.76.Y36
Yanzi
Religions: BL2480.Y34
Yao
Religion: BL2150.Y25
Ya'qūb (Biblical patriarch)
Koran: BP133.7.J33
Yashts: BL1515.5.Y28A2+
Yasna: BL1515.5.Y3A2+
Yatvyags
Early religions: BL945
Year
Hinduism: BL1215.Y43
Yelammedenu (Midrash):
BM517.T35+
Yellow Cap
Lamaism: BQ7530+
Yemen
Hadith literature: BP135.8.Y46
Yemenite rite
Judaism
Liturgy: BM672.Y4
Yesha'yah (Midrash): BM517.Y4+
Yezidis: BL1595
Yi guan dao: BL1943.I35

Yin-yang cults
Chinese religions: BL1812.Y55
Japan: BL2211.Y56
Korea: BL2236.Y55
Yin Yang symbol
Religious symbolism: BL604.Y5
Yixuan, d. 867: BQ9399.I55+
Yoga
Hinduism: BL1238.52+
Jainism: BL1375.Y63
Yoga Association for Self Analysis: BP605.Y64
Yoga, Tantric: BQ7800+
Yogācāra School of
Buddhism: BQ7480+
Abhidharmapiṭaka: BQ2920+
Relations to Mādhyamika School: BQ7471
Yogācārabhūmi: BQ3050+
Yogacuḍāmaṇyupaniṣad: BL1124.7.Y63+
Yogananda, Paramhansa, 1893-1952: BP605.S43Y6
Yoginīhṛdaya: BL1142.6.Y65+
Yoginītantra: BL1142.6.Y66+
Yogis
Hinduism: BL1241.57
India, Religions of: BL2015.Y6
Yogoda: BP605.S36
Yom ha-zikaron prayers: BM675.Y55
Yom Kippur: BM695.A8
Liturgical books: BM675.Y58
Yom Kippur Katan prayers: BM675.Y6
Yom Kippur sermons: BM747.Y65
Yonah (Midrash): BM517.Y7+
Yonghwagyo: BL2240.Y64
Yonitantra: BL1142.6.Y68+
Yorah de'ah law
Halacha: BM523.4+
Yoreh de'ah
Halacha: BM520.86.A54+, BM520.88.A54+
Yorubas
Religions: BL2480.Y6
Yoshida Shintō: BL2221.9.Y67
Yoshikawa Shintō: BL2221.9.Y6
Young adults
Buddhism
Devotional literature: BQ5585.Y5
Religious life: BQ5460
Young married couples
Buddhism
Devotional literature: BQ5585.Y5
Religious life: BQ5460
Young men
Buddhism
Devotional literature: BQ5585.Y7
Religious life: BQ5470
Young women
Buddhism
Devotional literature: BQ5585.Y8
Religious life: BQ5475
Youth
Buddhism
Devotional literature: BQ5585.Y6
Religious life: BQ5465+
Hinduism
Religious life: BL1237.52
Islam
Devotional literature: BP188.3.Y6
Religious education: BP44+
Religious life: BP188.18.Y68
Judaism: BM540.Y6
Religious duties: BM727
Sermons: BM742
Lamaism
Religious education: BQ7568
Religious life: BL625.47
Youth clubs management
Synagogues: BM653.7
Yoẓerot: BM670.Y69
Yu lan pen jing: BQ2220+
Yuan jue jing: BQ2230+
Yuddhavijayatantra: BQ2180.Y83+
Yuga concept
Hinduism: BL1215.H57
Yugapurāṇa: BL1140.4.Y87+
Yuiitsu Shintō: BL2221.9.Y67
Yuktiṣaṣṭikākarika (by Nāgārjuna): BQ2910.Y84+
Yūsuf
Koran: BP133.7.J67
Yūzū Nembutsu: BQ8760+

Z

Za bao zang jing: BQ1600.T73+
Zadokites: BM175.Z3
Zahirites: BP195.Z18+
Ẓāhirīyah: BP195.Z18+
Zaidites: BP195.Z2+
Zakat: BP180
Zamzam Well: BP187.48
Zanz
  Hasidism: BM198.56.Z35
Zanz rite (Judaism)
  Liturgical books: BM672.Z36
Zayn al-ʻĀbidīn ʻAlī
  ibn al-Ḥusayn, d. 710?:
    BP193.14
Zealots (Jewish party):
    BM175.Z4
Zela
  Religions: BL2480.Z37
Zemirot: BM675.Z4
Zen Buddhism: BQ9250+
Zend-Avesta: BL1515+
Zeus
  Classical mythology: BL820.J8
Zezuru
  Religions: BL2480.Z4
Zhan cha shan e ye bao
  jing: BQ2240.C39+
Zhang shou mie zui hu zhu
  tong zi tuo ni jing:
    BQ2240.C43+
Zhen fo (Sect): BQ9800.C48+
Zhen kong jiao: BL1943.C5
Zhi chan bing bi yao fa:
    BQ1529.5.C55+
Zhiyi, 538-597: BQ9149.C45+
Zhuangzi: BL1900.C45+
Ẕikrī: BP195.Z54+
Zinza
  Religions: BL2480.Z56
Ẓiẓit: BM506.4.Z5+
Zizith (Fringes): BM657.F7
Zodiac
  Anthroposophy: BP596.Z6
  Greek religion and
    mythology: BL795.Z63
Zohar
  Cabala: BM525.A5+
Zohar ḥadash
  Cabala
    Zohar supplements: BM525.A6Z6+
Zohar supplements
  Cabala: BM525.A6A+
Zongmi, 780-841: BQ8249.T78+
Zoology
  Anthroposophy: BP596.Z66
Zoroaster: BL1555
Zoroastrianism: BL1500+
Zoroastrianism and
  Buddhism: BQ4610.Z6
Zoroastrianism and Judaism:
    BL1566.J8
Zulgo
  Religions: BL2480.Z75
Zulus
  Religions: BL2480.Z8
Zunz, Leopold, 1794-1886
  Judaism
    Biography: BM755.Z8